MEMOIRS OF A DEDICATED AMATEUR

David Perry

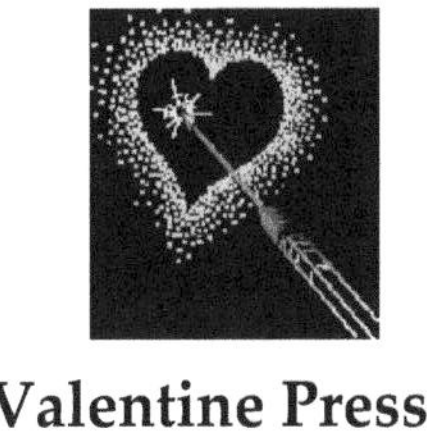

Valentine Press

First published in Australia in 2014

Valentine Press
P.O. Box 527,
Bellingen NSW 2454
www.valentinepress.com.au

National Library of Australia Cataloguing-in-Publication entry:

Perry, David, 1933-
Memoirs of a Dedicated Amateur / David Perry.
ISBN: 9780987506344 (paperback)
Includes index.
Photographers--Australia--Biography.
Painters--Australia--Biography.
Motion picture producers and directors--Australia--Biography.
770.92

Printed and bound in Australia by Lightning Source Australia

Cover painting *The Coast of Brittany*, 1972, by David Perry

Text, photographs, paintings and drawings are all by David Perry unless otherwise indicated.

Some of the images in *Memoirs of a Dedicated Amateur* were originally in colour. These can be viewed online in colour at the Valentine Press photo gallery:
http://valentinepress.com.au/?page_id=553

A large collection of images of other works by David Perry which are not contained in this book can also be viewed in the online gallery.

A Reader Comments page has been included on Valentine Press website where your feedback on *Memoirs of a Dedicated Amateur* would be welcomed: **http://valentinepress.com.au/?page_id=562**

INTRODUCTION
Jane Mills

David Perry writes very much like many of his films and paintings. Their sensory effect is akin to a synaesthetic flurry of warm snow: he writes words and you feel colours; he describes images and you taste letters; he uses metaphors and you hear concrete sounds. His words and verbal pictures overwhelm your senses and, at the same time, make vivid connections to your cognitive, sense-making processes. At least, that's how I experience David's films and paintings, and how it feels to read this book: I see echoes and hear shadows that take me beyond the surface of the word.

As I write, I can hear the ever-curious, slightly bemused, always to-the-point David telling me that this is not how he envisages the relationship between himself and his reader. Whenever I launch into a professional, theoretical analysis of a film or book, David offers an alternative perception that doesn't complicate ideas in the way that I do. How he expresses what he sees, thinks and dreams in his art, films and writing, enriches the sensorium. David's ways of looking and thinking come from someone who is openly and proudly an amateur - that is, he approaches a subject with an open mind precisely because of his lack of formal training and his financial disinterest. I particularly treasure our discussion - a disagreement that's become a joke over the years - about my initial interpretation of the UBU experimental film, *Bolero,* for which his cinematography is an amazing mix of filmic art, technical skill and courage that only an amateur dares. As he describes in these pages, to the sound of Ravel's intense erotic music, David's camera slowly and inexorably moves up a long street towards a waiting woman before climaxing in a swift edit and a shot that penetrates her eye. I once referred to this as rape; David mildly suggested I should rethink my ideas about lovemaking. I like my rhetoric as it offers focus; but I like David's ideas more because they open my vision to wider horizons and less literal understandings.

I first met David inthe mid-1990s when I arrived from the UK to head the Screen Studies department of the Australian Film & Television School (AFTRS). A Pom who knew almost absolutely nothing about Australian cinema, I suspect if I'd been asked about Australian experimental cinema I would have snorted in disbelief: British cultural imperialism (and ignorance) is deeply ingrained in British academics. I was expected to teach a course on Soviet cinema, about which I knew zilch. Fortunately - for the students, for me - David had been asked to step in until I could take over.

Upon hearing him lecture, I recall feeling shocked. Not that he didn't know what he was talking about - he surely did - but because he spoke as... well, as an *amateur*. That is, a *lover* of Soviet cinema. This is the first of many things he taught me: that you can talk to students not as an expert but as a student yourself and as a lover of films, their ideas and images. I was captivated, humbled, by how he enriched the students' experience. I had never dared talk about cinema in such an intimate, amorous way. Afterwards, we went to a pub where he talked about love: his love for cinema and the cross-over between words and images, his love for his partner, Lydia, who he described as "the love of my life" and, although he didn't expressly say so, his love for sharing his knowledge and learning with others - for teaching, in other words.

I discovered David had another strong love - for audiences. He was scathing of the canon of classic films that had been selected for the students. The films of Eisenstein, Pudovkin, Vertov and Dovzhenko were superb, of course, but shouldn't Australia's future filmmakers see the films that the Soviet people actually wanted to see? David gave me the courage, just two days into my new job, to insist that we change the screenings to include popular Soviet cinema. And, as if he hadn't already given me more than enough, upon learning that I had written a couple of dictionaries, he sent me a small artwork comprising the bold words: "Cunning linguists talk in tongues."

When I told a friend that I was writing this introduction he said - in high hopes: "I suppose it's all about sex." And yes, there is a fair amount of fucking in this book. Which is clearly part of David's delight in everyday pleasures: a bewildered student once asked him why UBU filmmakers were so obsessed by sex and, equally bewildered, he responded by asking the student if there was anything more important in life. But mostly, this book is about love - as one might expect from something written by a dedicated amateur, a word that entered the English language in the late 18th century from the French *amour,* ultimately from the Latin *amare* meaning 'to love'.

Associate Professor Jane Mills
School of the Arts & Media
University of New South Wales
Sydney
August 2014

CONTENTS

INTRODUCTION by Jane Mills v

PART ONE **1**

A Few Words To Start With ... 2

The Suburbs ... 4

Work And Career ... 6

Colour (and Dufaycolor) … 16

Friendship … 18

Painting and drawing … 21

Sex, betrayal and love … 22

The Push … 24

Films and film making … 26

Marriage … 30

New Zealand … 33

Our first child … 37

Country life … 38

Jazz … 42

Nostalgia … 43

Worrying about style and professionalism … 45

Back home, we find the Push again … 46

A really big change ... 63

After Blunderball … 67

Extreme abstraction on films … 70

Harbour … 72

Abigayl … 75

Cinematography … 78

Big changes coming … 86

The birth of Rachael ... 88

Juggling commitments ... 89

Marinetti and after ... 92

Thinking of leaving the country ... 100

Raising money to get out of Australia ... 103

Album ... 106

Exile or Flight ... 109

PART TWO **111**
Adventures on a Boeing 707... 112
Early days in London... 116
A trip through France... 123
The birth of Homer... 130
Friends in London (and politics)... 134
A personal loss of "moral confidence"... 144
Another crisis... 147
What is to be done?... 149
Let's get out of here... 155

PART THREE **161**
In Sydney again ... 162
New friends ... 165
Plenty of water and homest men ... 168
Queensland ... 178
DDIAE ... 184
Home ownership made easy ... 189
Toowoomban politics ... 193
Abby comes to Toowoomba ... 196
I start to "lose it"in Toowoomba ... 198
Leaving Toowoomba... 207
Back in Sydney... 209
The Harbour Bridge Series ... 215
The Pentax gets stolen... 219
Fairlight... 225
Contact remade ... 235
Manly ... 240
The Bunker Series... 244
Panoramas... 248
Now the Mamiya is stolen ... 250
Lydia ... 253
Life with Lydia ... 255
The Manly Mural Project ... 268
The Refracting Glasses ... 270
Doctor Jazz, an exhibition, another script ... 279

Hill End … 282
Lydia in China … 285
An exhibition proposed … 288
Postscript (by Lydia Fegan) 289
A few words to end with … 294

INDEX OF IMAGES **297**
Paintings and Drawings 297
Photographs by David Perry 299
Photographs and other images not by David Perry 302
Films and plays 303

PART ONE

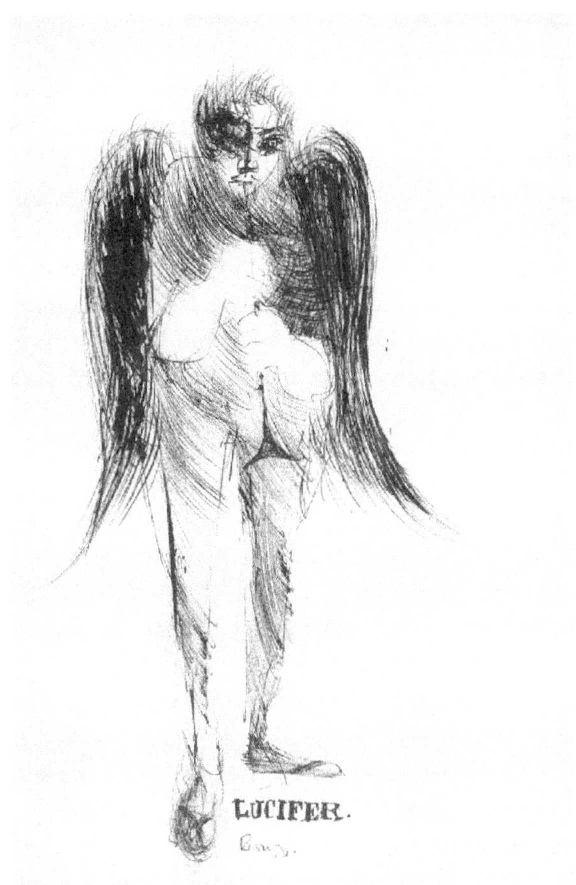

Self Portrait (Indian ink on paper), c. 1955

A few words to start with ...

I am almost entirely untrained as an artist or a film maker, yet it is by those two professions that I define myself. That's why I call myself a "dedicated amateur".

I am also a photographer with a thorough training in some of the technical processes of photography. My photographs will tell much of this story. Paintings, drawings and occasional film stills will add to it, but reproduction of those things on a reduced scale and without colour may not do justice to them. Photographs, being more suited to mass reproduction than other images will, I think, work best in this book. And some effort has been put into reproducing works in colour on the book's website. If you really want to know how good (or bad) my other work is you need to see the originals, or in the case of films, to see them in a cinema.

There are of course other factors than image quality involved. For example, Ken Quinnell, writing in 1971, said of one of my favourites of my early films, *Album*:

Perry does not preoccupy himself with the spaces between the images, the terrifying void that threatens us in the films of some of the American experimental film makers ... the moments of assured identity represented by the photographs are a guarantee of continuity ...[1]

I'm not so sure about that. What I'm more sure of is that photographs themselves are melancholy things. They freeze certain traces of life in silver-gelatin emulsions, or ink on paper, or in other more modern media. These traces form images of past experiences, past or changed relationships. But nothing or nobody in a photograph can be reactivated. That is why I say they are melancholy. Is that, in fact, what Ken Quinnell meant by "the terrifying void"?

And yet photographs make up a large part of this book. Photographs are considered to be more objective records of "reality" than any painting

---

1 Extract from Ken Quinnell's review in *Nation*, 12th June, 1971.

or drawing, no matter how "realistic". It's hard to argue against that view but one has to argue anyhow against the description: "objective". No doubt (in most cases) the thing or person photographed did exist, but there's so much more to a person's life than a frozen moment, or in the case of film, a sequence of frozen moments.

Contrary to popular opinion, photographs are not objective records of people, places, events photographed. They are records of the relationship between photographer and his/her subject. And even the records are mutable. Different prints from the same negative can create a very different atmosphere, a different mood, a more or less convincing formal trace of the "subject".

The Suburbs...

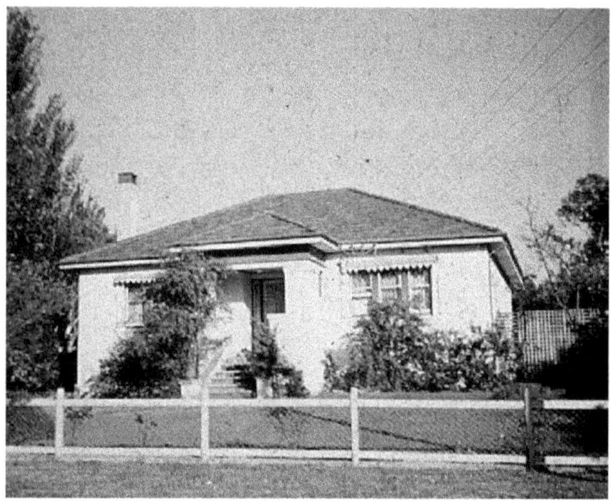

Family home in East Lindfield

This is the house in East Lindfield where I grew up and lived till my early twenties with my parents, three brothers and two sisters, in what was just a two bedroom bungalow. It's now hard to remember just how crowded this house became. At the same time I have to admit to our family having pretty middle-class values since what I remember as a crowded house would have seemed very comfortable to people in other parts of Sydney, let alone in the wider world. Nevertheless, as soon as I had an income I wanted to move out, to live in "the slums", which would have granted me no greater space but certainly more independence. My mother wouldn't hear of it. No doubt she needed the board I paid as soon as I left school and began work. But regardless of financial matters, and we were certainly poor, my mother seemed not able to let me go. Without doubt I was a "mother's boy".

I was born in May, 1933, on the same day (I believe) that the Nazis had their first awful bonfire of books. My parents never spoke of politics (or sex for that matter) and what I knew of these things I learned from other kids and movies - in the case of politics particularly, from newsreels. Newsreels, especially captured German ones, gave me my first awareness of the power and beauty of photographs, especially moving ones. I must confess, too, that I loved animated cartoons (my first 16mm film was an animation) and to being seduced by the deep blacks and rich tones of the beautifully lit images of the American and English feature films that were, as we know, evidence of Australia's unquestioned colonial status.

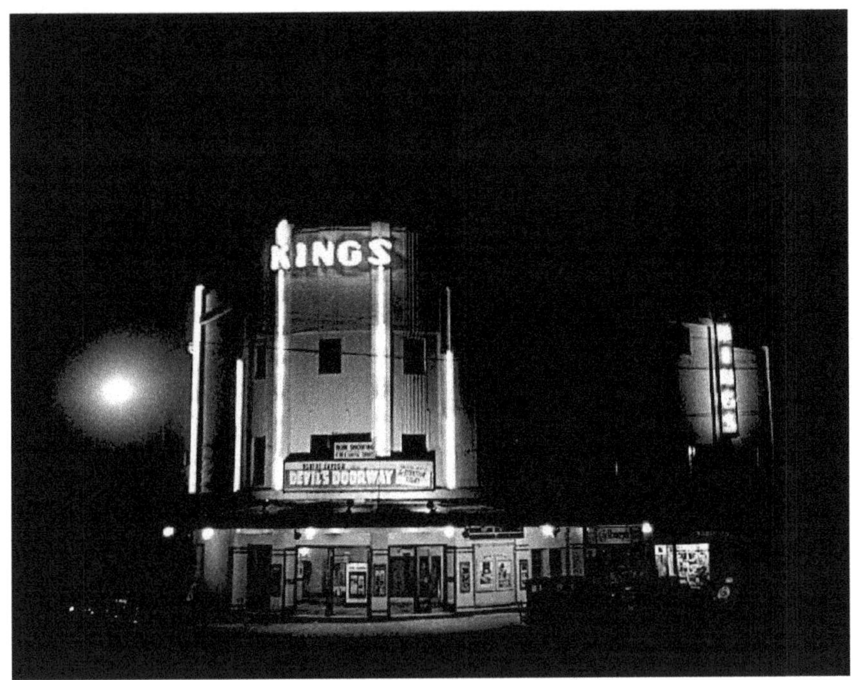

Kings Lindfield in the early 1950s

There were three cinemas that I went to almost every week: Kings Lindfield, Kings Chatswood and The Arcadia, also at Chatswood.

Of course I devoured newspapers too (you might question the "of course", but as I dig into my memory "of course" does seem the right phrase to use). *The Sydney Morning Herald, The Sun* and *The Bulletin* were the papers I most often saw, and from the illustrations and cartoons I saw in those papers I decided from my early teenage years that I wanted to be a newspaper artist.

Work and career...

To have a career as a film maker was an unimaginable possibility from the perspective of my adolescence, although the cinemas were my universities, at least until I discovered Art and the European avant-garde.

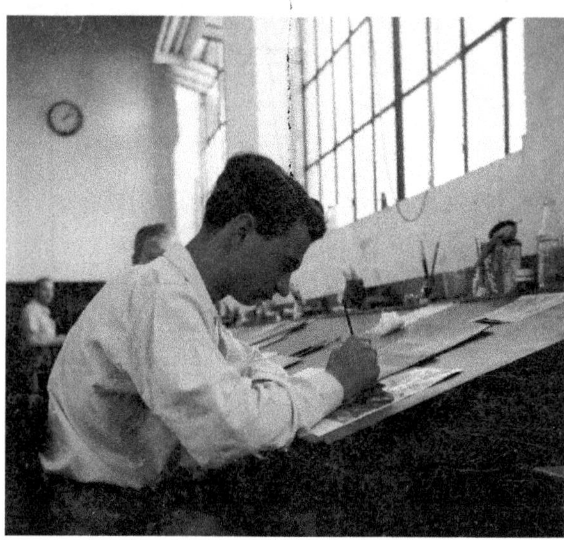

DP as an apprentice retouching paper negatives in the early 1950s. (Photographer unknown)

Before I could discover those things, though, I had to go out into the world. As soon as I was legally old enough at fifteen, I left school and applied for a job as an illustrator at Associated Newspapers where I was told I'd have to do three years at art school before I could be a newspaper artist. There was no way my parents could have supported me through art school, but at the suggestion of the personnel manager at Associated Newspapers I agreed (no doubt at my mother's urging) to be apprenticed to the printing trade. I had to wait till my sixteenth birthday before that could happen, and I waited out my time as a "copy-boy" earning £1/10/- per week. Being a copy-boy entailed carrying large canvas bags of copy (photographs, artwork and text) from the Sun building in Elizabeth Street, across the Domain, past the Art Gallery and down to Sungravure in Woolloomooloo. The world of magazine production and publishing was a revelation to me. There I learned the technical skills of photography and imbibed a love of composing pages of text and images by compiling them according to other people's layouts.

Looking back it seems to me that the composition of pages in a magazine has a parallel with composing images and sounds in a film, although I know such a suggestion might be too far-fetched for some to accept. The people I was meeting were from worlds I had never known. The social pressures to "get women back into the home" had not then become entirely irresistible so there were women and men working together in ways that would soon become unthinkable. The older people seemed immensely older than me, although they could have only been in their twenties or early thirties. Many of the men had been in "The War", flying bombers through flak over Germany or fighting in jungles much closer to home. Like I said, I was a "mother's boy" and a lot of these people's experiences, when they spoke of them, were pretty well incomprehensible to me.

There were a lot of pubs in Woolloomooloo and lot of the men at Sungravure were pretty hard drinkers, so another part of my apprenticeship involved drinking beer (never wine, nor for that matter, spirits). More germane to this story is the fact that half a dozen or more people at Sungravure were serious artists. One or two worked in oils, the others were watercolourists. Many lunchtimes they would go as a group to Woolloomooloo Bay, taking drawing pads, colours, pens or pencils to make quick sketches of the waterfront or the parkland nearby. Later they'd work them up into paintings. At least two of them submitted watercolours for the Wynne Prize just up the hill at the Art Gallery. Their works were almost always hung. I don't think a watercolour ever won the Wynne Prize (nowadays there is a prize specifically for watercolours) but to be hung was honour enough.

"Sunday painters" they may have been but they were no less serious about their work for that. Sometimes these artists invited me to join them on their lunchtime excursions. One of them, who I'd guess to have been middle-aged then, told me that when he was much younger he'd gone away on a painting weekend with Syd Long, a successful artist since the early 1900s. Syd made a pass at my friend, which was rejected but made no difference to the regard in which Syd Long was held.

I only had one or two passes made at me in those days. I'm not sure if the lack of passes was due to shyness being seen as stand-offishness or if I was simply unattractive. As you can see on the next page, I myself thought I was pretty spiffing.

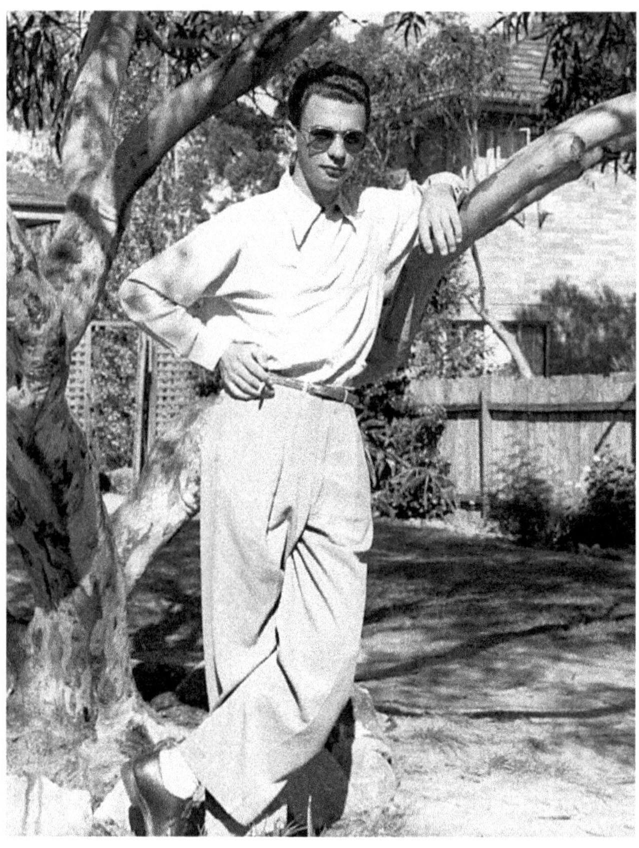

Self-portrait in new clothes, 1952 or '53

By 1952 I was earning enough money to buy myself some stylish clothes but much bigger changes than that were happening to me. I had taken up painting. I told myself at the time it was to overcome my sadness at my rejection by a nice girl from Rose Bay but, in fact, art had been brewing in me for longer than my testosterone and it was more than just a distraction, even if my first paintings were dreadful. By 1953, however, I think I was starting to get the hang of it.

Around that time too I could afford to buy myself a "good" camera. All the photographs from the 1950s in this collection were taken with that, a Voigtländer twin-lens reflex. A year, or maybe two years later, I was given a clockwork 8mm camera (standard-8, not super-8, which was unknown then). Once I had that I had at hand prototypes of all the tools that have served my purposes ever since.

With my new Voigtländer and growing skills at exposing and processing film I began to record places, things, people around me. I could take photographs with a reasonably good sense of composition and an eye for the moment, but I had no idea that photographs might be valued in the world of art, to which I aspired. I had no knowledge of the work of Max Dupain or Harold Cazneaux, for example, photographers who by this time had created significant bodies of work. I had no awareness of the sensuous, velvet tonalities that a silver/gelatin print could display, no knowledge of the darkroom skills and equipment that were needed to bring those qualities into existence. As a corollary of that I treated my negatives with something like contempt. It's a wonder that any of them have survived.

I think, if I'm honest with myself, I have to say that I was floating around in an intellectual void with a vague passion to be an artist. No doubt this passion got some of its energy from repressed sexuality (still dormant at the age of twenty!) but the passion for art was, nevertheless, genuine and, as I enter my seventies, has outlasted the passion for sex. "Dedicated amateur" indeed! But now I think it might be best if I let my photographs do the talking for a while. Paintings, apart from this one below, will get their chance later.

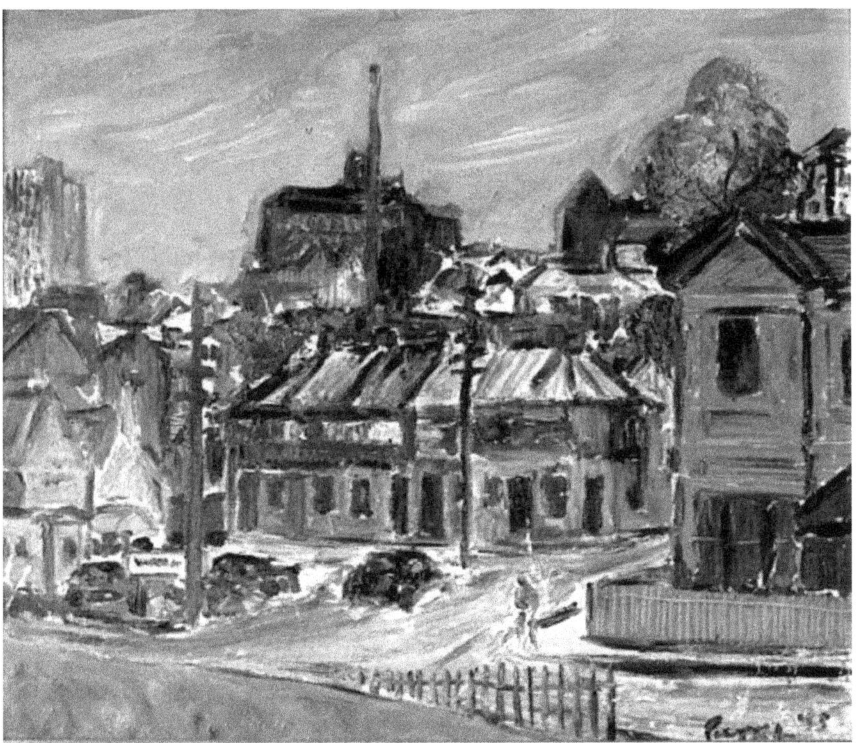

Woolloomooloo near Sungravure *(oils on canvas), 1953. In possession of Georgia Ireland. In colour on website.*

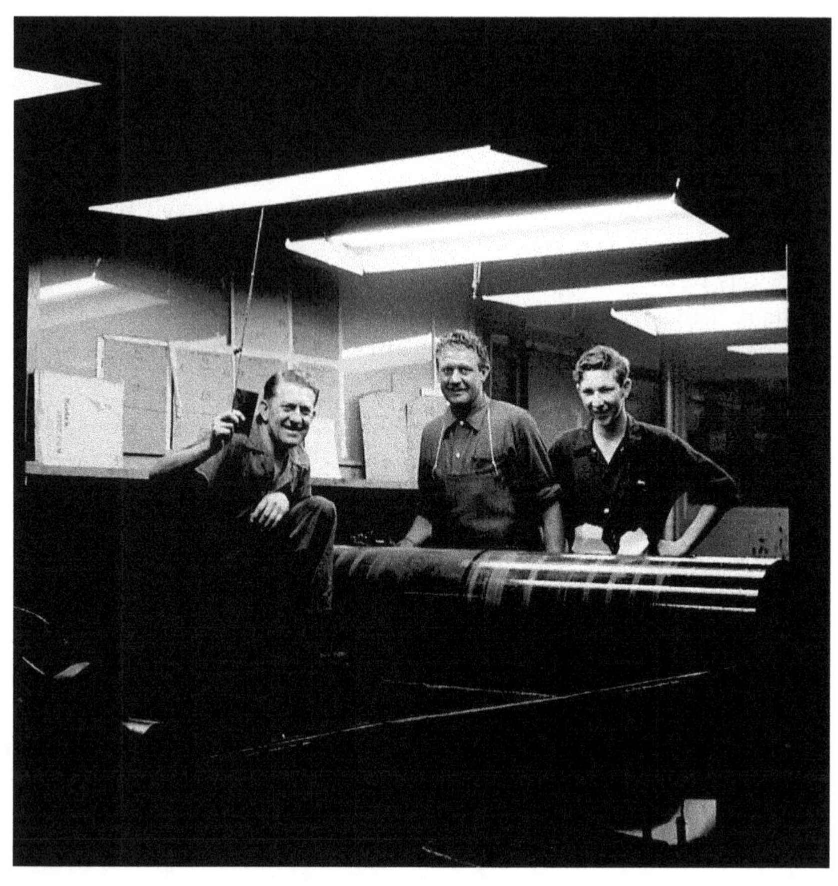

Etchers at Sungravure (Alf Carrigan, Jack Rogers and Bob Cogger, a fellow apprentice), c.1953

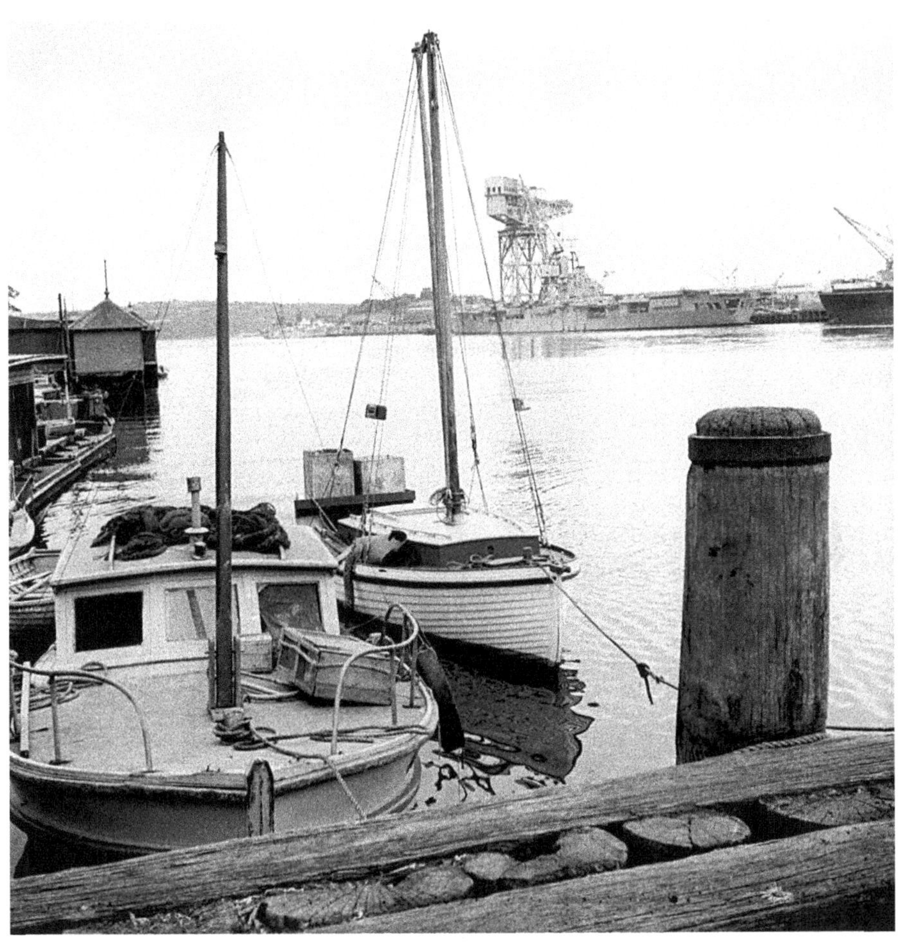

Fishing boats in Woolloomooloo Bay, c. 1953

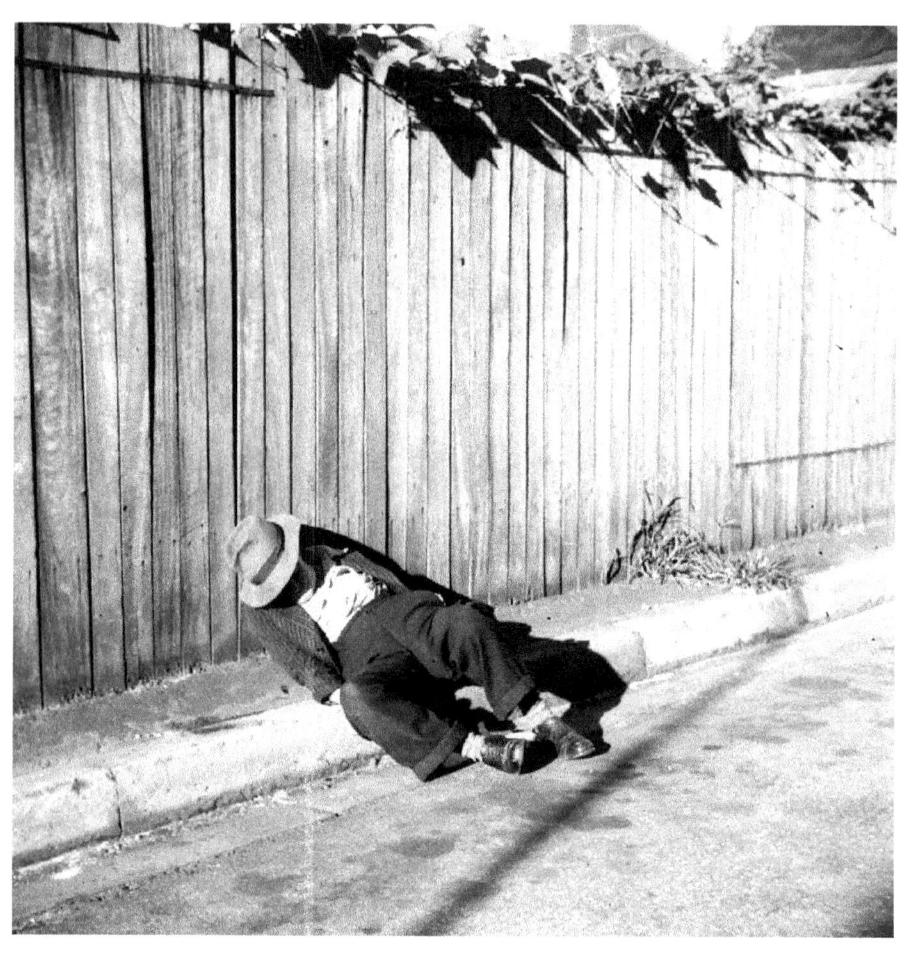

A drunk sleeping it off in Lindfield (even!), c. 1954

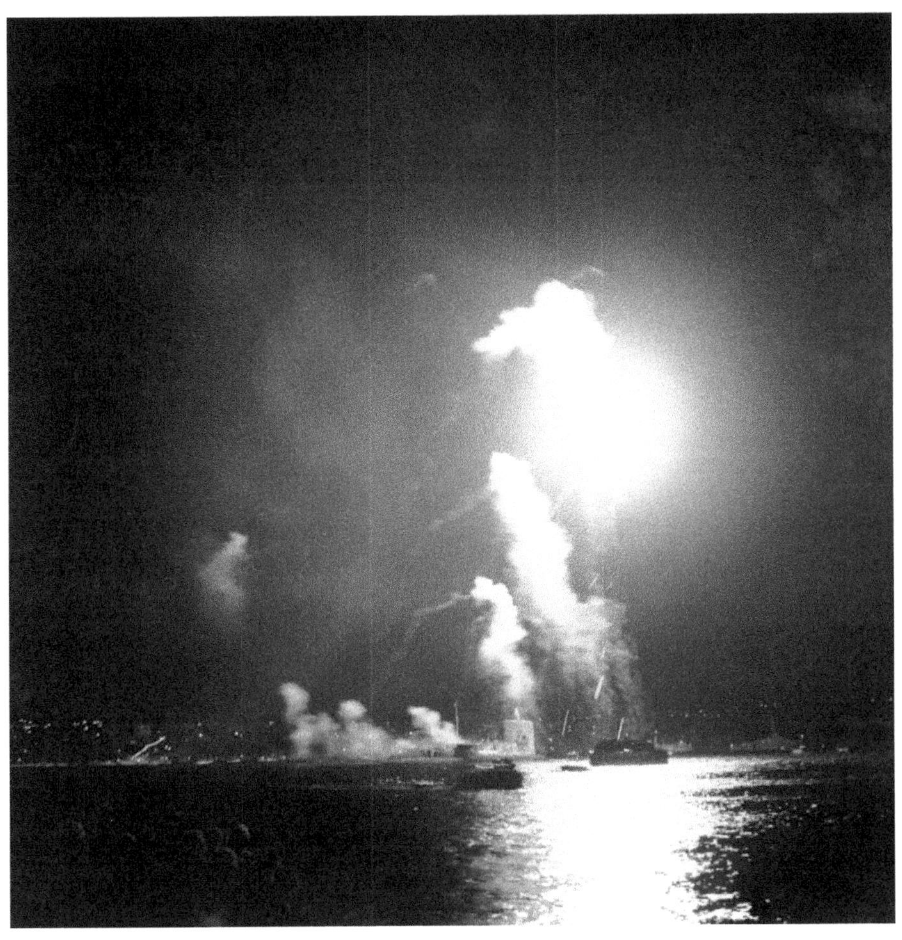

Fireworks on Sydney Harbour celebrating the Queen of England's first visit to Australia, February, 1954

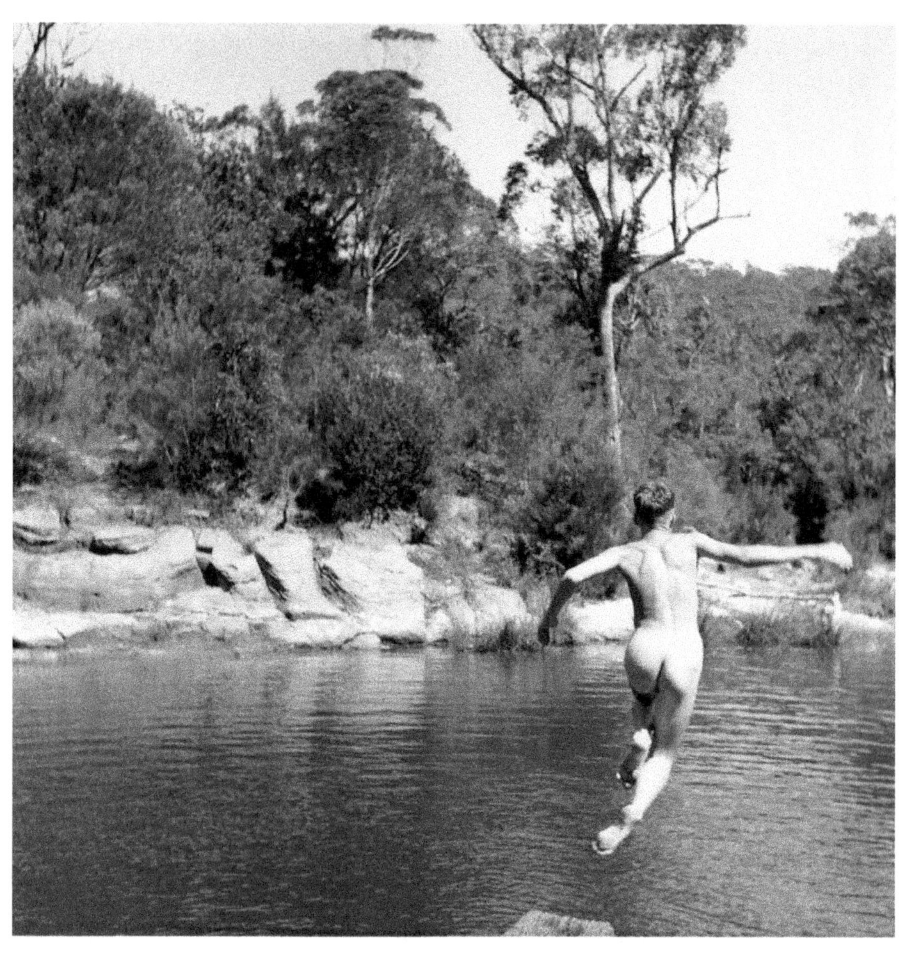

Jumping In (to our favourite swimming hole at "The End" of Middle Harbour), c.1954

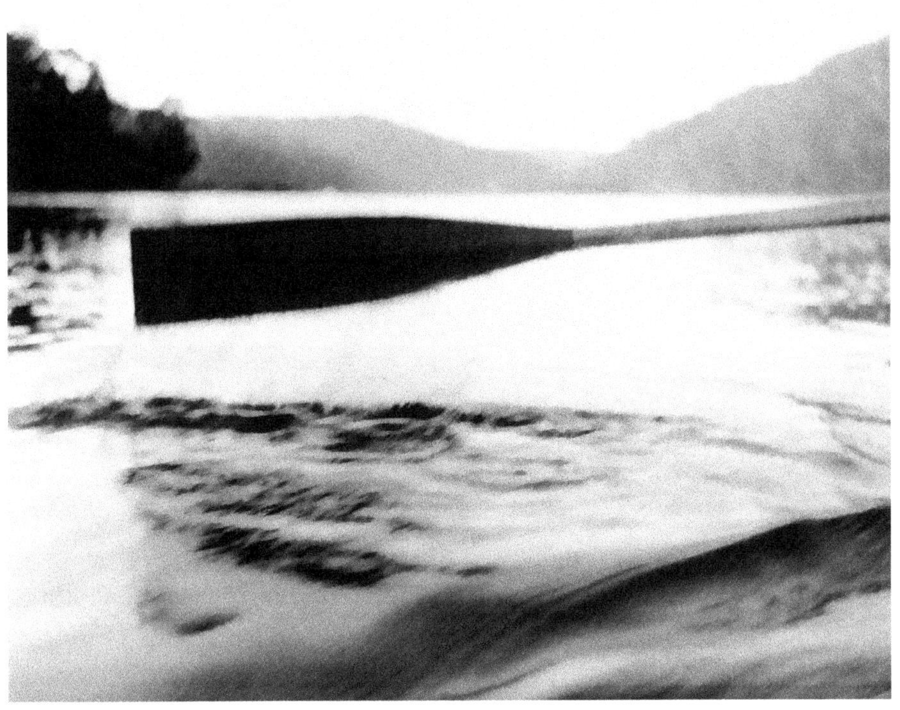

Rowing on Middle Harbour, c.1954 (toning added later – you can check this out at valentinepress.com.au)

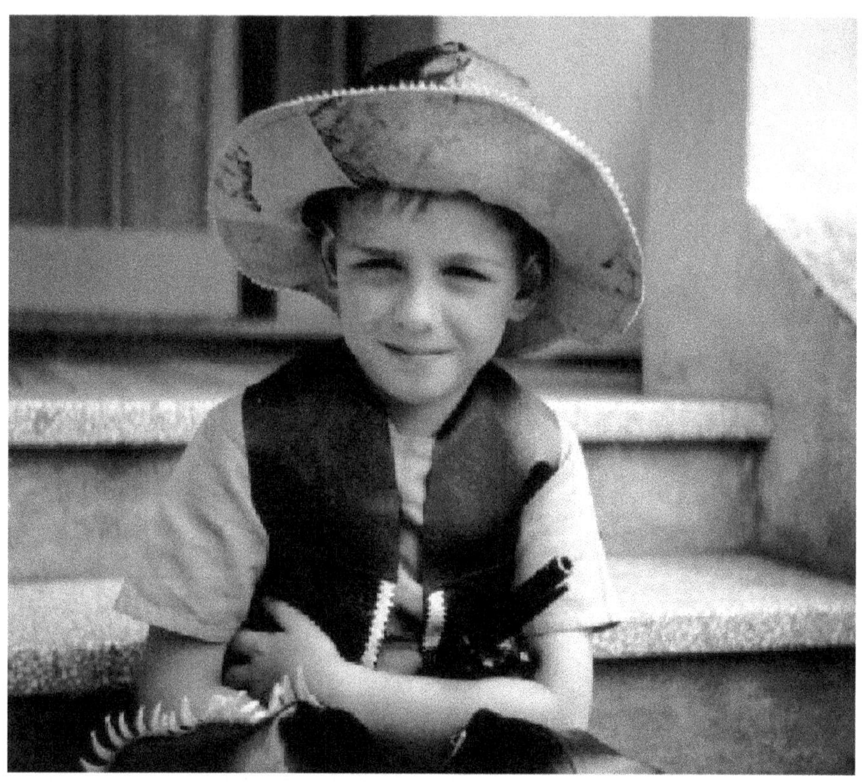

John (Dufaycolor transparency), c.1954. In colour on website.

Colour (and Dufaycolor)...

For as long as I can remember I've been aware of my colour blindness. It's not that I can see no colours, but I see them differently from other people. If the colour balance of some images in this collection seems "wrong" you can put it down, if you like, to colour blindness. At primary school my teacher ridiculed me for painting something in the wrong colours. In later years I've made quite a study of the physics of colour perception and colour reproduction, no doubt to help me to understand and compensate for my perceived limitations.

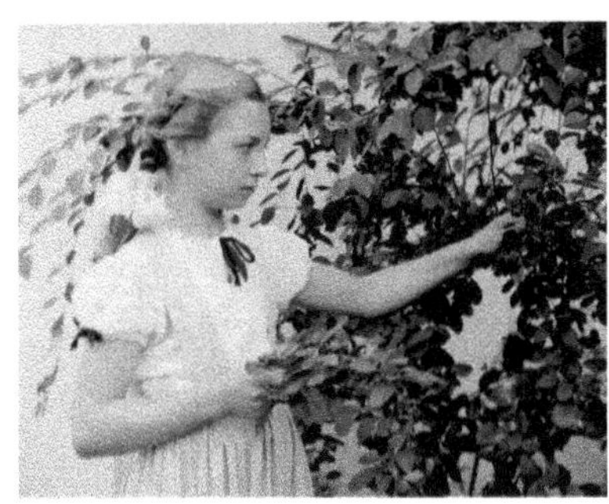

Patricia (Trish), early 1950s. (Toning added later.)

The photograph of my young brother John opposite was taken using a material known as Dufaycolor, which predated by many years such materials as Kodachrome, Ansco and Agfacolour. Dufaycolor used a reversal process, that is it produced a positive image on the original camera film (in that it wasn't unique). Tiny filters on its surface separated the exposing light into the three primary colours and also divided the viewing light into those same primaries, while the microscopic portions of positive silver image under each filter controlled how much of each primary colour reached our eyes. Dufaycolor images look quite dark, but when plenty of light is pushed through them for reproductions, they are infinitely more "natural" than any of Dufay's competitors at the time.

At Sungravure, large-format (eight by ten inch) Dufaycolor transparencies were used as the originals for illustrating cookery pages for Woman's Day. Dufaycolor was an English material that had some affinity with the French Autochrome process (invented just after the turn of the 20th century by the Lumieres of Cinematograph fame).

With a film speed of approximately ASA 3 it was considered far too slow to be used for hand-held photography or for moving subjects, although I don't think I had a tripod when I made the portrait of my young brother, John using 120-roll film in the trusty Voigtländer. Slow as it might have been it was obviously manageable. And Dufay's colours didn't fade horribly like most of its later, more high-tech competitors.

Friendship ...

Paul Rixon was my closest friend from the late 1940s until about 1954 or '55. There were social differences between us, but they weren't a barrier. Paul's father was an executive for a Sydney department store. He was also a musician, had his own vocal group, The Rixon Singers, and was the chorus master of one of the predecessors to Opera Australia. My father was a clerk for the North Shore Gas Company. Obviously family incomes were not comparable. Before I was earning enough to buy my own clothes I was pretty shabbily dressed. I remember that only from the fact that Paul's mother at least once, maybe more often, took pity on me and gave me Paul's old clothes.

Paul went to Barker College, I went to North Sydney Technical High School. When it came time for us to do our national service in the 1950s Paul was called up for the air force, I was called up for the army. I can think of nothing that more clearly indicates public perceptions of differences in our social class. But these social differences never impinged on our friendship.

My love of art was something that developed from indefinable elements in my own background, but from Paul's family I became aware of music. We went to operas and concerts. With Paul I listened to his father's substantial collection of recordings of classical music. These recordings of course weren't compact, they were on 78 r.p.m. discs, heavy and brittle. A symphony could take up a lot of twelve-inch discs in paper sleeves, all bound between covers of very heavy cloth-covered board, gold-embossed.

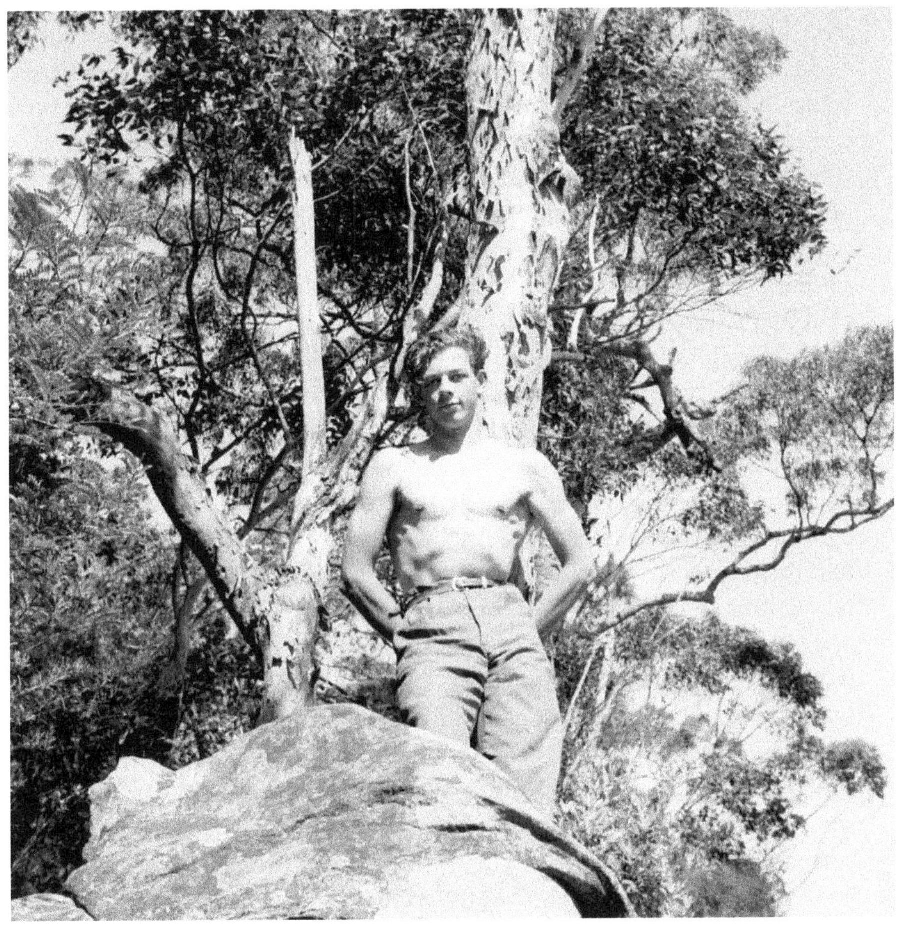

Paul c.1954

At my place we listened to at least one of Mr Rixon's recordings on a radiogram that I'd bought from my earnings at Sungravure. (Microgroove discs were just coming in and radiograms of the time had to be able to play three types of disc: the old 78s, seven-inch 45s, and ten and twelve-inch 33 r.p.m. discs that were relatively light and could hold at least 25 minutes of music on one side; 50 or more minutes on one disc!) Late one evening Paul put the bound set of 78s we had been listening to - one of Beethoven's concertos - on the luggage carrier of his bike. He had to ride home to West Lindfield with some steep hills on the way. Going down these hills you could get up to pretty high speeds. Close to home and at such a speed, Paul fell off his bike. Of course the records fell off too, and being brittle, they all shattered. Paul's father was shattered also.

In 1954 I completed my apprenticeship which meant that apart from being a fully qualified tradesman, the deferral of my national service came to an end. I was called up by the army for a three-month period of "basic training" in one of the army camps at Holdsworthy. That was one of the most miserable times of my life. I hated the army. The best way I can explain my feelings is to say that I remember making drawings of a soldier holding close to his body a hand grenade with the pin pulled. Not a pretty picture.

Basic training was followed by various weekends and two periods of two weeks given over to training as an artillery gunner. This wasn't so bad, I enjoyed the hard physical work and the practical achievements of accurately aiming the twenty-five pounder cannon. I must have been a not entirely unsatisfactory recruit, because at one stage I was approached by a couple of officers offering me the chance to go into officer training. I told them candidly that I wasn't interested and that I didn't like the army. No doubt there is a report on this mouldering away in the army's archives, along with a report of how I went to sleep while guarding one of the precious twenty-five pounders. Did I fall asleep because I knew we were only playing soldiers, and there was no real danger? National servicemen were called "chocos" (chocolate soldiers) by "regular" soldiers and although the Korean War was raging we chocos were kept right out of it. I was extremely glad of that, not only because I was shit-scared of being in real conflict, but because in a real war zone I could easily have been summarily shot for going to sleep on guard.

The officers who interviewed me the next morning about my dereliction must have been real gentlemen. They didn't abuse me and it seemed to me that they understood I was hopelessly out of place in the army.

In 2004, looking at the photograph (opposite) of me in 1955 is a disturbing experience. My expression looks extremely uncomfortable, in fact I think I can see a coarseness in my features that isn't evident in quite the same way in photographs taken before or since. Am I reading too much into it, or did the army have that effect on me?

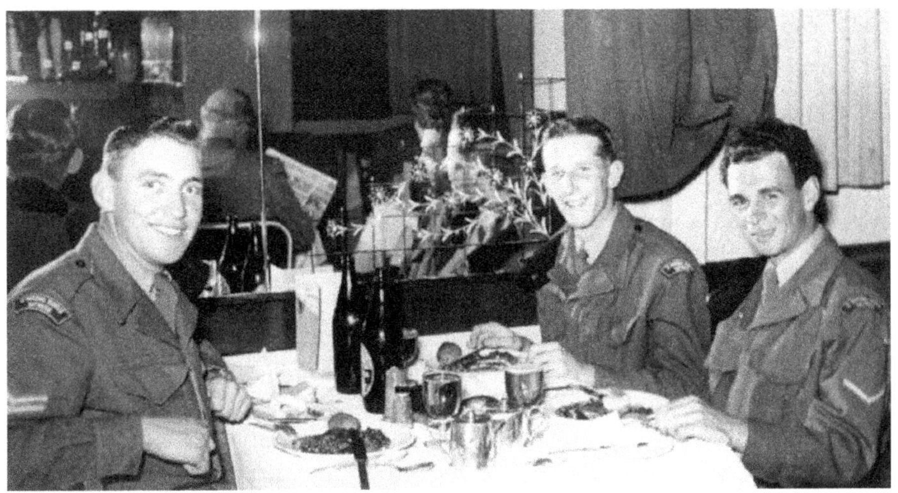

DP (far right) at a Sydney restaurant with two other "chocos", c.1955. (Photographer unknown)

Painting and drawing ...

I had been painting and drawing, mostly landscapes and still-lifes, since 1952. I can't locate many of these works today, and I never sold one, although I felt especially honoured during the early 1960s when a small picture that I was very proud of was stolen during a party at my house.

In the 1950s I joined the Contemporary Art Society (CAS) and showed work with them in their Sydney exhibitions as well as with the Society of Artists. In the 1960s abstract painting gained strength in Sydney (although not in Melbourne). I often attempted to paint in abstract modes, as I have again in more recent times, but it isn't something that came easily to me then. I remember with a lot of amusement a moment in a tea break at a CAS meeting when a well-known abstract artist and critic, Elwyn Lynn, stood next to me at the urinal and as we pissed together he told me he thought I was "the best realist artist in Sydney."

Sex, betrayal and love ...

Paul had a very active sex life from very early on in our friendship; I didn't. In the photograph of Paul on page 19 I think you can see that he thought he was god's gift to women. Even if you can't see it I know that he did think it. He had a girlfriend of whom he was very fond and the relationship between the three of us was such that at least once, while Paul and Judy made love, I sat on the edge of the bed picking out notes from a guitar.

Judy was as passionate as we were about music and art. She was all of seventeen and must have worried her parents desperately by staying out late. One night she stayed at Paul's even later than usual. As always there was music and intense talk.

But I remember something else: there was something entirely animal in the air, I can describe it no other way. Something entirely non-verbal was going on between Judy and me. The memory lacks detail. The one thing that's absolutely clear is an atmosphere of pure desire. But there was no physical contact, we didn't even kiss.

By about four or five in the morning Judy wanted to go home. I had a little two-stroke motor bike and I offered her a lift home. Nearing her house we turned away towards the bush and found a flat expanse of rock well above the road where we sat to watch the sunrise.

I don't remember if we spoke at all, perhaps there was no need. I don't remember us taking our clothes off but I vividly remember Judy lying beneath me. I was gone. She took me into herself. Of course it was all over in a flash. (As one of the characters in a Lawrence Durrell novel said: "I'm never any good the first time.")

Since this is not a novel I'm not about to flesh out the story with details synthesised from many experiences. I took Judy home, then rode my bike back to Paul's place, told him what had happened. It broke his heart. If for no other reason, I know because the same has happened to me more than once since then. But of course I knew right then what I - what we - had done. I suppose that at the same moment I was being inducted to the world of sex I was also being inducted to the world of moral ambiguity. I was ready for it. God held no meaning for me, nor did the communist party.

Judy and I formed a passionate relationship almost immediately. Our natures led us to leap into things with no premeditation, but this situation, driven by youthful hormones too long repressed (in my case), was more intense than anything I had ever experienced. Judy may have felt another, earlier, less earthly passion of equal intensity; she told me that at a slightly earlier time she had intended to become a nun, although at this distance in time I can't vouch for the seriousness of that intention.

The Push ...

We sought out places where we could meet like-minded people, "bohemians" we might have called them if we thought about it. One such place was a little café in Kings Cross called The Arabian. Paul and I had hung out there when we were still good friends. In The Arabian you could meet small-time artists and poets and small-time crooks, listen to bebop, cadge methedrine tablets (to keep us awake all night) and occasionally be approached by older men looking for sex with younger men.

But The Arabian couldn't hold us for long. I think we found the arty denizens too "up themselves", too pretentious "wankers" although we wouldn't have used those terms then. Somehow or other we heard about a pub in the city called The Tudor, where it was said you could meet "real" intellectuals, students and academics and anarchists. We went to The Tudor for the first time on a Saturday afternoon some time in 1955, it must have been.

This was more like it. And the atmosphere was hugely inclusive. We had hardly sat down at a table in the bar on the first floor when we were greeted by "Appo" (Dick Appleton) and Johnny Earls. I can't remember who else we met that afternoon, although there were many people there, drinking beer, talking loudly. We had stumbled into something unique in Australia (although Melbournians might dispute that description). We had found The Push. A more detailed account of this disparate group of individualists is appearing, at the time of writing, in Appo's memoirs,[2] currently being serialised in the photocopied, privately circulated journal *Heraclitus*.

The most immediately striking thing about these people was that men and women shared the same space (virtually unheard of in Australian pubs then, and indeed until many years later), and that men and women

---

2 *Appo: Memoirs of a member of the Sydney Push*, subsequently published by Darlington Press in 2010. A new story about the Push has since been published, *Witch Girl and the Push*, by Lyn Gain, Valentine Press, 2013.

shared the same language, an earthy, vulgar and very direct language that called a fuck a fuck. Although not everyone was the same, many people talked vociferously about politics, art, books, movies, and they discussed these things with a sceptical realism that mocked the mystification, preciousness and sheer bullshit that usually attended these things (sadly, still does). Authority figures, from the police to the Queen, and all between, were regarded with contempt.

Some people from the ranks of The Push went on to hold influential positions in politics, academia and the press. In politics some push people found roles as advisors to ministers. Only one, so far as I know, attempted the role of "politician", a despised category.

Academia was undoubtedly the favoured domain of Push people. Academia was in those days a realm where "disinterested enquiry" could still be spoken of seriously. I never experienced university life, although being in The Push conferred on one much of the status of student, I always felt. I say in all seriousness that I believe I am better educated, due to The Push, in areas of philosophy and politics than most students of modern, or should I say post-modern universities are now.

Artists - visual artists, that is - were thin on the ground in The Push. John Olsen was there for a time, as Appo relates, but Olsen had dropped out of Push life by the time Judy and I turned up. Later, other more and less famous figures from the art world were drawn, fairly cautiously I think, to take some part in Push life, but they rarely stayed for long. Perhaps that was because artists, in my experience, have a terrible propensity for talking bullshit and for being drawn to irrational "theories" and beliefs. I haven't been immune to this propensity myself, but I hope I'm not kidding myself when I say that I have always drawn back from the brink.

Some of the friends I made in my early days in The Push are still friends, almost fifty years later. When we meet we still laugh, drink and talk with the same scepticism, affection and respect for differences.

Films and film making ...

Several years before falling in love with Judy and falling out of friendship with Paul, I became a film maker. This may seem like a ridiculous statement; the first film that I'm publicly known for, *Swansong in Birdland,* was made and shown in 1964. But I had made a lot of films before then with my little 8mm camera, given to me by Ern Moxley, a worker at Sungravure.

I had been going to the Savoy cinema in Bligh Street since the early 1950s and Ern Moxley must have been prescient in seeing the connection between my artistic bent and my interest in films. Film making then was generally considered to be purely an industrial/commercial process, so expensive that it could rarely (if ever) occur in Australia, a colonial outpost, where the British and/or United States models were considered the only way to go. The Savoy was the only place in Sydney where one could see contemporary European films, and its name is honoured in my "business name", L.W. Savoy Productions. (What a joke, me as a businessman!)

There was another place that was for me even more influential than the Savoy: the Roundhouse, the library of East Sydney Tech, the only public art school at the time. The Roundhouse held regular screenings of pre-war avant-garde films, organised by a man whose name I can't remember clearly, although I'll call him "Kaplan" because that name rises up from vague memory. (I sometimes think that so many changes were happening to me that my memories have become fragmented and schematicised like a "synthetic cubist" painting. This is not a complaint, nor a bid to be seen as a crazy person. It is simply a statement of fact.)

With my little clockwork camera I started shooting movies. At first I just pointed it randomly at things that took my fancy but I quickly became more ambitious. Screenings at the Roundhouse, the Savoy and at the Sydney Film Society (the predecessor to the Sydney Film Festival) were my inspirations. Under the influence of D.W. Griffith's *Intolerance* (you see what I mean by "ambitious"), I started shooting the first part of an epic to be called *The Wheel* (of life, no doubt) which featured Paul and my sister Trish. Trish represented "goodness" while Paul was "evil". In Kodachrome, Trish was seen doing something vaguely ritualistic before an altar made from half an old car axle (the bowl, formed by the differential casing, held cloths soaked in kerosene and set alight), while Paul crept up and attacked her - symbolically - from behind, and overturned the altar.

Another entirely different film was a documentary about my childhood playground, Middle Harbour. (I re-made the film about fifteen years later, under the title *Harbour*, on 16mm colour film). The later version of that film contains a lyrical sequence in which a friend and lover at the time, Ellen White, walked naked through the bush. There was a sub-text to that sequence which it was of no benefit for anyone to know about then. I'll reveal it now, not because it throws any light on the film at all, but because people have notions that the 1940s and 1950s were universally puritanical.

The story goes like this. Around 1950, a friend and I had walked through the bush to go for a swim in a little creek that ran into Middle Harbour. At high tide it had some sandy pools deep enough to swim in. Probably its real advantage was that we could swim nude there with very little chance of being disturbed. Because of the place's seclusion, we were surprised to hear a dinghy being rowed towards us. We got out of the water and hid behind some bushes, hoping the intrusion would be brief. A young couple pulled their dinghy up to a flat rock and very soon took their swimming costumes off. What boys of fifteen or sixteen could ignore this opportunity? Acting out fantasies we'd had a few years earlier, of spying on Japanese soldiers, we climbed a tree opposite the couple's mooring. To our amazement we watched as the woman masturbated her friend. Luckily one or both of us didn't fall out of the tree.

The lovers then moved a blanket on to the flat rock. We couldn't hear anything they said, maybe they said nothing, but it seemed a very short time before the man lay on his back and the woman straddled him. Holding his cock she lowered herself on to it. They seemed to lie there like that for a long time, making slow undulating movements. No sex education, even if it existed, could ever have been so instructive.

Eventually the couple uncoupled, got into the water and made enough noise to cover our climb out of the tree. I'm sure the lovers never knew they'd been watched the whole time and since this is almost certainly the first time the story's been told (I can't vouch for my friend) they could have held their own memories of that time as a wonderful, innocent, extended moment. Life is strange and may have dealt them terrible blows, or it may have not. I hope they had long and passionate love lives.

A hugely influential exhibition came to Sydney in 1953: *Modern French Painting* opened at the so-called "National Art Gallery of New South Wales". It was a short walk from Sungravure and I went often. The exhibition contained paintings by virtually all the artists of the "School of Paris", artists whose work I had only seen up to that time in generally small and poor reproductions, usually in black-and-white, in art books which I pored over at every opportunity. The exhibition was massively inspirational to me, and I think to every artist and student who considered him or herself a modernist.

There were, of course, many conservatives in the Sydney art world who were disgusted by what they saw as bad painting, even as decadent art (were they in fact fascists?). Another problem for these people was that the exhibition had temporarily displaced from the gallery's very limited wall space most if not all of their beloved 19th century paintings certainly not "old masters" but they had a slick professionalism - scenes from mythology and British history, or the half-hearted "impressionism" of Streeton, Roberts and their contemporaries.

One man (by the name of Hinton, I think) caused a disturbance by shouting abuse at the modern paintings or the organisers of the show, or both. I believe he was firmly escorted out of the gallery (I wasn't there at the time, so my memory is of reports from newspapers, not first person observation).

Apart from the sheer excitement of seeing, for the first time, some truly contemporary art, what was so marvellous for me was to see the scale and texture of these works. In those days we all tended to make fairly small paintings, maybe, at least in part, because virtually everything we knew about the work of European artists we learned from small reproductions. There were paintings by many of the super-stars of the "School of Paris": Picasso, Braque, Dufy and so on. I don't hold any memories of the work of some of those artists. Perhaps, being young and not well informed in these matters, I wasn't well attuned to much that I saw. What I do remember are works by Dufy, to be sure, as well as by younger artists such as Mannessier, Estéve, for example, whose works were quite abstract in appearance, and a nude by André Marchand that scandalised one of my bosses at Sungravure when I showed him the catalogue. (I sometimes wonder whatever happened to Mannessier, Marchand and many others in the exhibition? I suppose they retreated into merely regional importance, although seeming to be world famous at the time.) I've had other inspirational experiences since then, but the passionate feelings aroused by that show are unforgettable.

Within a short time I was attempting to emulate the French artists. At this time too I almost completely put aside my interest in making films.

The painting below, photographed for me by one of my co-workers at Sungravure, is an example of where I had arrived by the mid 1950s, by which time Judy and I had married. (The painting was almost certainly done from a sketch drawn during our "honeymoon".)

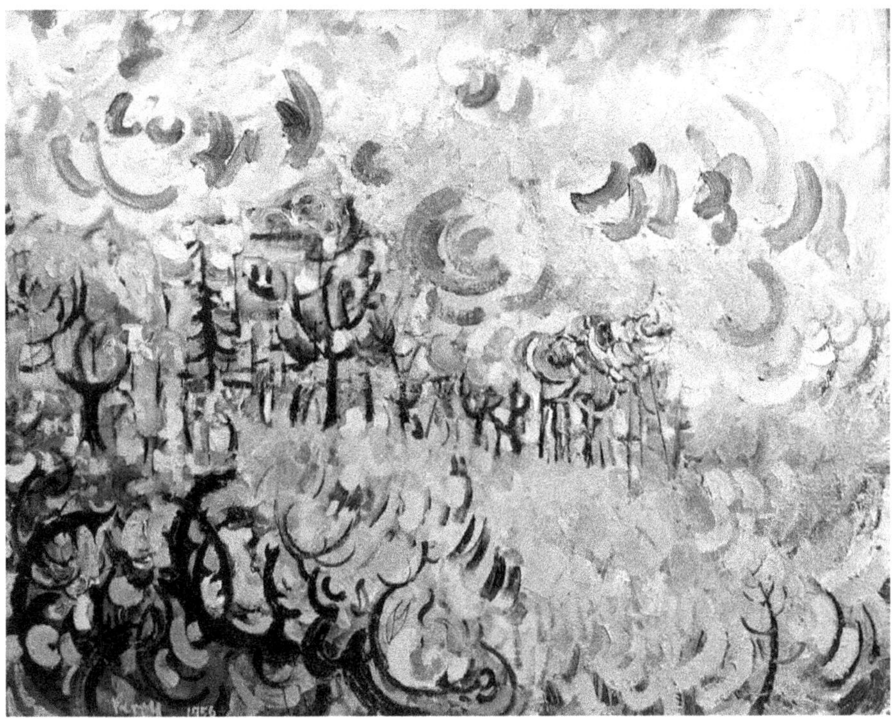

Blue Mountains Landscape *(oils on canvas, 75cm. X 100cm), 1956. Photograph by Ted Ashby. In colour on website.*

Marriage ...

Judy's parents were devout Catholics. They certainly didn't approve of our relationship, and they must have known that we were being "sinful" every time we met, which was very frequently. For us to simply live together would have been unthinkable to her parents and probably to both of us too. Although we were rebellious neither of us wanted to hurt our parents by doing something so scandalous to the morals of 1956, and Judy's parents tried hard to accept me. To try, I think, to escape the stresses of parental disapproval, we decided we wanted to get married. I did the proper thing and asked Judy's father for permission to marry her; an awkward moment for both of us, I think.

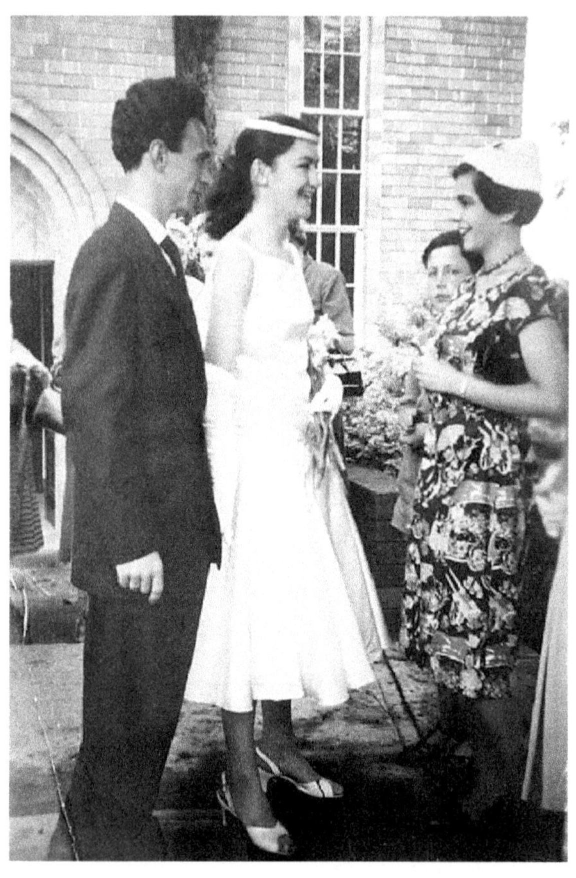

Outside Lindfield catholic church, 1956. (Snapshot by unknown photographer.)

And so, in the end, we were married. Before that could happen , as a non-Catholic I had to have lessons from the priest at Lindfield, basically, I think, about how virtuous Catholics should go about their lives. The only thing I can remember about those lessons now is the strong smell of whisky on the priest's breath.

Our train journey to the Blue Mountains is especially memorable to me for the intense feelings of expectant desire, made sweeter by the knowledge that we were no longer subject to social disapproval. Even though we gave fervent lip service to not giving a damn about that, we did, I'm sure, feel some relief that we were now socially acceptable.

As we fell together on our hotel bed (within moments of closing the door, it seems to me) there was something unspoken and supremely romantic in our expectations of our love making. Although she was an intensely sexual person, sex, at least with me, didn't automatically lead to orgasms for Judy. Somewhere in the back of our minds there may have been an acceptance of this as the result of going against the teachings of the church (in her case) and of respectable society (in my case). But this is an almost 50-year-old memory, and I don't intend any of this to be construed as accurate reportage. And yet, on the other hand, I do think such experiences were almost universal, at least in our social circles, and can possibly be blamed for a lot of sadness and hostility in personal relationships. I do remember that we were so worried about this that we together asked a family doctor about it. His response was great embarrassment and no useful information. It's one of the great natural injustices that while male orgasm, or at least ejaculation, is almost always a necessary precondition for the making of babies, female orgasm is entirely unnecessary for the same result. Thus it had come about that Judy was pregnant when we got married. We had successfully avoided pregnancy for more than a year by using the "rhythm method" (otherwise known as "vatican roulette") but as our marriage approached we must have decided this was an unwanted intrusion in our sex life.

Regardless of what I've just said, I remember our life together as harmonious. We shared a great love of painting, music and English poetry. I was something of a clean slate in regard to poetry, but Judy gave me at least a partial appreciation of Gerard Manley Hopkins (probably taught to her by nuns at Kincoppal) and of Dylan Thomas whose work was probably more naturally attractive to me since, as far as I remember, it lacked supernatural overtones.

I've known many painters since then who espouse various beliefs in the supernatural, but for me the great pleasure of painting lay in its materiality. I admired (admire still) the French artist Georges Rouault, whose paintings almost always depicted religious subjects. What appealed to me was the rough-hewn quality of his images; the very physical presence of his work: thickly-painted layer on layer of rich colour, heavy contours that were said to be influenced by stained glass windows. Of course, there is another kind of presence too in the work of Rouault: the religious events that he depicted have strong political meanings. The Jesus and other figures of Rouault's images are revolutionaries struggling against the Roman empire. Such an interpretation is of course projected backwards on the work, from an understanding more recent than I could have had in the early 1950s when, to be blunt, my feelings were stronger than my knowledge. (Please don't think that I'm representing myself now as an intellectual, but an accumulation of all those years of experience can't have left me as innocent as I was then.)

But even then, as I was voraciously reading art theory and looking at paintings, mostly in books, I was becoming permanently attached to Picasso's and Braque's cubism and to Paul Klee's abstraction. No doubt some people will point out to me the mysticism espoused by many abstract artists and claim I am wrong to call myself a materialist, which I do. If that happens I'll shrug and say: "I can handle the contradictions (if that's what they are), so you'll just have to do the same."

New Zealand ...

While living in Lindfield we felt suffocated by suburbia. It also became obvious that not even marriage could ensure our independence from parents and relatives. We still needed to run away and we hit on the idea of moving to New Zealand. I don't really know where this idea came from but I got hold of New Zealand newspapers where jobs were advertised for couples to work on farms, with accommodation being included as part of the "package", as we'd say now. I wrote to apply for some of these positions and fairly quickly had a response from a dairy farmer in the North Island.

In those days people almost always travelled by ship, and that was what we did. We booked our passage to Auckland on an old and creaky steamship that made its way slowly across the Tasman Sea. For most of the journey the swells lifted us high on crests one minute, then dropped us into troughs the next. Our cabin was deep inside the ship, close to the engine room. I didn't quite get sea-sick, I think I avoided it only by spending a lot of time on deck. Looking over the side I could see the massive height of the swells which sometimes were almost level with the deck, then the water fell away to reveal row upon row of portholes. Being in the fresh air and able to see what was coming, and thus being able to predict the ship's next move, kept the sickness at bay. I have read somewhere that the Tasman Sea is one of the roughest in the world. I can believe it. Down in the cabin there was no escape from the constant movement, nor from the creaking steel plates and thudding of the engine. Somehow we managed to get at least some sleep and to keep our food down.

After disembarking in Auckland we stayed in a hotel for several days. At that time a major exhibition was being prepared in Auckland Art Gallery. The exhibition contained a comprehensive collection of sculptures by the Englishman Henry Moore who was at that time at the height of his fame. In the gallery we could see glimpses of Moore's remarkable bronzes. The show was to open a day after we were booked to leave Auckland and somehow or other I managed to contact a senior curator (were they called that then?) who gave us special dispensation to have a private viewing.

This was a remarkable experience. We were free to roam amongst the many large sculptures and to get an intimate contact with the work that would have been difficult, if not impossible, to get as ordinary exhibition visitors. I am not the greatest fan of Henry Moore's work but at the time my taste was probably more catholic (less calcified?) than it is now. Even so, I'm not about to retrospectively denigrate the monumental power of those works or the incredible craft and imagination that went into their making. Several days later we saw an article and letters in the Auckland press that poured philistine scorn on the work, not unlike the responses to the *Modern French Painting* exhibition in Sydney a few years earlier.

After that remarkable introduction to New Zealand we went south by bus to take up the farm labouring job near Te Puke, a town not far from Tauranga and situated in lush dairy country. In those days, with imperial ties still strong, New Zealand farmers had a lucrative guaranteed market in Britain for butter, cheese and other dairy products.

We had only been on the farm for a very short time before the farmer realised that Judy was pregnant. He reminded us that one of the requirements of our position was that Judy would be needed to help with haymaking, which she wouldn't be able to do as a pregnant woman. He would have to let us go.

We urgently consulted the newspaper again and applied for similar positions a little further south. This time we made our situation clear and found a farmer who was willing to employ me without the expectation that Judy would work. Thus we found ourselves on a farm some miles out of Opotiki, a town placed at the junction of two rivers at the point where they emptied into the Bay of Plenty.

So began in earnest my life as a farm labourer, a life that gave me, skinny runt that I started as, a seriously strong physique, rude good health, and not a few lessons in life. I quickly learned to milk cows and to drive a tractor, to dig drainage channels across the boggy coastal country (the most unsatisfying job on the farm), to build fences as straight as a ruled line and to plough furrows almost as straight (these jobs I loved very much; I felt as if I was drawing directly on the landscape).

Drawing on paper kept me busy on many evenings. Sometimes I drew from memory, sometimes directly from the subject, almost always with a fine mapping pen dipped in Indian ink. These tools had the advantage of speed and of graphic clarity. I must have been extremely fit and healthy because I was able to work all day on the farm and still be able to draw most evenings. On a dairy farm there is no escape from milking, which has to happen twice a day, seven days a week if the cows' milk is not to dry up. Between the two daily milkings all the other farm work had to be done: fencing, ploughing, harvesting and so on. This meant starting work by sunrise or earlier and finishing at sunset or later, even on "days off". A "day off" meant that the time between milkings was my own. On such days I sometimes drew the landscape *en plein aire,* as they say in France .

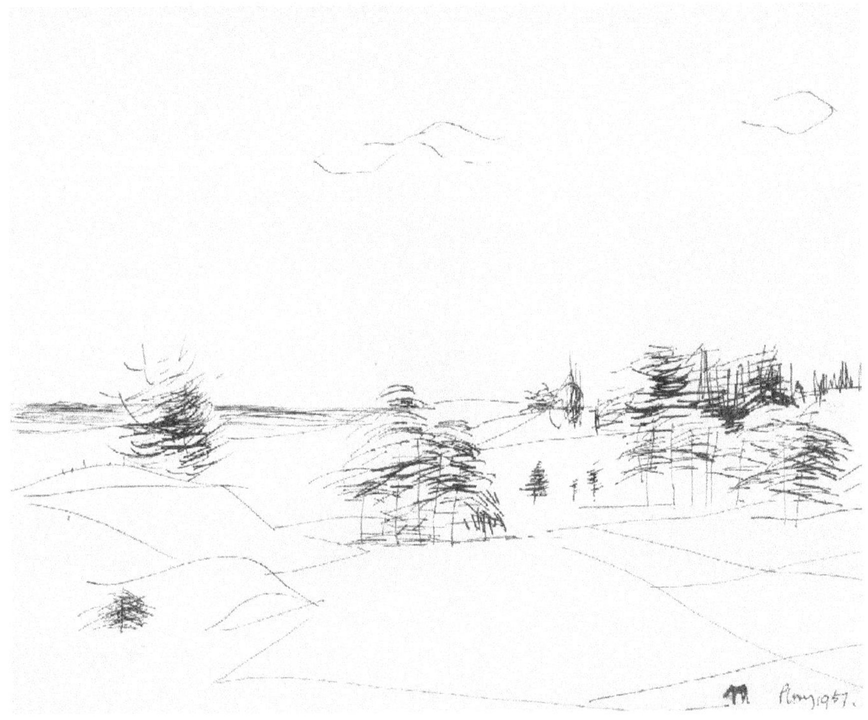

The Bay of Plenty (Indian ink on paper), 1957

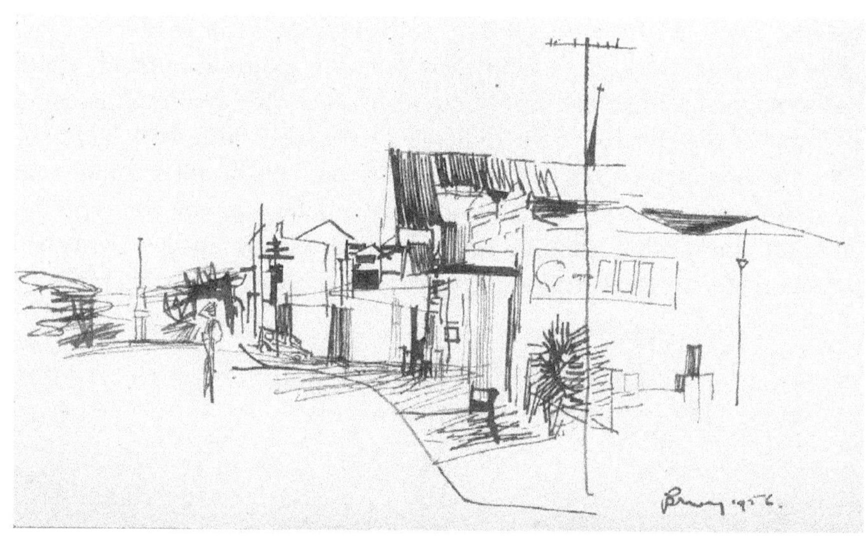

Opotiki (Indian ink on paper), 1956

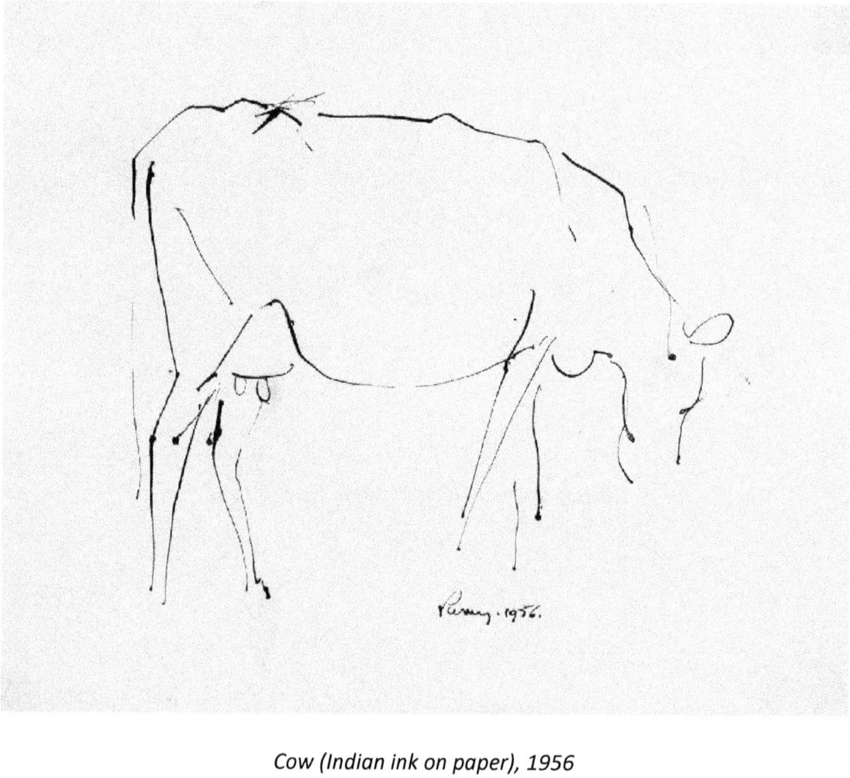

Cow (Indian ink on paper), 1956

Our first child....

On 24th December, 1956 our son Simon was born in the little hospital at Opotiki. In those days (until much later, actually) it was unheard

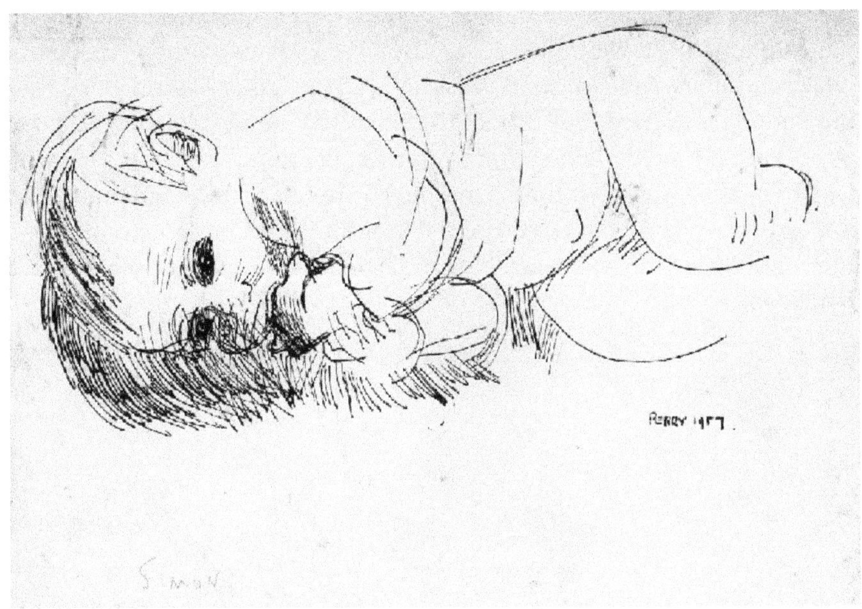

Simon (Indian ink on paper), 1957

of for fathers to be present during the birth of their children, so I was sent home to spend my first night alone since our marriage. On the same night the whole Bay of Plenty area suffered a significant earthquake (it's not for nothing that New Zealand is called "the shaky isles"). All houses in our part of the country were made of timber because it resists twisting forces far better than brick walls do. As if to demonstrate that, the earthquake demolished all brick chimneys in a nearby town. I woke to feel the bed rocking as though it was sailing on a very heavy swell. There was as well a loud creaking of the house's timbers and (is this memory or fantasy?) a deep subterranean rumble. A dramatic beginning to Simon's life, and, if you like, a prediction of the rocky relationship of his parents in later years (although that's getting a bit ahead of the story).

Country life...

Judy always seemed to be completely unfazed by child birth and child raising. This is not to say she was in any way uncaring. Just that she took such things as they came, without drama or preciousness. These were characteristics that I admired greatly, and which probably helped to keep me emotionally stable too. We were in New Zealand without friends or relations, apart from a short visit by Judy's father. Farm work was unrelenting and hard, but that didn't seem to stop me drawing at every opportunity. I took no photographs during that time, or at least I have no negatives now from that time. I'm pretty sure I had my Voigtländer with me but even if I'd wanted to use it I wouldn't have been able to afford film or paper or processing chemicals, and we had no space for a darkroom.

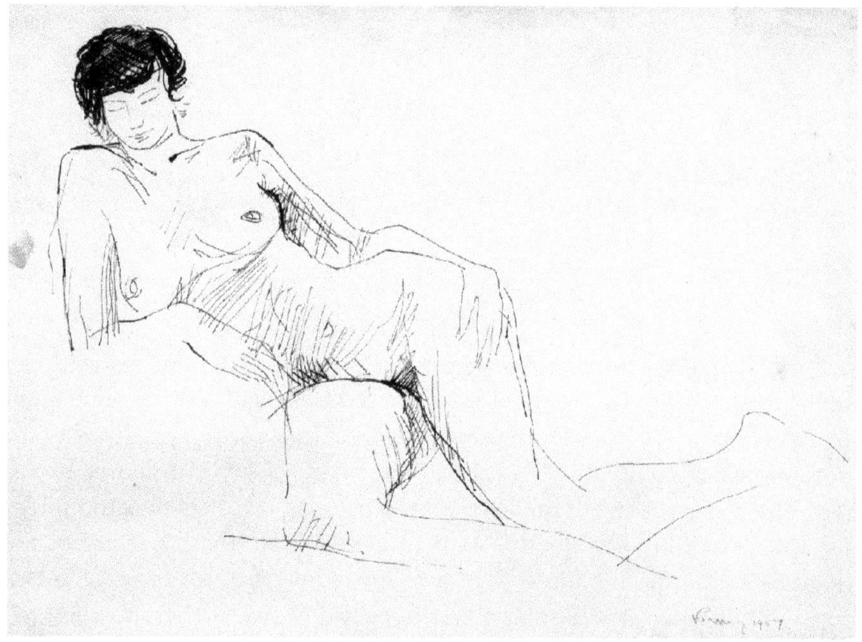

Judy (Indian ink on paper), 1957

As I think back to that time it's probably more accurate to say that my priorities were to spend what little money was available on drawing materials. I don't think there was ever a time in my life when I was more single-mindedly committed to being an artist as that word was understood in the 1950s. Although I continued to draw with a fine nibbed pen I was also looking for a more rough-hewn quality. I also had my 8mm camera with me and I made one attempt to make a film: an abstract animation based on coloured graphics. I remember being disappointed with the result of that and the film may have been discarded soon after it came back from processing.

Be that as it may, it's entirely irrelevant at this distance in time. What does interest me is a drawing I did of the truck (below). Apart from its documentary charm, if I can call it that, it is what's on the back of it (next

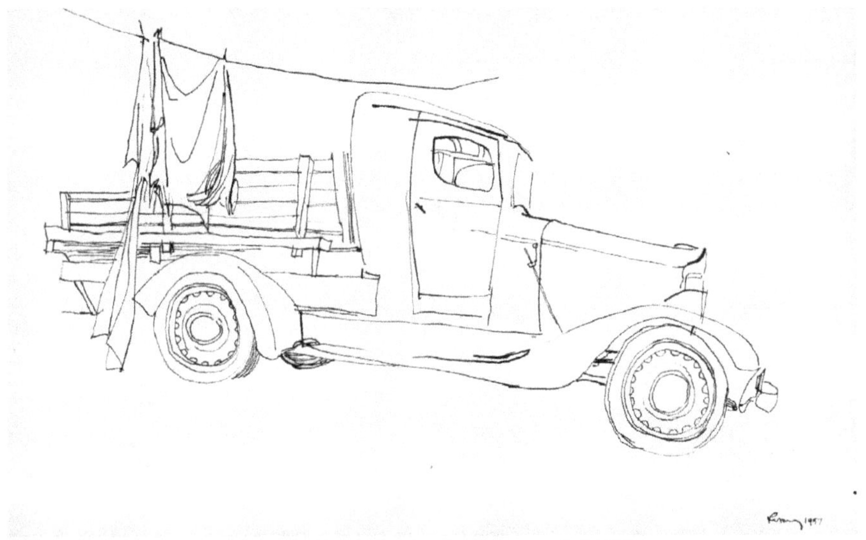

Our Truck (Indian ink on paper), 1957

page). It's a completely different kind of drawing, hard to think of as the work of the same person. But it is, and on the same sheet of paper. We artists are expected to maintain a consistent "style". By doing that we make it easy for collectors to develop a liking for our work, thus encouraging them to buy it, preferably in quantities of more than one. Such consistency reassures a collector that he or she has part of a body of work with reliable continuity, ensuring that the work will retain, or preferably, increase its value.

That continuity is something that I've always found hard to maintain. Presumably the panel labelled "The Cynic" in the drawing on the back of *Our Truck,* a not very well-disguised self-portrait, is a clue to how I saw myself at the time. But cynical about what? Art itself? Art theory? The market? Life? I can't help you with a definitive answer unless it's to say

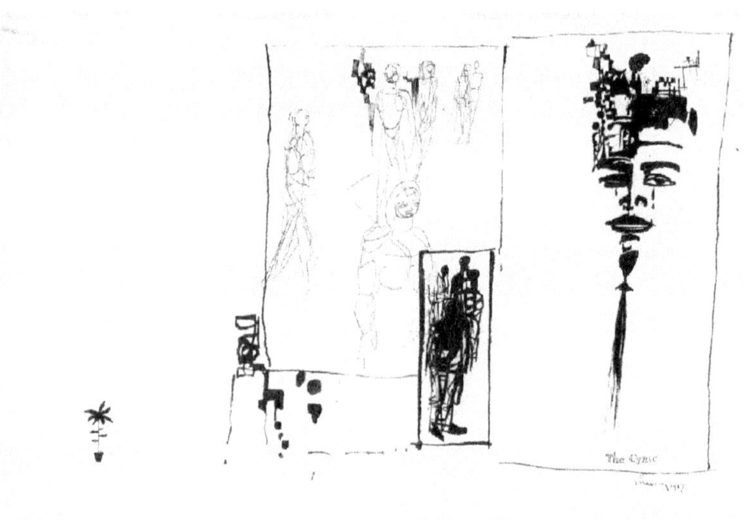

Obverse of Our Truck 'The Cynic' *(quill pen and Indian ink on paper), c 1957*

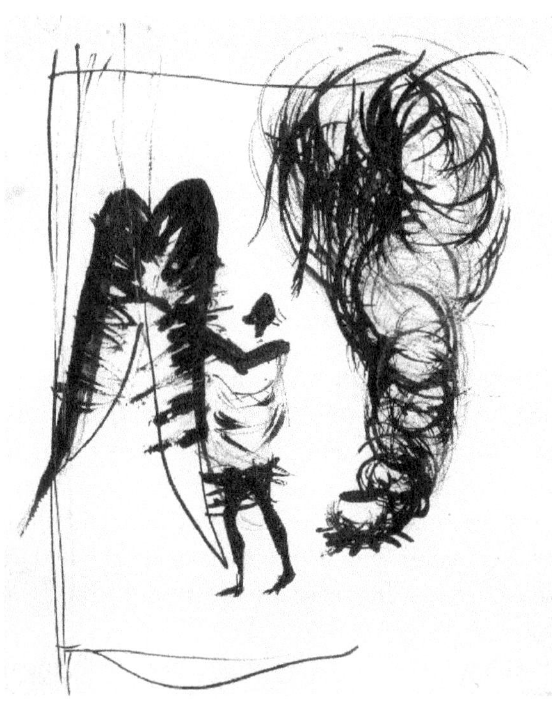

Icarus making his wings (quill pen and Indian ink on paper), c.1957

that the idea of myself as a cynic was probably serious self-delusion, a romantic fantasy brought on by reading too much Somerset Maugham and other writers from the English upper classes. Nowadays, the same lack of consistency still haunts the salability of my work in painting and in film making. Maybe I should call it "post-modernism"? Now, there's cynicism!

I struck on the idea of using a quill pen made, not with the traditional goose feathers, which weren't available on the farm, but with ordinary chook feathers. By carving out part of the bottom end of a feather's shaft with a razor blade, then cutting a slit in what was left, I could make pens that gave this result - see image below.

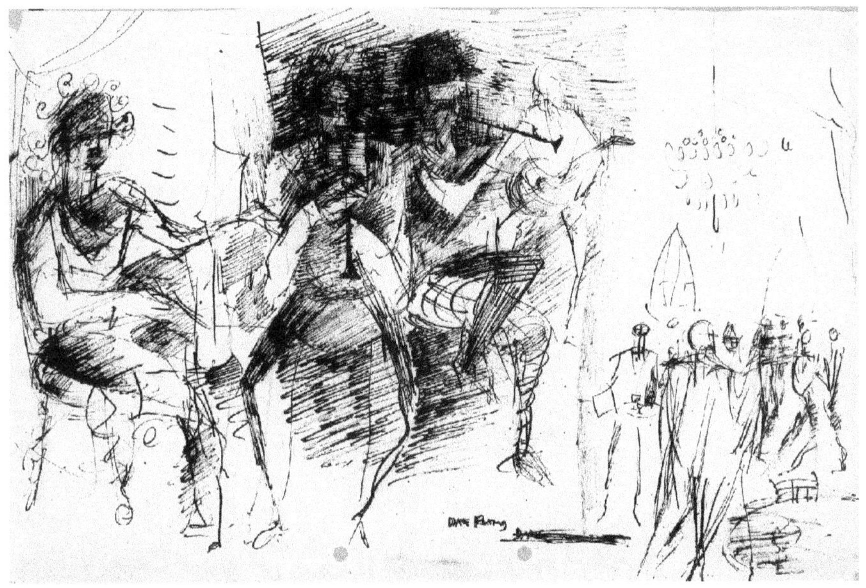

Jazz band (quill pen and Indian ink on paper), c. 1957

Jazz...

Judy and I listened often to the radio where we heard regular playings of traditional jazz and contemporary jazz. Listening to that reminded me of nights spent in Sydney much earlier, at the Sydney Jazz Club, listening to some quite beautiful traditional jazz, in which the clarinet, trumpet and trombone wove improvised melodies around each other in ways that I have never forgotten and have always regarded as perfect models of artistic form in any medium as well as models of social organisation, loose, co-operative and non-authoritarian (a bit of a load for the music to carry, but there you are, I'm often prone to read a lot into things).

This drawing based on memories of Sydney experiences while the fantasised ballroom setting is based on locations described in Eddie Condon's book, *Hear Me Talkin' To Ya*. (Many years later I learned from a friend and hugely knowledgeable jazz aficionado that *Hear Me Talkin' To Ya* is not regarded as a good or reliably informative book. However, it was all I had at the time and anyhow, I don't believe it was all self-serving bullshit, as my friend seemed to imply.)

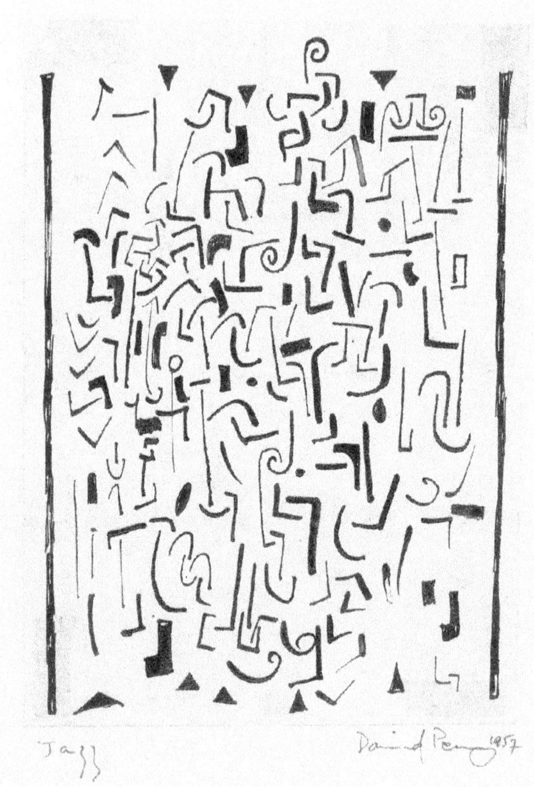

Jazz (quill pen and Indian ink on paper), 1957

Nostalgia...

Nostalgia, not only for the city but specifically for the world of art began to intrude on my thoughts. And then I started thinking that my work could never develop fully unless I went to art school. I know myself well enough now (you'd hope so, wouldn't you, after all these years?) to know that I have these crises of confidence regularly. But I didn't then, and there we were, we had exiled ourselves in New Zealand which was at least allowing us to assert our independence. We would stay there for another year or so before making our escape.

Maybe "escape" is too melodramatic a word. The photographs on the next page (which give the lie to my thought that I had no photographs from New Zealand) show us in the euphoria of new parenthood as well as my farm labourer's physique. We certainly don't look as though we wanted to escape to anywhere. The most remarkable thing to me now is how young we were. It may not have been so unusual in the 1950s, but when writing from the perspective of 2003, the responsibility we had taken on looks daunting indeed. Of course work had to continue, on the farm and on paper.

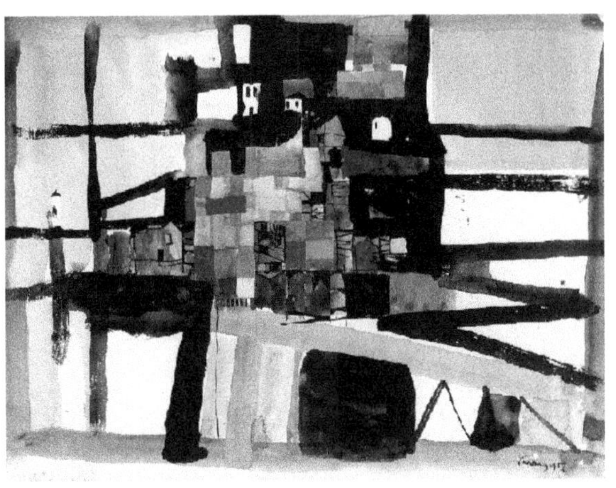

City (gouache, wash and Indian ink on paper), 1957

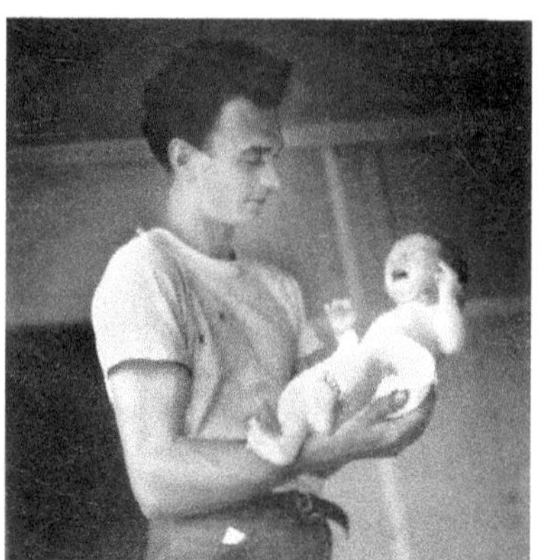

Myself with Simon early 1957 (photographer uncertain, probably Judy)

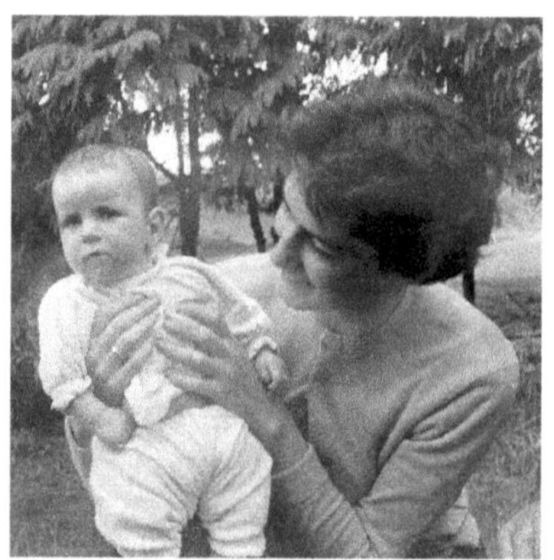

Judy with Simon early 1957 (photographer uncertain, probably me)

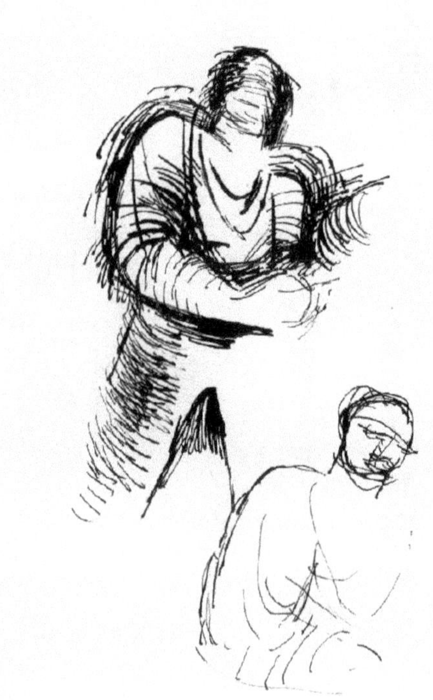

Farm workers (Indian ink on paper), c.1957

Worrying about style and professionalism…

Clearly, I had taught myself well enough to draw in pen and ink, but I worried about my lack of consistency, I worried about colour blindness, and I worried about what I thought of as my lack of professional skills. I began to believe that these worries could only be dealt with by returning to Sydney and enrolling at East Sydney Tech.

By 1958 I had become determined that that was the only solution to my anxieties. Of course my pay as a farm labourer couldn't stretch to cover our fares. I can't remember how we eventually raised the money to get back. Did we get it from my parents or from Judy's? In the meantime of course I just kept drawing whenever I had time off from the farm work. There must have been many more drawings than I've collected here, but these and a few on the website gallery are pretty well all that remains of my work in New Zealand.

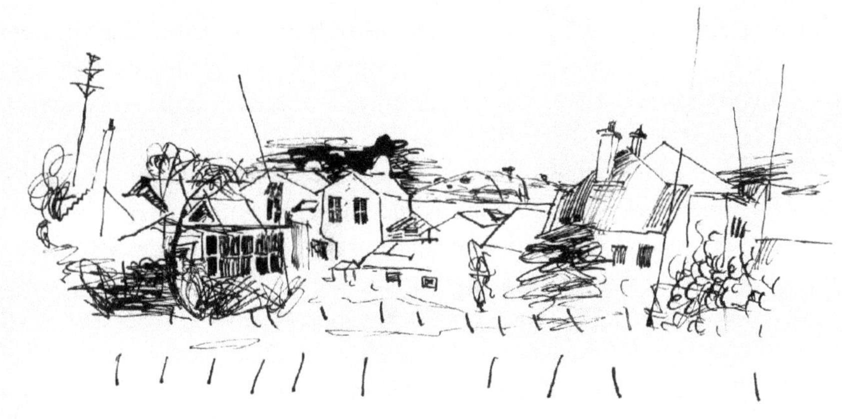

Backs of houses in Opotiki (Indian ink o paper), c. 1957

Back home, we find The Push again ...

We returned to Sydney in 1958 by and Judy was pregnant with our second child, Jane, who was born quite soon after we got back. Obviously I had to get a job as soon as possible. This was a time of full employment and finding work wasn't difficult. I must have been reluctant to go back to my old job at Sungravure because I took a job at a company in Sydney that specialised in making large photographic copies of architects' drawings and many other kinds of images: maps, photographs, drawings. These "blow-ups" were used as murals, for example, in restaurants and other places. It wasn't the most prestigious job in Sydney, nor the most lucrative, but it would do for the time being.

The dream of going to art school proved to be just that, a dream. I can't remember what we did at first for a place to live but eventually, after living in Katoomba for a while, we rented a barren little house a long way from the railway at Auburn, a western suburb of Sydney.

We had already made contact with our old friends in The Push. They had moved briefly to other pubs and then on to a more permanent venue, The Royal George, when The Tudor closed down. Throughout the 1960s and beyond, The Royal George was the pub of choice for the "lumpen intelligentsia" as Jim Baker called the group of Libertarians, whether from the universities or otherwise, who found a haven and release from conformism in The Push.

As Appo[3] had written recently: "The Push ... was a family, though a rather vituperative one." No one could disagree with Appo about that, although it's a good thing it was only figuratively a family since if there'd been blood ties it would have been an incestuous one. Promiscuity was a matter of course in The Push and never kept "under the covers", as it were. It was only a matter of time before Judy and I were drawn into this.

Who would go first? As it happens it was Judy. She "got off" with Don Ayrton, folk singer and poet and, as I remember him, a charming rogue. I'm fairly sure that in keeping with The Push's ideal of openness in personal relations Judy told me what she was going to do. I may have appeared blasé but in fact when it happened I was shattered. I don't think that having sex with another person and being "in love" are in any way the same thing but I do know that sex can have a very powerful bonding

---

[3] "Appo's Story" © Richard Appleton, 2004.

effect and breaking those bonds is usually a painful experience. If sex is passionate, tender and affectionate all at the same time, as it has generally been for me, there is no way to avoid that bonding. That is surely why there are such powerful taboos against adultery, "infidelity" or whatever else we want to call it. And yet, being human, and being driven by desires that are essential to our nature, we will, over and over, succumb to those desires, even at the cost of our well-being. A society that cannot tolerate those contradictions, that attempts to obliterate them by law and/or custom, will only create more pain for its members.

In The Push my pain was understood, no one told me I was a fool to feel it, my friends knew that it would pass even though I couldn't see it (it's like being ill with the 'flu: you can't remember what it felt like to be well and you can't imagine what it will be like to be well again).

People in my situation will call up all sorts of ways to cope. I did it by getting off with Don Ayrton's girlfriend, Judy Andrews (or did she get off with me to cope with Don's infidelity?). Judy Andrews and I became good friends and we remained so for at least twenty-five years. In time we went very different ways but occasionally we found ourselves in the same place and whenever it seemed appropriate we went to bed together. In all my subsequent long experience it seemed to me that our relationship was the most 'sensible' imaginable, friendship with sex, but this is only possible with very specific combinations of people. Such a friendship, like all relationships, is the result of interactions between people, never the result of just one person's attitudes or beliefs.

However, there was something that made the relationship between Judy Perry and me even more complicated: the presence of children. We already had Simon and Jane and soon we would have Caitlin. In spite of what moralists might say, we looked after them, got them to kindergarten and to school, kept them generally well cared for.

I continued drawing and painting and exhibiting at the C.A.S and the Society of Artists. Almost all of that work has disappeared with the exception of portraits of two Push identities, Johnny Earls and Dick Appleton (see following pages), and a photograph of one painting: *Table in a Bar of Sunlight* (next page), an oil in tones of blue, grey, brown and black; colours that I could work well with in spite of my colour blindness. I thought it was one of my best up to that time. When I exhibited it, it attracted the attention of dealer Barry Stern who came out to our house at Auburn to see what else I had and subsequently invited me to exhibit at his gallery in Paddington in a two-person show with John Bell.

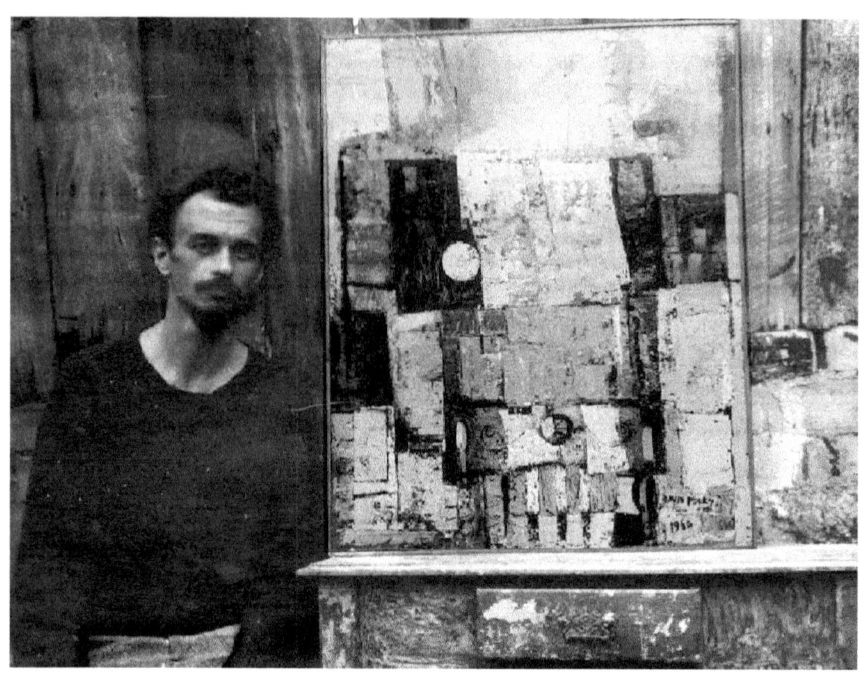

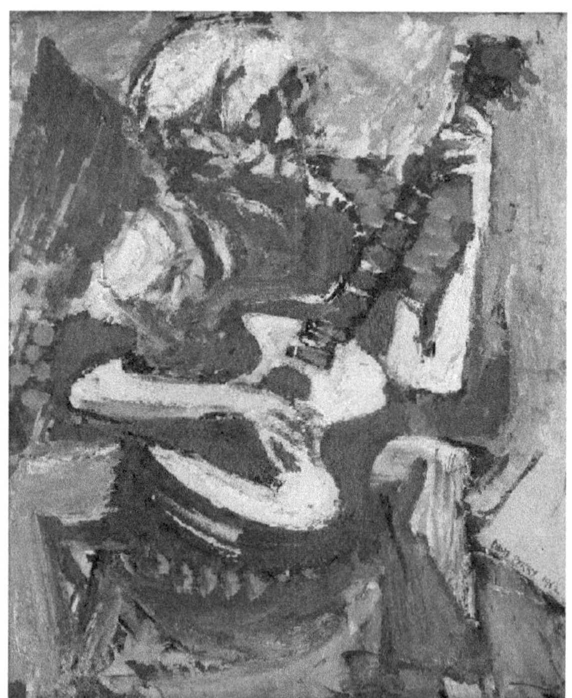

Above: Self portrait with painting Table in a Bar of Sunlight*, c.1960*

Left: Portrait of Johnny Earls *(oils on cardboard), 1963-64*

On opposite page: Portrait of Richard Appleton *(oils on hardboard), 1962*

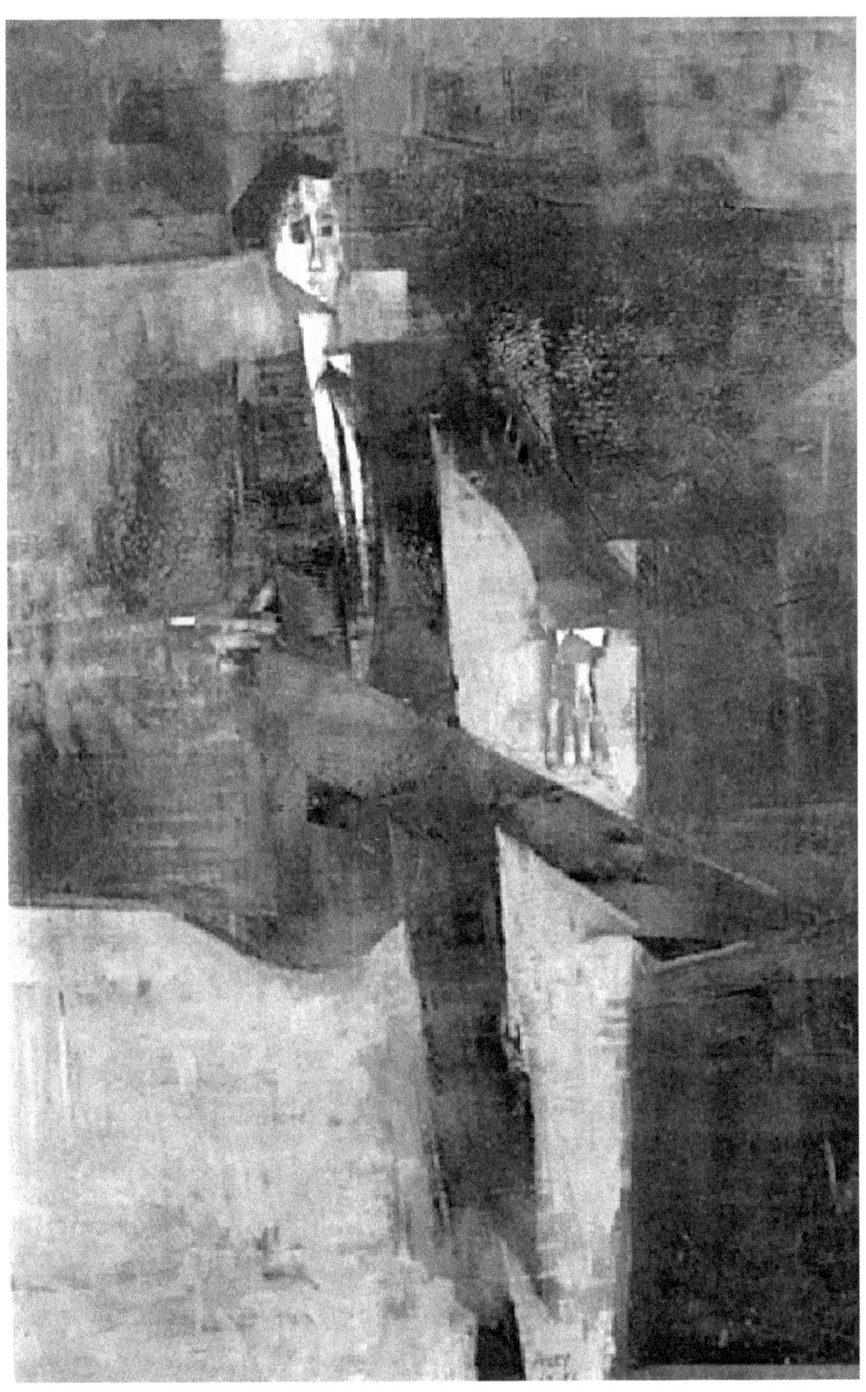

By 1962 I had returned to the printing trade, working at Sungravure's competitor, Conpress, owned by the Packer family and printer of the Australian Women's Weekly. The "Weekly" was envied all over the world for its penetration of the market; when Australia's population was 10 million, the Women's Weekly sold one million copies a week, which meant that each issue was seen by something like two million people. What used to disturb some of us who worked at Conpress - certainly it disturbed me - was that the paper and inks used to print it were so lousy that all the care we put into the magazine before it went to press was negated. This was confirmed when Frank Packer, before going to the States to compete in the America's Cup, had some special copies of the Weekly printed using good quality inks and coated paper. The result was a revelation. Even though it was done at the end of a run, when the rotogravure cylinders could be expected to be worn, the Women's Weekly could bear comparison, in appearance at least, with glossy magazines from America.

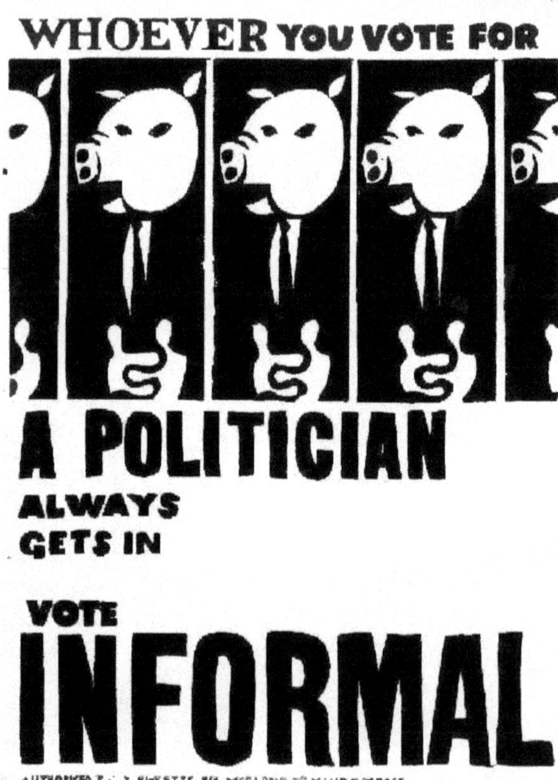

Around that time too I put my talents at the service of the Push. A federal election was coming up and in keeping with the realist/pessimist views of many in the Push I designed a poster where I drew a continuum of pigs (inspired by Orwell's *Animal Farm*) to go with the slogan "Whoever you vote for a politician always gets in". Hand-printed by silk-screen in fairly large numbers, the posters were put up in many parts of the inner city by many

Push people carrying big brushes and buckets of glue. One team used Araldite on at least some of their posters which meant that the posters stayed put for many years.

My pay at Conpress enabled me to acquire a mortgage on a tiny terrace house in Moorhead Street, Redfern. The house was indeed small. Because the land it was built on was steep, we entered the house from the first floor, and because the house was too small to allow the luxury of any kind of vestibule, the front door opened from the street directly into Judy's and my bedroom. Behind that was the children's bedroom and a narrow flight of steep stairs going down to the ground floor which opened onto a tiny backyard paved with concrete.

It suited me to work late shifts at Conpress, which I did as often as possible by swapping shifts with co-workers. Late shifts started at around three in the afternoon and finished around 11.15 at night. These hours made it possible for me to draw for a while before going to bed. I could then get up early enough to get the children to school and have a few hours of daylight for painting in the backyard. I no longer remember how Judy and I juggled all this and our social life.

I can remember coming home from work around midnight on several occasions to find the upstairs and downstairs parts of the house crammed with people, many of them drunk and loud.

Our marriage was starting to collapse. Sometimes I have put that down to my lack of ambition and self-assertion but I don't think I was fair to myself. On many weekends Judy disappeared to the pub, staying out till I had to go to work on Monday afternoon. For my own self-esteem I should have got out of this situation, but I worried about what would happen to the children if I did. As well, even though Judy was becoming very promiscuous I was still "in love" with her. This might be hard for people to understand but you'll just have to believe it. When she was at home we still made love.

Of course I became promiscuous too. Sometimes, when it was possible, I would go to the pub, then to a party and get off with someone or another. Or I would visit Appo and his partner Robin who shared a little waterfront flat with Sue Robertson. I formed a relationship with Sue and although the sexual part of it ended in the early 1960s we are still friends at the time of writing this.

One of the great things about The Push was that you could be friends with an amazingly disparate group of people. As I said earlier there weren't many visual artists in The Push. In fact I think that the hard-drinking anarchism would have been too coarse and threatening for most artists. Bob Hughes was there for a while before he shifted from being an artist to writing about artists. There were several folk singers who often entertained us with rousing political songs. Johnny Earls for example sang songs from the Spanish Civil War, removing on the way any references to "communism" and inserting "anarchism". There were several doctors, at least one of whom has gone on to be obscenely rich (while still calling himself an anarchist). There were professional gamblers who found The Push very congenial because, I imagine, The Push was opposed to such moralistic notions as "free will" and attracted to the idea of chance as a determining factor in life. And there were academics of every stripe.

I had changed my job, at a drop in pay, to one at the Telerecording Department of the ABC. Judy, inspired no doubt by the intellectual ferment of The Push, became determined to go to university. Not long after she started she met Michael McDermott, an extremely bright student. It wasn't long before Judy fell in love with Michael and it was only a little longer before I was relegated downstairs to a dingy little room where the only light came from a window that looked out on a ventilation shaft. Upstairs Judy and Michael fucked vigorously and frequently.

Judy still continued her promiscuous ways and one night when I came home from work there was a party raging, but more to the point I found Judy in my hard little bed with an unknown man.

I cracked. I went outside, collected two large beerbottles, went back into the room and hurled the bottles one after the other at the ceiling where they smashed, covering the floor with beer and broken glass. I must have wanted to make a gesture rather than to injure anyone and I seem to remember coldly making a decision to smash the bottles where I did rather than over the bed. I'm glad I did. It's been a hard enough memory to live with, but if I'd caused actual "grievous bodily harm", as the cops used to say, it would have been much harder.

Without looking back I went out of the house and started walking. I don't know if I had any plan at first but soon I found myself heading for the Harbour Bridge. The city streets and the footpath across the bridge passed in a blur. I knocked on the door of Appo's and Robin's flat. I must have looked dreadful. Robin immediately gave me some Valium which knocked me out, I don't know for how long.

I sometimes wonder if it might have been better if I hadn't been drugged to sleep, maybe then I would have been able to think about what I'd done. But the fact is I was so freaked out, both by what had just happened and by our lives in general, that I don't think anything could have made a difference just then.

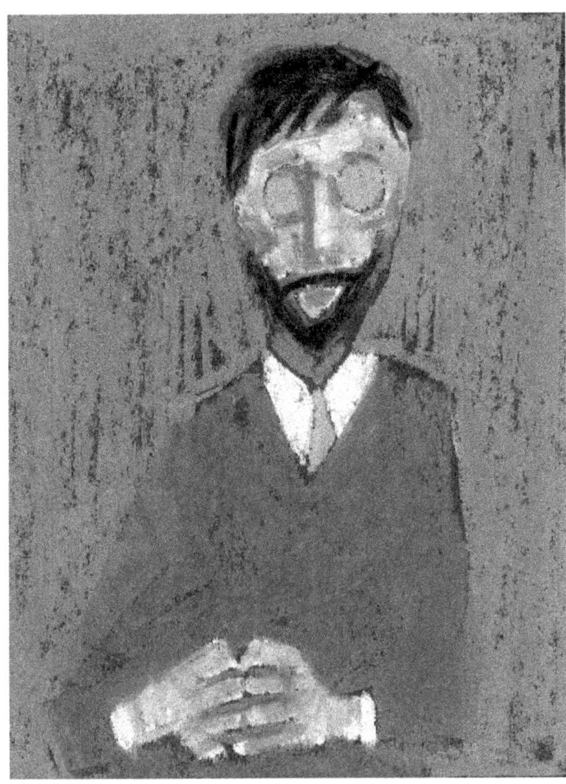

Portrait of Bill Psychs (pastels on cardboard), c. 1962

In the Push around that time there was discussion of the oppositions between Freudian and "behaviourist" psychology. Inspired by these discussions I began a series of drawings that had a decidedly narrative intent with Bill Psychs as the protagonist. I don't think there's any doubt that Bill Psychs is some kind of *alter ego* for me, although the drawing here is pure fantasy. I have never shown any interest in (or skills at) therapy of any sort. As the series proceeds, Bill undergoes a serious breakdown.

Apart from (or in spite of) the state of my relationship with Judy, this period was actually pretty fruitful for me. I did a lot of drawing and painting, most of which I can't locate now, and in my dreary downstairs bedroom (where I eventually smashed those bottles against the ceiling) I made my first 16mm film, *Swansong in Birdland,* with some indispensable help from Carolyn Barkell who became a life-long friend.

The chronology of the period surrounding my breakdown is hazy. It's easiest for me to determine dates from inscriptions on the backs of paintings or from filmographies (I was soon to shift nearly all my attention to film making on the basis of what I perceived as insufferable pretentiousness in the art gallery scene - little did I know that a similar characteristic was firmly entrenched in the film scene!). The image below is one of a series of monotype drawings called B*irds of a Feather* which I did before making the film, *Swansong in Birdland.* The two stills on the opposite page are from *Swansong.* There are more in the website gallery.

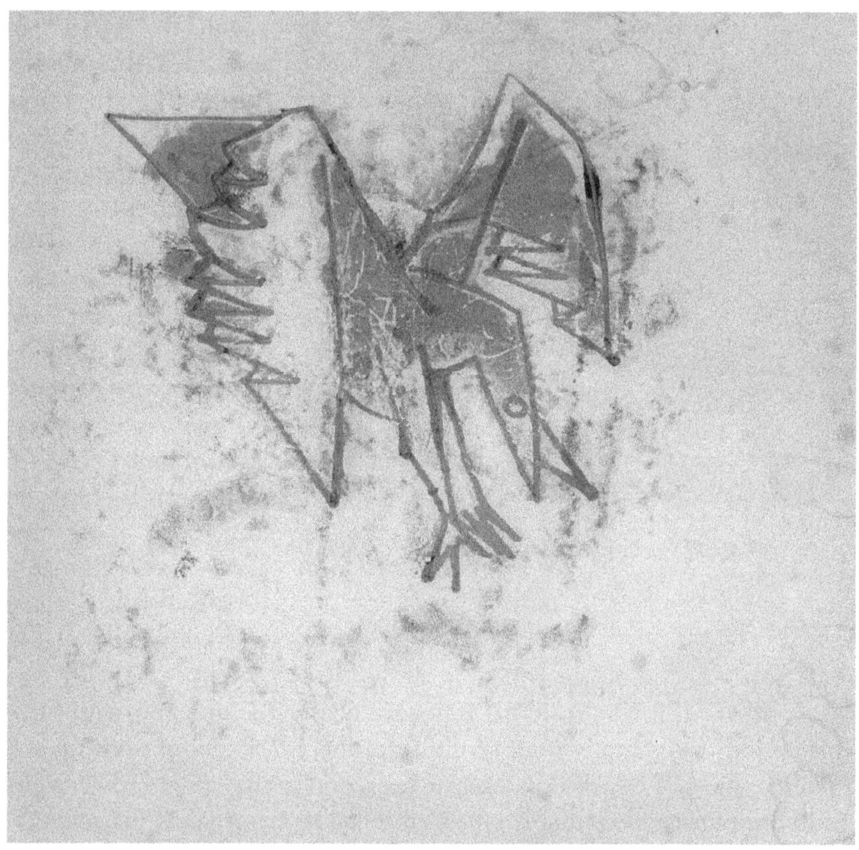

*Birds of a Feather No. 5 ("*Unpleasant Bird*"), monotype using oil paint on newsprint, July, 1964*

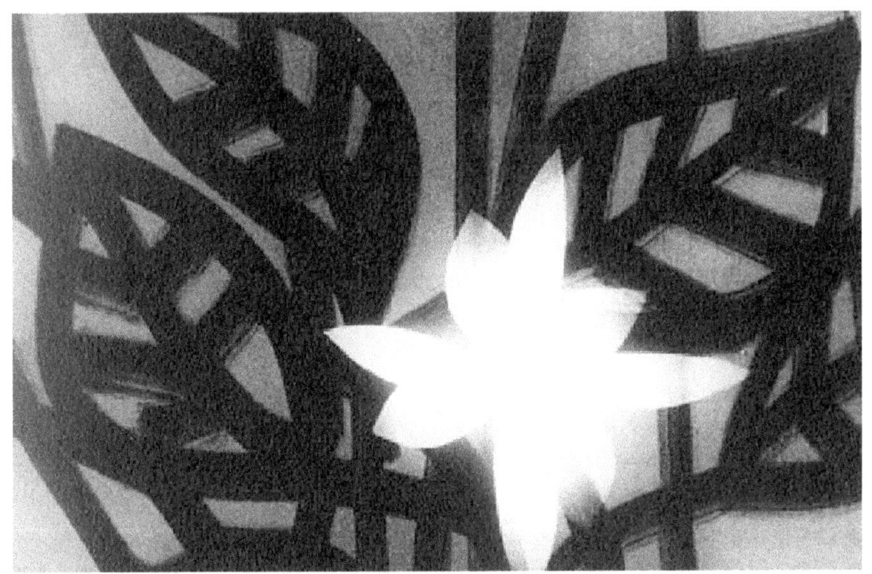

Frame blow-up from Swansong in Birdland*, 16 mm. film, 1964*

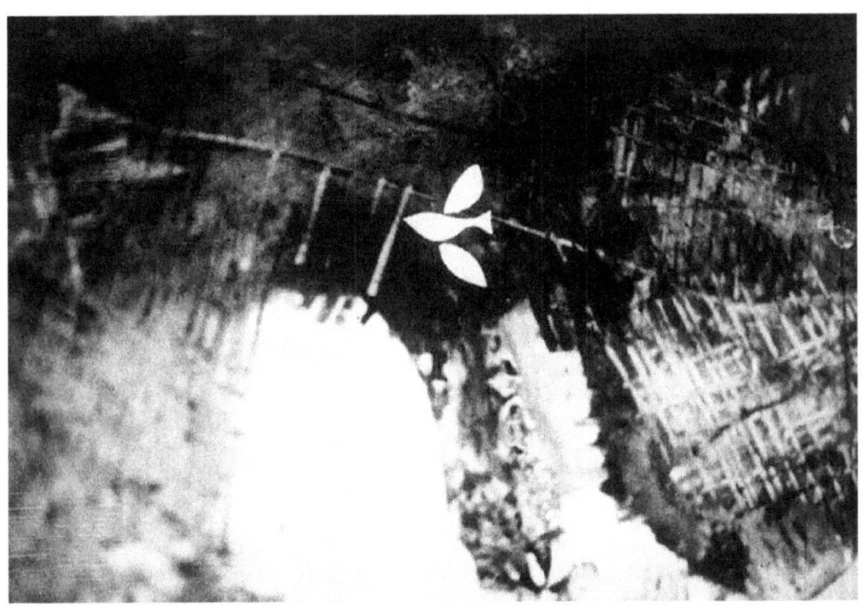

White Bird high over the land (Frame blow-up from Swansong in Birdland), c.1964

It might seem superficial to write about what was undoubtably one of the worst things I ever did and to wrap it around accounts of my art and film making as if my violence was inconsequential. The fact is that it was more than half my present lifetime away and it is now impossible for me to quarantine one part of my life then from another.

As well as that, painting, film making and photography can't just be put aside as if they are mere decorations to a person's life.

And so, the story of how *Swansong in Birdland* came about: I must have been thinking about it since the days of the Cuban missile crisis when there was a palpable fear of nuclear war. The white birds in my film were conceived as agents of "goodness", as that quality was defined by the clichés of popular culture, while of course the black birds were, by the same token, "badness". It appealed to my cynical nature, nurtured by the Push, to have "goodness", driven by revenge, to be the agent of the world's (nuclear) destruction.

The predominance of birds in my imagery at that time was not the result of symbolism, neither of the surrealist nor of the socialist realist sort. Both surrealism and socialist realism had their adherents at the time, but I was inspired by the birds in Georges Braque's magnificent series of *Studios*. I now have a book of Braque's paintings in which, as well as all the *Studios*, there's a little painting of flowers called *The Painter's Despair*. Attempting to emulate Braque's mature period paintings could lead to similar despair, although I have to say that when I worked within my own limitations what I produced was very good. I was especially pleased at the time with the "Birds of a Feather" series I mentioned above - the whole 16 monotypes were all done in one late night session after coming home from night shift at Sungravure.

I would like to have been able to include many more paintings and drawings from that period in this book, or at least to have more to choose from - there were certainly plenty of them - but sadly they are now almost all lost. And that has to be at least partly due to the chaotic state of my life.

After recovering a certain amount of composure at Appo's and Robin's flat I made my way back to Redfern. The mess I had made had been cleaned up and the house was quiet. Judy immediately presented me with an ultimatum: I had to move out. She had even found me a place to live: a room at Geoffrey Whiteman's house in Darlington. There was no moralising, no questioning: "Why did you do such a thing?" That was for my own internal moralist which has sniped at me, on and off, ever since.

A more pertinent question might have been: "Why didn't you move out long ago?"

I have no real answer to that. I am not the most decisive character at the best of times. At that worst of times, my decision-making, my self-preservation must have been paralysed. One could have – and some would have - blamed the Push's amoralistic stance for this schmozzle, but I found that the people I was closest to were entirely supportive in the best way possible: their sympathy was clear, if unspoken. There was no criticism of anyone. I was as fully accepted as ever I had been.

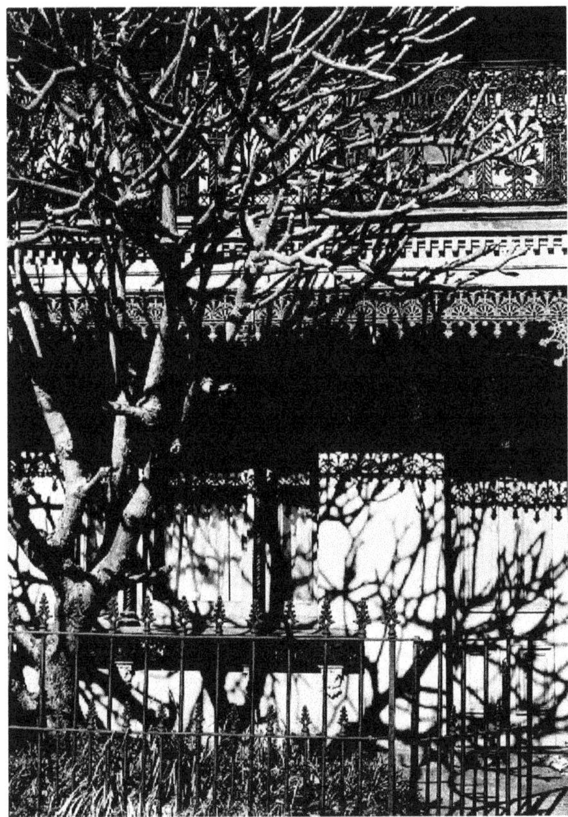

Geoffrey Whiteman's place at 125 Darlington Road, Darlington, c.1965

And a new life was beginning for me as a film maker after showing *Swansong in Birdland* at the Sydney Film Festival.

I had been working for a while as a film technician at the ABC. That was how I'd been able to make *Swansong in Birdland*. I had found some cans of outdated 16mm negative film which was otherwise to be thrown out. I took it home and started shooting the animation for *Swansong* with it, having borrowed a Bolex from Bob Ellis who also worked at the ABC. (Some time later - I'm not sure if the film had even been shown then - Bob asked me to return his Bolex on the grounds that I was using it to get famous and he wasn't!)

After *Swansong* was screened at the Sydney Film Festival I was invited to the Commonwealth Film Unit where I was offered a job. I would probably have taken the job except that I didn't have a university degree and thus my pay would have been even less than I was earning at the ABC. I just couldn't afford to take the job, and it's probably a good thing I didn't. I would seriously have been a cultural misfit at the Film Unit, later known as Film Australia, (where I would have been no less a misfit).

Albie Thoms was another person working at the ABC at the time, as a trainee producer (television-speak in those days for "director"). I had met Albie through the Push and on the basis of *Swansong* he made me an offer I was delighted to take up. While at the ABC Albie was also working with Sydney University Dramatic Society (SUDS), preparing an ambitious production called *The Theatre of Cruelty*, which was to be, in effect, a review of European avant-garde theatre up to the then present day, the early 1960s. One of the items on the programme was to be based on a script by Antonin Artaud, a piece called *The Spurt of Blood.* What was called for in the script seemed impossible in the live theatre, things such as clothing becoming entirely transparent or people defying gravity. On the other hand, such things are very easy to achieve in film, even with very low-tech equipment. All that's needed is imagination and some technical understanding.

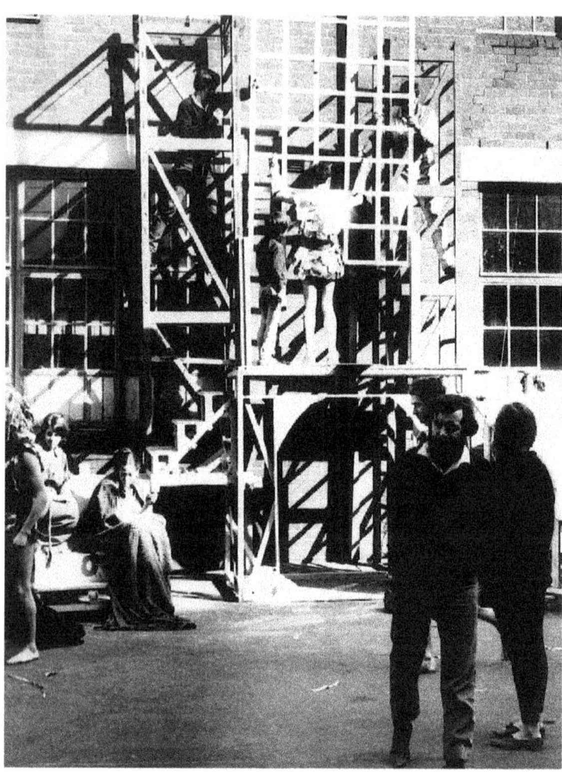

Building a set for Theatre of Cruelty *(Albie Thoms and Sue Howe lower far right)*

That was how I came to be inducted to the production team for *Theatre of Cruelty*. In the first place I was Albie's DOP (we didn't use grandiose terms like that) but later I took a lot of photographs of the production as well as becoming the projectionist for the film screening. One of those photographs of sets being built (opposite) shows the clear influence of the early Soviet Constructivist period of stage design. All of this work, as well as rehearsals and shooting of *The Spurt of Blood*, took place in and around Sydney University's "Deaf and Dumb Institute" as it was then called. I enjoyed enormously my work with SUDS. It was my first experience of collaborative work on a large scale. I had worked in the theatre before, as a graphic artist and programme designer for Frank Strain's theatre-restaurants, but there I was as a kind of observer making quick sketches of the performers. Now, with SUDS, I was an integral part of the team. And the work produced was much more to my liking, more in sympathy with my feelings about art and life.

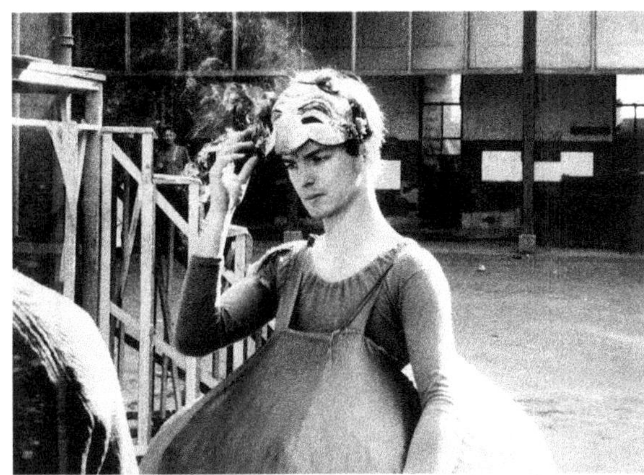

A break in rehearsals for Theatre of Cruelty

Of course during weekdays I had to go to work and on weekends it was likely I would have one or more of my children with me (underneath this mask is Simon, by then getting on for eight years old).

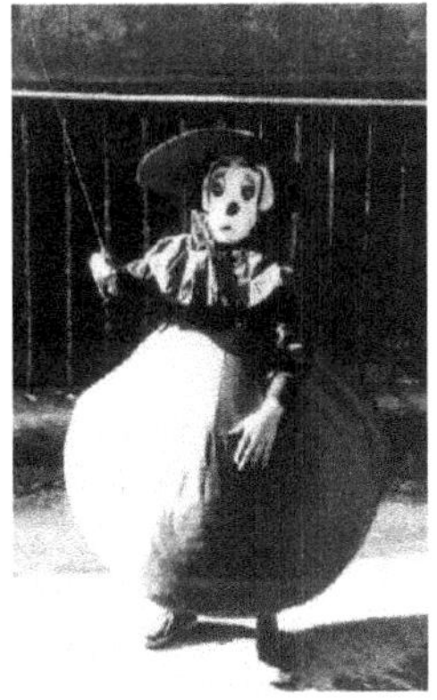

Darlington, when I moved there, was in the process of being taken over by the rapidly expanding University of Sydney. I have always been attracted to towns and buildings in decline. There must be a strong streak of the Romantic in me, as in the English artists who were in earlier centuries drawn to paint the ruins of Rome.

This group of buildings below, awaiting demolition, was just down the street from where I was living with Geoffrey Whiteman. All around us old houses and small factories were being demolished. By the time these photographs were taken I had bought myself a Mamiya twin lens reflex camera, but I also had access to a 35mm camera, which explains to some extent the different character of these two images. The one below, taken with the Mamiya using moderately fine grain 120 film, shows a lot of detail. The one opposite was taken on very fast (therefore grainy) 35mm film. In processing these images in the computer I made some effort to emphasise the differences between them. (Although computer processes are electronic they are in fact little different in effect from the photo-chemical processes that I used when I originally developed and printed the photographs.)

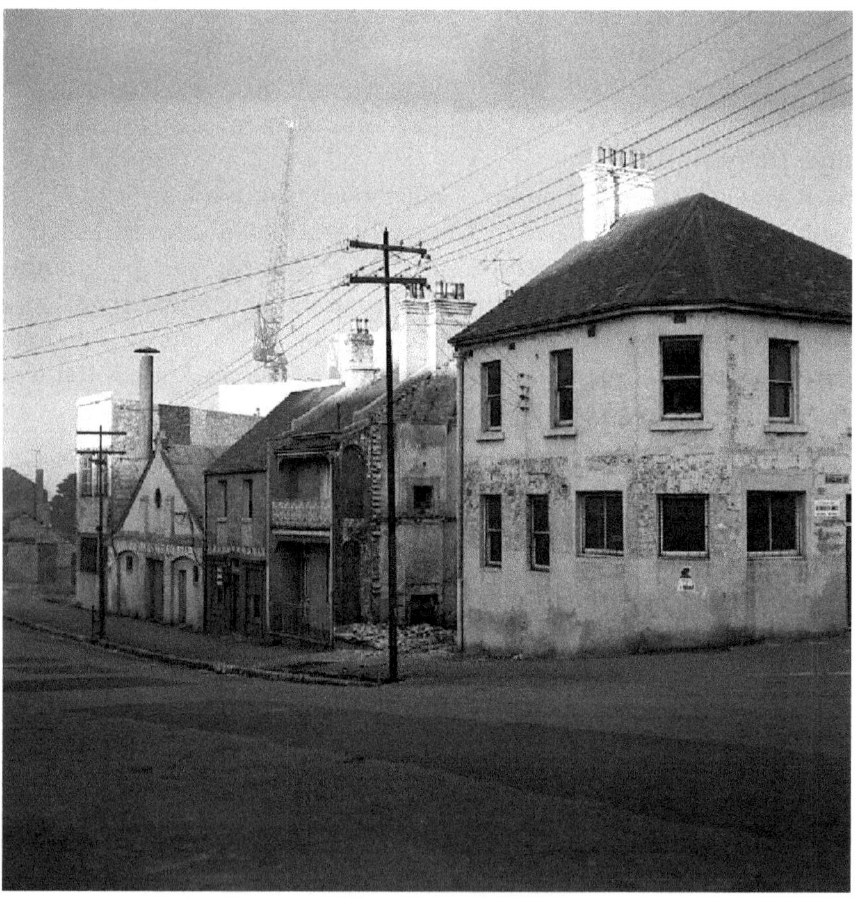

Sunset in Darlington, 1966

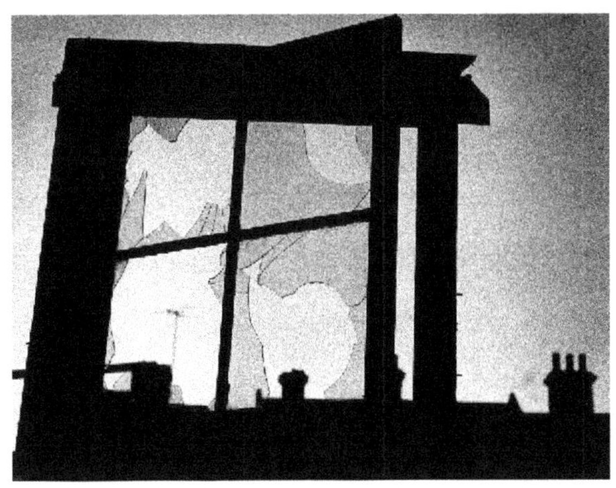

Demolition in Darlington, c. 1965

The two photographs on the next page, on the other hand, demonstrate something entirely non-technical: the extremely disparate nature of people who were attracted to the Push. I knew virtually nothing about Bill Pope when I took the following photograph, perhaps nobody did. We were all amazed to discover that Bill had taken up a contract to kill somebody, which he apparently carried out without a hitch. He would never have been caught had he not walked into a police station to confess. The "hit" had apparently taken place before I took the picture. Somebody told me, so I can't vouch for this, that Bill had wanted to find out if doing "evil" felt any different to doing "good". I'm not sure if he learned anything from his "experiment", but I do know that he did a lot of time in gaol. There has never been anyone in the Push who could compare with Bill Pope. In fact the Push's amorality was only skin deep. As somebody said, "Scratch a libertarian and find a moralist." This was true then, and amongst the people I know now, it's still true.

Women nowadays will very readily acknowledge this contradictory aspect of the Push. This is not to say in so many words that "all the men were bastards," but to acknowledge that they were human. Ellen White and I experienced this first hand. Let me tell it this way: Ellen was recognised as a girlfriend of Geoffrey Whiteman; Geoffrey had a constant stream of women coming to his bed (which apparently Ellen accepted); Ellen and I were attracted to each other and began a relationship; when Geoffrey became aware of this he told me I'd have to leave his house. (At least he didn't want to kill me or beat me up. He, like most Push people, was entirely non-violent.)

Of course it wasn't just men who were inconsistent in this way, but I think I've told enough tales for the time being.

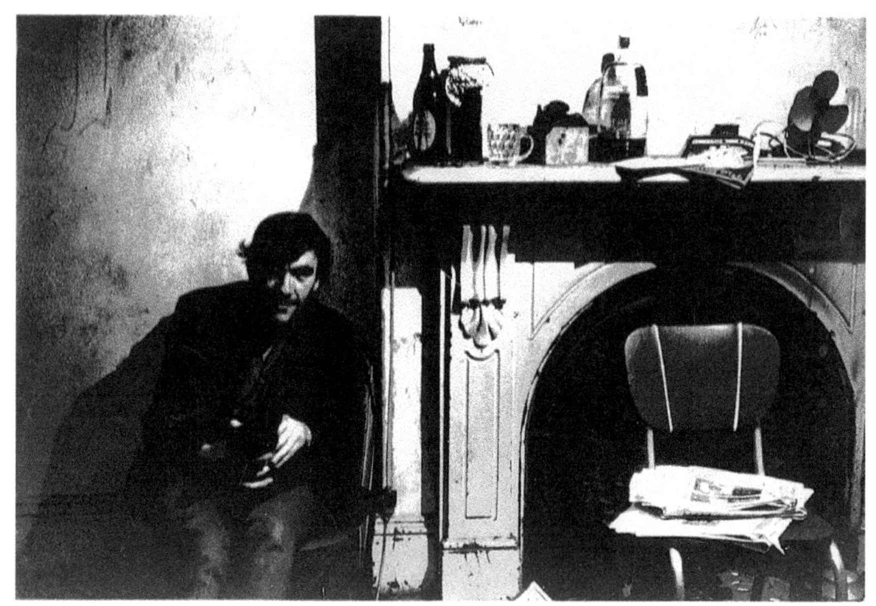

Bill Pope at Darlington Road

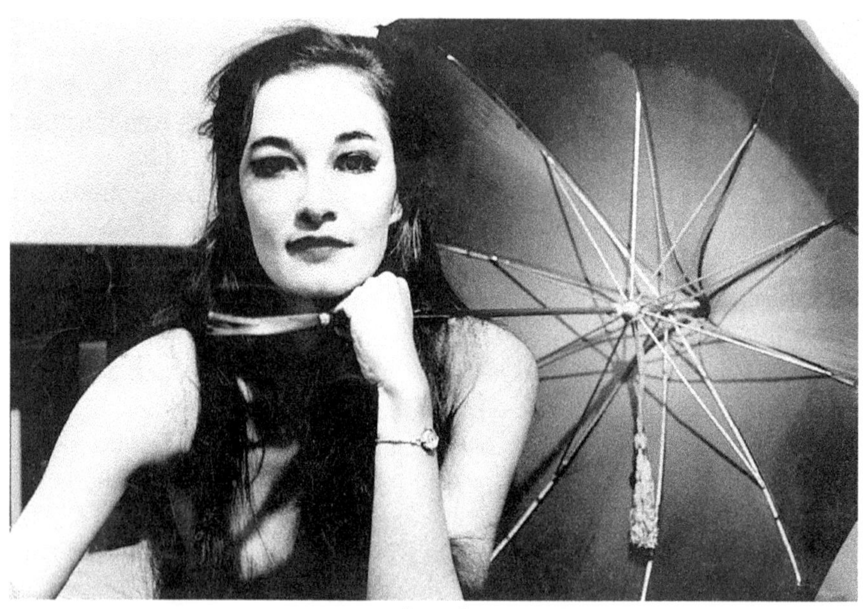

Ellen White

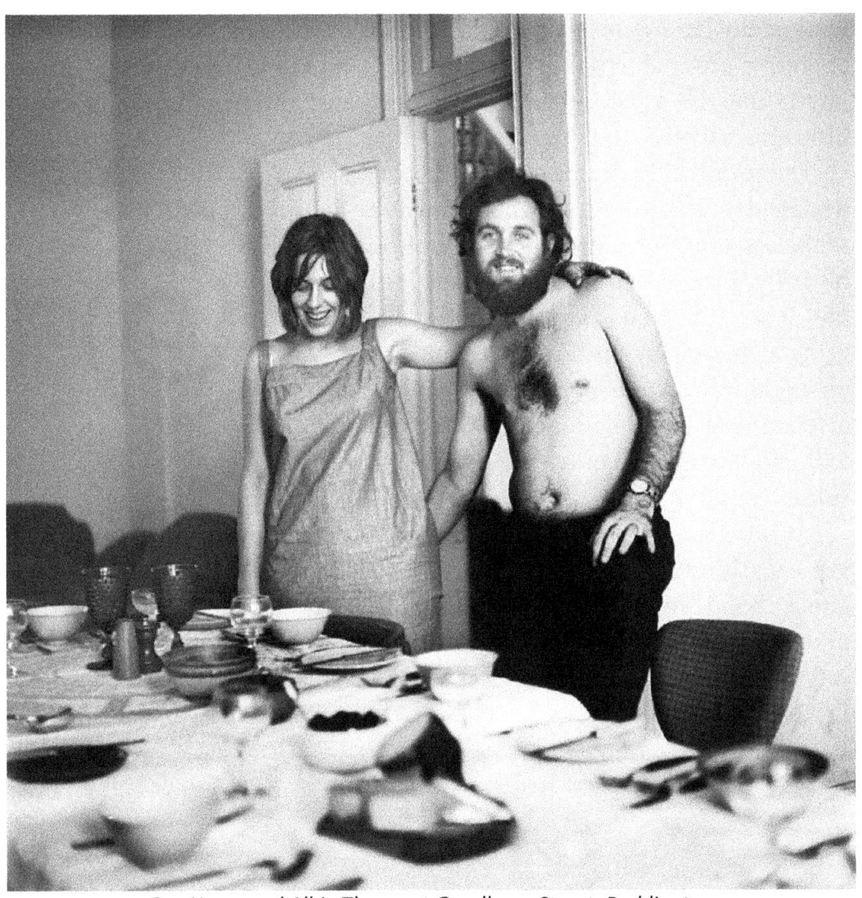

Sue Howe and Albie Thoms at Goodhope Street, Paddington

A really big change…

After Geoffrey gave me the shove, I asked Albie if there was room for me at the house he shared with Sue Howe and several others in Goodhope Street, Paddington. There was room, and this move proved to be decisive for me in a number of ways.

Albie and I had developed a good working relationship over two films for *The Theatre of Cruelty*. And Sydney itself was changing: this was a very affluent time and Sydney's unique character suited us well.

With Albie being extremely entrepreneurial and my being anxious to do some more film work we got together with two other people who had worked on *The Theatre of Cruelty*, John Clark and Aggy Read, to form a co-operative group that we decided to call "Ubu Films", named after Alfred Jarry's *Ubu Roi*, a play that Albie had produced and I had seen and liked a little time earlier.

The original costumes for *Ubu Roi*, designed by Pierre Bonnard, had Ubu as a shapeless lump bearing a huge spiral on his belly. I loved this spiral and used it as the logo for *Ubu Films*, creating the original graphic by putting a sheet of card on a gramophone turntable, then with the card turning while holding a fat felt pen to it, moving the pen outward to draw the spiral.

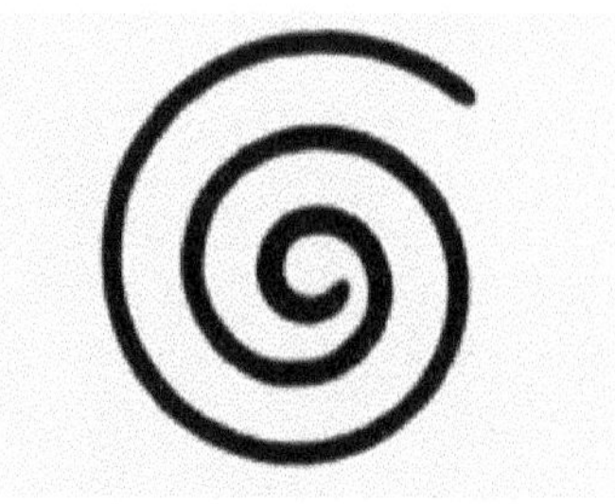

At our first meeting we determined to do something to raise money. We eagerly took up Albie's suggestion that we make a send-up of the James Bond films. Albie, who was already an experienced writer/producer/director of television programmes, wrote the script which contained parodies of scenes from all the Bond films to date. I was to be DOP, with John Clark (who had his own Bolex) as my camera operator.

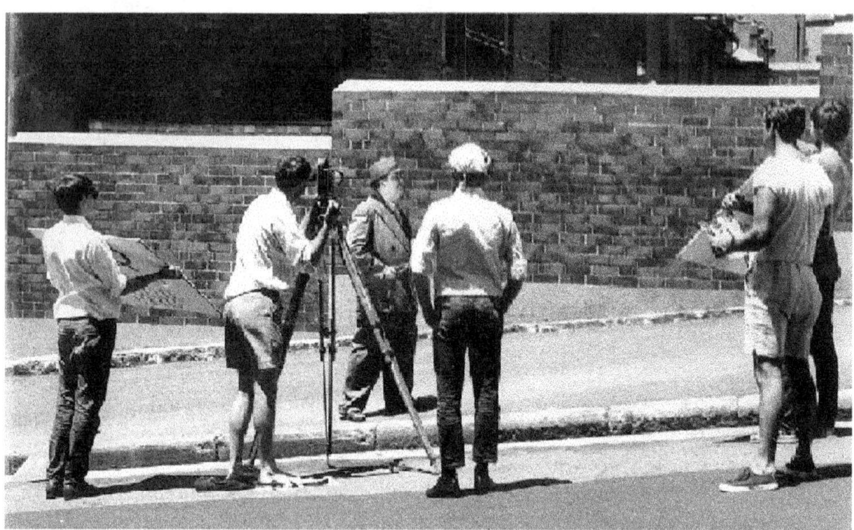

Shooting Blunderball. L. to R: Michael Steel; John Clark; Terry McMullen; Albie Thoms; Keith Whitely; Aggy Read.

The film was to be called *Blunderball* and featured Terry McMullen, a friend of ours from the Push, as a bumbling, incompetent Jim Bond. In

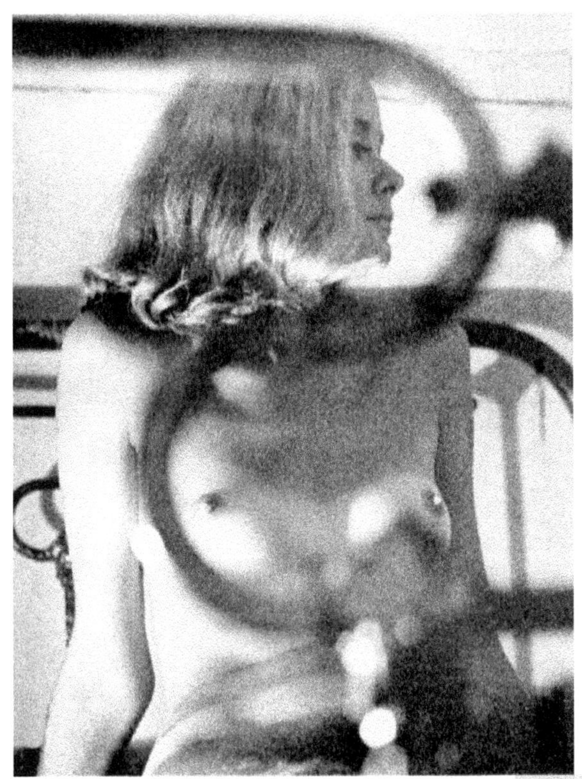

Sue Robertson, Blunderball *publicity still*

fact almost all the characters in the film were played by people from the Push, to which Albie was as firmly connected as I was.

In those days there was little, if any, theatrical film production happening in Australia. Feature film production had dried up at the start of the Second World War, so there was little marketing expertise for us to draw on. Of course, for film making to be successful there has to be publicity. We had to make it up ourselves. I think this is what made *Ubu Films* unique. While we called ourselves "underground" film makers we had no compunction about employing all the hype and publicity methods we could manage with our very limited finances. To this end I took many photographs of the production and, for placement in certain (very tame) Australian "girlie" magazines, I took nude photographs of some of the women who had parts in the film.

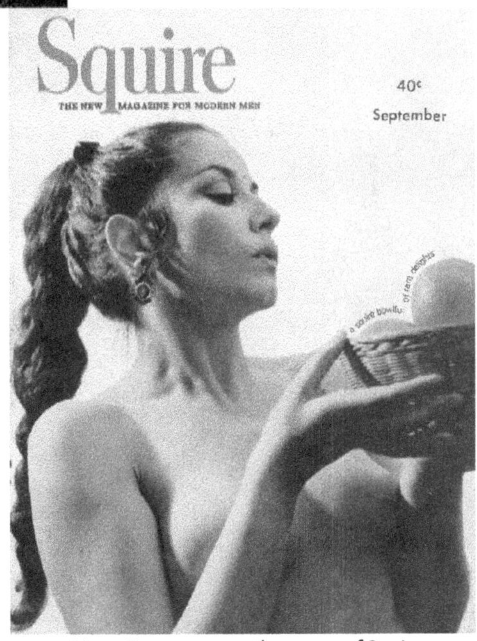

Mary Patterson on the cover of Squire

Looking back on these photos now they seem remarkably sweet. I think there's a direct and unembarrassed looking going on there). I like to think that in these photographs there's none of the vulgar posturing and sexual dishonesty of the usual publicity material. If I'm right it seems that, much as I thought I wanted to be, I wasn't really cut out to be blatantly commercial.

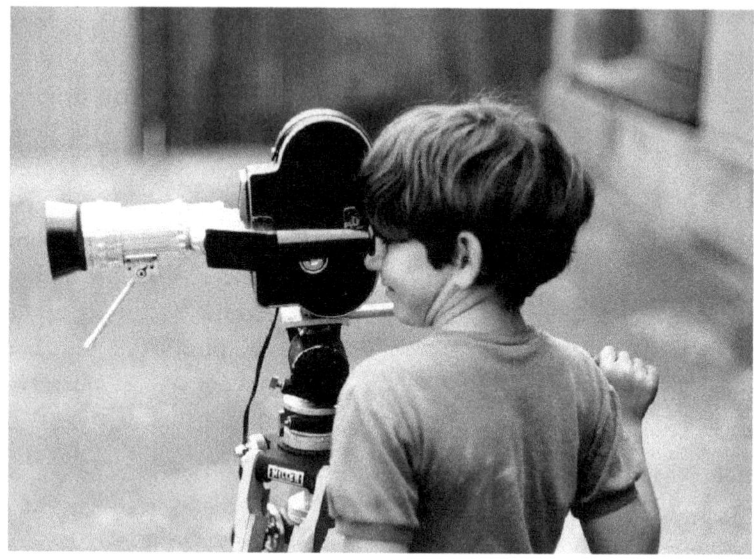

Simon tries out the Bolex at one of the locations for Blunderball

After Blunderball ...

After *Blunderball,* which left us all enthused about the processes of film making (including the marketing and screening), we were ready to start on more of the same. Or should I say we were anxious to improve on what we'd done so far?

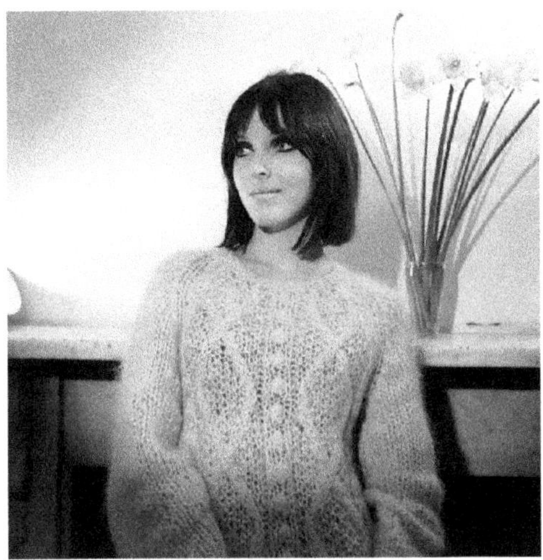

Rita clothed, publicity still for Rita and Dundi

One of the problems of working with very limited budgets is that personal standards of quality can be swamped by other requirements, at least they were in my case. Of course I can't deny that my personal standards for photography were originally formed in the context of commercial magazine production in the 1950's rather than "fine art" photography. Whatever the merits of that self-assessment, the work done under the umbrella of *Ubu Films* is described in extreme detail in Peter Mudie's book, *Sydney Underground Movies.*

The camaraderie among all of us in the Paddington house was fantastic to experience. The end of 1966 was probably the high point of our sense of community, which the photo on the following page clearly documents.

And although I was deeply involved in photography and film making I hadn't lost my love of painting. For some years, although my "lifestyle"

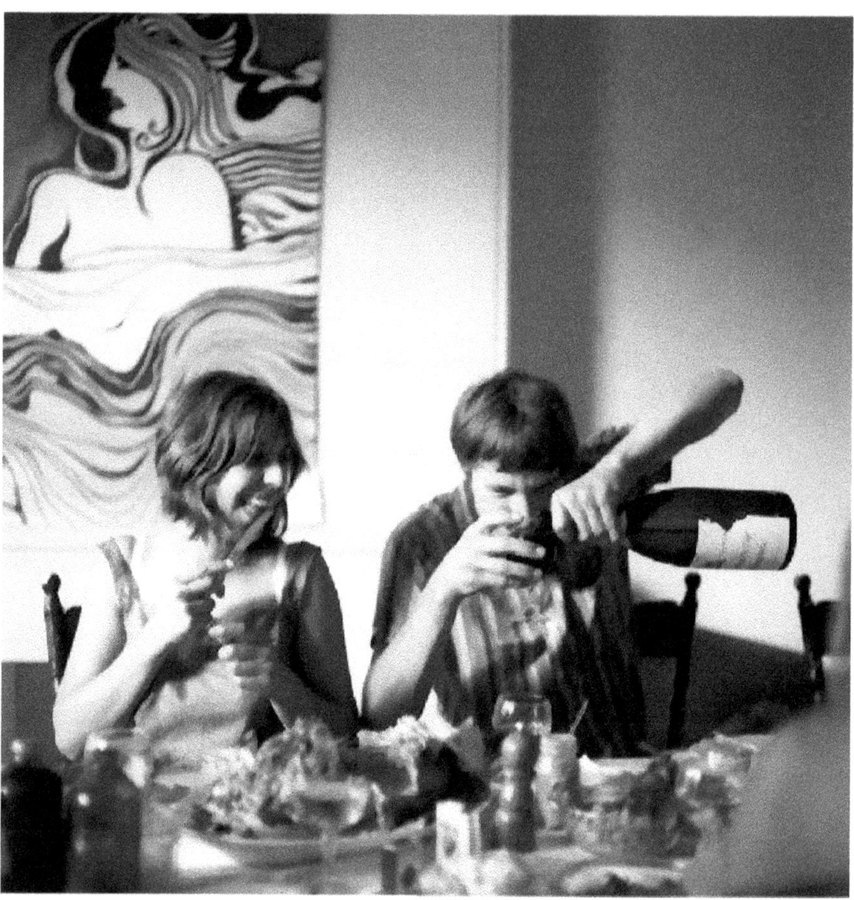

Sue Howe and Aggy Read at Boxing Day dinner at Goodhope Street, 1966

and financial situation made it difficult, I had been attempting to base my imagery on "pin-up" or "glamour" photographs I came upon while I was still working in the printing industry. There are obvious similarities here with the "Pop Art" being done in the United States, although I came to my subject matter independently. The painting on the wall behind Sue is a good example of where I had come to in the mid-1960s.

However, although it doesn't really show in the above example, I began working like this not in emulation of the Americans but in direct response to what I perceived as looks of unease, even unhappiness on the faces of the models for the photographs I took as my starting points. I have always valued an honest direct expression of sexuality, and that is certainly what you *didn't* get in "glamour" photography. These rather rough proofs from my wood blocks of a few years earlier show something of what I was trying to express when I started finding my imagery in popular magazines. The style is obviously heavily influenced by German Expressionism. There were more of these wood cuts and at least a few oil paintings influenced by Picasso's post-war Cubism. None of those paintings nor any of the wood blocks these images were printed from exist any more. Sadly, I took little care of my own work in those days.

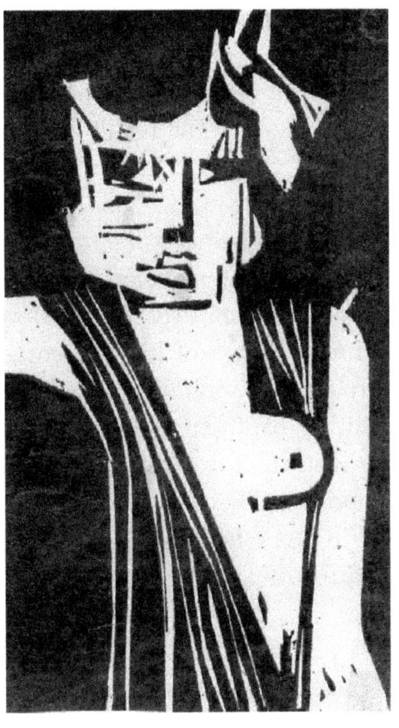

Woman I (proof), 1963

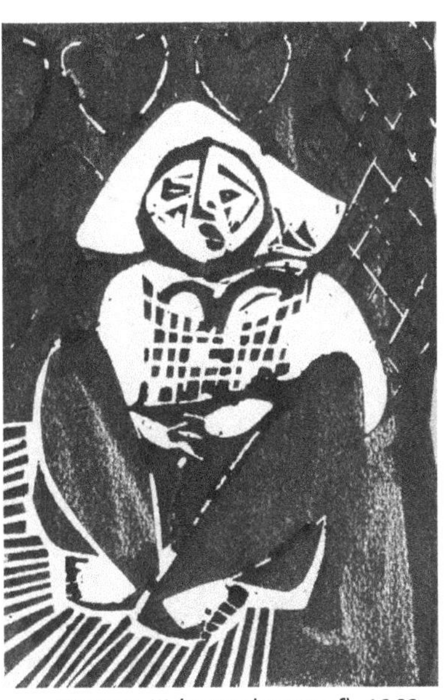

Woman III (gouache proof), 1963

Extreme abstraction in films ...

Ubu Films and before that the *Theatre of Cruelty* had given me the opportunity to take up again and develop on 16mm film some techniques I had first tried out on 8mm some years before. These techniques could be described as "animation", although certainly not animation as people brought up on a strict Disney diet might recognise.

In the very early 1960s I had exploited this effect when I filmed a wall in Redfern with my 8mm camera. Instead of running the camera continuously I stood close to the wall and shot numerous "still" frames of related details of torn posters, peeling paint and so on. The result when I projected the processed film delighted me. The images were extremely dynamic "dancing" I might have said as well as being, I like to think, a very vivid form of "social realism". (If that description offends a lot of Australian film makers I'm delighted. Many of these people have worked with such a limited idea of the expressive capabilities of their medium, and have criticised any work that doesn't conform to their notion of cinema as illustrated literature ... but I won't go on, I'll just wind myself up into a spluttering, resentful old windbag, and that won't do, will it?)

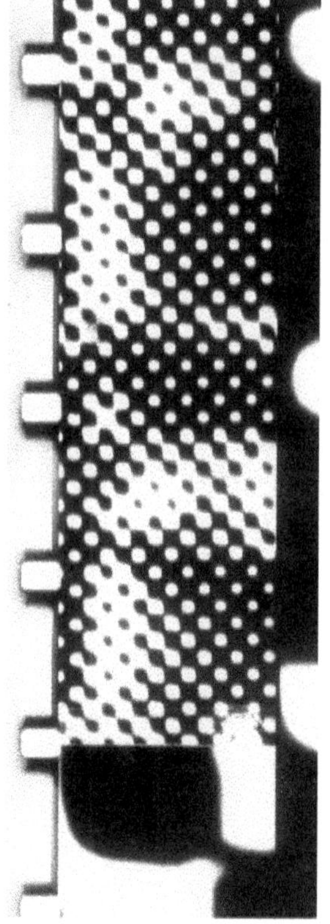

Filmstrip from Halftone *1966. Photographed by Peter Mudie*

The human eye allows us to see movement that isn't there. A case in point: the pattern of dots on the filmstrip reproduced to the left is just a static pattern, but when it's run through a projector our brains make of this a floating, shimmering pattern. Any finely detailed pattern would achieve a similar effect, although it's always necessary to run the images through a projector to see if the result's aesthetically satisfying.

In the case of the little film, *Halftone,* the strips were printed from a halftone[4] negative through an enlarger onto strips of 16mm film, so that the original dot patterns were spread across the full width of the strips and thus covered the soundtrack area as well as the image area. After editing, I asked the lab to run the film through the printer twice, printing the image area first, then to wind the original and print material back to the start and print the soundtrack area with the image starting twenty-eight frames earlier, to allow for the offset between picture start and audio start on a standard 16mm print. The result was a film in which the pattern you saw on the screen also created the sound you heard from the speakers.

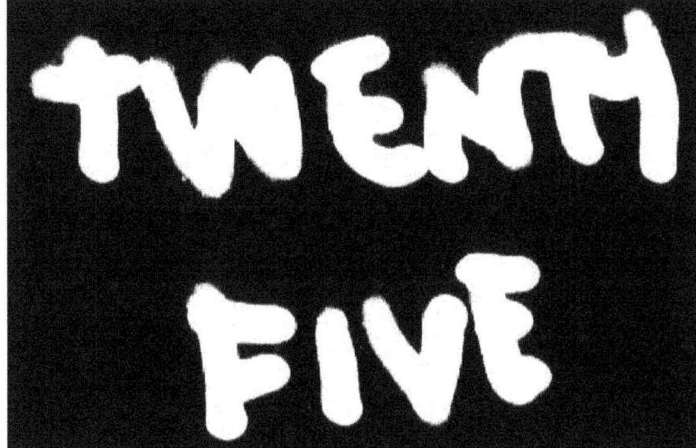

Frame from Poem 25, *1965*

Halftone and *Poem 25* (hand drawn directly on film) were two of a large number of films made without cameras in the Ubu period. We called them "synthetic films". *Poem 25,* like most synthetic films, was drawn directly on blank film and was only truly effective in the theatre where a performer spoke numbers in sync with the hand-drawn numbers dancing on the screen.

4 A "halftone" image is used in printing to convert tonal images to varying sized dots of ink, usually in regular patterns.

Harbour ...

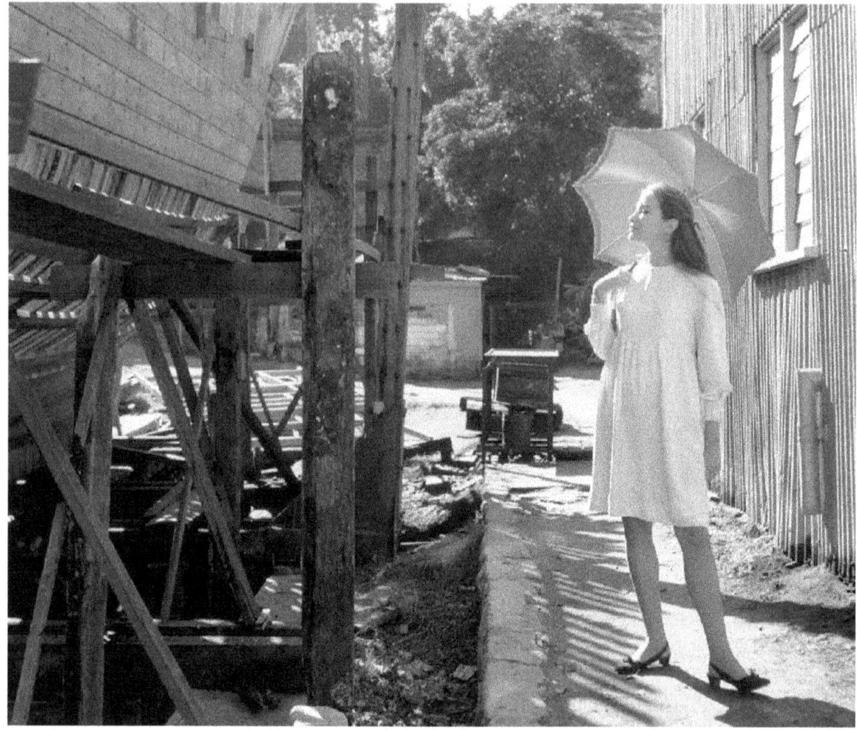

Ellen White (publicity still for Harbour*), 1966*

Towards the end of 1966 and early 1967 I worked on two films virtually back-to-back. These were *Harbour,* our first experience of working with Eastmancolor negative film, and *The Tribulations of Mr DuPont Nomore. Harbour* was to some extent a remake of a film I'd made many years before on 8mm black-and-white film, while *Tribulations* was developed out of a momentary incident while I was still living with Judy; it was an escape fantasy (and fairly crass at that).

However *Harbour* is the one I want to talk about here. Featuring Ellen White, it was shot for me by John Clark in basically two locations around Sydney Harbour: the industrial docklands and a little backwater of Middle Harbour known to my father, uncles and aunts as "Shotmachine Creek", now more prosaically identified on maps as "Gordon Creek".

Harbour taught me a few good lessons. Although it was shot on colour negative film, the workprint, to save money, was made on black-and-white stock. My first discovery was the problem this created in editing the film. After the colour answer print was made, I found that the timing of many cuts was too abrupt in colour, although it was appropriately "snappy" in black-and-white. I put my timing errors down to the fact that there is quite simply a lot more to take in from colour pictures. In colour my editing should have been far more leisurely. However so many things, including the marvellous guitar music by Terry Driscoll, had been locked in by the time I saw the first colour print. By then it was too late to make any changes.

One lesson I learned was to trust my own perceptions of how to go about shooting a movie, and to be more assertive about putting those perceptions into practice. After all, although virtually unknown to anyone, I was already an experienced cinematographer and film maker from long before the days of *Ubu Films*. I had originally wanted to shoot many of the inner harbour scenes, the usually ignored industrial locations, from close to water level from a slow moving boat. This would have required shooting from a motorised dinghy and resulted in close-up views of rusty metal and stained timber, effectively expressing an intimate relationship - almost a love affair - with the location. In the end I got little of this from the water because I mistakenly allowed John to convince me that we should shoot from a larger, more comfortable boat.

When we worked from the land, we got much better shots as Ellen moved amongst mangroves and old, discarded machinery. But it's all such a long time ago that nitpicking is totally irrelevant, except as a way of recognising that I have made many wrong decisions, both personally and career-wise, during my adult life. Maybe the very title of these memoirs says something about this.

But I'd prefer to be more positive. One of my favourite photographs from this period (on the following page), both for its technical quality and for the fact that it documents a long gone Sydney, was taken while we were working at one of the locations for *Harbour*. Nowadays the skyline dwarfs the AWA radio mast, and the industrial waste-land of Darling Harbour has been reclaimed and turned into a consumer's paradise.

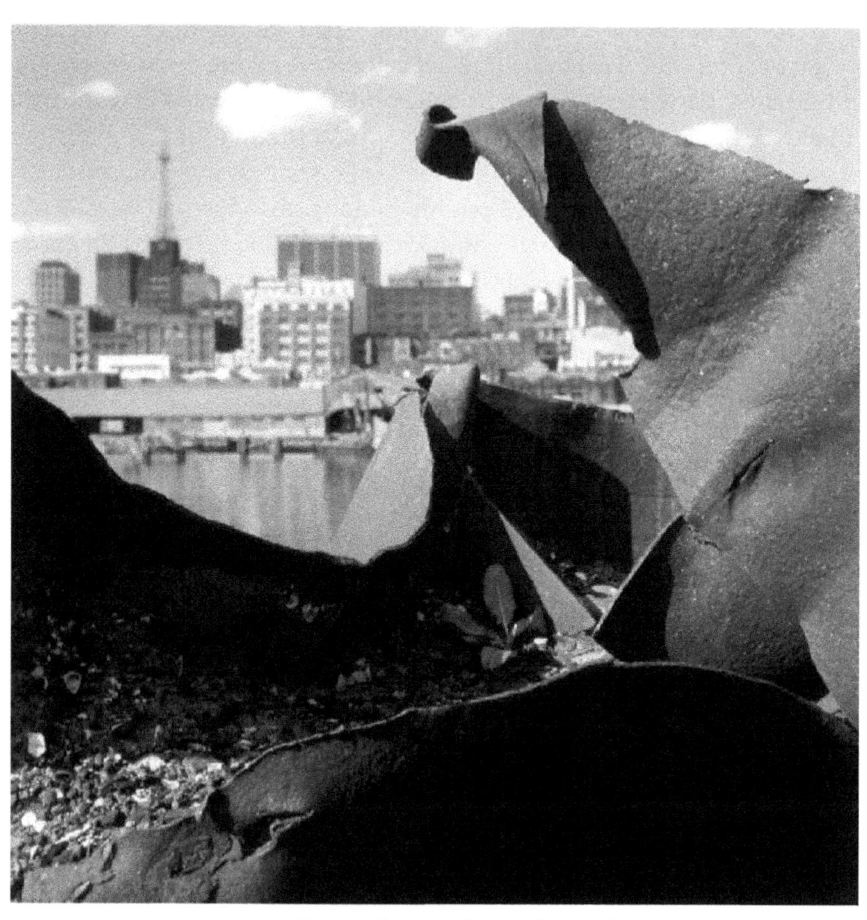

View of Sydney from Darling Harbour, 1966

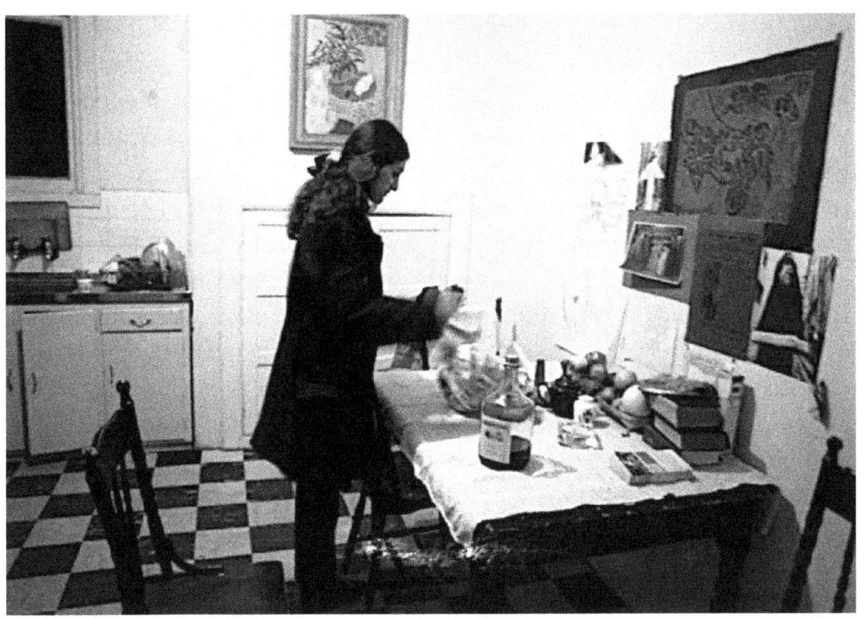

Abigayl in kitchen at Goodhope Street

Abigayl ...

Early in 1967 I formed a passionate relationship with Abigayl Day, who had been, a few years earlier, a close friend of Judy's. I had known Abby for several years since I first met her at Redfern before that household fell apart so spectacularly. After that I saw her occasionally at the Royal George, the Push's favourite pub.

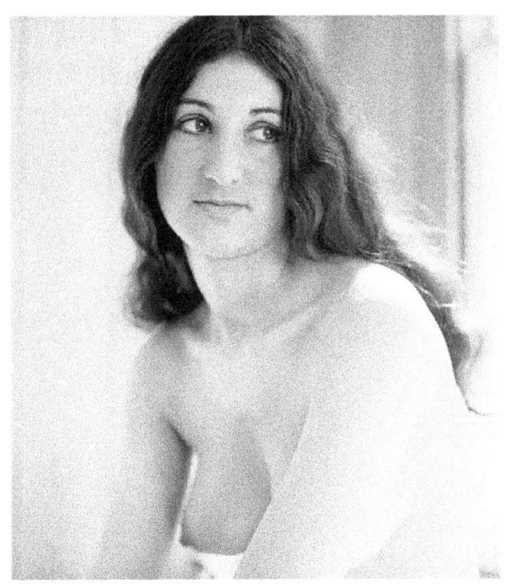

Abigayl at Goodhope Street, 1967

Abby and I found ourselves talking together one night at the bar. There was a clear sexual attraction between us and I invited her home to my room at Goodhope Street. This was a pretty basic place, my room, it had a mattress on the floor and paintings and drawings pinned to the walls, although I doubt there was much else in the way of furniture. We were all pretty well inured to the rigours of bohemian life so I think the state of my room hardly mattered. What I remember most of all about that night is that on our way to bed we left a trail of discarded clothing on the stairs and across the floor leading to my room. From that moment our relationship quickly grew into a fully formed love affair which stimulated every aspect of my creative life. It was truly a life-changing event

I no longer have access to the originals of the reproductions on the following page, so I can't show the qualities of the lines that were drawn, if I remember rightly, with a fine pointed, relatively hard pencil. But poor as they are these reproductions can give an idea of the subject matter I was working with.

Innocent as they might look, these images were deliberately offensive to the prevailing views of decency and of what could be shown in the popular press, movies and so on, although this wasn't the only reason I did them. However, *Ubu Films*, along with others of the time, was soon to be engaged in frequent battles with censorship. As I write this there are, and have been for some time, many signs of moral panic in Australia. It looks as though all the battles will have to be fought over again. This shouldn't really surprise me since the idea of continuous, linear social progress has proved over and over again to be an impossible dream.

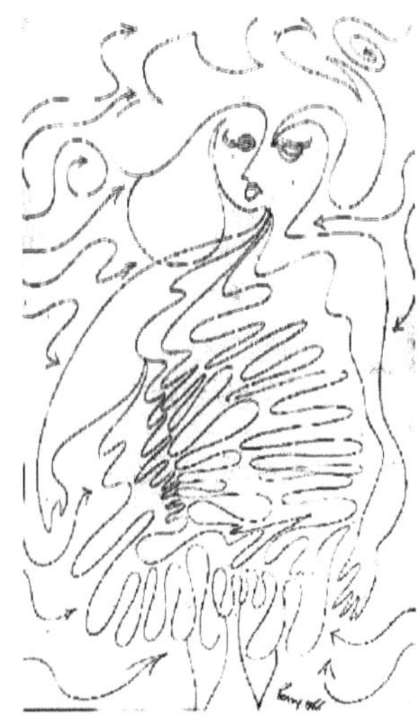

Girl in a wind (pencil on paper), 1966

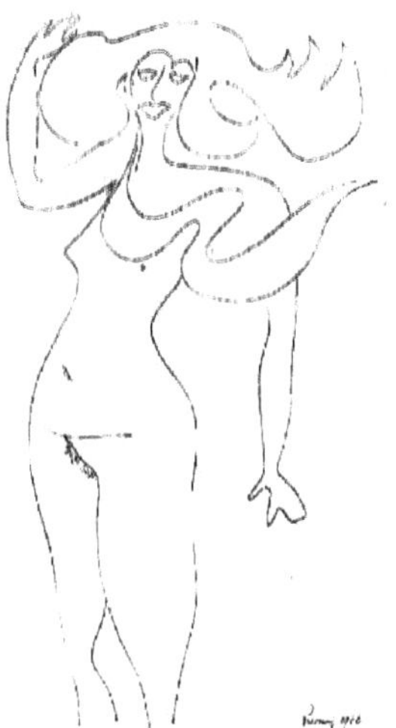

Girl waving (pencil on paper), 1966

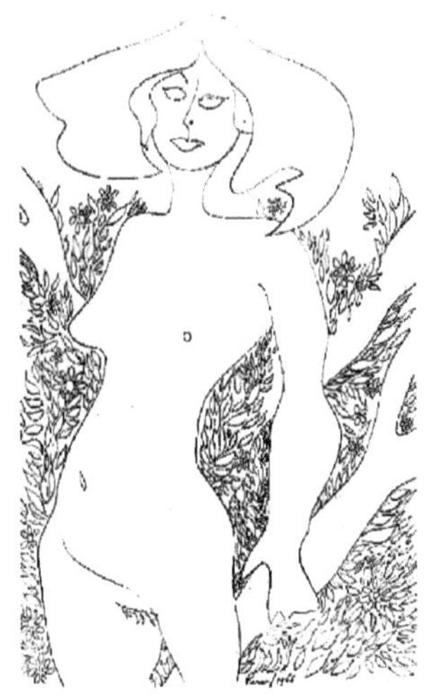

Girl in the bush (pencil on paper), 1966

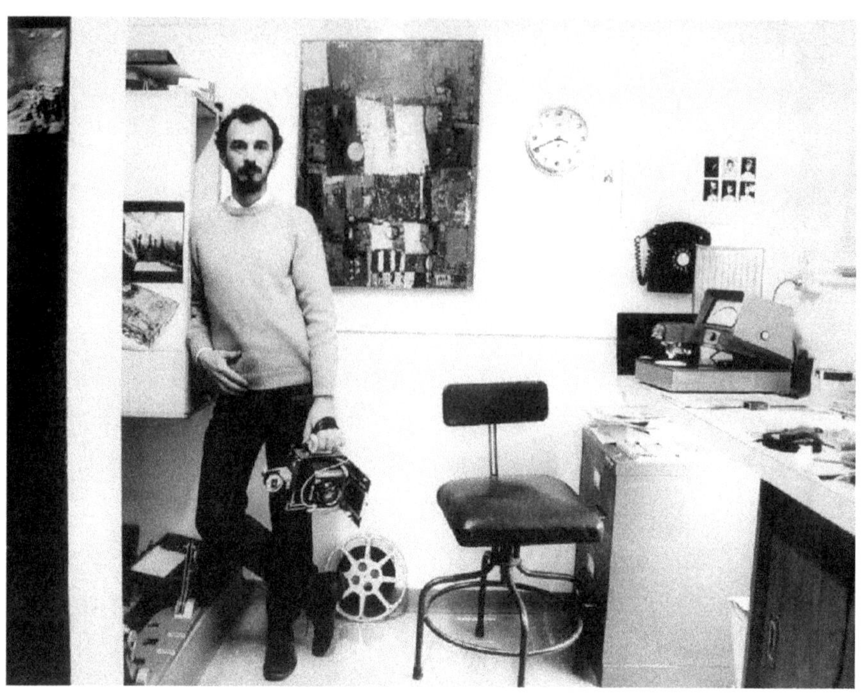

Autoportrait at the ABC

Cinematography ...

By 1967 cinematography was the dominant activity of my working life, both at the ABC, where I had landed a highly technical job in the Federal Engineering Laboratory, and in my after-hours work with *Ubu Films*. At the lab I gained a great deal of knowledge about the fundamentals of video and chemical photography and the close relationship between the two processes. I was always conscious of the theoretical possibilities of marrying these processes as is now done in large budget films, but in those days the technology was too crude to have acceptance in the "industry". Nevertheless, what I learned at the ABC, added to the craft skills I had from the printing trade and my personal experience as a painter, put me in a very good position to take on a role as a cinematographer which I did with alacrity.

I shot all of Albie Thoms' experimental films between 1965 and 1969, including the notorious *Marinetti* which tested me to the limit. (I don't have many stills from that work which is covered anyhow in exhaustive detail in *Sydney Underground Movies*, Peter Mudie's book on the *Ubu* period.) My aim here is not really to revisit all that stuff but rather to tell a story that incorporates knowledge that may or may not make my career more explicable to myself, at least, if not also to friends, lovers, colleagues and children.

Just recently I heard a man telling tales about Albie's sexual exploits and my drug use, all of which might have had some basis in reality but which were such outrageous exaggerations about me (and probably about Albie) that I thought at the time that I'd like to propose an antidote to various people's self-serving mythologising.

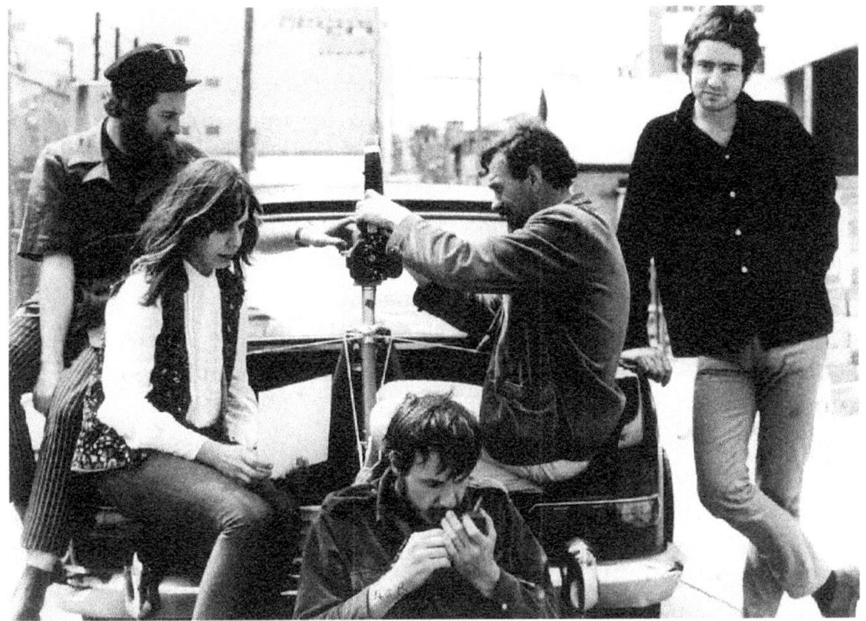

Setting up to shoot Bolero*: Albie Thoms; Sue Howe; Aggy Read; DP.; Nick Casey, 1967. (Photo: Mattt Carroll, reprinted from Peter Mudie's* Sydney Underground Movies.*)*

But back to the main story. In 1967 Albie conceived the idea of making a film that matched Ravel's *Bolero,* in the sense that the structure of that piece of music is an undeviating progress to its conclusion. Albie's idea was that the camera would make an equivalent undeviating progress along a narrow street towards the figure of a seated woman. As the viewpoint came closer we would see the woman's face, her eyes and ultimately we would be so close that a reflection of the camera in her eye would fill the screen as the music reached its climax.

This was a serious technical challenge. We did tests to determine an appropriate lens for the camera and to see how well Aggy's Austin 1800 would work as a camera "dolly"

The shot on page 79 shows our setup. I used the *Arriflex* because we needed a camera with an electric motor and that would take 400ft. rolls of film and could be run in reverse (so we could start at the end position). As well I wanted to run the camera at 48 frames per second to slow our on-screen progress along the street and to help smooth out any bumps. Also to smooth bumps, Aggy let some of the pressure out of his tyres.

We were easily able to hide the necessary overlap between the two 10 minute rolls, but where I have always been unsatisfied with my shooting for Bolero is on the transition to the extreme close-up on the eye. That required a difficult "focus pull". I could not at the time find a lens that could continuously change focus from extreme close-up to "infinity" while maintaining the perspective needed for most of the shot, so we agreed to change lenses for the last part of the shot (the first part when shooting). The result of the overlap between these two parts of the shot is quite obtrusive and spoils the effect of undeviating progress at the worst possible moment: at the climax.

Bolero was a formalistic concept that, like all formalism, required a perfect match between its idea and its formal realisation. Sadly, the way I had to do it was like a grammatical gaucherie in an otherwise elegant sentence or a logical error in an argument.

In spite of that, the film was well received in experimental film circles and overseas screenings, even though some critics did point out the problem of the lens-change.

Speaking about "formalism" brings me to a story that has always irked me and left a smouldering resentment towards many people in the Australian "film industry". The story goes like this: since I first made *Halftone* I had dreamed of a much more ambitious project based on a similar idea. I wanted to use three superimposed strips of halftone patterning printed on colour film through primary coloured filters and, from those same three strips, I would generate three tracks of audio to be mixed in the way that film sound tracks usually are. I knew from my technical knowledge that if I got the combinations of patterns right I would generate a rich and potentially fascinating result, similar in some respects to, although more rigorously abstract than the "colour separation" films of the Cantrills, a highly-gifted film-making couple from Melbourne.

I talked to Albie about my idea. He was working at the time as a television producer and naturally had many contacts at the ABC. He set up a meeting for me with a senior man in the film department, with the idea that I would seek funding for my project, which would have cost peanuts compared with the ABC's usual diet of documentaries and naturalistic dramas or comedies.

The outcome of my meeting with the ABC man was totally unproductive. I might have got out a few sentences trying to describe what I intended to do and what I thought it would look/sound like, but almost immediately my hoped-for benefactor launched into an hour-long monologue about a new TV series he was working on, a series of *cinema verité* docudramas, a new concept for Australian television. He seemed totally oblivious to the fact that *cinema verité* was just about as far as one could get from what I had come to talk about. I have seen a number of films made along those lines, some of them very good indeed (my tastes are catholic). It's just that I have never wanted - especially didn't want, at that time when I and my colleagues were "on a roll" with our new-found film/formalist beliefs - to make *cinema-verité* films. Had I known about it, I may have been more enthused about what the Soviet *avant garde* called "kino-pravda" (which translates to exactly the same verbal meaning as the French phrase although the end results are very different), but in the end the meeting with the man from the ABC was exactly like my later meetings with many other people from the film industries of Australia, England and even Russia: I was subjected to a lecture on how films should be made. These lectures always seemed to assume that I was ignorant of all film history and would benefit by being "put straight" by the "lecturer". You shouldn't wonder that there is a hint of anger in my attitude to people who identify themselves with the "industry".

Ubu Films continued producing and screening films. Our audiences were generally young and radical in late-1960s kinds of ways. We felt very pure in that we weren't market-driven, but perhaps we didn't need to be since we were a part of our own market and knew it intimately. That being true, it was also dangerous, in that the culture we were part of would inevitably mutate and fragment and leave us isolated as individuals. In a few more years that is what I believe <u>did</u> happen. In the meantime there were a few good years left for apparently disinterested idealism.

Around about 1967 Albie started to tell me about a major film he was planning. This was to become the film that I described several pages back as the "notorious" *Marinetti*. "Notorious" for several reasons: one being that after its premiere it was judged to be entirely lacking in narrative content (which it wasn't); another being that Marinetti, the Italian futurist whose ideas the film ostensibly was based on became a great supporter of Mussolini and the Italian fascists. At the time we were making *Marinetti* the politics of virtually everyone in the art world through to most in the film "industry" even, covered the spectrum from moderate to far left - the right wing had little or no support at all. What this meant in practice was that most people who had been Albie's supporters till then, even if they had no knowledge of politics at all, and even if they thought it had "no narrative", picked up a "vibe" from the film that they interpreted, albeit inarticulately, as "fascist".

I said that *Marinetti* was "ostensibly" based on the ideas of Marinetti because that was what Albie said it was, and I'm not saying here that he was fooling himself. It is nevertheless an article of faith for me that once one has made a work of art (this also applies to written texts), the work takes on an independent life and is free to be interpreted in far more than one way. Speaking for myself alone, I have always thought that *Marinetti* was an expressionist work rather than a futurist one, because of its extremely personal, confessional nature. I have always thought that the ideas articulated in the film were anarchist rather than fascist. I know that some of my left-wing friends would say there is little or no difference although I don't agree. All this might seem obscurely academic nowadays, but at the time the influence of Leninist thought was pervasive.

When I lived in London a few years later that influence was particularly strong, but that part of the story will have to wait its allotted time, as will the story of my own film, *The Refracting Glasses*, dealing with left wing tendencies in the Australian art world. For now I'll only say that *RFG* (as I've come to call it) disappeared like a stone in the rapidly draining lake of formalist film culture.

But enough digressions: by the time *Marinetti* was complete Abby and I had firmed our relationship to the extent that we decided to have a child.

This was a momentous step for me, since after my break with Judy there had been a divorce when I had willingly agreed to pay a significant part of my income as maintenance for our three children.

To complicate matters Abby had a falling out with Albie. I have no memory of what it was about but the outcome was that we had to find somewhere else to live. We did that with little trouble, moving to a little old stone cottage in Balmain that is by now, I'm sure, an extremely valuable middle class residence. Even then, in 1968, the gentrification of Balmain was under way.

I myself had become a slum landlord, although no doubt one of the least businesslike in the world. Some time after our divorce Judy and Michael moved out of the Redfern house and for what it was worth (very little) I was free to put it on the rental market. The woman who then lived in it was often late with the rent and I was always a sucker for her hard luck stories. Eventually somebody made an offer to buy the place from me (for less than I paid for it). I was so relieved to be free of the hassles that I accepted the offer. At least I was able to be freed of all debt and to be able to buy a little car which served Abby and me well for a couple of years.

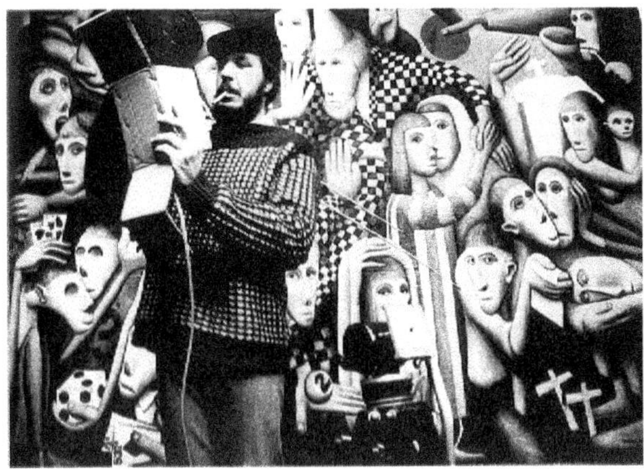

Aggy unpacking lights for Looby *shoot, 1968*

Around that time I got to know Keith Looby, an artist who had been overseas for some years (as Australian artists were wont to be). Maybe I should have remembered him from earlier days of the Push, but I can't say that I did. No matter, Looby now proposed that *Ubu Films* make a short film promoting his paintings, which we did with me directing and John Clark shooting.

Looby's paintings at the time were crowded with often grotesque figures loaded with symbolic meanings and painted with great craft. Not for nothing had he been studying the "old masters".

Abby and I became good friends with Looby and his partner, Helen Beresford. Many weekends we visited them at their house in the country overlooking the Hawkesbury River. Out there I photographed Looby with his paintings for at least one magazine article and sometimes just recorded everyday activities. When Looby and Helen were married at the Windsor court-house I took their wedding pictures.

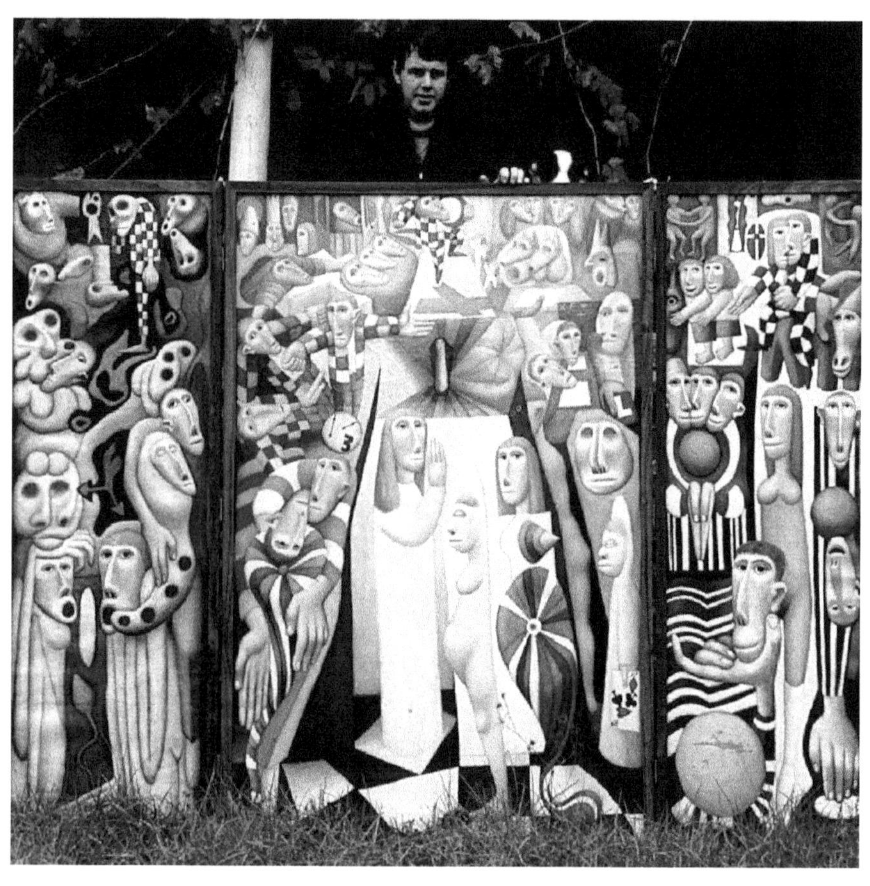

Keith Looby with God made all this, *photo 1968*

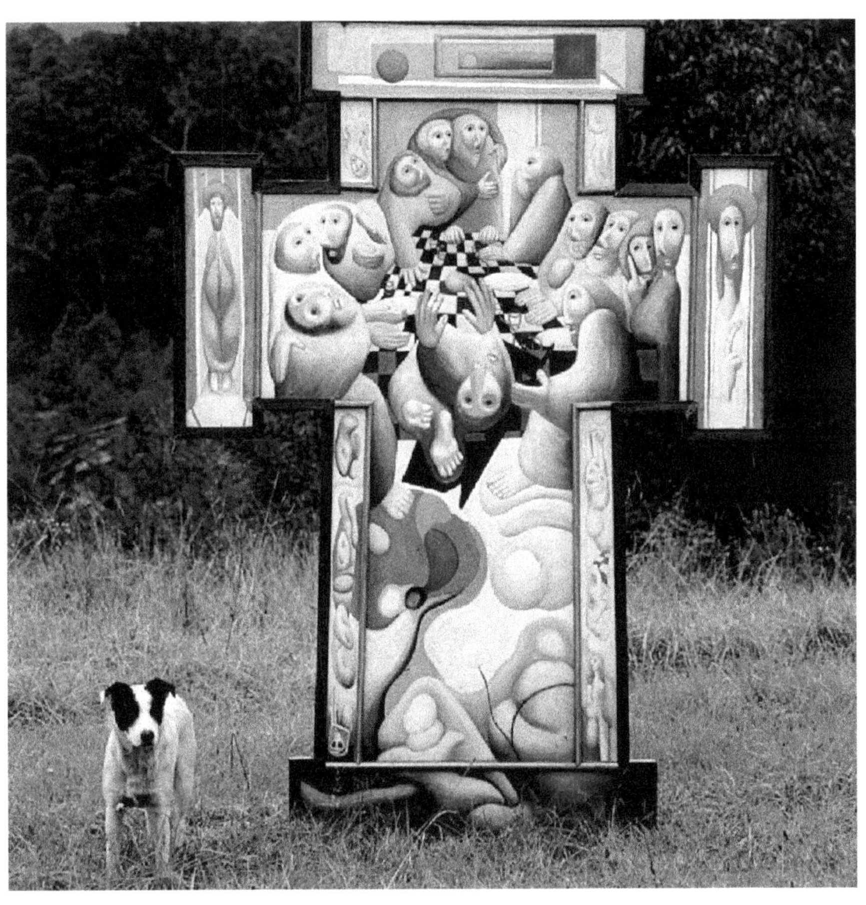

Looby's painting Last supper, *photo 1968*

Big changes coming ...

Big changes in many aspects of my life were in process. To start somewhere, although not necessarily at the beginning, my approach to film making changed. I moved away from the strict formalism of my abstract work to something more like humanism, although certainly not the humanism that was found in *cinema verité* docos or the French "New Wave". Somewhere I had seen a short animated film by a Polish artist, Walerian Borowczyk, which made a huge impression on me. The film was called *Angel Games*. Its imagery implied a never ending series of prison cells with drain pipes that ran with a strange blue fluid. The viewpoint continually shifted up, down or across. Disturbing sounds implying a chopping action could be heard. Eventually it became clear that winged creatures with blue blood were being hacked to pieces. Hence, doubtless, the title. Undoubtedly, too, an expression of the Polish obsession with religion and "nobility". Much later I saw other films by this artist, all different from each other, some contrasting a humanist viewpoint with a formalist structure. Later still Borowczyk made feature-length films that some people called "pornographic".

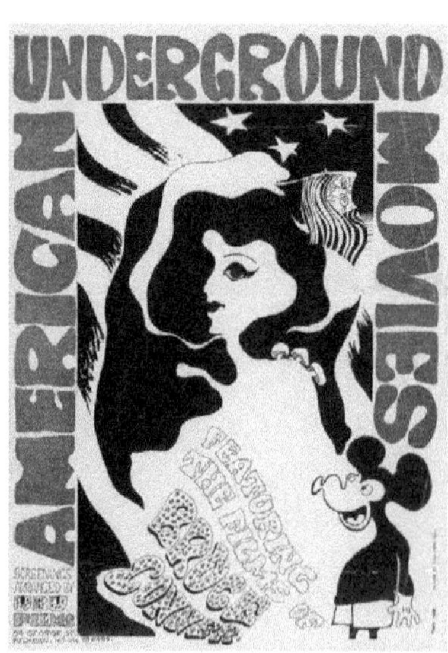

Flyer for the Brisbane screening

But it was *Angel Games* that pushed me first in a new direction, basically I think because I saw that it was possible to deal with highly emotional subjects while retaining a strictly formal structure: for example regular, repetitive movements, simple drawn shapes, the modernist "grid" and an absence of literal, photographically represented symbols. It was a long time ago now and my memory may be playing tricks about just what it was that impressed me but I have no doubt that that film was a major influence. Another influence was the work of the American, Bruce Conner, which I learned of through a print of Conner's film *Cosmic Ray*, brought to Australia by an American expatriate named Gladney Oakley who came here as a "nuclear refugee" at the time of the Cuban missile crisis. (*Ubu Films* subsequently featured a number of Conner's films in shows at Sydney and other places - see the flyer on previous page.)

All of this was going on while Abby was pregnant. I was driven to record on film aspects of her pregnancy as well as some enactments by Abby of her feelings, pleasures and ambivalences which she had told me about while her belly swelled. I called this little film (it ran about two and a half minutes) *A Sketch on Abigayl's Belly* because that's what the film was

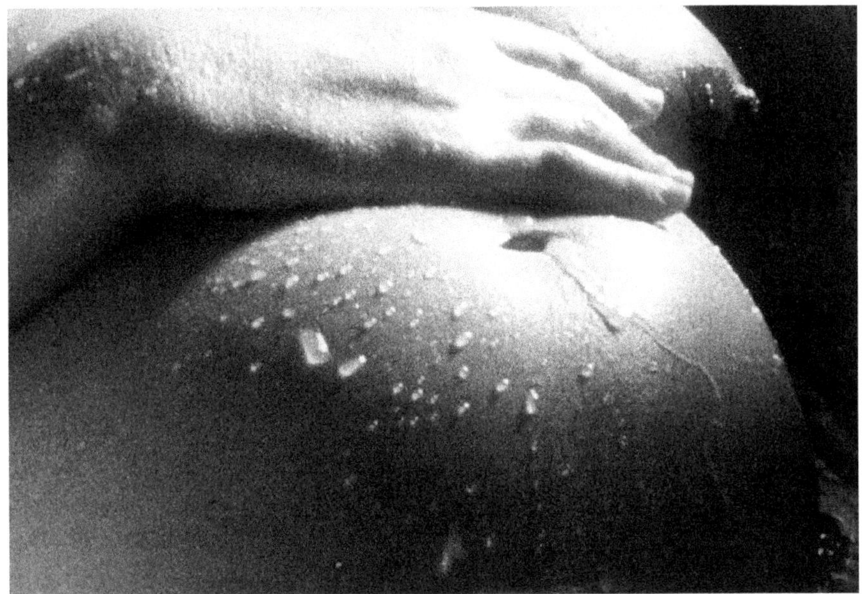

Frame blowup from A Sketch on Abigayl's Belly, *1968*

- a sketch; a documentary sketch quite unlike anything the ABC would recognise as a documentary.

The first screening of this film was a wonderful experience. I was in the theatre and almost from the start I could feel the audience's total absorption. It was just as the cliché says: "You could hear a pin drop."

The birth of Rachael ...

On the 2nd October, 1968 our daughter Rachael was born. We had decided only a few weeks before then to get married. I'm not sure what precisely our reasons were, They weren't really for "respectability", although in those days that could certainly smooth the way along various paths of bureaucracy. We certainly didn't care what ordinary people might have thought.

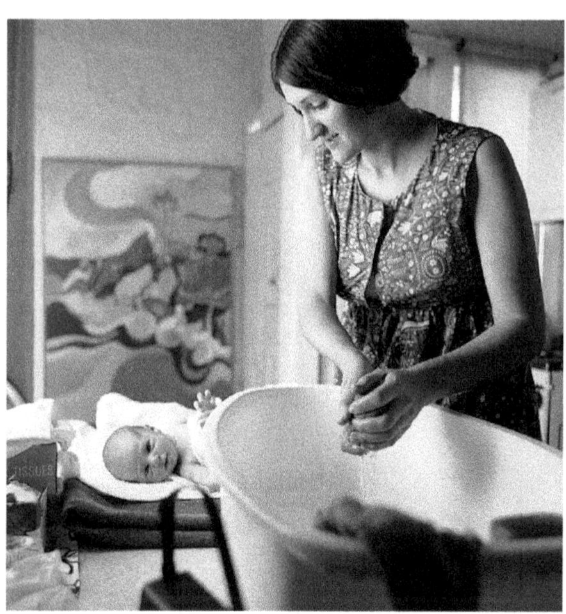
Abby bathing New Rachael, 1968

In those days (that phrase again) childbirth was still considered to be an entirely medical procedure. When the time for the birth came there was no way fathers would be allowed to share in the experience and I was sent home without ceremony. The birth was slow and difficult and I could only try to imagine what it was like for Abby. However, like the majority of other births, at the end of their time in hospital Abby and Rachael came home in very good order.

Juggling commitments ...

My relationship with Abby didn't mean that I stopped seeing my children Caitlin, Jane and Simon. Abby and I took them for outings in our little VW when they were sometimes "handfuls" (in the nicest possible way). I remember once they pulled down their pants and showed their

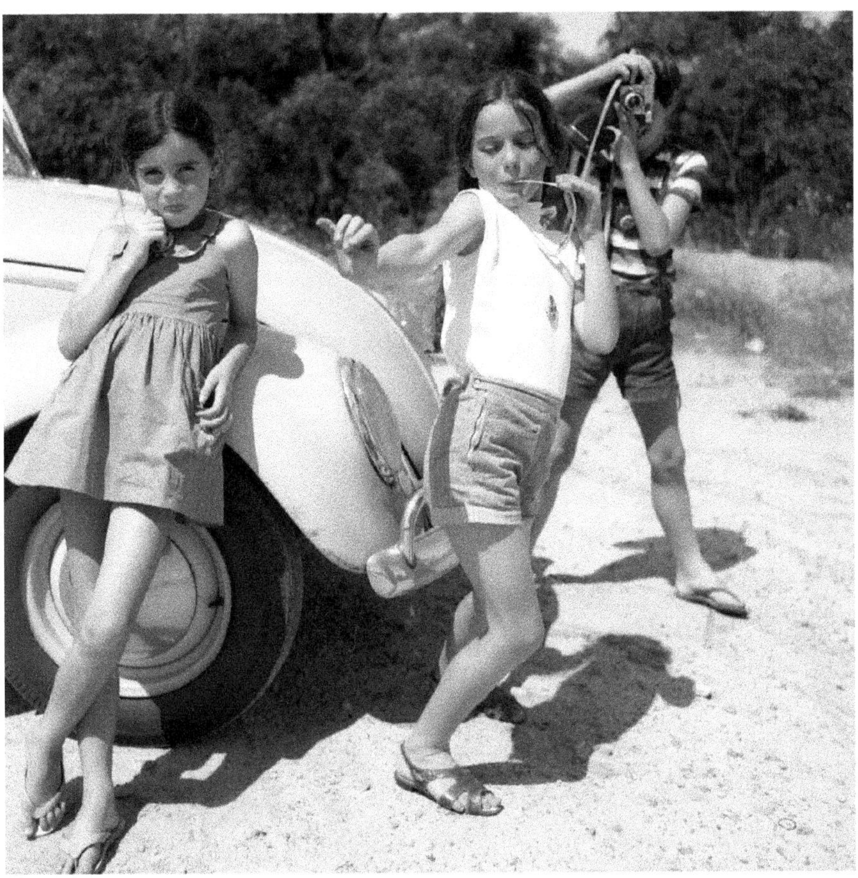

Caitlin, Jane and Simon, somewhere in the Blue Mountains, c.1970

bare bums through the back window to following motorists (there were no seat belt regulations then to restrain them).

Simon seemed to be following in my footsteps as a photographer. As I'll relate later I lost contact for some time with these children, a truly painful time, but I had "made my bed and was obliged to lie in it" as I think the saying goes. Unfortunately the children too had to "lie in it" without having any choice in the matter.

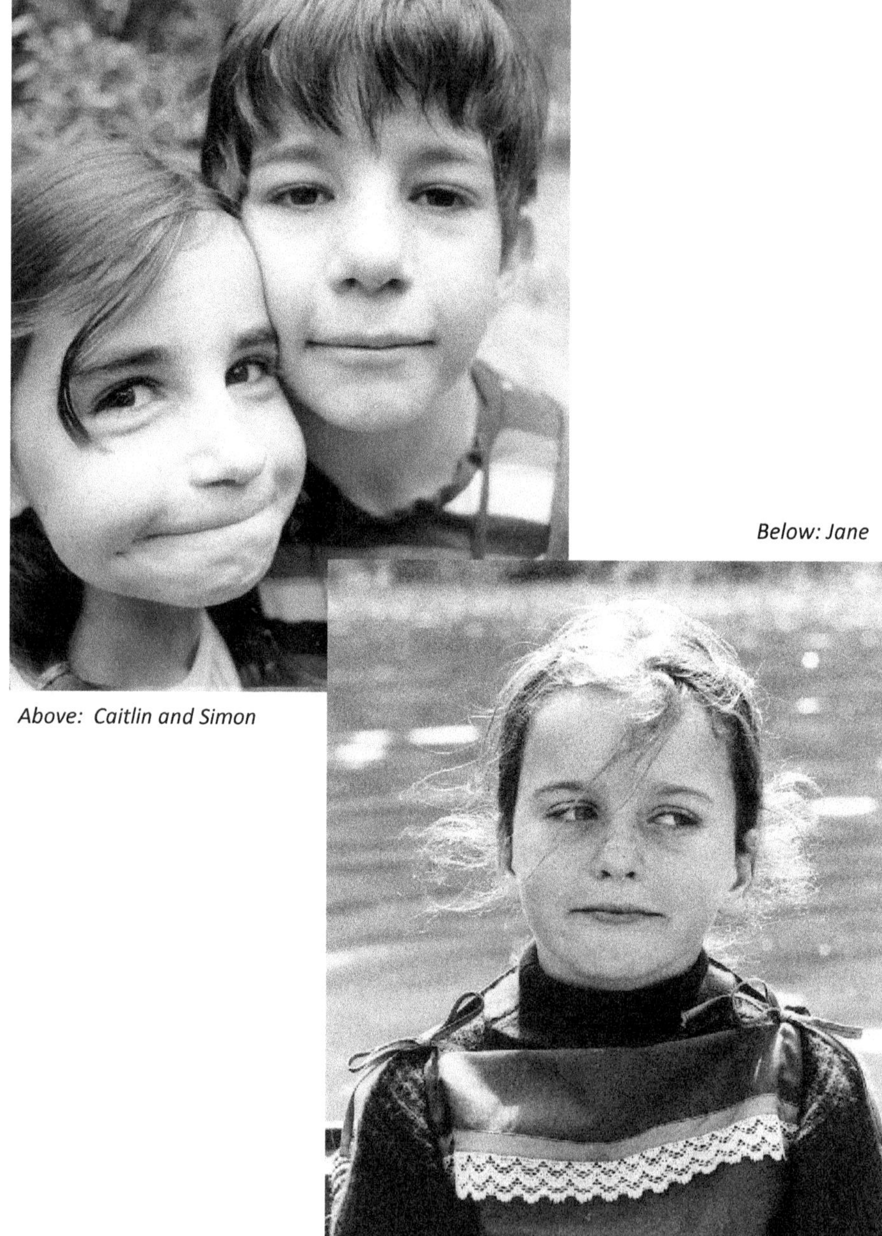

Below: Jane

Above: Caitlin and Simon

For the time being, though, everything seemed to be going well, Abby and I were very happy together with Rachael, I worked on weekends with Albie, shooting *Marinetti*, or on my own photography or on graphics for *Ubu*.

On the subject of *Marinetti*, it was only when we were well into the project that I really worked out what its subject was, as distinct from its structure. Albie's style of directing was basically to set practical, technical, problems for me to solve, which of course I loved to do. Psychological things he kept to himself.

After a while though I'd have been pretty stupid not to see what was going on. Albie's long-term relationship with Sue Howe was falling/had fallen apart and he had fallen in love with Clem Weight. The psychological impact of all this is fully documented in *Marinetti*, expressed in tableaux depicted with sometimes elaborate staging and richly coloured lighting, and using visual effects created entirely in the Bolex.

I was beginning to "hit my stride" as a photographer and cinematographer, by now well able to get the results I wanted without much risk of failure. (In compiling this book I have gone back to my negatives from that time and I have to say most of them have been a joy to work with; and now I don't even have to get my fingers wet with chemicals.)

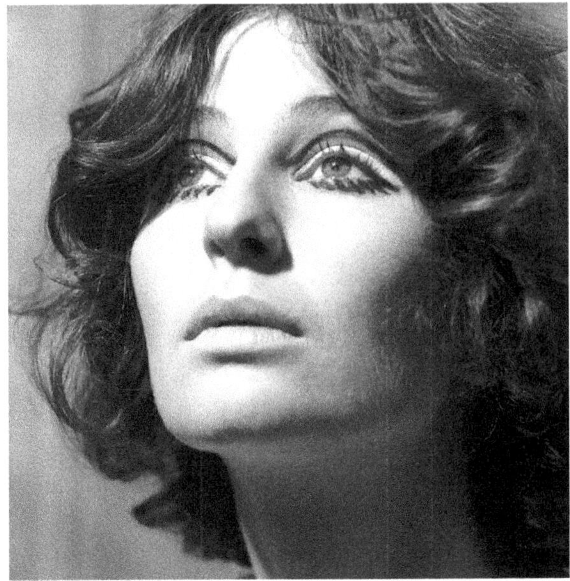

Clem Weight (part of a publicity series for Marinetti), 1969

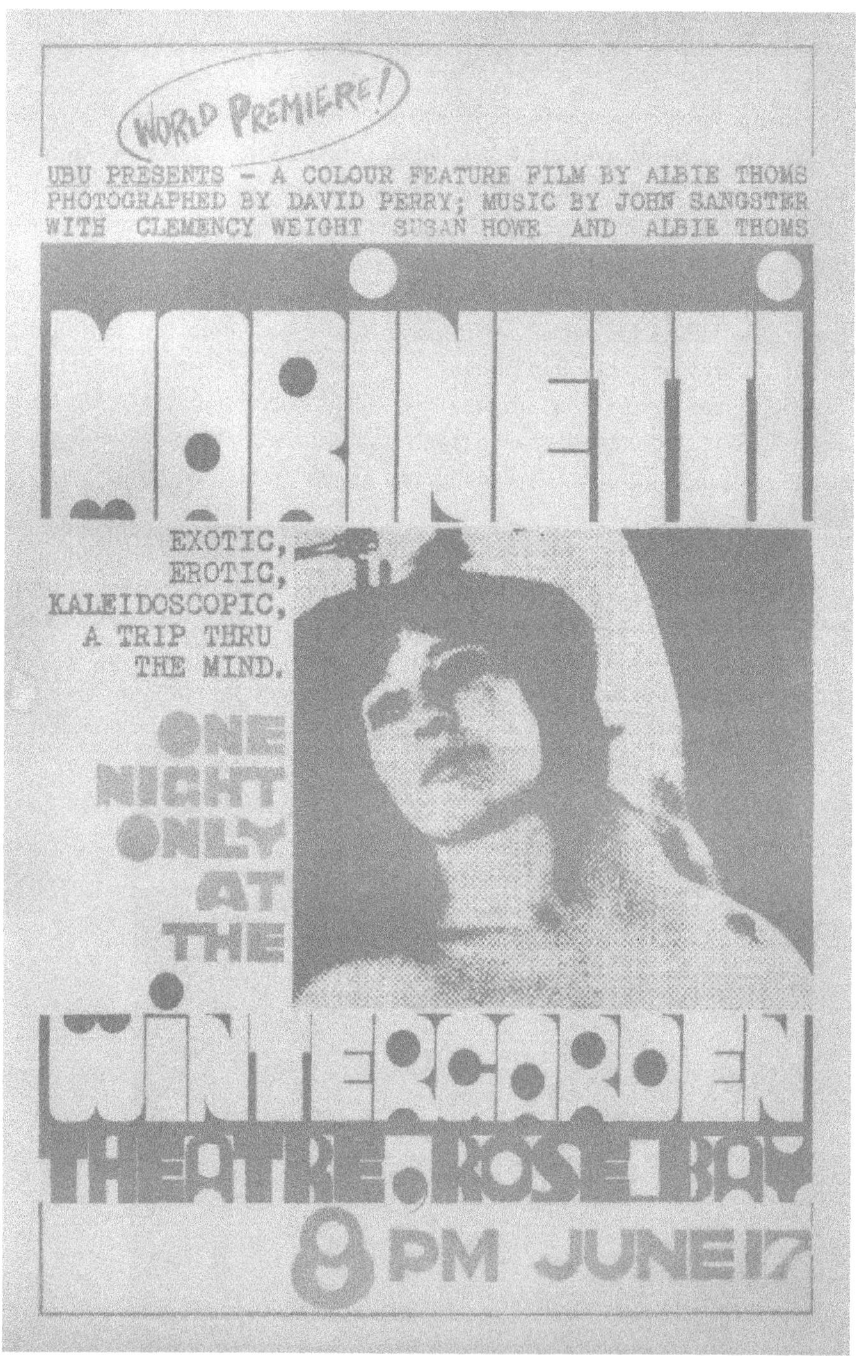
WORLD PREMIERE!
UBU PRESENTS - A COLOUR FEATURE FILM BY ALBIE THOMS
PHOTOGRAPHED BY DAVID PERRY; MUSIC BY JOHN SANGSTER
WITH CLEMENCY WEIGHT SUSAN HOWE AND ALBIE THOMS
MARINETTI
EXOTIC,
EROTIC,
KALEIDOSCOPIC,
A TRIP THRU
THE MIND.
ONE
NIGHT
ONLY
AT
THE
WINTERGARDEN
THEATRE, ROSE BAY
8 PM JUNE 17

Marinetti had its premiere on 17th June, 1969. The audience was divided with, I'd say, many more than half being negative in various ways, some just uncomprehending, others opposed because it didn't look to be the herald of the much hoped-for renaissance of the "Australian film industry". There were probably more varied expectations in the Sydney audience, all fanned by publicity in press and television. Looking back on that stuff now it seems clear that all the journalists involved projected their own expectations on *Marinetti* without taking any account of the fairly provocative work previously made and shown by *Ubu*. Albie was even ridiculed by a cartoon on the leader page of the *Daily Telegraph*, pretty bizarre really when you know that the *Telegraph* was pitched at a readership that had no interest in, or was hostile to, whatever we might have said or done.

An indication of the derisive attitude to our work held by many old fogeys working in cinemas and TV stations at the time can be found in the fact that a slide was projected at the start of every short in the first half of many of *Ubu's* earlier films, and at the start of *Marinetti*, saying: "A 16mm presentation." I presumed that this was really saying: "You can't expect much of what you're about to see."

I don't think there's any doubt that the reactions to the screening cemented many peoples' perceptions of us as unsuitable for any place in "the industry", such as it was. At least in the short term, my own view was that there was no place for me there.

While we were finishing *Marinetti* I had also been working on other projects. One of these was the shooting of Clem Weight's film portrait of her son, *Tobias Icarus Aged Four*, and the shooting and then editing of Phil Noyce's first film, *Better to Reign in Hell*. Phil had become involved with *Ubu Films* while still at high school, and even then his talent, self-confidence and drive were unmistakable. Without those, of course, he could never have become the highly "bankable" film director that he now is, and has been for many years.

As my "day job" I was still working at the ABC's Federal Engineering Lab. At one stage I was given the job of producing thousands of feet of 16mm film containing a minuscule test pattern for calibrating telecine systems. It had to have small patches in the centre of every frame,

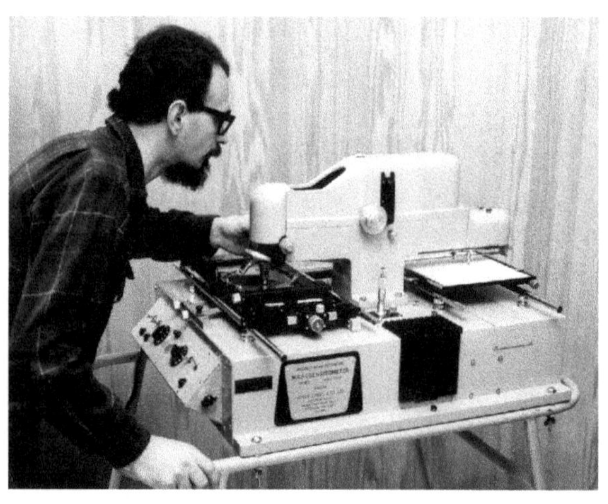

DP with microdensitometer, c.1969 (photo by Scott Meynert/ABC)

a "grey scale" running the gamut from "TV black" to "TV white". This was extremely demanding, with very limited tolerances. The patches were so small that before I could measure their densities the ABC had to buy me a microdensitometer, a highly specialised device that scanned the film so that when properly calibrated it gave a readout of densities across the frame. I decided that I would have to use reversal film for the job because using a neg/pos process would introduce variables that would make getting the desired accuracy virtually impossible.

The photograph above shows me operating the microdensitometer. I think the fact that the photograph was taken for the ABC's Annual Report to parliament indicates how valuable the equipment was. It might also indicate how prestigious the test pattern project was. It was being done for all the broadcasting organisations of the [British] Commonwealth of Nations, where the BBC still reigned supreme.

Censorship also still attempted to reign supreme over a popular culture that was ever more determined to throw off the hypocritical moralism of a conservative establishment. The corruption of that establishment, and the links between sexual politics and politics generally, had been making itself clearer to people at least since the "Profumo Affair". Of course the British establishment (and no doubt, in a faint echo, the Australian establishment) contained quite a few idealistic people working from the inside to destabilise, even to destroy, its power. I'm thinking of people like Philby, Burgess and Maclean. Then there were novelists like Graham Greene and Lawrence Durrell who described with what appeared to be clinical detachment, the activities of their class brethren in various colonial locations.

By the late 1960s the Vietnam War had generated irresistible anti-establishment forces in the societies of Australia and the USA. This explains the idealistic optimism of the so-called "counter-culture" to which we in *Ubu Films* felt we belonged. I felt that my films and drawings were weapons to use in the struggle against illiberal, oppressive laws. In their various ways so did everyone else involved with *Ubu*.

A year or so earlier I had made *A Sketch on Abigayl's Belly* which eventually won for us a small victory in the war against censorship. It went this way: the film, being able to fit into a very small can, was sent by air mail to a short film festival at Oberhausen in Germany. It was accepted into competition and screened at the festival attracting positive comment.

While *Sketch* was only screened in Australia it was not subject to Commonwealth censorship laws, which applied only to imports. Censorship of locally-made films was usually only applied after someone complained to the State police, or some member of one of the States' "vice squads" stumbled onto a screening. In fact *Sketch* had been shown a number of times around Australia without complaint, but when it came back after Oberhausen, it became an import subject to Customs Department censorship (that was their interpretation, anyhow). The film was viewed and found to be "indecent" or "obscene" and therefore banned. We were entitled to appeal this decision, which we did. This time I was permitted to sit in on the screening. When the lights came on a man - a "Mr Prowse" as I remember it - said the appeal would not succeed. When I asked why he said, simply: "You can't show something like that." *Sketch* now became something of a *cause célèbre*. Questions were asked in Parliament and eventually, to quell embarrassment, the Minister for Customs was replaced by a more liberal member, Senator Don Chipp. My little film had given us a scalp. The film was unbanned.

Ubu Films, to promote its films and its anti-establishment line, had been for some time publishing its own newspaper. I didn't have a major role in its production, although I designed its most frequently used masthead (see next page). However, when *Sketch* became a victim of censorship I was inspired to do several drawings expressing my contempt for that activity. The most virulent, the most deliberately ugly one of those ended up on the front page of *Ubu News*. In making such drawings my experience with the printing trade was useful. I knew from photographing drawings for cheap printing processes that subtle tones or delicate pen lines would almost certainly be lost. To avoid that I took to making drawings with a pen designed for technical drawing. Loaded with Indian ink, the pen was held vertically to the paper. The "knib" was

Front page of Ubu News *No.15, June 1969*

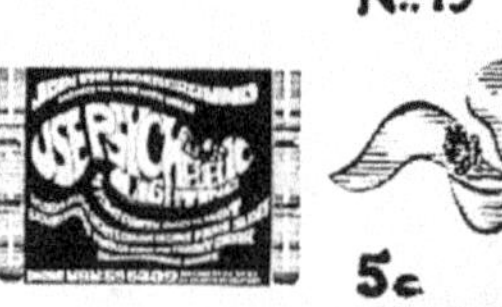

No 15

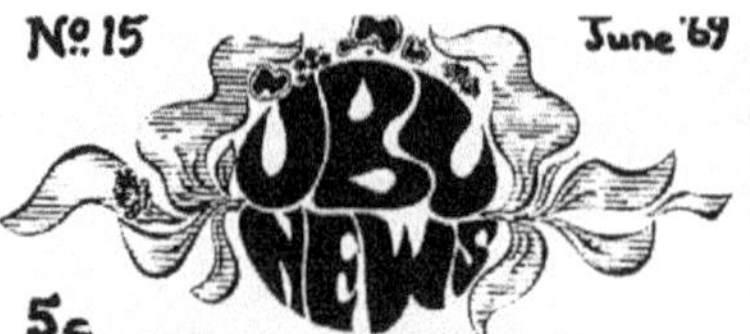

June '69

5c

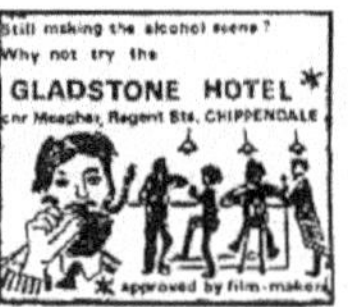

DEFEAT CENSORSHIP!

IMAGINE A DARK ROOM. A MAN SITTING ALONG WATCHING LIGHT FLICKER ON A BEADED SCREEN. THE PATTERNS MADE BY THE LIGHT RESEMBLE A NAKED WOMAN. IMAGINE A WARM SENSATION BETWEEN THE LEGS. FEEL AN ERECTION COMING ON. STOP THE FILM! BAN IT! NEXT FILM.

The censors are riddled with sex guilt. The idea of someone getting an erection from watching a film is hideous to them. How horrible to enjoy sex? Shave that woman's pubic hair! Airbrush her pudenda! Cut off that cock! Film passed!

Pregnancy is a reminder od sex guilt. If she's pregnant she must have had a fuck. How horrible. Ban it.

1968 - A SKETCH ON ABIGAYL'S BELLY - 3 minutes 16mm color - a film by David Perry of his wife's pregnancy. Banned! But the film has been shown publicly without complain. Irrelevant. The film cannot be exported. The film cannot be shown in the state of Victroia. Banned. That pregnant woman has pubic hair. She is enjoying her pregnancy. She is not ashamed, Banned.

1969 - A SKETCH ON ABIGAYL'S BELLY screened in the finals of the Oberhausen (germany) Film Competition. But that film is banned - how did you get it out of the country? I posted it. You what? You realise that under section 28 of the Customs Regulations Act you are liable to prosecution.... Go shave off your Customs Regulations Act. Castrate yourself with your censors' scissors.

1969 - I LOVE, YOU LOVE sent to Australia by the Swedish Government. A pregant woman talks to her lover. Cut! Cut! You cannot show that scene in Australia. Australians do not approve of such things. What things? Simulated intercourse. But those people aren't fucking. Out! Out! You filthy foreign pervert. We do not permit Australians to see pregnant ladies, or pubic hair, or cocks, or cunts or arseholes. We don't have sex here. We are all born by autogenisis. So piss off".

1963 - IT DROPPETH AS THE GENTLE RAIN - Banned.
1967 - RITA & DUNDI, THE FILM, THE TRIBULATIONS OF MR DUPONT NONORE - banned. Not fit to be shown on a lavatory wall).

PEOPLE WATCH THESE FILMS. SEE THEM & WALK ON THE STREETS AS FREE PEOPLE. DO NOT LET THE CENSORS CUT OFF YOUR BALLS. DEFEND YOUR SEXUAL APPETITES. DO NOT BE ASHAMED THAT YOU FUCK, & THAT THIS LEADS TO PREGNANCY, & THAT THIS LEADS TO LITTLE CHILDREN.

LOCK THE CENSORS IN THEIR DARK ROOMS WITH THEIR PAINFUL ERECTIONS LET THEM RAVE & PRONOUNCE SEX A SIN. BUT IGNORE THEM. DENY THEM THE POWER THE STATE HAS GIVEN THEM. MAKE FILMS THAT GLORIFY & REVEL IN SEX. WATCH THEM. DEFEAT THE CENSORS' ATTEMPTS TO FORCE THEIR NEUROTIC OBSESSIONS ON US ALL. LET THEM CONSUME THEMSELVES WITH THEIR OWN GUILT!

NEXT UBU SCREENING - ANZAC AUDITORIUM. June 26,27,28,29 For programme details contact Ubu: 696489, 6991285.

Portrait of a Censorious Person

CENSORSHIP

THE ELEMENTS - A, not suitable for TV (verbal notification)

UNSTRAP ME - AO, not suitable for TV with cuts - WE WILL NOT ALLOW THIS FILM TO BE CUT and will appeal as soon as we have written confirmation of the cuts required.

IMAGO and HEY MAMMA - The Minister has upheld the censors refusal to register these two films.

ADVENTURES OF X Trailer - TV'G'

ADORATION OF SUSIE - TV'G' (verbal notification)

RUBBISH PEOPLE - Educational dramatic, not suitable for TV, not suitable for children.

NEWSNEWSNEWSNEWSNEWSNEWSNEWSNEWS

Colin Campbell, former Chief Censor & recently Appeals Censor has retired. Tom Cadwallader is now Appeals Censor. He is a "film man" - 47 years with Universal Pictures. One hopes he will not refuse to reverse the decisions of the censors as Colin Campbell did.

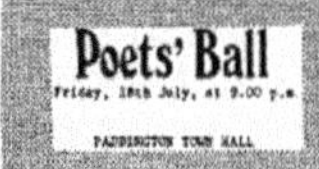

NEW CO-OP – NEW FILMS

The Sydney Cinema Journal, which hasn't been published for some time, raised money on a coop bas basis to finance THE AMERICAN POET'S VISIT (Mike Thornhill, 1969). This 15 min B&W film was premiered last month along with other films which form the basis of the SCJ Coop. One of these films is BALMAIN (Kit Guyatt) which may be available from Ubu shortly.

THE AMERICAN POET'S VISIT is a gutsy piece, satirising intellectuals, and the Sydney Push in particular. However much of the savage satire is a put-on, as the Push act all the parts themselves.

Also shown was David Minter's HEY AL BABY, which come across as gutless and insipid in comparison to the other two films (BALMAIN in 'films coming'). Revealing minor key changes in human personalities, it has an anthropological quality, dutifully recording the variety of nuances of human behaviour. Dialogue is improvised and the loose structure decidedly non-dramatic.

These films reveal the incredible range of independent filmmaking taking place in Australia. Unfortunately these films went unobserved by press, radio, or TV. And, of course, only small a audiences attended. The carry-on about indigenous film production seems pointless and nonsensical when films such as these are ignored.

The law of the Karma is long my friends, long, much longer than life.

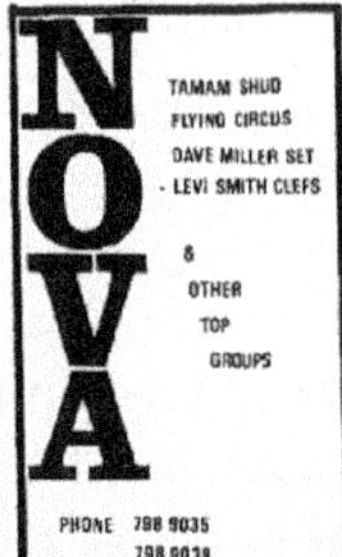

a fine tube with an even finer needle inside it. Light pressure on the paper pushed the needle upward, releasing a flow of ink through the tube. The resulting line was very even in thickness and, so long as the knib was kept clean. It was very firm, and very easy to reproduce.

The drawing of the following double page spread (see next two pages) was also reproduced in *Ubu News*. You'll find in it a number of sardonic references to sexual politics of the time, although they won't reveal themselves as explicit satire or commentary of the kind that might have been understood by the generation that followed us in challenging the establishment.

I'm jumping ahead a little here but this feels like the right place to do it: whereas Albie's and my politics had been formed by the Sydney Push, a libertarian movement - anarchist, if you like, although "anarchist" only roughly fitted many Push people - the sympathies of a lot of the people who came into the film scene in the 1970s lay more with international left-wing politics. If pressed, I have to say that my own sympathies are with the left. Nevertheless I am often uncomfortable in the company of "lefties" whether old communists or the "new left" whom I have often found to be puritanical moralists or bureaucrats or both. Especially when it comes to film work, I have often found these people to be unsympathetic to or uncomprehending of the way that I like to work.

If you want to know what I mean by "the way that I like to work" don't ask me to explain it to you in words, just look at what I've done.

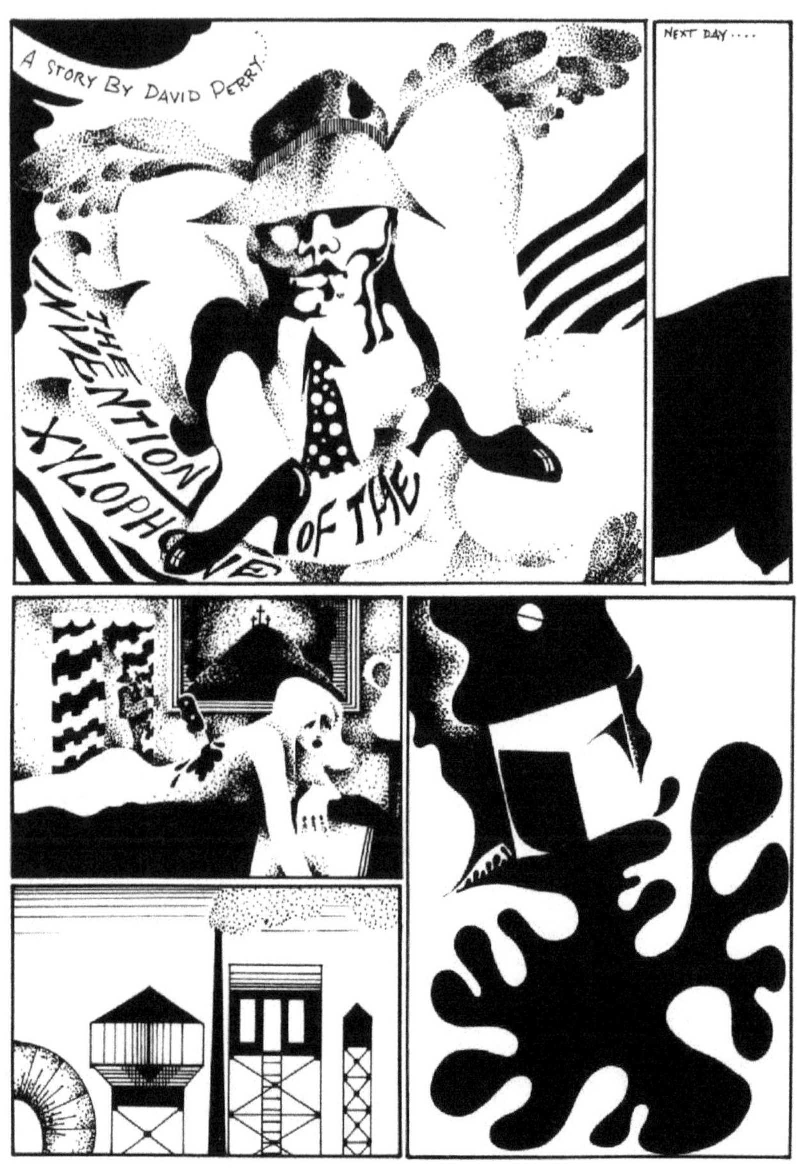
A STORY BY DAVID PERRY
THE INVENTION OF THE XYLOPH
NEXT DAY....

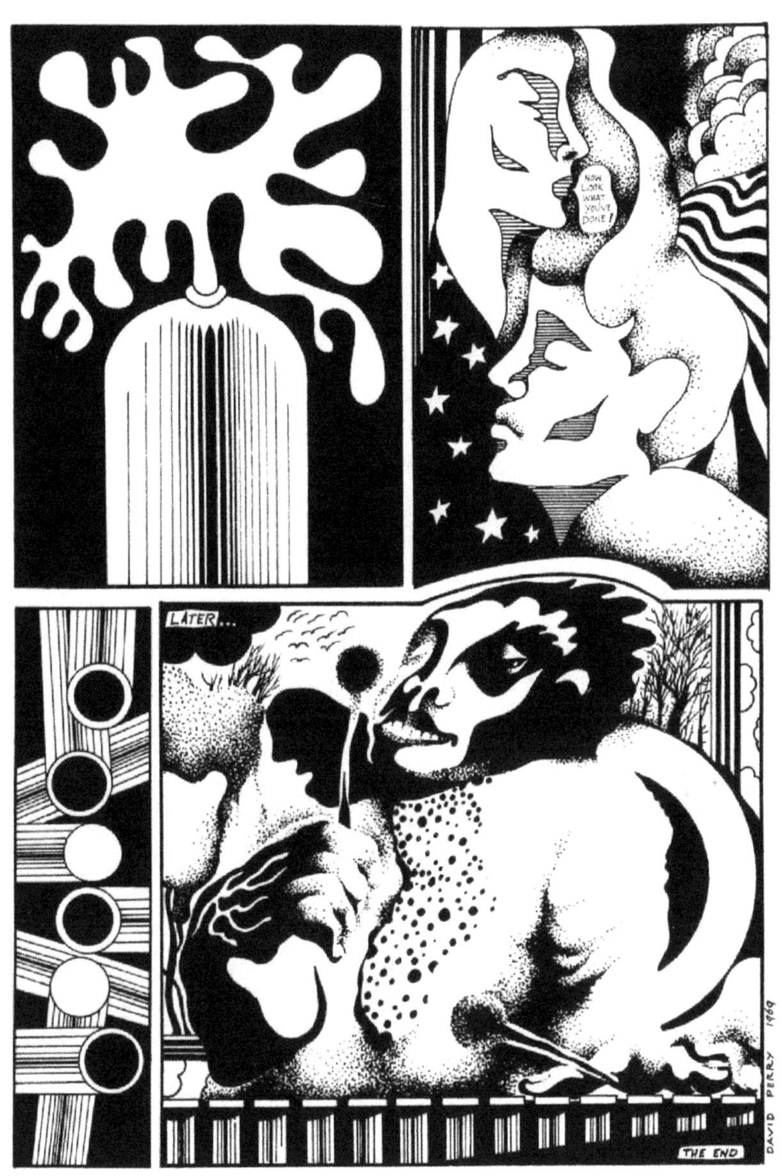
NOW LOOK WHAT YOU'VE DONE!
LATER...
DAVID PERRY 1969
THE END

Thinking of leaving the country ...

By the end of 1969 Albie had left Australia to show *Marinetti* in the US, England and Europe. Just before that *Ubu Films* had become Sydney Film Makers' Co-operative - a co-operative in legal fact rather than just *de facto,* now registered under regulations originally designed to cover co-operative farming organisations.

The drawing on the next page was incorporated in the cover of the Sydney Film Makers' Co-Operative's catalogue, which I designed with typography heavily influenced by the most modern styles of the day, themselves in turn influenced by Constuctivist posters and publications of the early Soviet Union. It's interesting now to see how the drawing expresses an idea of the film maker as conspirator, using the technology of film production as a weapon. Romantic dreaming, no doubt, but firmly held convictions at the time.

Australia in 1970 had had more than 20 uninterrupted years of conservative government by a coalition of slightly liberal capitalists and agrarian socialists, a highly paternalistic combination. It was hard to see any end to this state of affairs and a fair number of Australian artists and intellectuals had taken themselves off into exile in what seemed at the time less authoritarian, more arts-friendly places, London being the most popular destination. Abby and I started toying with thoughts like these ourselves.

We didn't have a lot of money, however, and one way of adding to our resources seemed to be to hold an exhibition. In my crazily idealistic way I had virtually stopped painting in the mid-1960s in favour of film making with a little bit of graphic design thrown in. Now I started painting in earnest again, working on large canvasses in acrylics, in a style heavily influenced by posters and graphic art. One of those paintings, on three canvasses 900x1200cm each, is reproduced on page 102. Although there is a superficial resemblance to American Pop Art, I don't think there was much celebration of American pop culture in that painting or any others I did at the time.

Even after the formation of the Co-Op., *Ubu Films* continued under new management now registered as "Ubu Pty. Ltd." In this new guise

Ubu had a very different agenda. It was to attempt to be a money-making venture, largely because the old Ubu owed a significant amount of money to various businesses in Sydney. John Clark and I undertook several "commercial" film making activities but they didn't come to much, I suspect because neither John nor I are commercial animals. John might seem to be more so than I but really he is just as much idealistic dreamer as I am. This, of course, is not a guarantee of financial failure. Nor is it much help towards success.

The photograph on the following page of my painting 'The Comet', was taken in a house where I lived many years after the painting was made.

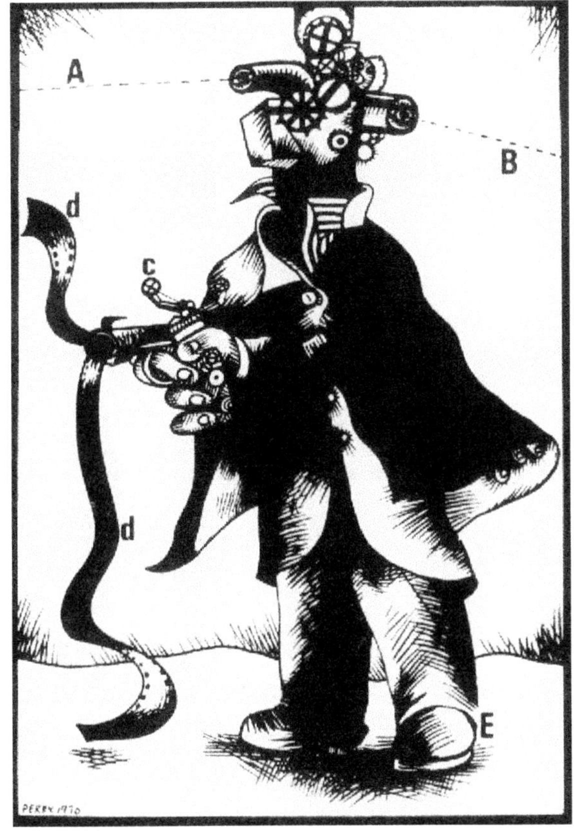

Drawing for the cover of Sydney Film Makers' Co-operative catalogue (Indian ink on paper), 1970

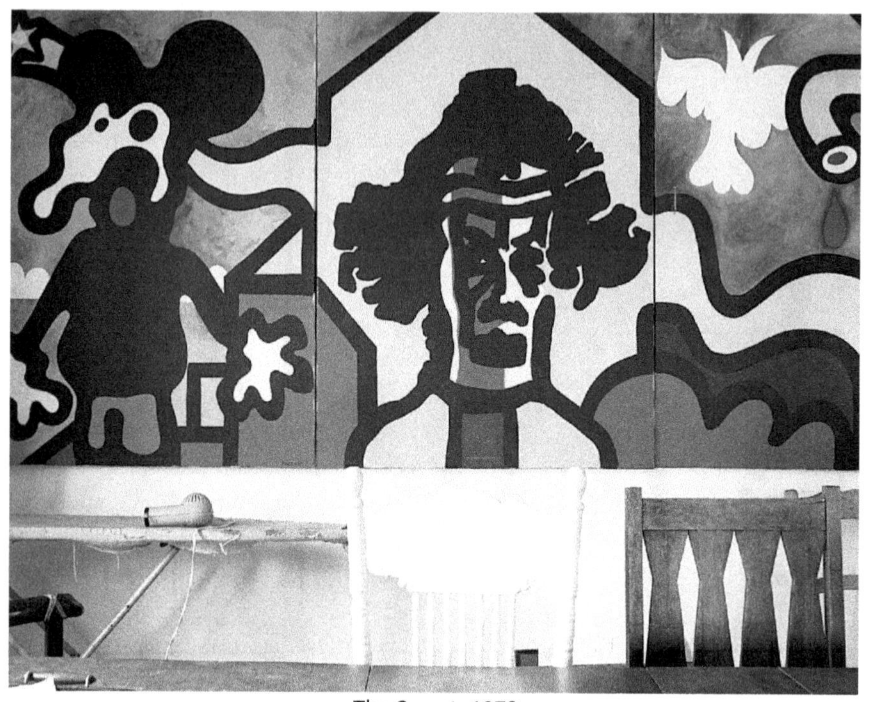

The Comet*, 1970*

Raising money to get out of Australia ...

Some time during 1970 Abby and I made a fateful decision: we would leave Australia, never to return, we thought at the time. As it turned out I did return and Abby did not.

One of the ways that we scraped together enough money to pay for our air tickets was through selling some drawings at an exhibition of my work at The Rocks Gallery near Circular Quay in Sydney. To introduce an unprecedented note of objectivity to this document I'll quote a review of the exhibition, written by Phil Noyce and published in *Honi Soit* of March, 1970:

*David Perry is perhaps better known as a film-maker. He has made nine films of his own and photographed all of Albie Thoms' ten filmed experimental movies, including the ninety minute colour feature, Marinetti. His first exhibition of paintings, at present on show at the Rocks Gallery, is characterised by all the sensual originality of his films.**

To David mystery plays an important part in art; mystery is communication because the viewer participates in supplying the answers. An image can be either very specific as in political or advertising art, or so mysterious as to imply something different to every viewer. David's paintings are in the latter category.

Two examples: Four sets of images, in four different squares; a Mickey Mouse and a star, two single stars plus a star and a bird. When viewed under an alternating green, blue and red coloured light, the tone-values of the images keep reversing. Part of one image may completely disappear into the background, or two images may blend to form a third. The Mickey Mouse and star square under a blue light shows up only as Mickey Mouse. Under a red light it appears as Mickey Mouse with a star-shaped head. And with green the image becomes Mickey Mouse silhouetted against the star.

A Rural Tragedy depicts (?) a macabre country scene of truck wreckage on a green-pastured hillside. The twisted wreckage inspires images of beaten entangled bodies. The sky's blue is interrupted by a blood-red cloud which drops bloody rain onto the wreckage. In film-making style, the artist cuts from a general wide-shot to a more specific close-up; the divided bottom quarter of the painting represents a close-up of the wreck. We see (at least, I saw) what looks like a foot, a nipple, blood-streaks and a human torso.

For all the mystery of these two and other paintings on show, what definitely emerges is that David Perry's work represents one of the art discoveries of the year. Well worth a visit by all art enthusiasts.

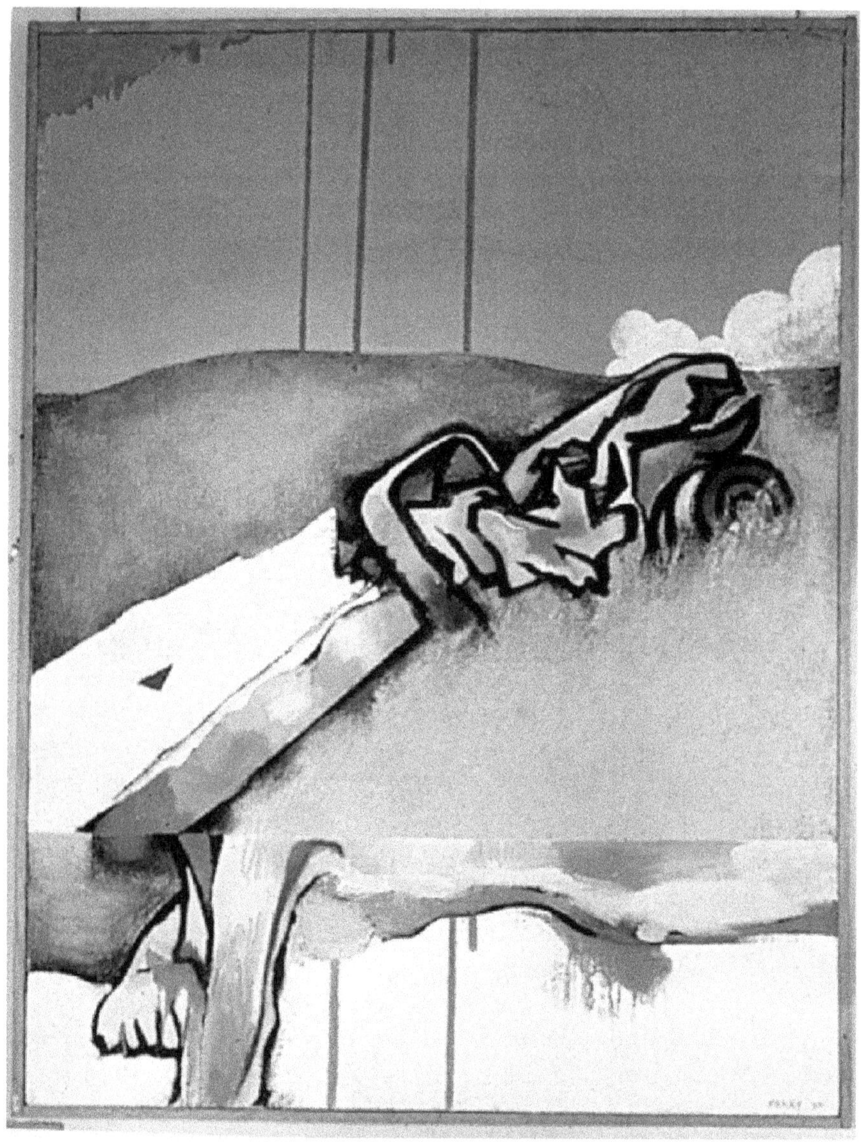

A Rural Tragedy *(acrylics on hessian, 1200 cm x 900 cm, 1970.*

After the exhibition Abby and I, with Rachael and Henrietta the cat, took a holiday at Hartley Vale, a tiny spot on the maps of the slopes just west of the Blue Mountains. While there I took some of the most self-consciously "artistic" photographs I had made up till that time. All of these were taken with the camera that had served me well for years now: a Mamiya twin-lens reflex that had an extension bellows that enabled extreme close-up photography.

Never one to pass up a kitschy opportunity, I certainly couldn't let this one get away. Henrietta was an inner city cat, having lived all her life in Balmain. There is a belief that if you transplant cats to a new environment you have to put butter or some such on their paws to stop them running away to where they came from. A number of times I've found this to be nonsense. In Henrietta's case we put her in our car in a cardboard box and let her out at Hartley Vale.

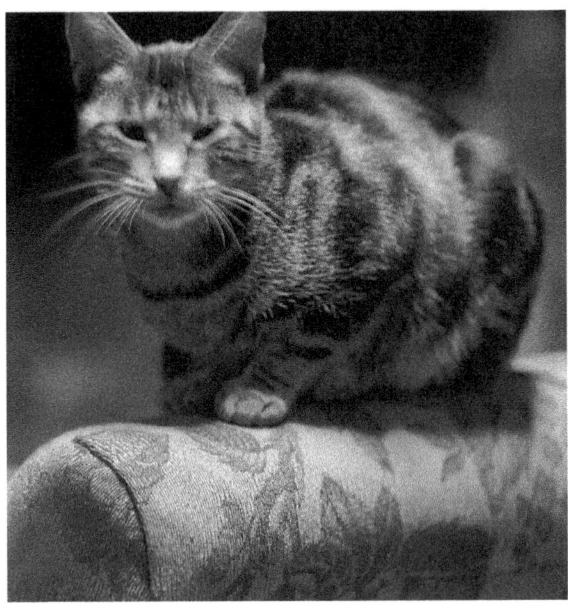

Cat (Henrietta) on a Sofa, Hartley Vale, 1970

After a good feed she had a sleep, then started to explore her new world without any sign of anxiety. No doubt "anecdotes" are not "scientific evidence", but the number of anecdotes that I have must be the beginnings of statistical data (QED?) (just joking).

Album ...

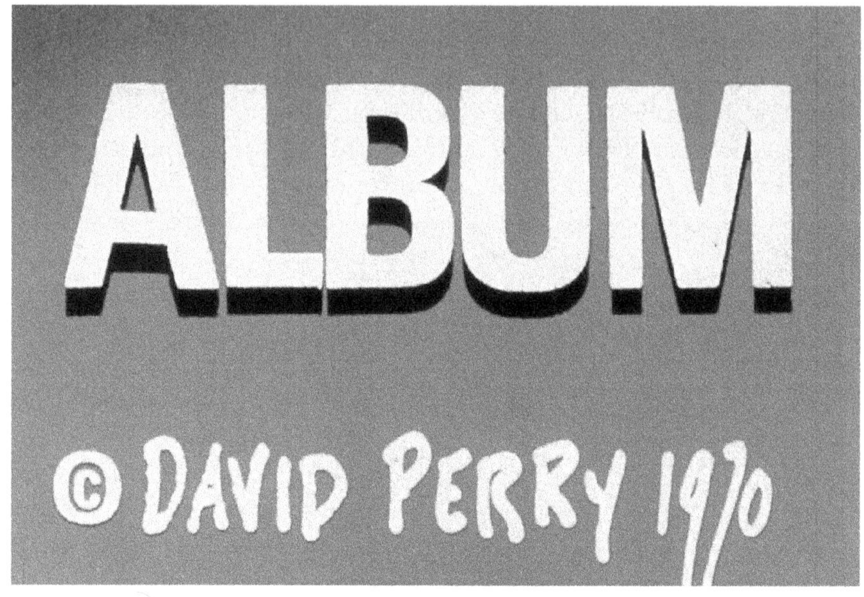

Frame blow-up from Album, *1970*

In 1970 I completed the film that, although short (six minutes approximately), was the most ambitious thing I'd done up till that time. *Album* was composed of short clips from most of the films I had then made, intercut with old and new photographs modified by optical effects done in the camera, the whole thing sparingly accompanied by a narrative commentary in my voice. In addition transitions and links between sequences were accompanied by a few abstract sound effects that I created. My ambition was to apply optical effects to some of the moving pictures but doing that was far beyond the reach of my technical or financial resources at the time.

No matter, the results were highly satisfying. *Album* is like a cubist collage, with all sorts of stylistically disparate bits stuck on. This memoir is being constructed by virtually identical means. The films made since *Album* that I like best were constructed in much the same way.

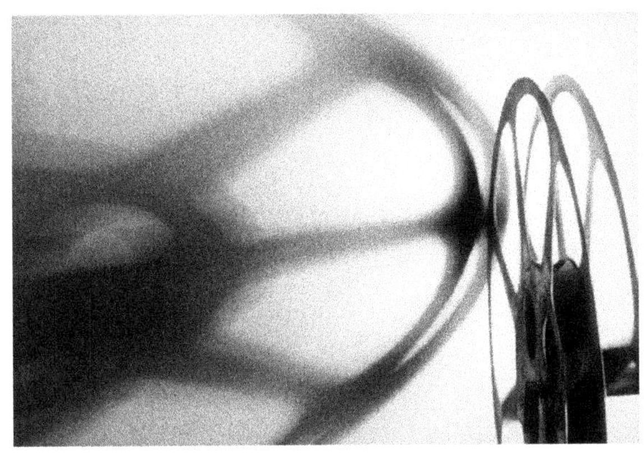

Frame blow-up from Album, *1970*

"Self-referentiality", for example, the images of projectors and cameras in *Album*, is a modernist mode that I took to with great pleasure. Pleasure, too, is something that I like to offer my audiences. It might surprise many of the critics of our "underground" films to find that I actually do/did consider the audience. The idea of making films (or any of the other things I am doing/have done) just to push some ideological or intellectual point is never at the front of my mind, although I'm not suggesting that my work has no "content".

Now the time has come to wrap up this part of the story. We had our passports and our tickets ready to fly out of Sydney. I had given paintings and drawings to friends for indeterminate safe-keeping, which at the time I really thought would last forever.

It was strange to see my canvasses in the back of a friend's utility truck, disappearing around the corner at the end of our narrow Balmain street. Well, not so much a street really, just a lane lined with small old houses on one side and the high brick wall of a bleak catholic school on the other side.

As I said a little while back, Balmain at that time was undergoing rapid "gentrification" and before we committed ourselves to this journey Abby and I had seriously thought about buying one of the marvellous old houses that were coming on the market. With my salary from the ABC and Abby's part-time income as a nurse we must have thought we could manage a mortgage. We looked at at one house at least in what is now a very desirable part of Balmain that we could have bought for, if I remember correctly, around $20,000. As I write this such a house would bring about $700,000!

Before we left I found myself photographing sights (sites?) I was fond of, no doubt storing up tokens to remind me of what we were about to leave behind.

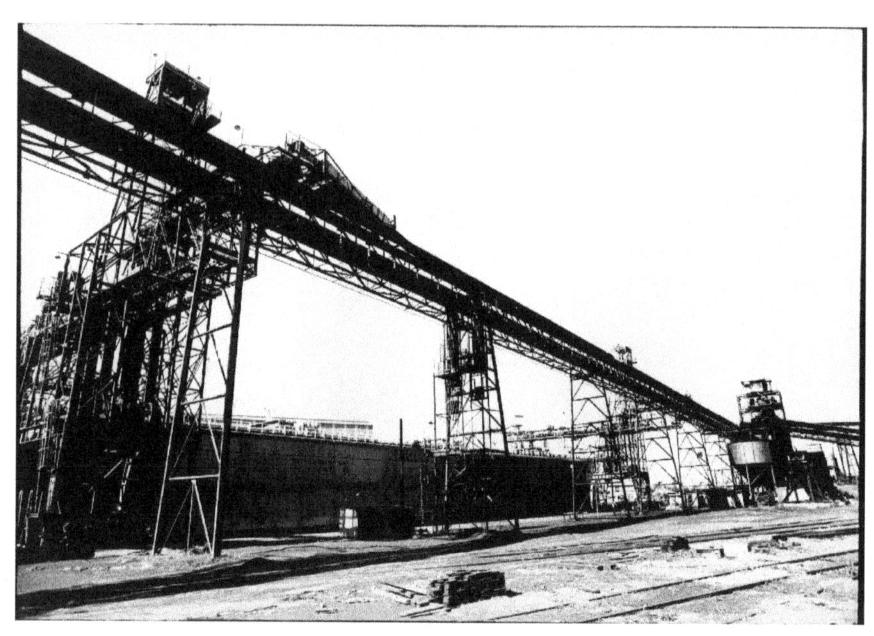

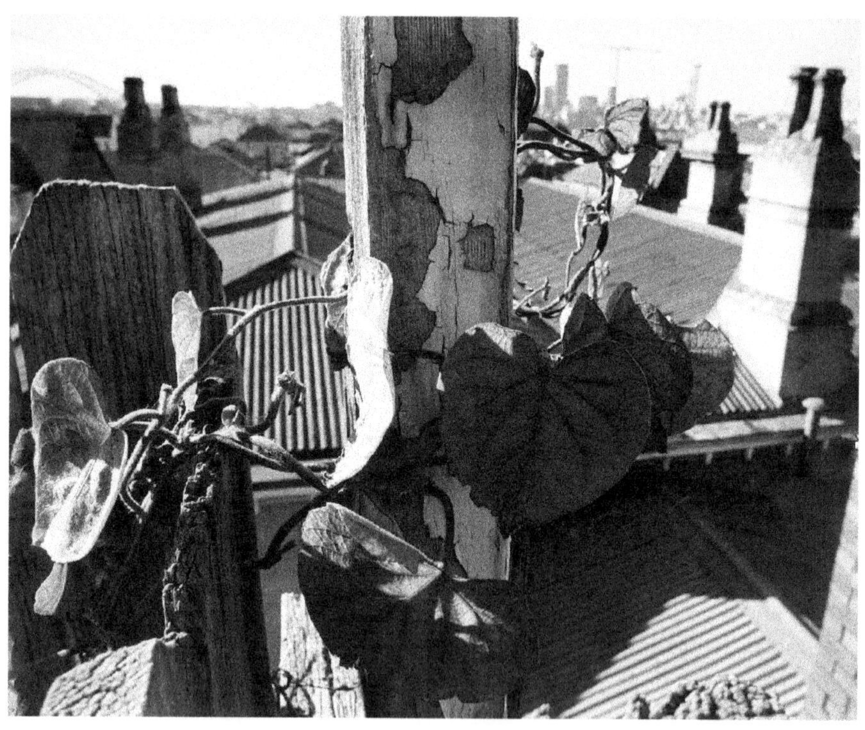

Exile Or Flight?

Who can say how our lives might have turned out if Abby and I had bought a house and stayed in Australia? But we were both very impulsive (not only then, I might add) and we had committed ourselves to escape what then appeared to be incorrigible philistinism.

But there was another motive for our move: since our divorce I had been paying maintenance to Judy to help with the upkeep of our children. After Rachael was born, Judy wouldn't agree to reduce the amount so I applied to the divorce court for a reduction. The application was successful but the legal bills for that, which I must have been paying by instalments, added to our costs to the extent that even though the maintenance was less, almost the same amount was going out each fortnight.

My lawyer, the same one who had acted for me in the divorce, reminded me that he had said the first time around that I was "too much of a gentleman". I'll try to explain what he meant: in those days divorces were usually granted on essentially punitive grounds, that is, a person seeking divorce had to prove that the other party destroyed the marriage. "Adultery" was the most likely ground for achieving this. Now there were innumerable instances of adultery on Judy's part and probably nearly as many on my part, but since Judy was perfectly willing to be divorced and I didn't want any more unpleasantness than could be avoided, we chose a single adulterous event which a friend agreed to say he had witnessed (to have seen two people in bed was enough).

My lawyer knew the truth was more than that and during the original divorce action he urged me to really lay it on, listing many adulteries. As I understood it, his aim was to ensure that Judy received no sympathy from the court and thus would be granted minimal maintenance. Being "too much of a gentleman" meant that I would have to pay more than I would if I were punitive.

Anyhow, after some time of paying the court-ordered reduced maintenance, Abby and I together conceived the idea that by just disappearing we could avoid paying anything. For us to be able to leave the country without alerting Judy to what we were up to required a conspiracy of silence amongst all our friends who knew our plan. I had little enough sympathy for Judy but what I truly felt awful about was knowing I'd lose all contact with the children. I don't expect anyone to have sympathy for me but the thing that has burdened me with guilt ever since is that I just skipped out on the children without even a farewell note. I had suppressed my anger at Judy for far too long and it just spilled over onto Caitlin, Jane and Simon without my even being aware of it. What an arsehole!

PART TWO

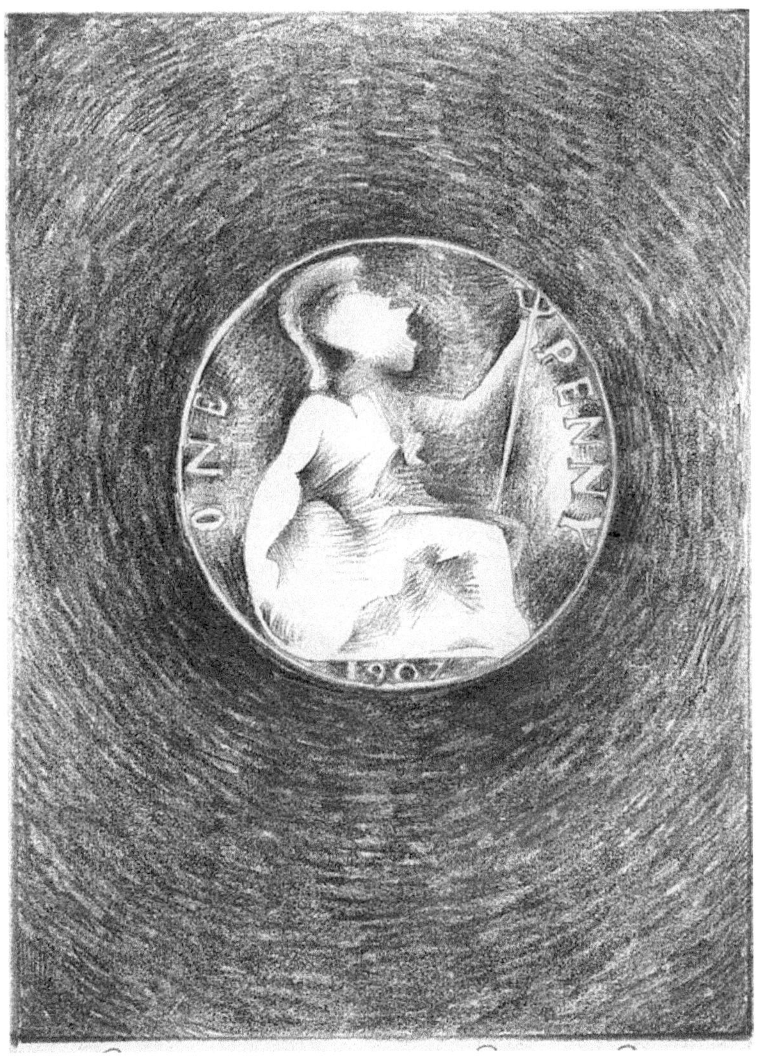

Old English penny, pencil on paper, 1970

Adventures on a Boeing 707 ...

The Boeing 707 was a sleek jet plane: four-engined, cigar-shaped, with a central aisle and three seats either side. I have always thought no passenger aircraft should ever be bigger. But nowadays even domestic flights use larger aircraft on which "tourist" class might be more honestly named "steerage"; international flights are even worse.

But I should stick to my story: on 1st October, 1970, after a delay of several hours we finally took off from Sydney airport, heading for London, with Rachael about to turn two in a kind of bassinet mounted on a bulkhead in front of our seats. Our plane landed to pick up extra passengers in Brisbane, where the transit lounge was a galvanised iron shed, hot and stuffy.

Next stop was Manila. In the early hours of the morning we flew in low over what appeared in the dark to be interminable jungle. Little settlements, tiny clusters of lights were scattered randomly over a very large area. But suddenly, seemingly out of nowhere, a six lane highway appeared. Soon after that we landed. My only other experience of a country outside Australia was New Zealand which involved only the mildest of culture shock. This time I was entering a truly different place. The Manila transit lounge made this very clear. At the risk of seeming terribly corny I have to say that I felt as if I'd landed in an American western movie, or perhaps, even, a "spaghetti western" where America was even more mythical than it is in American movies. I went into a bar where a couple of sullen characters sat. These memories may be richly coloured by romance so I can't vouch for their accuracy, but it seems that I ordered a whisky which the barman slid across the bar's zinc top. After that I wanted to go back to my seat on the plane but I was confronted by a very large man at the door with two pistols on his belt. He said: "Where you going?" I replied: "To my plane." His bulk and his pistols made his response unarguable: "No you're not!" I'm not sure if Abby had stayed on the plane to sleep, but I was obliged to stay in the transit lounge until called to re-board just before take-off.

Our next scheduled stop was to be in Hong Kong, where we had arranged for a two-day stop-over. Our travel agent had booked us into a very exclusive small hotel. Some of the guests at this hotel were Americans who had enormous amounts of luggage in trunks that could surely have only been carried by ship; the size and weight of any single trunk would have far exceeded the limits for air travel, even in First Class. These Americans seemed to us to be wealthy beyond our wildest dreams. In Australia in those days such ostentation was inconceivable.

From our hotel window we looked out at a huge, storeys-high banner depicting heavily armed Red Army soldiers, painted in the prescribed compositional style of diagonal forms signifying revolutionary political dynamism. [5] A slogan, in English, across the banner proclaimed: "POLITICAL POWER GROWS OUT OF THE BARREL OF A GUN!" Later, on a building as long as a city block and facing the waterfront, we saw an enormous expanse of scarlet-enamelled panels. There was not a word to be seen. They weren't needed, the meaning of this display was unmistakable. At the centre of what seemed to be acres of red there was a huge portrait of Chairman Mao, topped and surrounded by softly fluttering flags, also in pure unadorned scarlet. It may have been almost 40 years in the future before Hong Kong would be formally absorbed into mainland China, but the signs were there that such absorption was already well advanced.

Our next stop-over was to be in Rome. In those days jet planes couldn't travel as far as they can now before having to refuel and because we had apparently been making heavy going against headwinds, and would have run out of fuel before we got to Rome, we had to make an unscheduled landing at Beirut.

The airstrip ran alongside the Mediterranean Sea. On one side the landscape was beautiful: low hills and small, sandy-coloured buildings. On the other side, between the also beautiful sea and the airstrip, there were many burned-out tanks. As soon as the plane came to a stop a small group of extremely handsome young soldiers moved through the aisle checking out everyone on board. To add to the romance of the situation (at least for me), each of the soldiers wore ammunition belts criss-crossed over his chest. All we passengers must have passed whatever test was

---

[5] These may have been the result of the "Six-Day War" of 1967 or the so-called "War of Attrition" of 1967-70 or the "Israel-Palestinian Conflict" of 1960 to the present. No doubt all these are parts of one continuing conflict including the "Gulf Wars" of 1991 and 2003.

being applied to us, as our fuel tanks were replenished and we continued on to Rome.

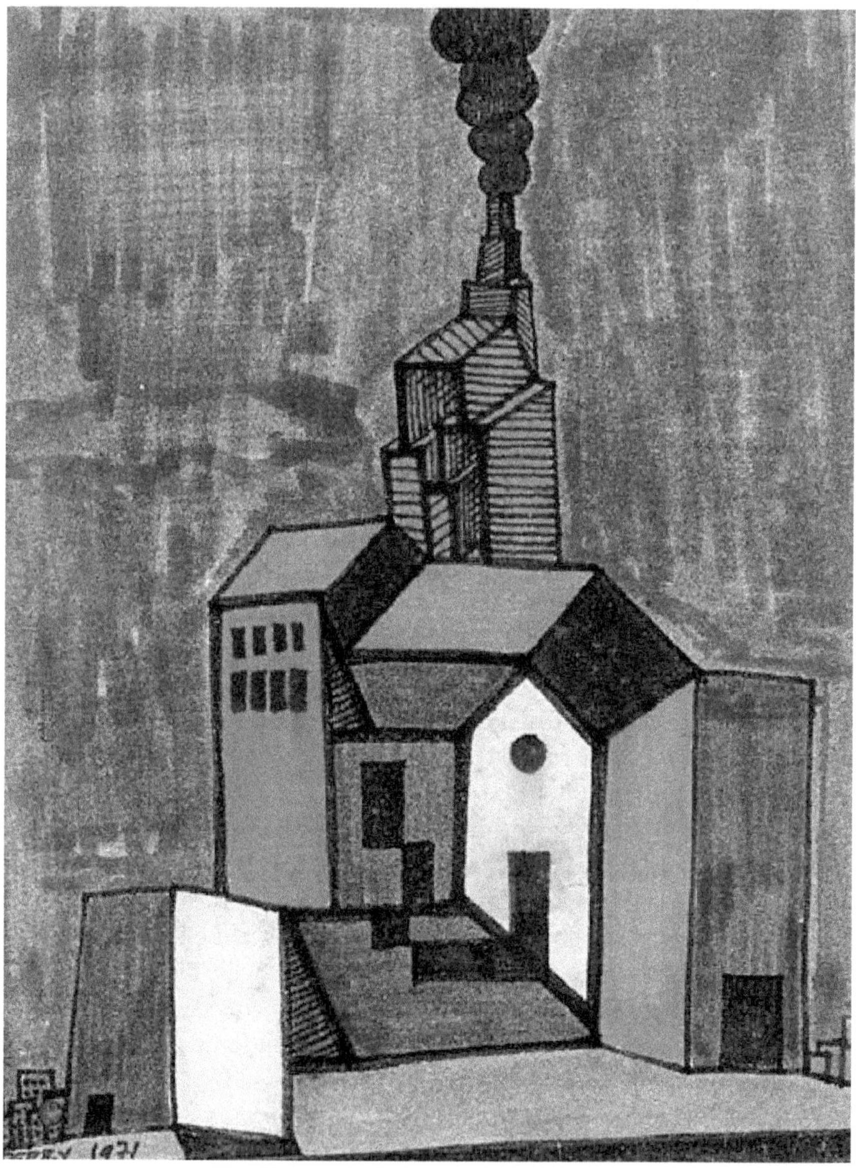

Rome *(felt pens on paper), 1971*

Of all the revelations we were offered on this journey Rome was the most splendid. We had our first glimpses of what we had been primed all our colonial lives to see: the glories of ancient Rome and the stylishness of modern Rome (not, I think, that these things were illusory) and a palpable self-confidence on the part of most people we saw.

A memory that comes back to me now is of sitting in bright sunshine in the gardens of the Villa Borghese eating bread and olives. You might think that corny, or superficial, but the experience was so intense as to be unforgettable. No doubt everything we saw had connotations formed by past readings and mythologies. Abby found walking past the Colosseum almost unbearable: she could hear the prisoners screaming as the lions tore them apart. Once again you might think that was corny, but that was the sort of of person Abby was, highly sensitive to all kinds of sensations and their associations. Perhaps I was too, in my own way. The two drawings on these pages, done later from memory, do suggest that to me.

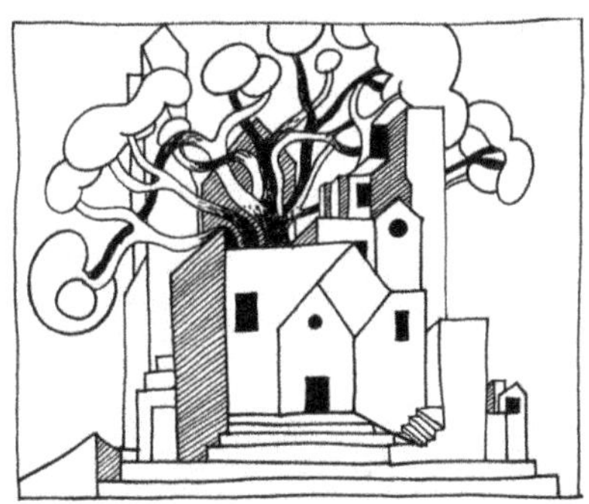
Rome 2 *(felt pens on paper), 1971*

I think we stayed in Rome for four days, after which we had to face up to our destination and get on the plane for London. Having left Rome in perfect weather we arrived over London in typical London weather. Below us we could see the tops of clouds extending to the horizon in all directions and shining white in the sunshine. I thought that once we pierced that cloud layer we would see London below. No such luck; before that could happen we had to pass through at least two more thick layers of cloud. It was hardly surprising that by the time we landed the atmosphere was grey. It would stay like that for me for the next three-and-a-half years with really very few breaks in the emotional clouds. It's not that London doesn't have a lot going for it, it was just that I had gone for the wrong reasons. And most surprising of all to me was the culture shock. Of course, I spoke English (of a sort) and had an Anglo-centric upbringing and yet I found London a stranger environment than Rome in some respects.

Early days in London ...

We found a comfortable flat in the North London suburb of Crouch End. This was an extremely middle-class area. (Can "extremely" and "middle-class" co-exist in the one phrase?) I must say that the name Crouch End always tickled me because I felt that many English place names denoted an original character or function of a place, most likely lost in a dim (and more earthy?) past, and having thought that, I wondered just what could be the connotations of "Crouch End".

Whatever geographers or social historians might have to say about my possibly bizarre question can be left to another time. Just then, at the end of 1970, London had something like "post-card" weather. It snowed a lot. The photograph below shows a view from Crouch End. All the other winters I experienced in London were pretty cold but they never had such picturesque snow falls.

I had never experienced snow so I put on my fur coat and gloves and went out on the street. I hadn't gone far when snow began falling again.

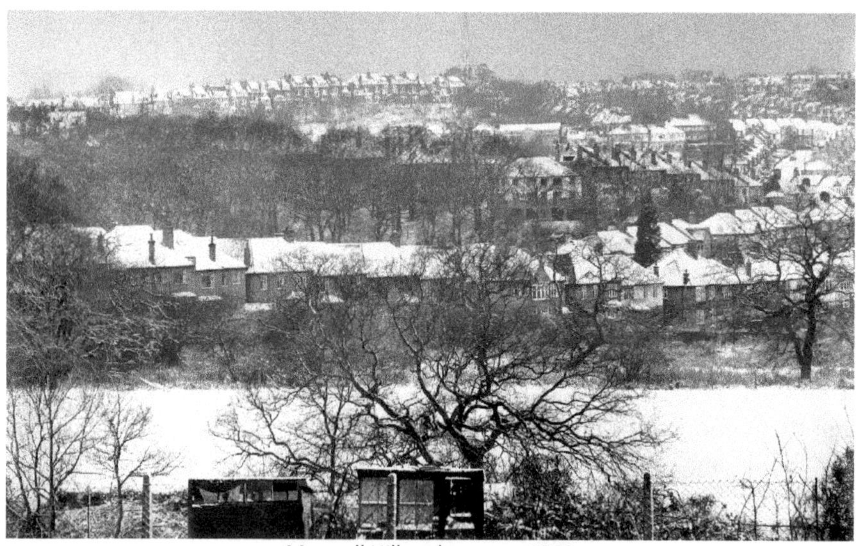

Muswell Hill under snow, 1970

The snowfall was only brief, I think, but it was so heavy that it obliterated everything around me. I found myself in a complete "whiteout". It was as scary as I imagine it is being in the total darkness of a deep mineshaft.

Our money was, of course, quickly running out. Looking through the local newspaper I saw a job as a delivery driver for a Crouch End furniture shop. I met the manager and told him a lie, that I had driven a furniture van before. It was a bit nerve-wracking, reversing such a large vehicle out of the garage using only the rear vision mirrors, and having done that, to be driving the narrow winding streets of London, sometimes slippery with snow. Since I quickly became adept at all that, my lie in that regard became irrelevant.

Another lie I told was a bit more devious and probably reinforced English employers' suspicions about Australians. When asked if I intended to stay employed by the firm I said yes, since the clear implication of the question was that if I said no I wouldn't get the job. Of course the truth was that I'd only stay there until something better came up. Which it did.

A job was advertised in a technical position at the Hornsey College of Arts film and television studio (in those days nobody made a distinction between "television" and "video"). My experience with the ABC carried some weight, as did my film making, and I got the job.

Hornsey College of Arts was a fairly typical school of fine arts. It taught painting, drawing, print-making and photography. It had a large number of students, some of whom could elect to do units in film or "television". There were also students majoring in film and television. Because film is a very expensive subject to teach, the only students who could study it had to have a grant from their borough council, or to come

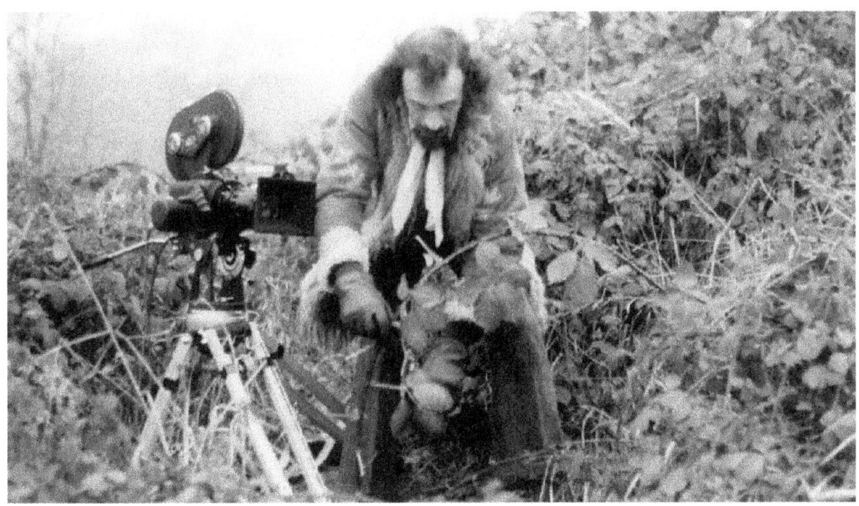

DP arranging "dingle" for a student film in London, c.1971 (photographer unknown)

from countries outside Britain that would pay their fees. If I remember correctly, having rich parents was not a qualifying factor - the funding had to be government to government. The end result was that I had students from all over Europe, from Iran, India, Canada, the US, even from Australia. A truly amazing experience.

How I became a "lecturer" at Hornsey rather than a mere "technician" is this: the man who ran the film school part of the college was an English doco maker named Douglas Lowndes who had no experience of working with video equipment. Since I'd worked in Australian television, albeit, once again as a technician, Douglas co-opted me into teaching in the "television" studio, a fairly low-tech replica of BBC studios. I must have done this adequately because I was quite soon invited to jump the class barrier between technician and lecturer, which I did with a corresponding jump in salary.

What I didn't know at the time was that in 1968, while there were student riots in Paris which filled the French establishment with fears of revolution, there had also been a student take-over at Hornsey. This lasted quite a long time but had eventually - somehow - been defused (I really don't know how), but the aftermath was that English academics and film makers had some kind of black ban on Hornsey and would not work there. No one I met spoke about this so that, although I thought of myself as politically aware and should have known, I didn't. In a country where so much is contingent on nods and winks I was, I suppose, a "scab". Perhaps with pragmatic realism nurtured by the Sydney Push I thought more about the financial desperation Abby and I would have otherwise endured than I did about political purity. This retrospective awareness has always left a shadow over my otherwise justifiable pride in my effectiveness as a teacher of "film and video".

One of the first projects that I involved my students in was a kind of installation set up in the corridor between the film and art departments. I took a lot of photographs as the installation proceeded, which I subsequently put up in the corridor along with a page of text that explained what I had been up to:

"On Friday, 17th November, 1972 I set up a small experiment in the corridor between the Fine Art and Film & TV departments of Hornsey College of Art. My idea was to use a television system as an object rather than as a medium, and to see what kind of interaction (if any) would occur between the object and its observers. A camera was placed to give a static view along the corridor and of any

events which might happen there. The picture was recorded on videotape for about one hour.

When the recording was complete I placed [...] two monitors on a table just in front of the camera and connected the output of the camera to one monitor and the output of the recorder to the other and replayed the tape. This meant that I was showing pictures of present events on one monitor and past events on the other, although both sets of events occurred in identical picture spaces. [...]

The effect of this was that as people walked toward the installation they could see their own picture on one monitor while on the other it might be somebody else's picture or just the empty corridor.

At first it seemed that nobody was going to take any notice at all of the installation but then several people became intrigued by it and eventually a large group gathered and obviously found it very engaging. I was watching and recording the entire event with two additional cameras and a second videotape recorder. [...]

In case it may be inferred that I have an ideological preference for television used in this way (as an object), I want to say that this is not the case. I have no puritanical notions about what is, or is not "good television". I have, and will, use it any way that seems appropriate to me. [Signed] David Perry."

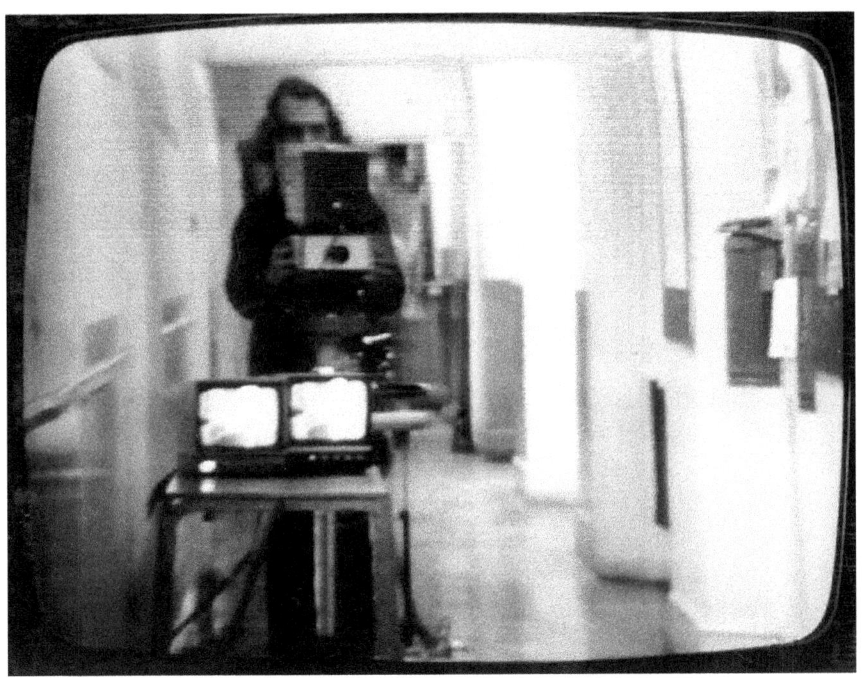

DP setting up for the installation, 1972

The previous picture and those below are a selection from the ones that I originally put up in the corridor. The "clunky" nature of the equipment we had then is obvious from these pictures.

To tell the next part of my story I need to jump around a bit in time and space. Not long before I left Australia I met a man who worked at Sydney University's computer centre who so loved his work that I think he rarely went home. I had the impression that he rarely slept. It seemed very odd in those days that an engineer fanatical about the future of computers would have anything to say to an artist but this man invited me into his territory, at that time a whole floor of a university building filled with large cabinets containing spools of magnetic tape shuttling back and forth. My host took me to a small colour monitor (a great rarity at that time) and showed me animated graphics that he'd been working on in his spare time. They had great beauty, to me at any rate. He told me proudly how he'd introduced "noise"- randomness - into the data that drove these graphics that made them sparkle with a kind of afterglow. I think this man's manic enthusiasm for computers, long before we'd heard of PCs or Apple Macs, must have added fuel to my own later enthusiasm for electronic technology as production tool. That wasn't my only influence, of course, but the fact that I remember this so vividly must indicate something.

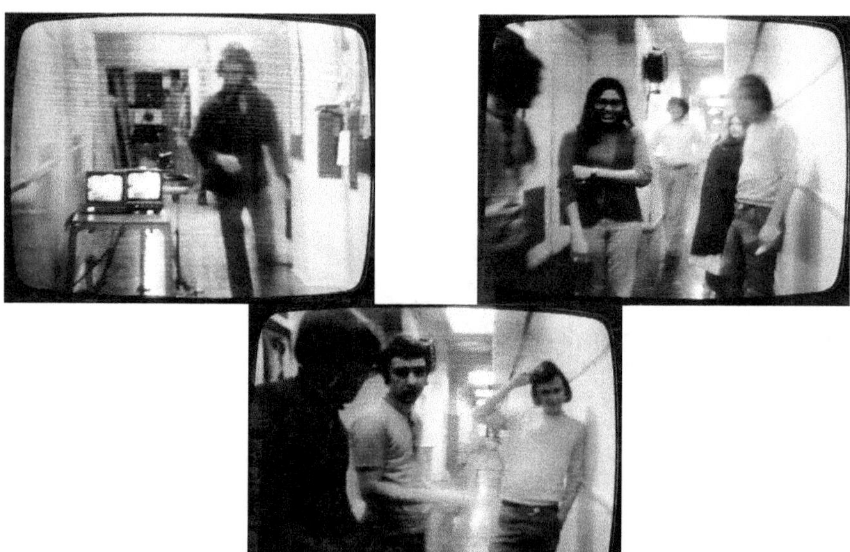

Thus when I went to a conference on electronics at Brunel University, on the fringes of London, I was somehow attuned to find this image, just outside the university. For those who don't know, the punched paper tape was used to enter data into computers of the time.

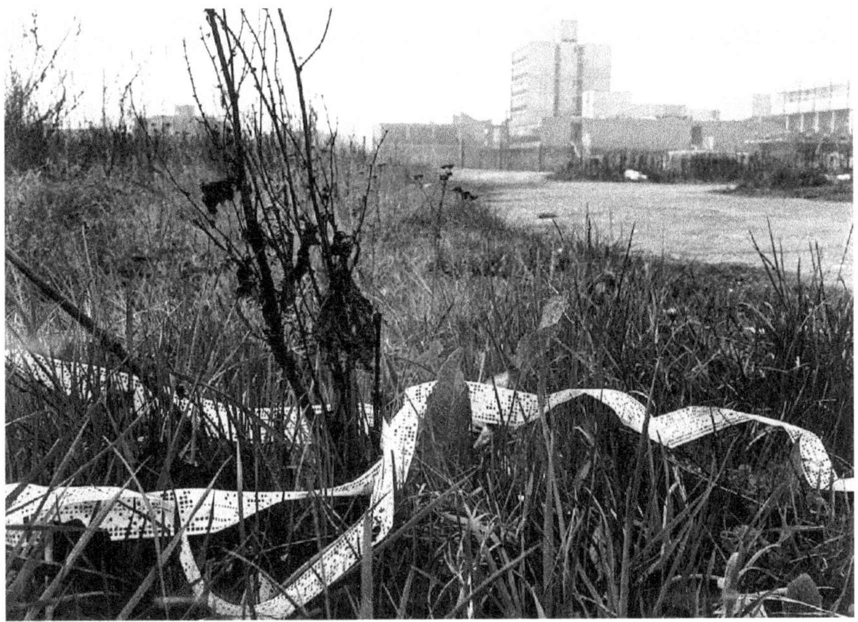

Near Brunel University, c.1971

Something else that was appearing on film makers' horizons was the portable video camera with a smallish video recorder attached by cable. These things were made by Sony, at least they were the only ones I was aware of at the time, and I'm firmly, if retrospectively, convinced that Sony "portapaks"as they became known were the prototypes of the "Betacam" system that eventually replaced 16mm film systems as the means of choice for all television news gatherers.

I encouraged Douglas Lowndes to order a portapak for the college, and quickly began experimenting with it, even though editing the material shot with it was a nightmare. But to be able to collect material shot anywhere on the streets or in dimly lit buildings and incorporate it with material from the studio was potentially a huge advance. Of course that could always be done with film, but film was very expensive to use and could generally only record 10 minute's worth of action in one magazine load, and it took time to process. Furthermore, the clear advantage that film did have, it's far superior image quality, was largely lost once film was converted to video through "telecine chains".

Portapaks, of course, could record pictures and sound for 30 unbroken minutes, although the problems of accurately editing portapak material would only be solved after a few more years, by which time the black-and-white, half-inch tape system of the portapaks was being superseded by better systems that recorded in colour. But, as I said, I believe it was the clumsy, clunky portapak, especially the user-unfriendly way the camera had to be operated, that eventually led to the Betacams and digital systems that are used now. In around 1972 I started shooting with the portapak, gathering material that I would later incorporate in several rough documentaries.

A trip through France ...

But I was getting ahead of myself there. Crouch End wasn't really our cup of tea and so, when some time in 1971 some Australian friends told us about a flat that had become available in West London, fairly close to Ladbroke Grove station, we jumped at the opportunity. It meant that I had to go to work by tube and bus, but I enjoyed that because it meant that every day I travelled with the enormous range of people who lived in London.

We had made contact by then with quite a number of Australians who were living and working in London. A small group of these were planning a motoring holiday through the French countryside and invited us to join them. They were Tony and Daphne Skillen and their daughter Tanya (the same age as Rachael) and Billy Tuck and Barbara Segal. We'd all travel in two cars. Abby decided not to come. She was expecting our second child and didn't feel up to it.

We all set off in midsummer on a British Rail car ferry. I don't remember which ports we left from or arrived at but looking at the map of France has stimulated a lot of memories. Although our journey left almost exclusively happy memories I do remember one startling, even scary sight. It was probably on our first day in France. Somewhere near Caen we saw a policeman standing on a rise beside the road closely watching the traffic (including us) approaching him. He was dressed, top to toe, in black, including his shiny leather leggings, belt and that military-style strap that goes diagonally over the chest and shoulder. His cap seemed identical with those worn by high-ranking SS and Gestapo officers. I was tempted to call him an "apparition" but that would imply that he wasn't really there, just something supernatural left over from the War. Since I don't believe in the supernatural the man was undoubtedly there. Why he was dressed that way I can't begin to imagine.

Throughout the entire three-week journey we didn't once have to spend money on accommodation. We had tents, sleeping bags, all the accoutrements of camping in Australia, including billy cans. During each day when we were on the road we would start looking late in the afternoon for a good place to camp. Often we found these in woods or fields. We ate wonderfully well: local cheeses, breads, ham, fresh fruits.

Sometimes we'd go out to dinner at a local restaurant. I know this must sound like romantic nonsense, but I also know it's the truth.

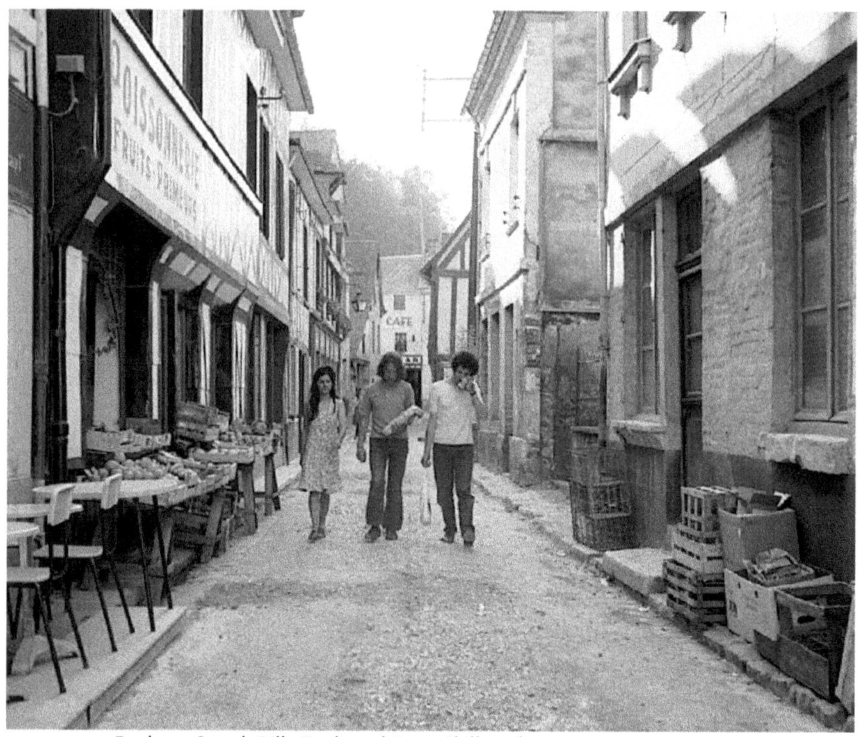

Barbara Segal, Billy Tuck and Tony Skillen shopping in France, 1971

One thing this trip did for me was to make me realise how ideology can render people blind to what should be self-evident; how that can afflict even the nicest, most intelligent people. I'm talking here of Tony Skillen, who was a highly intelligent person who'd had the added benefit of acquiring the sceptical realism of the Sydney Push before coming to England. One day, when I was taking one of the many pictures that the one above was selected from, Tony said to me: "Dave, anyone could take these photographs, couldn't they?" Since the pictures in question were still only latent negative images there was no way anybody could judge their quality and I don't think that was in question. I thought what Tony asked implied that no particular skill was needed to take photographs, or alternatively that the skills could be learned (which of course they must be) and that talent didn't come into it. I said "yes" to the question because I too was influenced by the prevailing ideology which

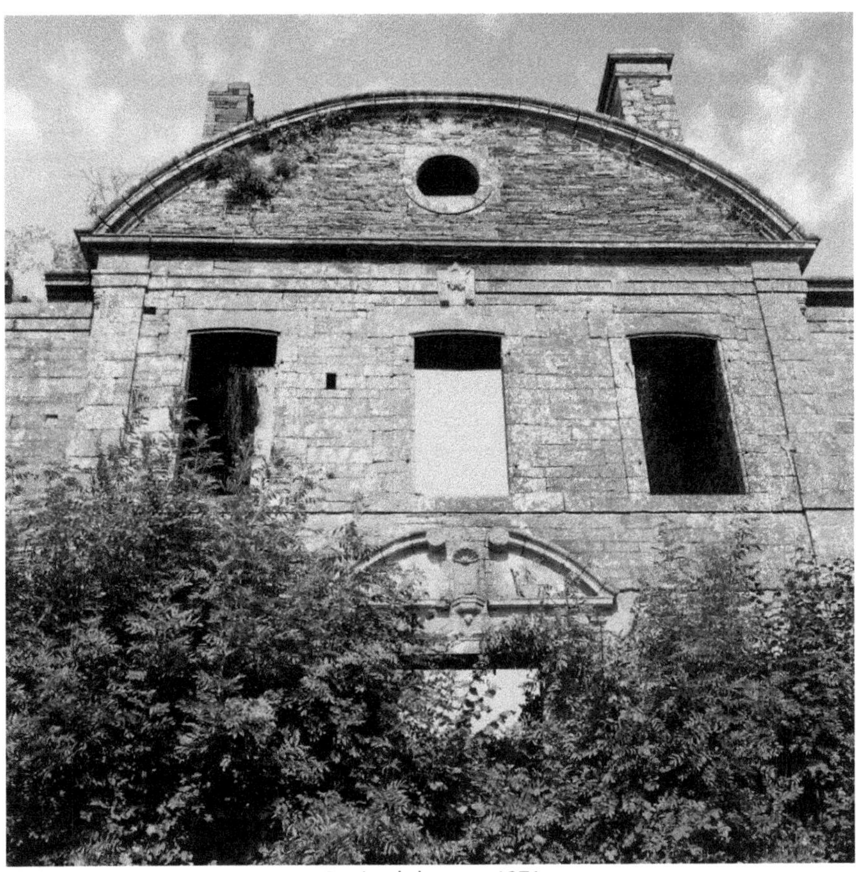

A ruined chateau, 1971

saw class - and nothing else - determining everything. Talent meant nothing. It was a relic of the class system.

I have always been ashamed that I didn't stand up for myself but I was intimidated by Tony's political self-confidence.

Many years later I heard a story that illuminated that episode only too well. A Russian woman told me about her father who had been a diplomat in the Soviet Union of the late 1930s. The man was dismissed from his post in a purge intended to "clean the apparat", and when he protested to a high official, saying: "But I'm a diplomat. I'm an expert in eastern countries," his protest was dismissed by the official's reply: "We're all diplomats now. We're all eastern country specialists."

I'm not trying to suggest that Tony was a Stalinist. Nevertheless, the egalitarian idealism that was so strong in those days was strongly influenced by the ideals of the Russian Revolution. The liberation

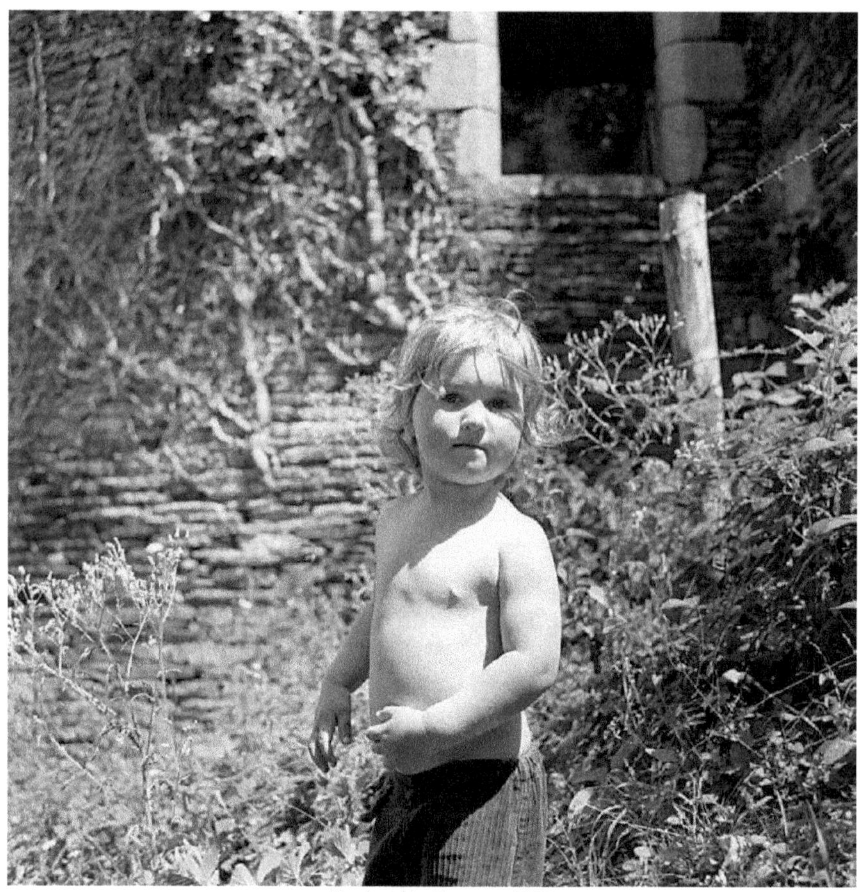

Rachael in France, 1971

movements of the time, which most of us supported in one way or another even if we didn't join them, took much of their organisational structure from Leninism.

Speaking for myself alone now, I think that being in France and seeing signs - subtle and not so subtle - of revolution and war may have stimulated me to identify with revolutionaries and resistance fighters to the extent that I was.

But to show that this trip wasn't really as earnest as it might be starting to seem, some pictures in an altogether different vein ...

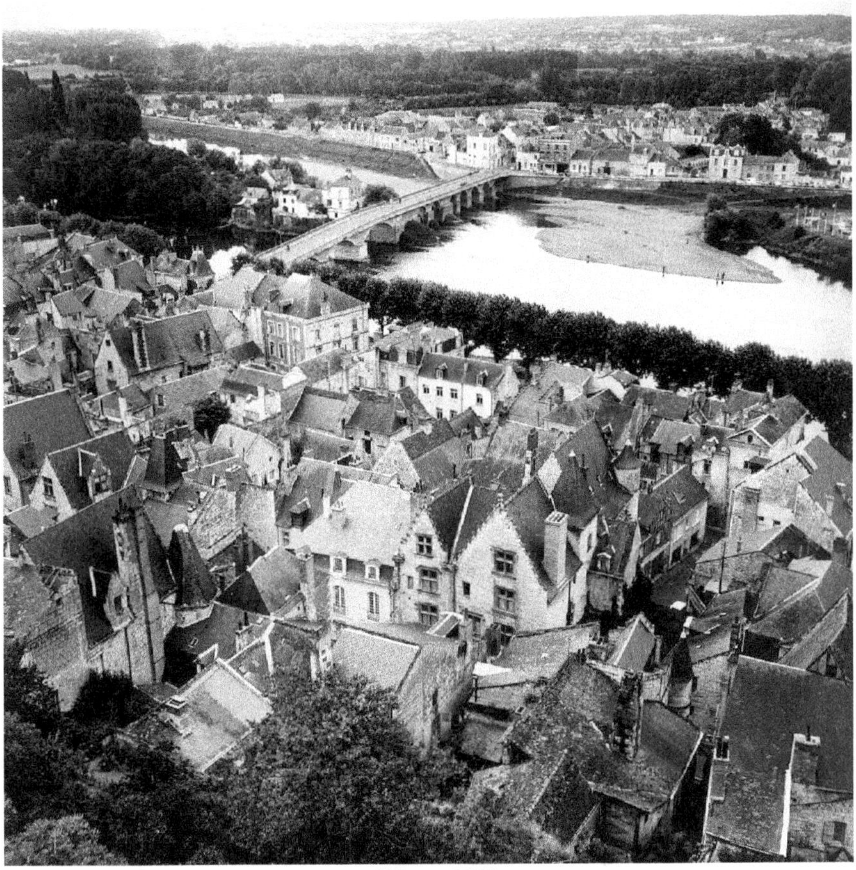

Chinon, 1971

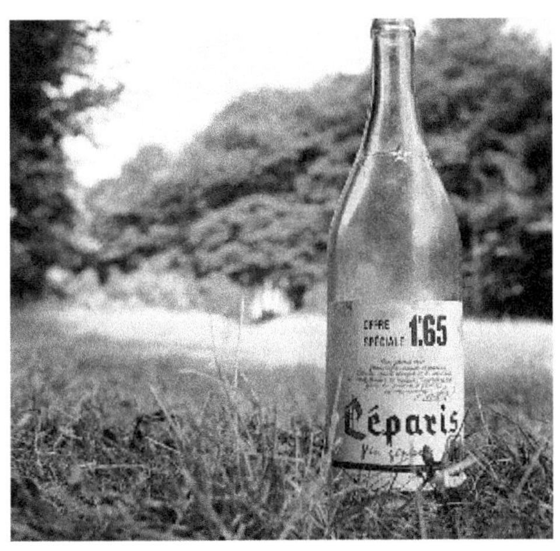

The cheapest wine in France (and the roughest?), 1971

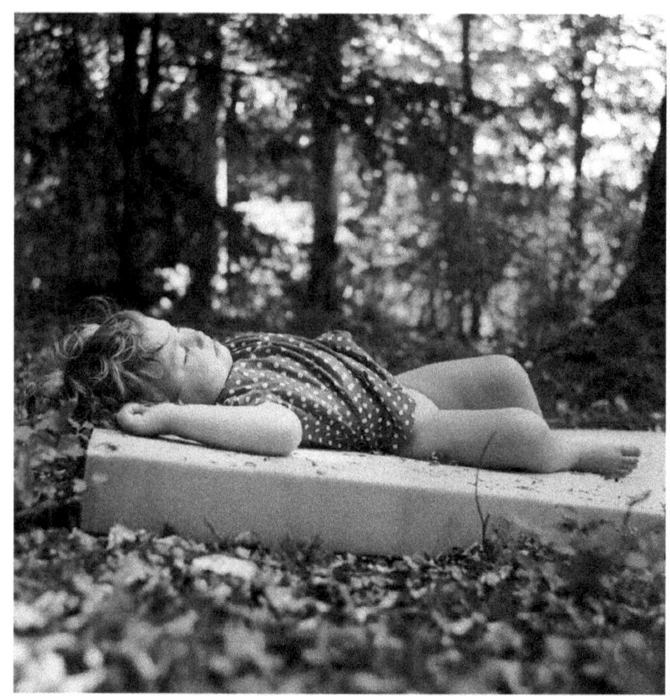

Rachael asleep in a French forest, 1971

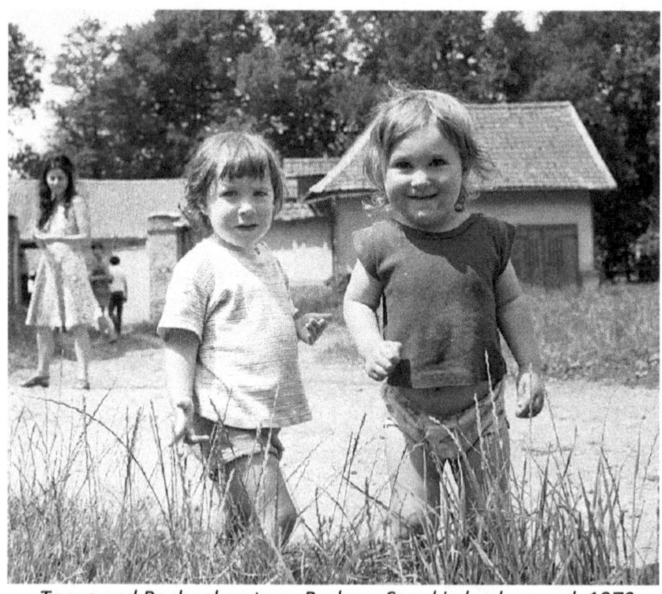

Tanya and Rachael on tour, Barbara Segal in background, 1972

While we were in Brittany I did some drawings of the landscape. A couple of years later an English artist who had befriended me gave me some of his unused (and unusually elongated) canvasses. I used the largest one of those, about two-and-a-half metres long, for this painting from one of the drawings. I have always intended to change the sky in the far top left to get rid of the dark red and blue areas, although thinking about it again one of the things that impressed me in Brittany was the drama of the skies. Perhaps I'll just leave it alone.

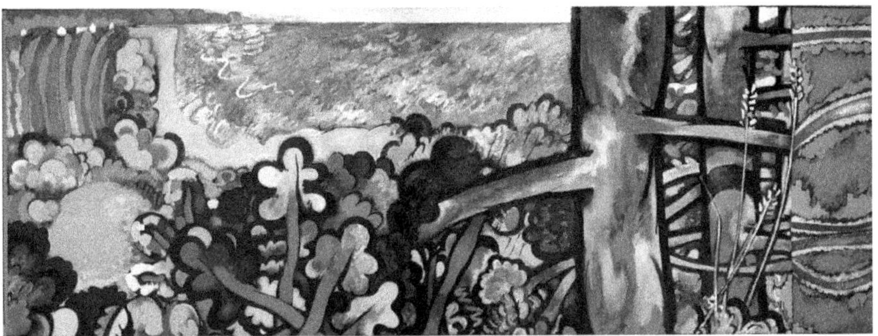

The coast of Brittany *(acrylics on canvas), c.1973 (Also the image on the cover of Memoirs of a Dedicated Amateur!)*

Of course our time in France had to come to an end. We could have made Paris our last place to visit but I think we all agreed that that would have put too many demands on our two three-year old girls, as well as on our finances. The road ahead gave us the option of passing through Rouen rather than Paris. Rouen was, for me, a wonderful choice since I got to see the cathedral with its astoundingly beautiful windows. You don't have to be a religious believer to be utterly enthralled by those. I can't remember if photography was forbidden in the cathedral, but since I was only carrying black-and-white film it would have been pointless anyhow.

The journey back across the English Channel by British Rail car ferry was an anti-climax, utterly. Having grown used to the delights of everyday French food we were confronted on the ferry by English cod and chips. Flavourless, greasy pap!

The birth of Homer ...

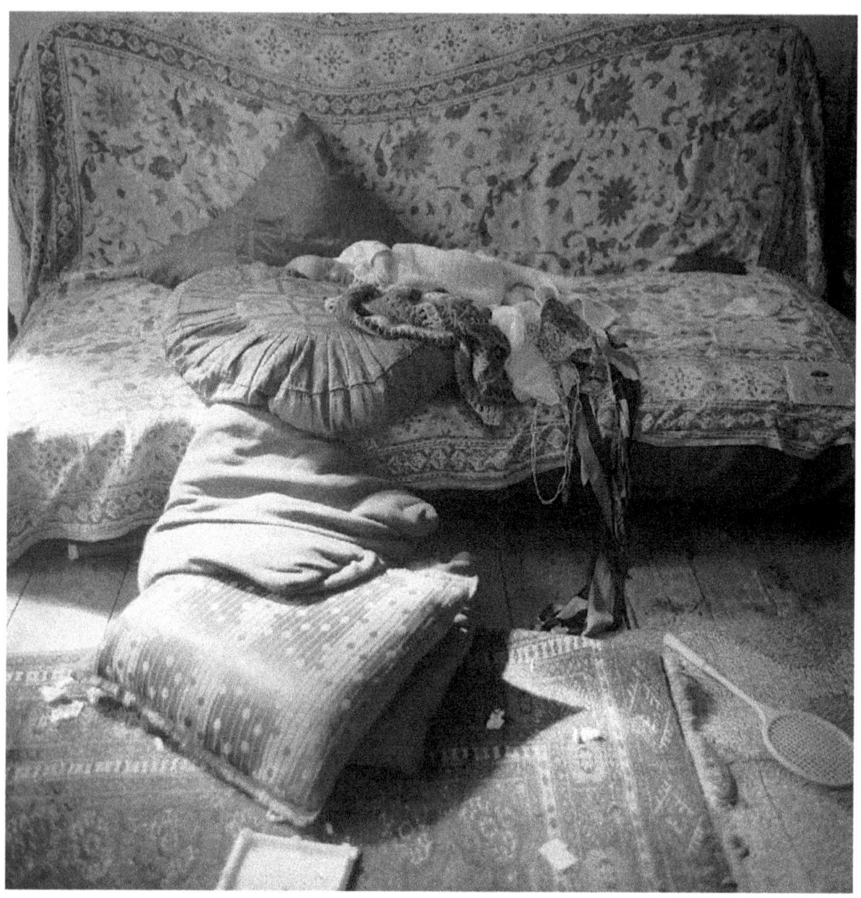

Homer asleep, 1971

The birth of Homer was for me an amazing experience. Unlike the births of all my other children I was permitted - encouraged, even - to be present. Thus I could see for the first time the animal passion and huge physical effort that takes over womens' bodies at that time. Of course I couldn't experience it in the same way that Abby did but at least I could take part in a way that had always been denied me before. I don't think this happened because England was more enlightened than Australia. I think that it was probably because, as in many other places in the world, old, conservative values were crumbling, particularly old conservative

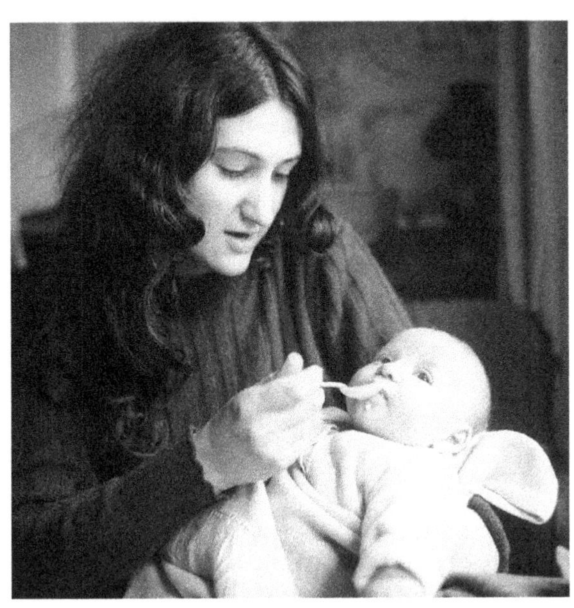

Abby feeding Homer, 1971

patriarchal values. This was the beginning of the Feminist Revolution as stimulating, and as terrifying (for some) as the French and Russian Revolutions, although this new revolution would not bring into play the murderous impulses of those other ones.

(When I told Lydia - with whom I've lived for over 20 years now - that I was writing this she nearly pissed herself laughing. She said words to the effect: "You're writing about feminism in the context of your own [indirect] experience of childbirth?!" Maybe I should have waited till later in this story to bring this up, or even just left it out, but all I can say is that it seems to me to be the right place.)

Anyhow, unlike those other revolutions, the feminist revolution didn't take place within national boundaries. It largely took place within domestic space, in a great many countries, although the so-called "liberal democracies" were undoubtedly the places where the revolution was most complete, most all-pervasive.

Feminism, like the Russian revolution in 1905, had a false start with the suffragette movement. The gains of the suffragettes were largely overthrown by the Great Depression and who is to say that the severity of the depression (I don't mean its cause) wasn't capitalism's reaction to the combined threats of socialism and feminism. I don't think you'll find that in any of the standard histories of the time, but I am trying to look sideways for other unacknowledged forces at work, particularly psychological ones.

I want to put on record that it was my mother who told me, when I was a young teenager, about the suffragettes, for whom she had a great admiration. If you'd known my mother you'd think this was very strange, inconsistent with her seemingly conservative attitudes about most things. However, contradictions abound everywhere, so I just accept them. My mother's admiration for the suffragettes rubbed off on me and I remember telling someone, as early as 1960, that I called myself a "feminist".

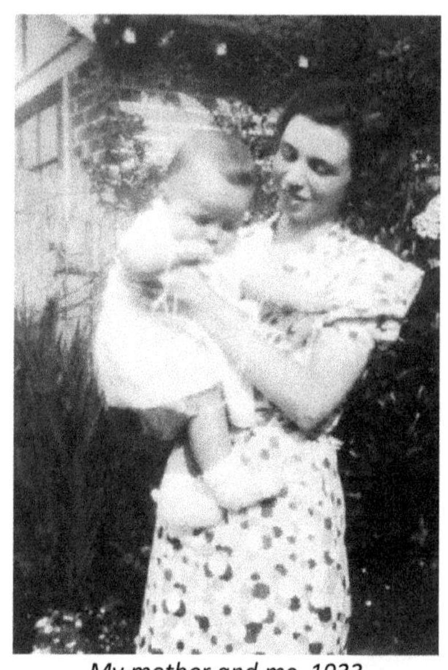
My mother and me, 1933

Around the time of Homer's birth we re-established contact with Clem (Clemency Weight) who had gone to London with Albie. By the time we met up Clem had parted from Albie and married a young Dutch film maker, Theo van Leeuven. Clem and Theo invited us to visit them at Christmas, in Amsterdam, and to travel with them for a holiday on Texel, a tiny island in the North Sea, off the far northern end of Holland.

Amsterdam is notoriously crowded - although frankly I found London even more crowded. I saw the visual expression of this crowdedness as our train pulled into Amsterdam. Alongside the railway there were apartment buildings, not very high, I think, but very numerous, and uniform in design. Every one of these buildings, it seemed, had identical "picture windows", and in each of these windows identical Christmas trees were on display festooned with pretty little lights. The feeling of conformism was daunting. I talked later with Theo about this (we got on very well) and he told me that when the Nazis occupied Holland they were delighted to find that the Dutch bureaucracy had complete records of everybody in Holland. Anyhow, that's how Theo expressed his thoughts about Dutch conformism.

The island of Texel was a delight; very cold, a picture-book version of Holland. The landscape was utterly flat, almost all reclaimed from the North Sea by dikes. Large windmills could be seen in the distance and, I presumed, were still used to pump out the water that seeped into the land. The only high ground was a line of sandhills which I think would have been, in the absence of the dikes, the only things to rise above the waves of the North Sea.

Amongst the windswept trees on the sandhills, Theo pointed out to us a large concrete bunker of rounded shape and with tiny windows, a relic of the German occupation. Also amongst the sandhills, a much more pleasant experience, Theo took us to a large wooden cafe, warm as toast inside, where they served good coffee and a kind of advocaat that I've never come across before or since. This advocaat was like an alcoholic custard, served warm and eaten with a spoon.

While on Texel I shot some 16mm colour film, which I eventually made into a little film that I called *My Dutch Newsreel*. I also did some drawing, although the one below is the only one that I can find now.

Some years later Clem and Theo moved to Sydney, where Theo found

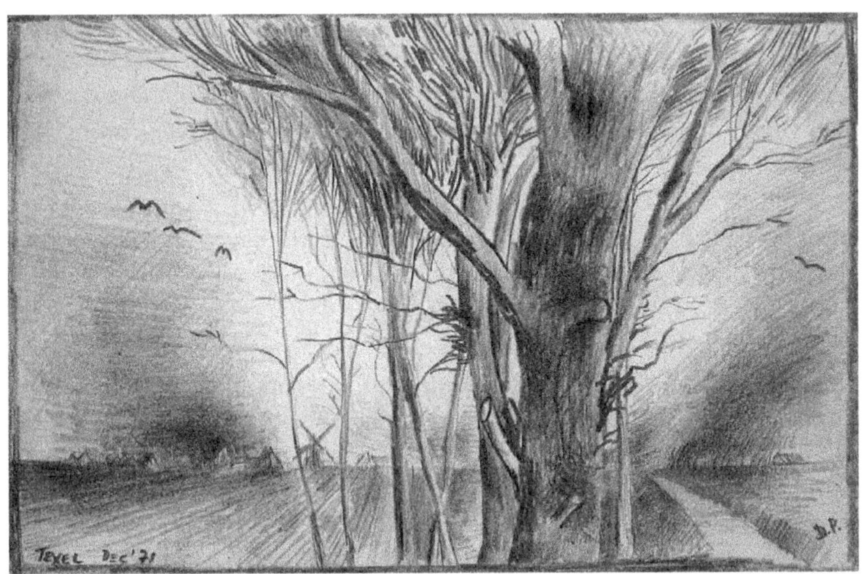

View of Texel (pencil on paper), 1971

a job at Macquarie University. He was a natural intellectual, whereas Clem - an artist – lived much more by her feelings, which was probably why they eventually parted. I don't mean to denigrate either of them - it's just that in the end they must have been working to very different agendas. I would like to have maintained contact with Theo but this was never to be.

Friends in London (and politics) ...

We were starting to find our way into friendship networks in London. Some of the people we met were deeply involved in politics. They believed that it was only a matter of time before a socialist revolution came to Britain. They were immersed in histories of Europe and Russia from which they drew intellectual sustenance. I would like to have been a believer myself but my natural skepticism, nurtured by the Push, protected me to some extent from the more passionate beliefs swirling around me.

One truly positive thing to come out of all that was our experience of collective child-care. We became part of a group of five or so families who had between us seven or eight children varying in age from about one to five years old. On each of the five weekdays, the kids were brought to whichever household was rostered for duty. The person, or people, from that household then looked after the kids between about nine in the morning and four in the afternoon, making sure they were well-fed and properly looked after. We called this mobile organisation "The Crèche". I remember once, when it was my day on, a couple of the men from the group turned up to help me. They were pretty useless, really, because they sat around most of the time talking earnest politics - even earnest childcare politics - but as for actually doing something, I don't remember anything like that happening. (Am I too cynical about political "activists"? I don't think so.)

This was a time when the IRA was very actively at war with the English, who maintained what was effectively an occupying force in Northern Ireland. At least one of the people in our childcare group was part of the large Irish immigrant community in London and our sympathies lay with them in their campaign to get the Brits out of Northern Ireland. The fact that Ireland was an oppressive theocracy hardly registered with me at the time and so, when a large demonstration was organised in London in support of the anti-British cause, I went in it.

Perhaps I was the only new face in the protest. That's the only reason I can think of for the very large number of photographers all jostling to get pictures of me. I have always assumed they were police photographers. Special Branch maybe, or one or other of the spooky organisations that operated, still do, of course, even more so in the background of ordinary life.

That wasn't my only brush with the English cops. Around the same time I was "befriended" in a pub near home by a couple of strangers - men who, by some ploy that I don't remember, invited themselves back to my place. They bought a small amount of beer and as we consumed it their "friendship" turned decidedly sour. They began by asking seemingly innocuous questions about what I did but quite soon their manner became increasingly hostile. I think that if they were "spooks" they were very amateurish in that they let their hostility show. (Once, in Australia, at a Push pub, I had met a man I had no reason to suspect of big-noting himself - who claimed to work for ASIO and who told me that the only skill required to be a "spook" was to be able to remember in the morning - no matter how drunk the previous evening - all the details of conversations with people of interest. That has stuck in my memory as a definition of "professionalism" in "spookery".)

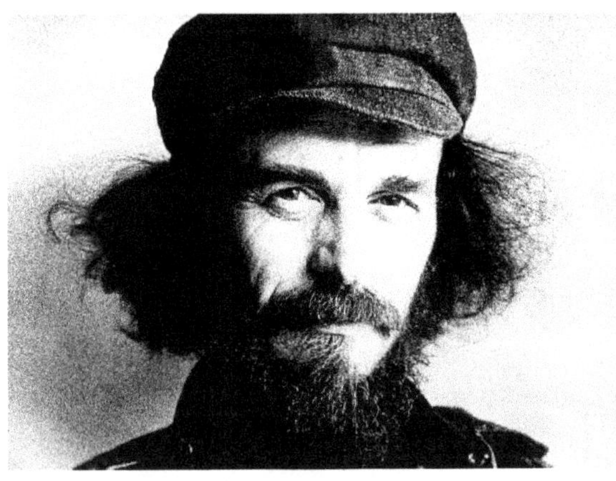

Portrait of DP (photograph by Gopala), c .1972

I don't remember how my evening with the amateurs ended. I can only assume they finally came to the conclusion that I was an idealistic artist who had no real grasp of anything that was going on in the London "underground". There was of course a lot going on, but there was no need to be "in the know" to know that. There were bomb scares that closed London's tube stations on more than one occasion. Television news and current affairs programmes were awash with stories from Ireland. More mysteriously and feeding my by now heightened sense of conspiracy, there were not infrequent explosions in the night that seemed to come from the direction of a suburb close to us that was said to be "full of Republicans". I feel a bit silly writing this because I can't for the life of me remember the name of the suburb.

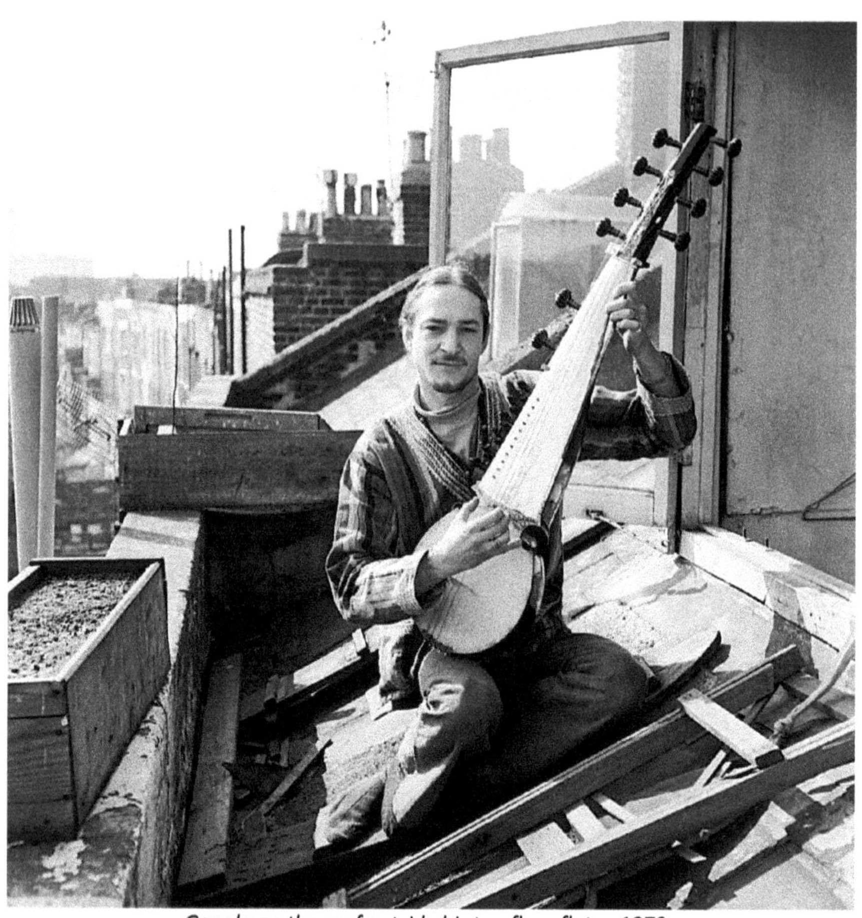

Gopala on the roof outside his top floor flat, c.1972

There were other reasons, too, for paranoia in London. There was the issue of "drugs". Now, of course, I liked an occasional joint in the evening after the children were in bed and I usually got my grass or hashish from an artist who lived in the top flat in our building. He was known as Gopala although his original English name was Richard de Villeneuve, or so I was told. (Gopala was part of a little community around an Australian band called "Quintessence", who had originally been known as "Phil Jones and the Unknown Blues". In London this band of hippies had been inducted to a Hindu sect and Gopala painted the elaborate designs for their record covers, meticulous "quotations" of a style of Hindu religious art. Gopala's partner was a young woman I only ever knew as Nisa.) Also living upstairs was the group's mentor, or guru, who had a constant stream of young women in long, silky dresses going upstairs to visit him.

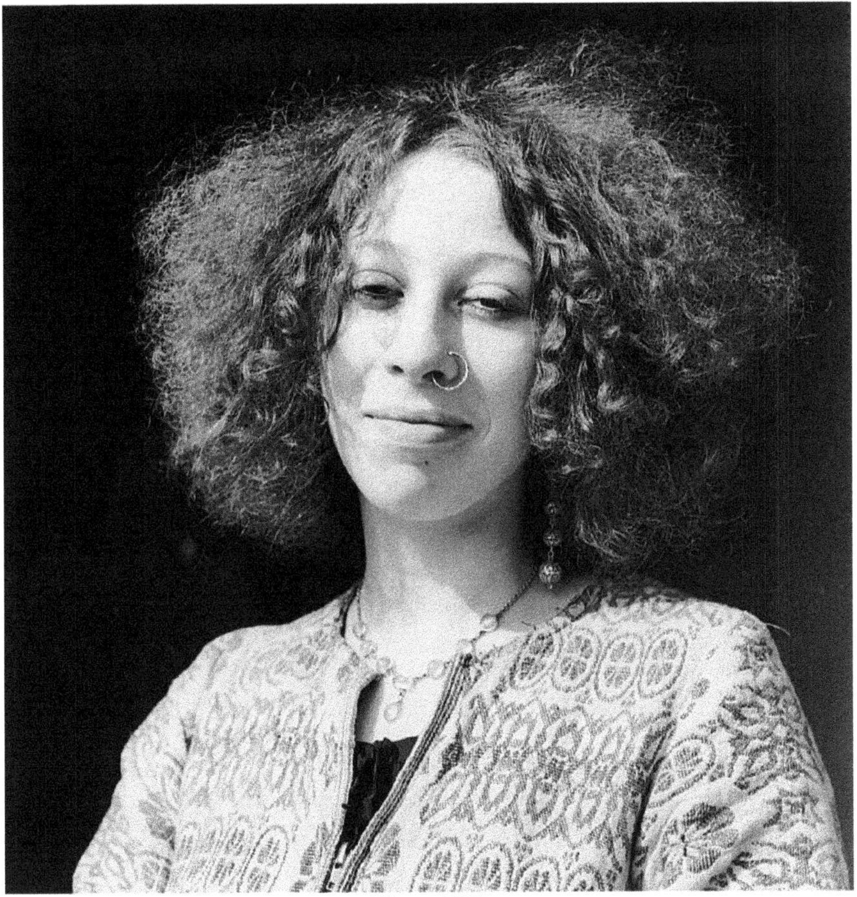

Nisa, c.1972

Now, that was a bit of a digression from the story about "drugs", but I think necessary colour. No doubt Gopala supplied people besides myself and inevitably the police knew about him. Early one evening there was a loud knocking on the front door of our building. Since our flat was the closest to the door I went to open it. A couple of plain-clothes policemen were there, asking for Gopala. Once again lack of professionalism comes into this, because although these cops flashed their IDs at me they had no search warrant. As well as that they smelled heavily of alcohol. I told them they'd have to have a warrant before I'd let them in. For a little while they tried to reason with me (although I don't remember what their "reason" was), but soon they pushed their way in and closed the door saying: "We're going to have a little word with you." I thought I was for it, and probably would have been except that Abby came out and began shouting at them in her best fishwife manner.

No one could stand up to Abby when she was in full angry flight, not even two London cops, who retreated immediately. In the meantime I ran upstairs to tell Gopala what had happened. There was a flurry of activity as Gopala, and possibly others, got rid of the evidence. An hour or two later some other, much more polite cops arrived, led by a senior officer in a civilian suit of impeccable cut. This time they had a search warrant, and I just stood aside to let them go upstairs. It must have been a frustrating raid for them because I don't think they found anything incriminating.

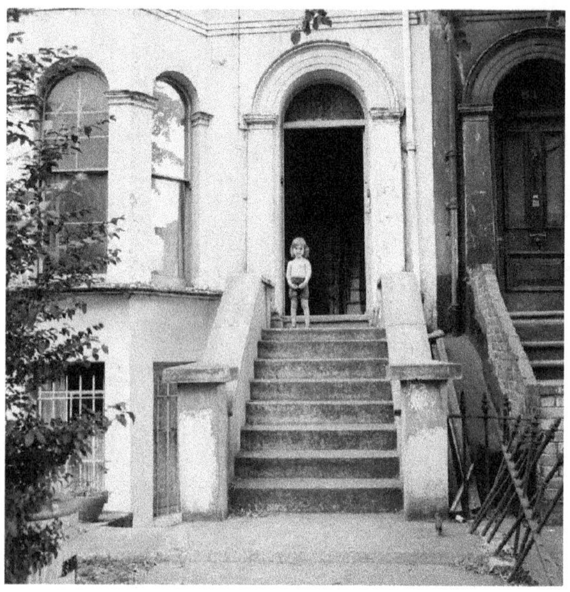

The entrance to our building, c.1972

The building we lived in, in Blenheim Crescent, W.11, was four or five storeys high. I don't remember who lived on the floors between Gopala and us although I do remember that directly opposite lived the Australian artist, Colin Lancely. Colin seemed uncomfortable with me but Abby got on very well with his wife. This probably reflects the fact that the womens' movement was in the process of changing a great deal about social relationships. Women who previously may have not had much to say to each other across conventional barriers of class, ethnicity and so on were finding a new sense of solidarity.

As I've already suggested London was swirling with political movements of all shades of red. Feminism was becoming the most prominent of those. Feminism seemed to draw its early supporters, and its rhetoric, from western leftist movements, but its influence spread far wider than that. Before modern feminism most of what I call the "moral confidence" that people felt in the justice of causes was found in left-wing movements that looked to the Soviet Union or China for inspiration. By 1970 or thereabouts such simplistic faith could not be sustained. However, until long after I left England, the broad "left", especially feminism, maintained its moral confidence.

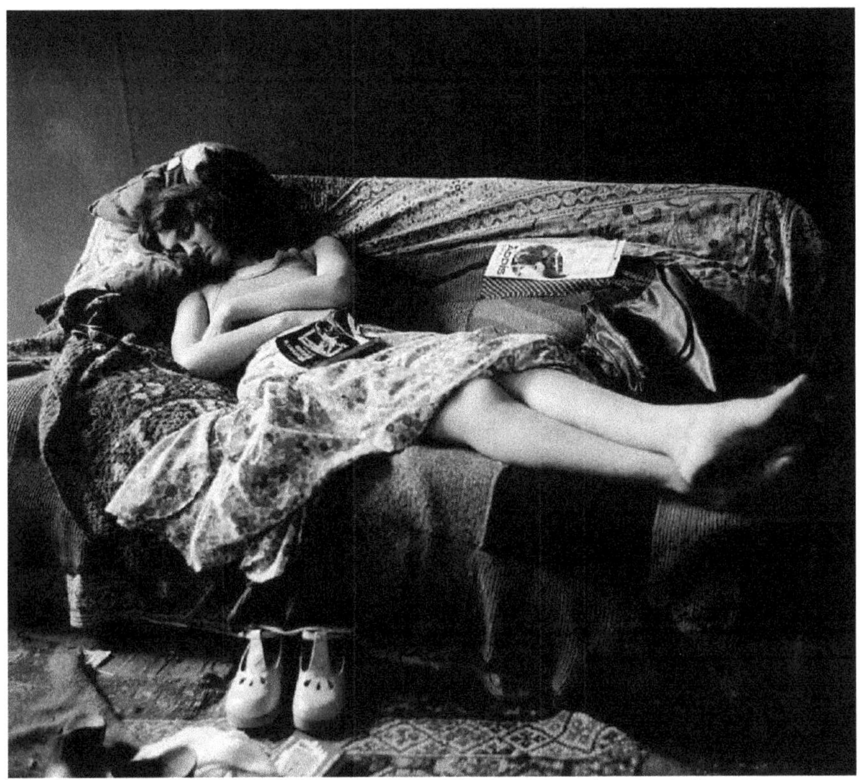

Abby napping while reading Women's Estate *by Juliet Mitchell, 1972*

Long before I met Abby my sympathies were for the left, although unfocussed. I have learned only recently that my paternal grandfather may have been a communist - perhaps my father was also, although he never really confided in me - and I've already mentioned my mother's sympathy for the suffragettes, so there must have been a lot of unconscious activity going on in my head.[6]

---

[6] In Sydney, way back in the early 1950s I found myself riding on the back of a truck with a lot of "Bodgies" (young men whose unconventionality was signaled largely by their "sharp" clothes). We were being driven to some long-forgotten destination and singing a song that contained the line: "We'll put all the squares in concentration camps when the great revolution comes along." ("Squares" were

If you add to that the influence of Abby's attitudes and the atmosphere in London at the time, it's not so surprising I thought of myself as part of the Revolution, and in a more hard-edged way than the anarcho/hippie way of our *Ubu Films* days. All around us were people who were deadly serious about this although if I had been put to the test I can't say what would have happened. Being an artist I hope I would have found an honest way to express my experiences. As it was, in the pre-revolutionary atmosphere not altogether unlike the atmosphere in some of Chekhov's work, there was room for a lot of romantic posturing.

Around that time I had been using the "Film and Television" Department's portapak to record a lot of scenes on the streets and in the London Science Museum which I later used in a production called *Utopian Memory Banks Presents: Fragments From the Past* (the longest title I've ever used). This piece, which is so technically rough that I rarely show it, was set in an indeterminate future after "The Interminable Struggle and The Greater London Fire". A presenter with a burn-scarred face showed the footage I had shot as if it was material "recently discovered in the ruins of a building in old North London".

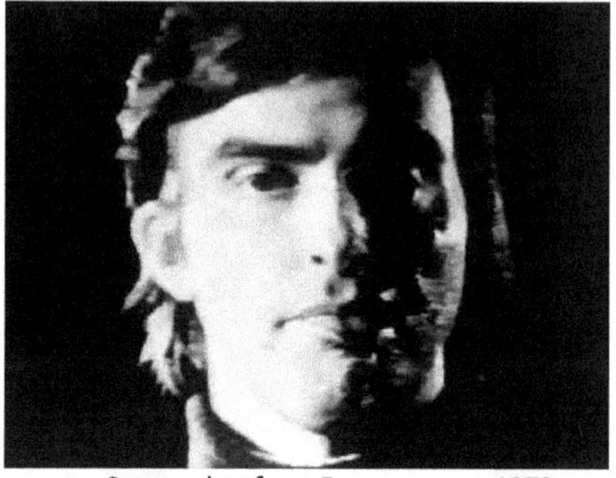

Screen shot from Fragments., c.1973

Fragments, to give the piece its short name, is an expression of pessimism about any political change. I've no doubt that that pessimism made me untrustworthy in the eyes of the political operators of London.

I loved going to the London Science Museum. It contained working examples of inventions going back to the beginning of the Industrial Revolution. Although, as a child of the industrial age I admired these exhibits immensely, I had no trouble imagining how the first steam powered engine could have struck terror into any person who had grown

---

the great grey mass of conventional people of the time.) That was the nearest I ever came to being overtly part of a political movement, although "Bodgies" would never have been dignified by such a term in their own time. They were just "juvenile delinquents".

up in the rural landscape of pre-industrial England. Eighteenth century technologists, just like their modern equivalents, dreamed of how much wealth was going to be created by these machines and were undoubtedly as impatient of the fears of the people of their time, as modern technologists are of modern fears. These engines were so big as to seriously dwarf a person. Black wooden beams connected large pistons to huge steel flywheels which in the past, in "dark satanic mills", must have been connected by belts and pulleys to terrifying and truly dangerous machines. The engines' huge beams rocked up and down as the pistons rose and fell, while scalding jets of exhaust steam made an inhuman hissing sound. (In the Science Museum the "engines", now simulacrums of themselves, were driven by electricity.)

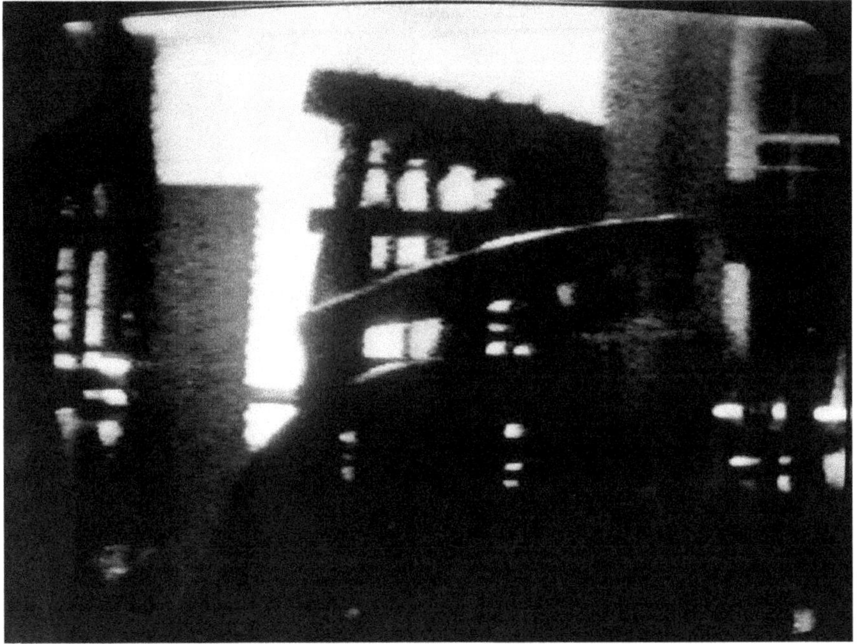

In the Science Museum (screen shot from Fragments), c.1973

A more recent relic was James Logie Baird's prototype for a television system which, incredible as it might seem now, was largely a mechanical system not an electronic one. What I was reminded of by the history of television is that pure science always precedes technology. An example: soon after the turn of the 20th century a group of English scientists gave a lecture to their peers, which described in theory how fluctuating light patterns could be converted to electrical impulses, transmitted along a wire or through space, and in the receiving apparatus converted back to fluctuating light patterns. It took more than 30 years for this fundamental understanding to be converted to practical technical devices that were at the heart of the first television systems. Then came the second World War and all the people working on television were diverted to radar research. I worked with a man at the ABC's Engineering Laboratory who told me of his first-hand experience of this. Then in the post-war boom period the 20th century went into hyper-drive, which I suppose, is one of the reasons that it became possible for Abby and me to get so easily to the other side of the world..

But I'm sick of this theorising. Below and opoposite are some drawings inspired, however loosely, by television and newspaper reports of the activities of the British Army in Northern Ireland ...

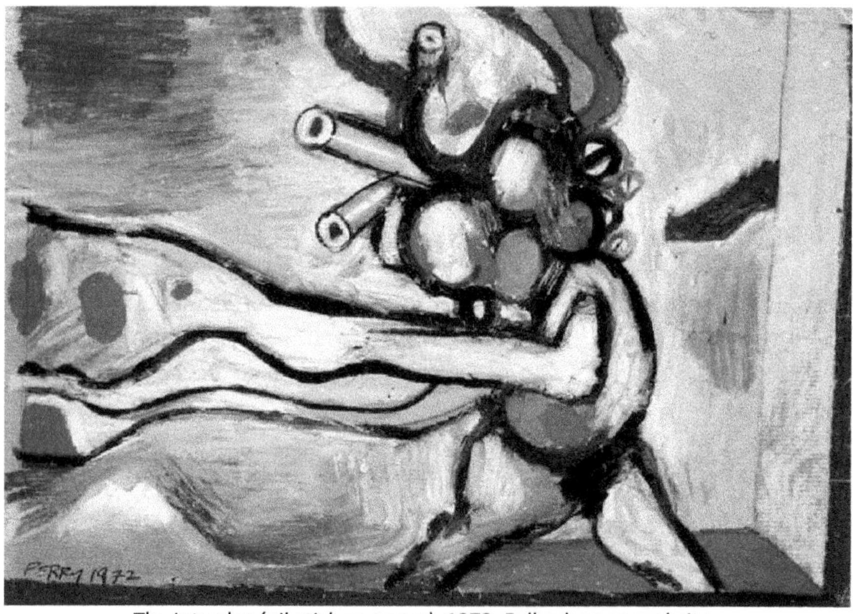

The Intruder *(oil-stick on paper), 1972. Full colour on website.*

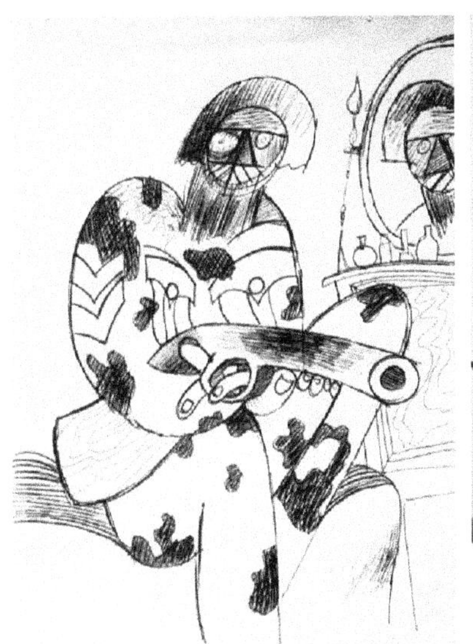

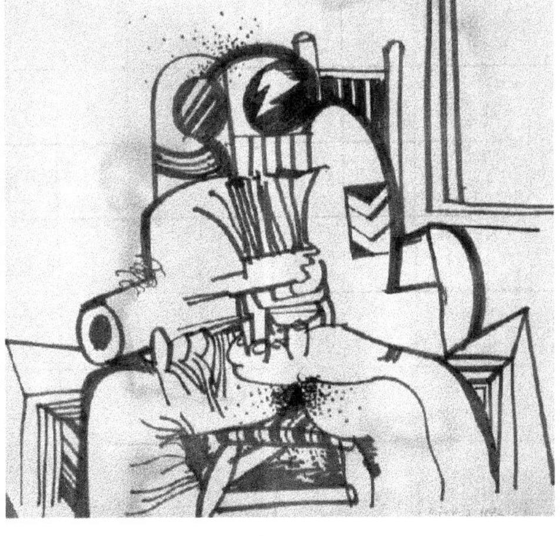

Sergeant Phuqnukle *(felt pen on paper), 1973*

Sergeant Phuqnukle in a house
(ballpoint on paper), 1973

… and a scene in a street near Blenheim Crescent. Parts of London looked as desolate as newspaper images of Northern Ireland.

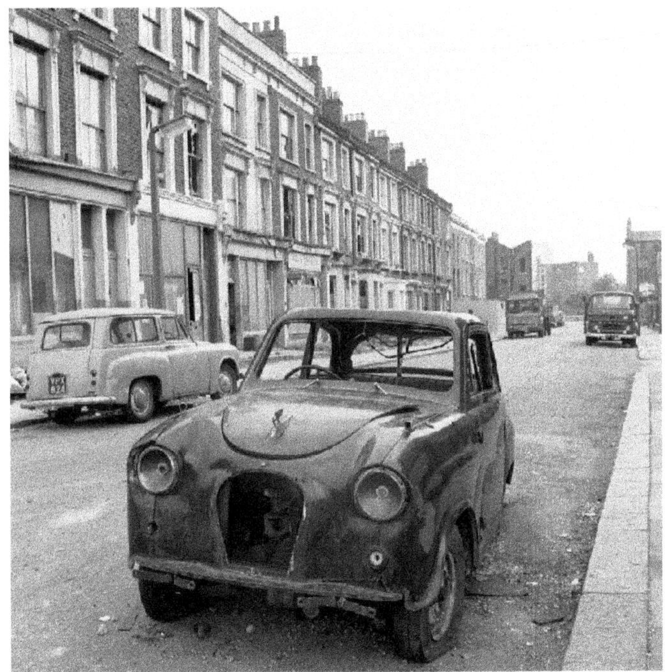

Ruined car in a ruined street, c.1973

A personal loss of "moral confidence"...

In spite of all the serious words on the past few pages I have to say that in truth I found it hard to engage with politics in England. When I look now at many of the photographs, like the one on the previous page, I don't think it was the landscape I was photographing. It was my internal desolation at being cut off from people who knew my history, and that includes of course the children left behind without a word. Although I had a sense of loss about that, it was going to take much longer before I would properly understand what I had done..

In retrospect the first indication of that was when an Australian friend brought me a letter from Simon in which he asked me for advice on photography. Simon must have been asking people about how he could contact me. It seemed to me that he understood that my relationship with Judy was utterly unworkable and there was no point in going through her to find out anything about me. He was about seventeen at the time. I wrote a letter in reply and entrusted its return to the same person who brought it to me. I know now that Simon never received it. The atmosphere of secrecy, conspiracy even, that surrounded this errand would have been funny if it wasn't so sad.

Of course it's only in retrospect that anyone can truly understand a life. But memory is an unreliable guide to one's motivations. Fortunately for me I have all these photographs, taken throughout my life, as some sort of guide to what has happened to me and to the people around me. And yet, as I said right at the beginning, I don't think photographs are objective records of anything other than the relationship between photographer and subject and anyhow, that relationship is always open to interpretations which will shift over time. Does this mean that we can never know anything about the past? Does this mean that "history is bunk"? Meaningless? The best answer I can give is one that I heard a film historian give to that question, in around 1993: "We know that something happened." I don't think that is so despairing as it might seem. I thought he meant the work of history was to continually worry about these "somethings", not to dismiss them out of hand.

And then, just before I wrote that last paragraph, I read something in the newspaper that might have some bearing on this: "Each time someone revisits a memory it gets revised, so that by the time they're dredging a memory up for the tenth time it may have very little resemblance to what happened in the first place."

I suppose that could mean that this memoir is meaningless. I don't accept that. It is, for what it's worth, a story. You don't have to accept it as forensically factual, just accept it as throwing some light on certain "somethings" that happened. (Incidentally, the words "history" and "story" come from the same Greek and Latin roots: istoriya. This means, to me, that history is not "his story". That popular misinterpretation is based on just a quirk of the English language. That men have been in charge of history throughout recorded history, although factual (unless you want to ignore the evidence) can't be supported by etymology.)

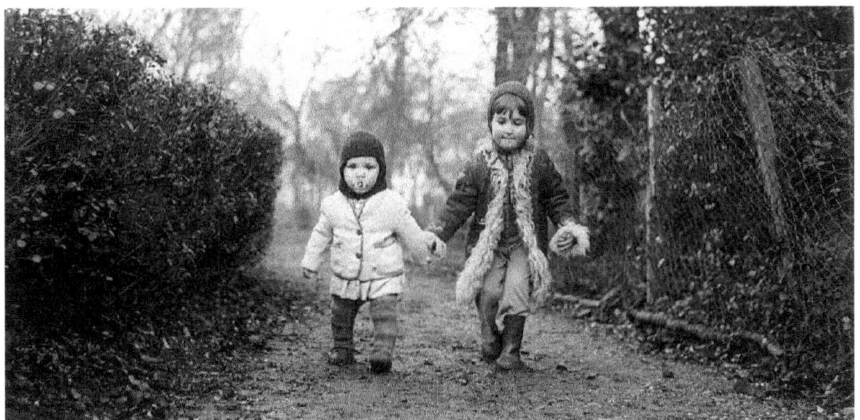

Homer and Rachael in the communal garden

Which brings us to the impact of modern Feminism on Abby's relationship to me. With all the qualifications about "memory" just alluded to, I have to say that in the early 1970s and for some time after, there was a widely-held view that "all men are bastards". I think it's more likely true that all people are bastards but perhaps it's better to accept that all people can be bastards. If we are going to sustain any relationships at all we have to accept that bastardry is not due to any intrinsic evil, just to circumstances which may be transitory or they may be deeper. Either way circumstances are usually complicated and difficult, even impossible to comprehend when their outcomes first arise.

In London, Abby had formed friendships in "revolutionary" circles from which my ambivalence kept me at arm's length. Our sex life became inactive. Not surprisingly, Abby became attracted to other people, although I'm not sure when she began to respond to those attractions. I remember one night when she came home late, got into bed with me and asked me to masturbate her. I presumed she'd had a very unsatisfactory experience although I didn't ask her outright. Anyhow, how could I refuse her? She was desperately attractive to me. I was still in love with her and would stay that way till many years later. And of course we had our children.

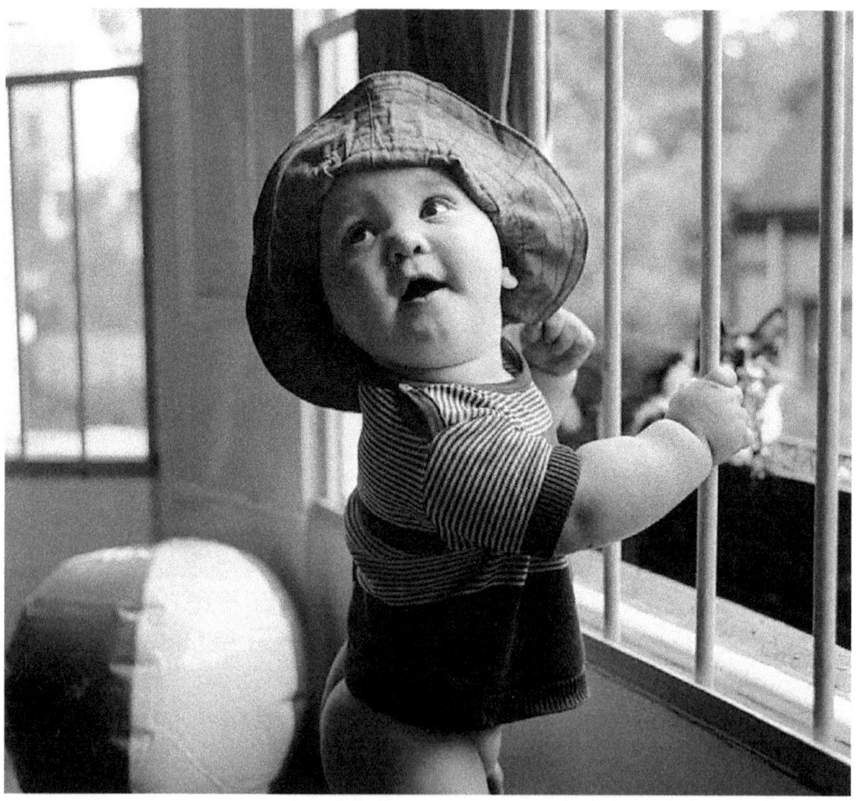

Homer in London, 1973

The reason for the bars that Homer is rattling is that, like all little kids, he was adventurous and had no sense of danger. One day, before he could walk, I had just gone outside for a moment to collect the mail, most likely, thinking he was totally safe - but when I came back into the room Homer had scrambled out through the open window and was holding on to the window ledge with his feet dangling over the drop to the ground one floor below. I somehow managed to get to him without startling him, grabbed his hands and pulled him back inside. I hate to think what would have happened if I'd been even a few seconds later.

Another crisis...

One evening we were invited to a party by a woman we knew through the crèche. Abby encouraged me to go although she wanted to stay at home. Not feeling all that comfortable about being with a lot of people I didn't know, I decided to go anyhow.

It was a friendly party with lots to drink. The woman who had invited us introduced me to her younger sister who was extremely attractive. Her Irish accent only added to the attraction. I was momentarily smitten. Of course all this was superficial but being sexually frustrated I all too willingly found myself making love with this young woman on the floor of her sister's flat. It was that sordid. I'm sure neither of us got much out of it. I let myself out of the house and stumbled home.

I had no intention of telling Abby about this, it seemed so inconsequential. Nevertheless there must have been something about my demeanour that gave me away (there always is) and, once she got an admission out of me, Abby's anger was unstoppable. She went for me with furious words and a carving knife. I have no idea how I escaped injury.

So began our estrangement. In my memory Abby's removal of herself from our flat was instantaneous. She had lots of friends who would take her in and undoubtedly stoke the fires of her sense of injustice. We must have soon enough been able to have some kind of civil conversation because we came to an arrangement under which I'd have Rachael and Homer with me at weekends and Abby would have them during the weeks when I had to go to work. At home I was desolated by incredible sadness at the loss of our relationship and the potential for losing another family.

There was, I think, only one person at the time who acknowledged my loss and actually tried to do something about it. This was Derek Wood, an Englishman who had gone to Australia and become a part of the Sydney Push, so he knew something of my background. He'd had an unfortunate marriage in Sydney and felt that he had to return to England. He empathised with me and on Sunday afternoons would turn up carrying several bottles of cider or Guinness. I don't remember what we talked about but I do remember that Derek's visits made me feel better, at least for a little while. His affectation of cynical detachment was a breath of fresh air.

Derek's manners and his accent were decidedly English upper-class although he had clearly detached himself from that and become part of what Jim Baker of the Push called the "lumpen intelligentsia", intellectuals without allegiances (my interpretation). Derek's fruity laugh and even fruitier accents can be heard on some video footage I shot when he and another Old Pushian, Johnny Earls, were visiting. This footage eventually became part of a short film, *Goodbye Richard Nixon,* which I completed after returning to Sydney.

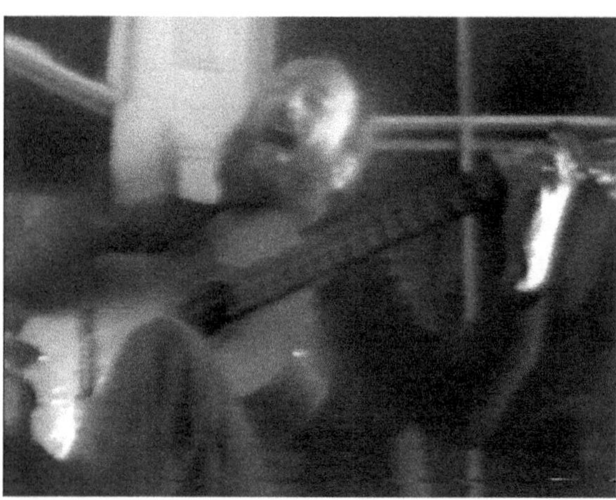

Johnny Earls in London (screen shot from Goodbye Richard Nixon*), original recording 1973*

It's amazing that I got this footage. We were all pretty pissed at the time from drinking what Derek called "sledge-hammers", a mixture of cider and bottled Guinness. At one point there is a brief shot of Homer, who must have been wakened by the noise, sitting on Derek's knee.

Johnny had very recently been in the States, where the Watergate scandal was starting to hit the fan. On the spur of the moment, and with little need for urging from us, Johnny launched into a song in which he improvised a whole lot of scurrilous innuendoes and insulting words about many of the characters from Nixon's cabinet who were involved in the bugging of the Democratic Party's headquarters in Washington.

What is to be done? ...

As I've already said, I was "a fish out of water" in London. The split with Abby only exacerbated that feeling. Abby herself had felt this in earlier times, probably more strongly than I; she was stuck at home with the children, a very serious problem in those days when the social structures assumed without question that "the woman's place was at home". I had told her that I would happily take over the primary child-caring role so that she could get a job as a private nurse, something she'd done in Australia. It wasn't exactly stimulating work but it paid quite well - probably not that different from my pay at Hornsey - and it would allow her a qualified freedom that she didn't then have. If that had happened my reasoning was that I would have more freedom for painting. My continuing involvement with the crèche made that a realistic possibility. I could see no possibility that I could make films. Video production at that time was exceedingly primitive and could not enable anything remotely like my film work in Australia.

As it turned out Abby didn't take up my offer and I had no real scope to develop anything consistent or substantial as a body of work in either painting or film. I did continue to take photographs but at that time, in fact right up to the present, photography was a very private activity, one that I had plenty of skills at but which never seemed to me to be any kind of career path.

Of course I was a frequent visitor to the National Gallery, the Tate Gallery and the Courtauld Institute where I could immerse myself in the entire history of European painting. There was, however, a major readjustment that I had to make before I was able to really see that work. It didn't look like the reproductions I had grown up with. The scale - and materiality - of the real things took some time to sink in, although when they finally did they were a revelation.

Another thing that eventually sank in was how deeply embedded British people were in their history. As an Anglo-Australian I had some vague notion of that history but no real idea at all of what it was like to feel yourself to be a part of it. Some probably quite superficial examples might give some idea of how I came to be conscious of this: I remember meeting a woman in a pub one evening who spoke about Oliver

Cromwell as though he'd lived in the immediate past; another time and this may seem truly superficial a man stopped me in the street and asked: "I say, are you related to Disraeli?"

These and other little fragments stuck in my mind as examples of non-academic history that you can only understand by being part of it. Most Australians in Australia have never felt that. Undoubtedly the only people in Australia who have such a deep sense of continuity are the Aboriginal people. For others history is purely academic. I certainly make no claims to be an historian: this account has too many gaps and, anyhow, is too personal to carry much weight as history. Even so, this next part of my story seems to me to embody at least one lesson about history apart from the ones just indicated.

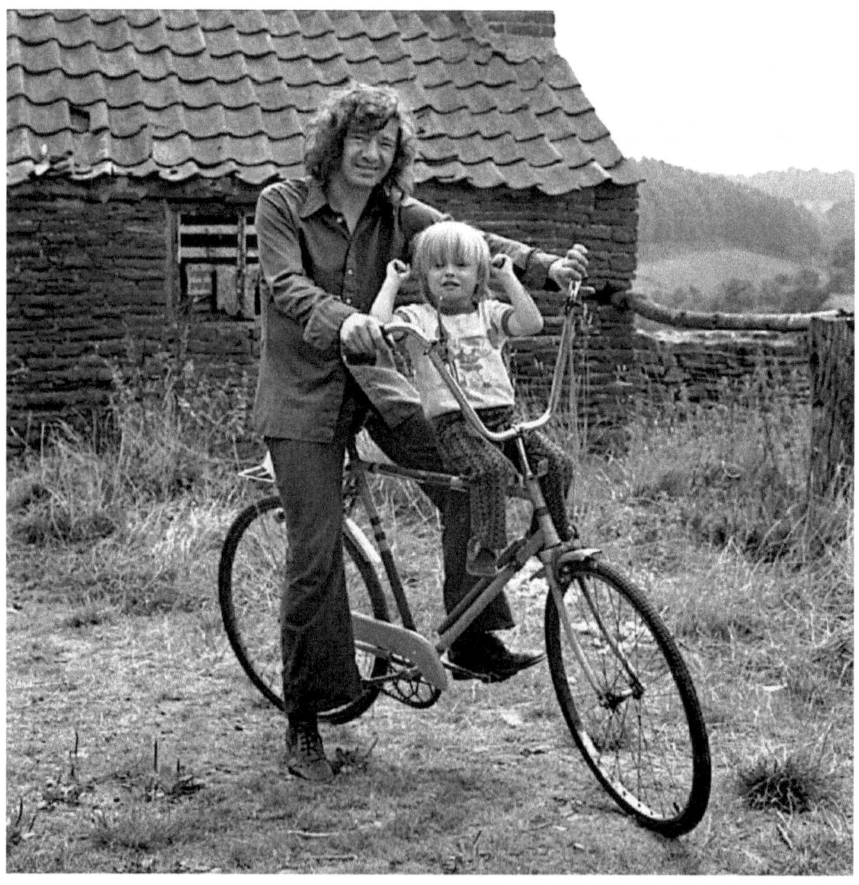

Tim and his son in Gloucestershire, 1973

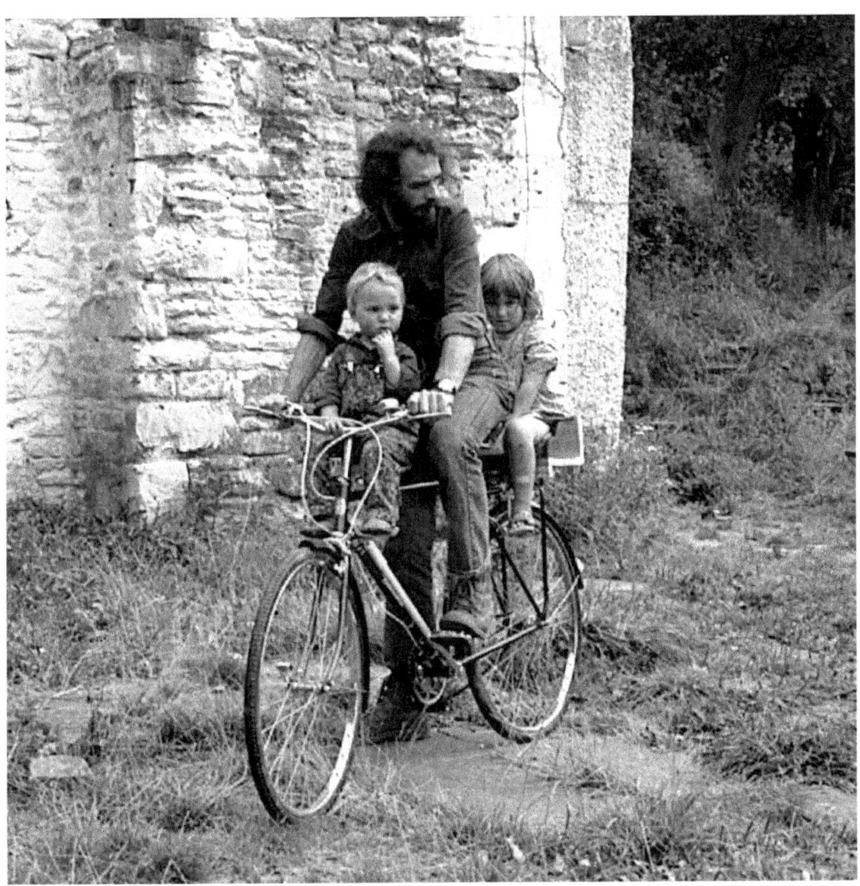

Homer, DP and Rachael in Gloucestershire (photograph by Tim)

I can't remember how I met Tim (Elliot?): he was certainly part of the political counter-culture of London and somehow or other we teamed up to take our kids for a holiday in the country. We modified our bikes with seats for the children and with minimal luggage and supplies caught a train to Gloucester. Through some of our contacts we knew we could stay in an old farm cottage a long way out of town.

I remember pedalling for what seemed hours along the narrow lanes of Gloucestershire with the kids aboard as the photo shows. Rachael's seat was well padded and Homer's was a comfortable small bicycle saddle. They both had footrests attached to the bike frame. I must have been fairly fit because I did the journey without being exhausted. Homer did the last part of it sleeping with his head resting on the handlebars.

Something I saw for the first time while I was positioning the shot on the following page, is what looks like an image of a face on the can inside the door of this shed, which seems to be intended as a lock-up for offenders, against the rules of what seemed to represent itself as a left/libertarian community.

The "face" on the can looks remarkably like a portrait of one of the many Old Bolsheviks killed during the Stalinist purges of 1937. I know this is just a coincidence, but it's an eerie one since, as I got to know him, Tim began to speak in the aggressively punitive mode of Stalinism. If I was to believe him he was only too willing to kill many of his political enemies. He seemed convinced that it was only a matter of time before he would find himself on some kind of revolutionary tribunal that would empower his itchy trigger finger.

As he got drunker Tim seemed to turn against me too, calling my camera a "rich man's toy." That was a bit rich, indeed, since he was no working class boy himself, rather he was a son of a very wealthy English merchant family. As I've come to know more about revolutionaries that seems to be a frequent pattern.

The bird of "Freedom" painted on, of all places, the wall of the "lock-up", seems to me to exemplify the paradoxical nature of revolution. In fact, if you look closely this bird has a very cruel beak. I've said before that I can live with contradictions, but I think I'll be selective about the ones I'll live with: this one I can live without.

Looking at the picture on page 154, the frieze around the window and the slogan painted next to it give a more benign impression. I don't think I ever met the people who owned this old farm house, but they clearly were idealistic dreamers given to expressing their dreams in clichés. I have to confess that I'm ready to forgive this kind of nonsense. Nor can I forget that the Thatcher/Reaganites of a few years later must have drawn their support from people rabidly critical of and punitively opposed to any such "nonsense". Of course, nonsense has a long tradition in English. It was expressed most famously in the 1960s and 1970s by the Beatles.

Not one of the photographs so far shown, nor most of the ones to come for that matter, was made with the intention of producing a work of "fine art". I suppose I was (am?) a conservative in that regard. That is, that if I were going to make "art", I would make paintings or drawings. Nor did I see these pictures as having any journalistic purpose. Clearly, I took them - and processed the negatives - with some care, but, if I thought about it at all, I only had a vague impulse to record something to do with my personal life. My sense of composition was informed by the conventions of painting or cinema. The choice of "moment", a skill I have nurtured, is quintessentially a still photographer's skill and has nothing to do with any other medium, since no other medium freezes moments in so commanding a way. Of course, any photograph, from the most innocent

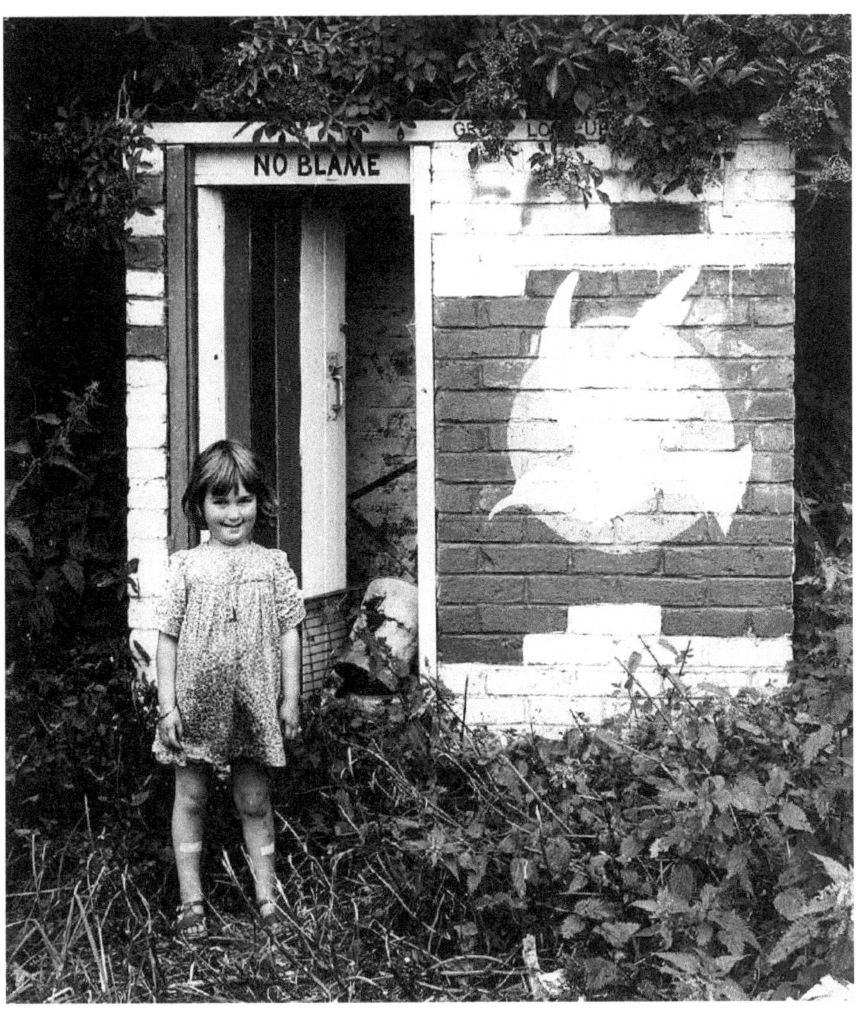

Rachael in Gloucestershire, 1973

snapshot to the most "crafty", most "arty" production, has the ability in retrospect to become an historical object. Whether or not a photograph does become an historical object depends a lot on the context that it's subsequently viewed in and the person viewing it. All the photographs in this book are historical in my eyes. What they represent to you is up to you.

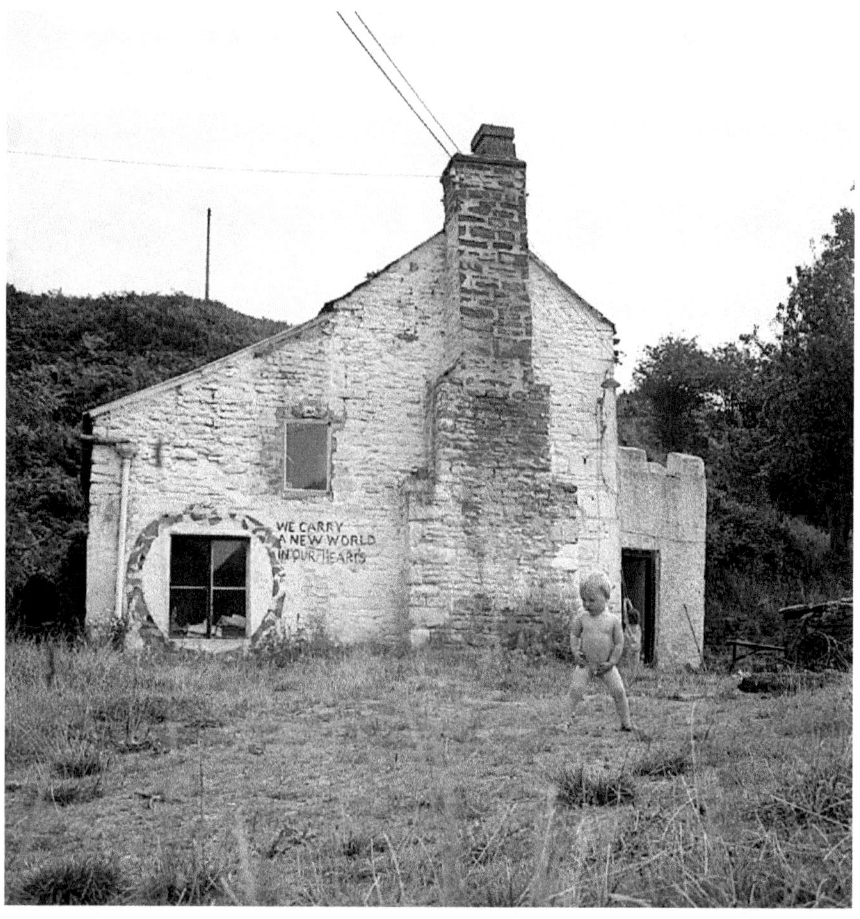

Homer pissing, Gloucestershire, 1973

Let's get out of here ...

I can't remember the order of events that follow. To be truthful the exact order of all events described here is open to question. They've been dredged from memory, but since I never kept diaries, none of my memories are annotated.

Not all that long after getting back from Gloucestershire I began thinking seriously about returning to Australia. One of my students had a strange theory about why I should do that. His view was that significant political events move around the Earth randomly, but they only happen once in any one place. He was Egyptian and said Egypt's moment of importance had happened three thousand years ago. Now it was Australia's turn. Gough Whitlam's Labor Party had beaten the Liberal/Country Party in the federal election of 1972, the first time in 23 years, and had immediately begun making radical changes to the way the country was run, including withdrawing Australia from the Vietnam War in defiance of United States foreign policy. My Egyptian student was duly impressed by this and, in keeping with his "theory" of the mobility of political power, urged me to return home to take part in this extraordinary development.

I thought his "theory" was the silliest idea I'd ever heard of, although I did take seriously the idea of returning home. The fact of the change of government was not unimportant, although my general unhappiness with my circumstances had a lot to do with it also.

Some time in the summer of 1973 Albie passed through London on a tour to promote his new film, Sunshine City. Someone once described one of my films as "breathtakingly egotistical" and, in that same vein, I might say of Sunshine City that I thought its visual qualities would have been better if I'd been there to shoot it.

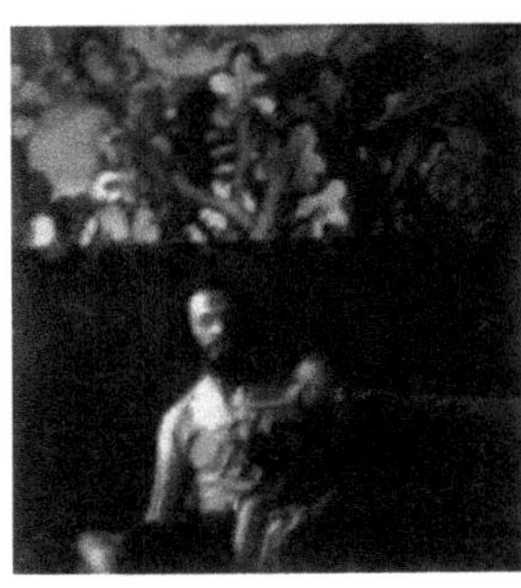

DP and Homer in London, 1973 (photograph by Linda Slutzkin)

With Albie was his new partner, Linda Slutzkin. They stayed together until Linda's untimely death in 2005. Linda showed me a small Polaroid print that she'd taken as a part of her visual diary, a picture of me in the London flat holding Homer sucking on his feeding bottle. Linda's photograph was probably taken at twilight which would account for the "moodiness".

By this time Hornsey College had been renamed as Middlesex Polytechnic. I can't remember what structural changes the new name signified. Whatever they were they had no impact on the work I did. I still had students from around the world: a very beautiful woman from Iran, an Indian princess who teamed up with a couple of German Marxists, several Israelis, a Canadian, an American, a couple of Australians and several English men and women. All of these students were post-graduates and made for the most incredible mix. Nor should I forget the Egyptian man who told me it was time to go home.

Two of these students opened wonderful windows of opportunity. Through the American I was "headhunted" for a position at a private college in one of the southern United States. I was interviewed in a large high-ceilinged mansion in a district close to Buckingham Palace, wearing a borrowed brown velvet suit. Incredibly I can't remember if I was offered the position, most likely I wasn't since it's very likely that I presented as a fairly unstable character.

A more interesting offer, and really right up my alley, was one where I would have designed and been in charge of a closed circuit video system (CCTV) on Israel's largest kibbutz. The idea was to enable all on the kibbutz to communicate with each other. I could have done it on my ear. It's one of the seriously lost opportunities of my life. The reasons for turning it down are not all that clear to me now but they were somehow entangled in the need to stay in touch with Rachael and Homer and not to alienate Abby more than I already had. I don't know if this makes any sense, maybe I'm forgetting other reasons, but it all seemed logical at the time.

Emotionally, I became something of a loose cannon, having one night stands or brief affairs with a number of women, including several of my students. I'd like to draw a curtain over that since I was a bit of a shit towards those women.

Eventually I met an English woman about my age with whom I formed a really good, passionate relationship. Her name was Rosemary and she had two children, a son about four or five years old and a little girl not yet walking. I remember strolling with Rosemary one summer day. Her daughter lay back in her push-chair sucking contentedly on her bottle which Rosemary had filled with Guinness. There was at the time an advertising slogan that said "Guinness is good for you" but I sometimes worry about what became of that little girl who would now be in her thirties. Did she become a serious alcoholic? Or did she defy all the fears of modern "political correctness" and grow up a prim teetotaller, or even perfectly normal?

For Rosemary there's no doubt I was a temporary lover, filling in for her real lover who was in gaol for some politically motivated crime against the British state. I never knew any details about this "crime", it might well have been bank robbery to finance the Revolution in the tradition of the Bolsheviks before 1917. If it had been left to Rosemary alone I may have been told more, even everything, since, apart from being lovers who spent many nights in each other's beds, we were becoming good friends.

One evening I arrived at Rosemary's place to find a meeting in progress around her kitchen table. None of the people there were familiar to me, but I think they were a prisoner support group. What was clear was that I was an outsider, and should wait outside.

It was probably very soon after that evening that Rosemary came to my bed and instead of making love as wonderfully as we usually did, Rosemary began crying. She told me: "I can't fuck you any more." She cried herself to sleep. I should have been more understanding but at the time this felt simply like rejection. I don't mean that I reacted with angry words, but I certainly withdrew into sullen silence. And that was the end of what had been, for me at least, a three or four week summer idyll. Through Rosemary I had drawn closer than ever before to an English culture that had previously been closed to me.

One afternoon in the National Gallery I found myself in a court devoted to English 18th century painting. Standing before a painting by Gainsborough, a painting of farm labourers, I could recognise in one of the young women on a hay wagon an unmistakeable likeness to Rosemary. I found myself crying tears of loss.[7]

I had been an inveterate gallery goer from the start in London. As I said, I had originally found it difficult to see the "old masters" with a clear mind. Over time, of course, the fog of strangerdom lifted. Gainsborough's landscapes (long before I met Rosemary) impressed me marvellously for the boldness of his brushwork. It seemed to me that he had painted the broad outlines of his trees with a huge brush, as large as we would use to paint the walls of a modern house. This wasn't obvious if

---

7 I have searched the web trying to find a copy of this picture to no avail. Possibly the painting wasn't by Gainsborough. I'm quite sure, however, I did see a painting of farm workers that brought on my distress.

you stood at a distance like a lot of casual visitors do. If in fact you just kept strolling as some do (I don't know why they bother), you probably wouldn't see this at all. (Although it may not be obvious, I think it was Gainsborough's brushwork that inspired the way I painted the landscape in *The Coast of Brittany* on page 129.)

Another painting I came to love in London was Titian's *Bacchus and Ariadne*. Titian's brush work and rich colours were revelations. I think the landscape in the background of that painting must have reminded me of a place in Sydney that I remembered fondly, Balls Head Reserve, with its views of Sydney Harbour. I bought a postcard of *Bacchus and Ariadne* which I later used to make several drawings.

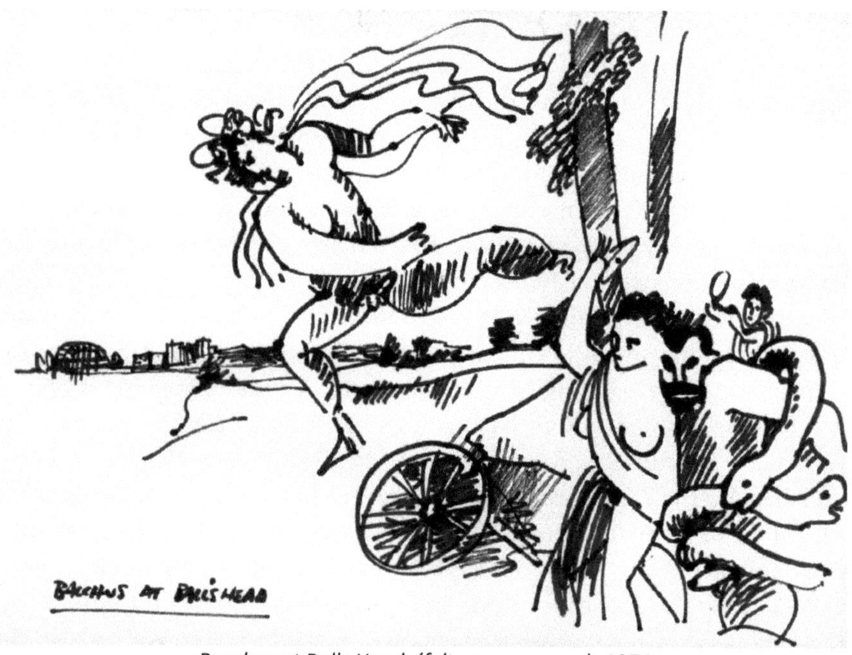

Bacchus at Balls Head, (felt pen on paper), 1974

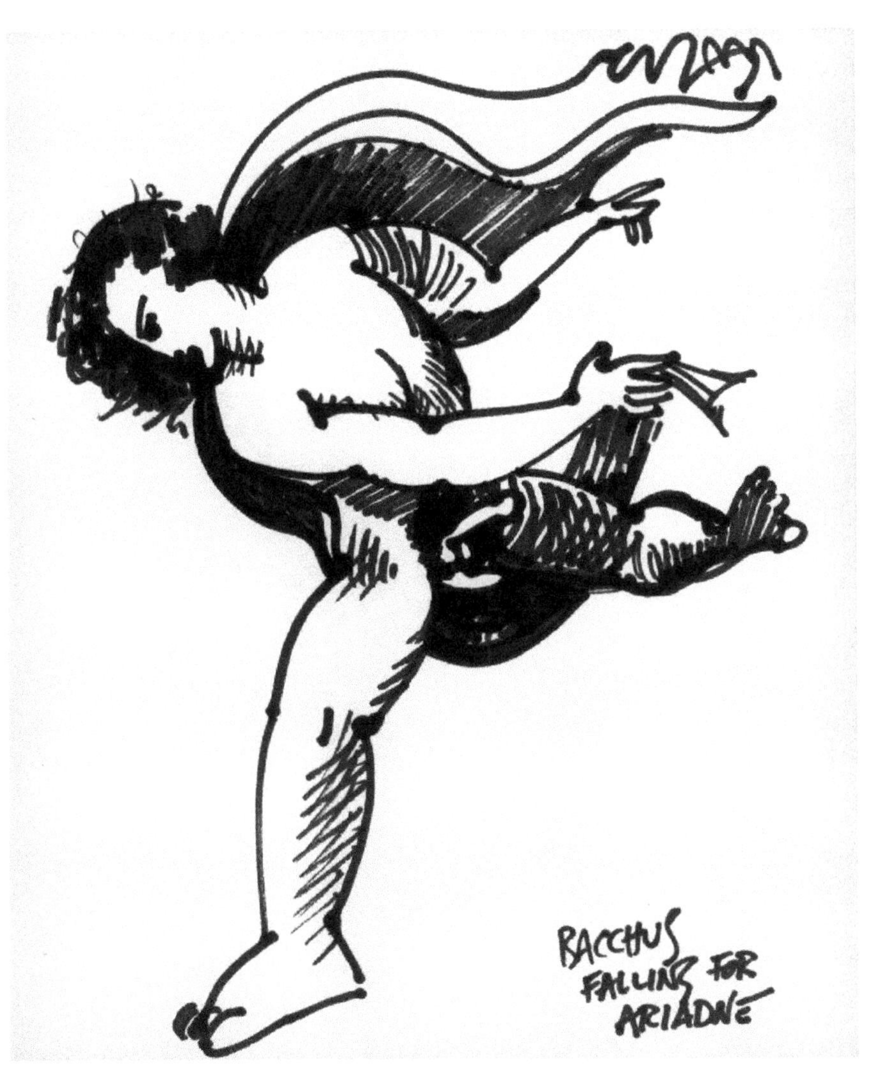

Bacchus falling for Ariadne *(felt pen on paper), 1974*

My determination to return to Australia became absolute. I was also determined to take Homer and Rachael with me. Another lost family was too painful to contemplate. I think I hoped I could get Abby to come back to me and that all of us would go back to Australia, if not together then separately and live reasonably close to each other.

In the end we came to a difficult decision: I would take Rachael to Sydney with me, Abby would keep Homer in London with her. I clung to the hope that Abby would herself return "home" soon enough. I had no idea if I could survive in Sydney as a single father - the concept was virtually unheard of in 1974. Maybe we could never have been lovers again but I did think that we could have stayed friends living in the same city. The photo below is the last I took of Abby and Homer in London and even now it is hard to look at Abby's eyes and the stoic acceptance in her expression.

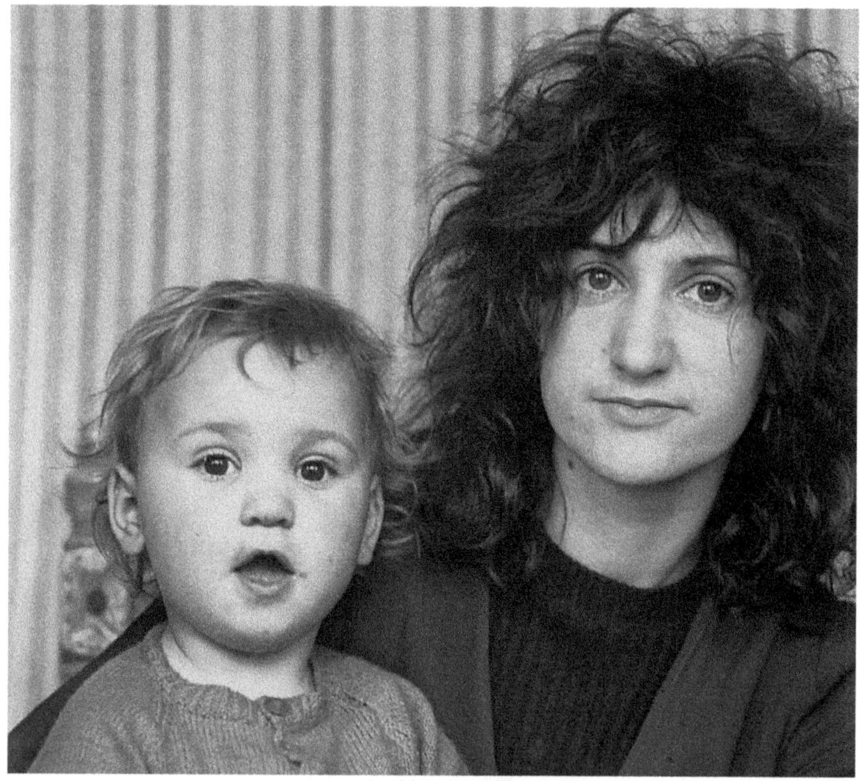

Homer with Abby in London, 1974

PART THREE

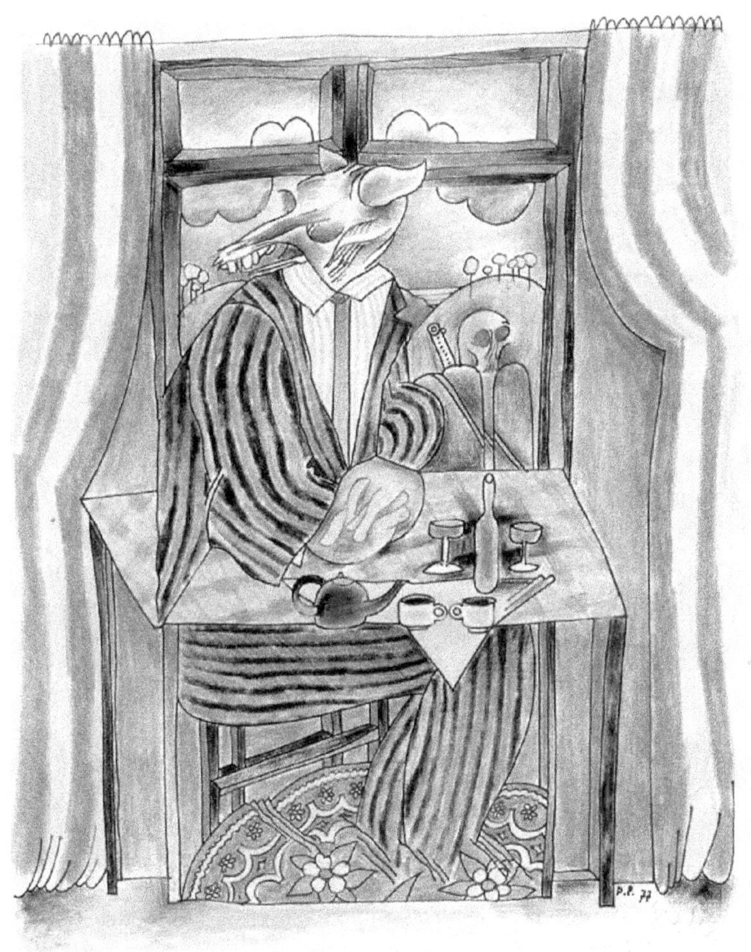

Nightmare in Queensland*, photocopy and coloured pencils on paper, 1977*

In Sydney again ...

Sue Howe had visited us several times in London and by now was an old friend. I wrote to Sue several times about my need to return to Sydney. Her replies were always encouraging. Eventually she sent me some money to help pay our fares and offered space for Rachael and me to stay in her house.

One evening in March of 1974 we flew out of London. The city below was a map of itself: the lights of the ring roads and radial roads etched a pattern that looked exactly like a spider's web. Before that impression could fade of its own accord, the ubiquitous clouds of the English sky wiped the cobwebs away forever, I might have hoped.

I've told the story of that journey before, in 1980, in a different format and another context. It's reprinted on the next page. There, there are anecdotes not told before, one at least already told, and some that pick up the story from the previous paragraph. This brings us to Sydney in the early autumn of 1974.

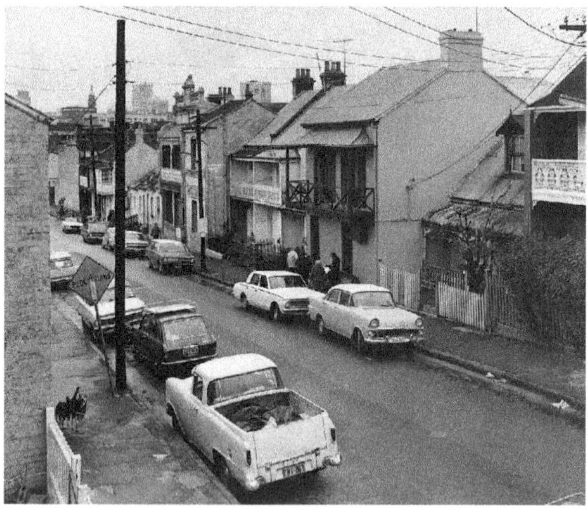

Edward Street, Redfern, 1974

Sue's tiny house in Edward Street, Redfern was exactly that - tiny. Rachael had a little bedroom upstairs, I had a narrow single bed in the downstairs front room. My bed doubled as a sofa when I wasn't actually sleeping in it. I didn't mind the tininess at the time, it was just so good to feel again the mellow caress of Sydney's air, to be conscious of an enormous and congenial space outside and to be in contact again with old friends. I know that sometimes (often?) I can give the impression of being thoughtless about people, but

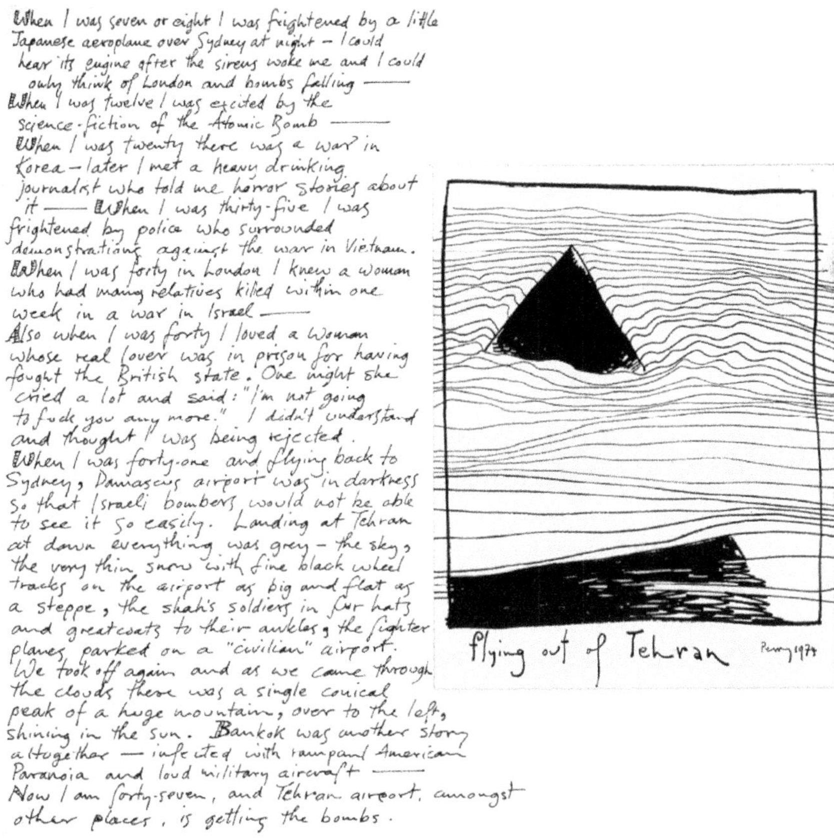

When I was seven or eight I was frightened by a little Japanese aeroplane over Sydney at night – I could hear its engine after the sirens woke me and I could only think of London and bombs falling ——
When I was twelve I was excited by the science-fiction of the Atomic Bomb ——
When I was twenty there was a war in Korea – later I met a heavy drinking journalist who told me horror stories about it —— When I was thirty-five I was frightened by police who surrounded demonstrations against the war in Vietnam.
When I was forty in London I knew a woman who had many relatives killed within one week in a war in Israel ——
Also when I was forty I loved a woman whose real lover was in prison for having fought the British state. One night she cried a lot and said: "I'm not going to fuck you any more." I didn't understand and thought I was being rejected.
When I was forty-one and flying back to Sydney, Damascus airport was in darkness so that Israeli bombers would not be able to see it so easily. Landing at Tehran at dawn everything was grey – the sky, the very thin snow with fine black wheel tracks on the airport as big and flat as a steppe, the shah's soldiers in fur hats and greatcoats to their ankles, the fighter planes parked on a "civilian" airport. We took off again and as we came through the clouds there was a single conical peak of a huge mountain, over to the left, shining in the sun. Bankok was another story altogether — infected with rampant American paranoia and loud military aircraft ——
Now I am forty-seven, and Tehran airport, amongst other places, is getting the bombs.

Last page of Four Drawings from a Journey, *text 1980, drawing 1974*

remembering how good it felt to be back in Sydney makes me realise how important it was to be "home".

Sue worked as a teacher at the local public school. She was a friend to the children of Edward Street, many of whom, especially the black kids seemed to regard Sue's place as a second home. Almost opposite there was a much larger house now converted into a community centre for the Aboriginal people of Redfern. One of Sue's most frequent visitors was a young teenager, Sally Haines, who said she was going to be a pop star. After I had sussed out access to video equipment, I talked (from behind the camera) with Sally about various things. Finally I asked her if her parents ever talked about life before the English came to Australia. Clearly I had overstepped a line: Sally's expression, normally happy and animated, went totally blank and she changed the subject. That image has been physically lost forever so I am obliged to try to hold it in my memory.

Life in Sydney in 1974 was utterly unrecognisable as the life we had left three and a half years before. There was in the air a friendly co-operativeness that I had never experienced before. Attached in some way to Sydney University there were darkrooms to which I had free access. That's where I processed and printed many of the pictures here (I only had to book a block of time and bring my own printing paper, no money was needed). There were also "Video Access Centres" where I could borrow a portapak and edit footage (also free of charge). These things were evidence of a huge cultural shift in Australia, given expression by the election of Gough Whitlam's Labor Party. For a while it seemed as if my Egyptian student in London was right to think that it was indeed Australia's turn for political happiness.

But of course "these things" were also evidence of a "dangerous left wing anarchism" which, if it wasn't stopped, would destroy business and anyone's ability to make profits. That was the view of the Liberal/Country Party, so thoroughly defeated in 1972 and now, just a year and a half later, manouvering to bring on another election.

This book surely is not a political history, there are plenty of those. I hope it is just what I want it to be: one person's selective account of his life in "interesting times".

Anyhow, an election was brought on, which the Libs didn't win.

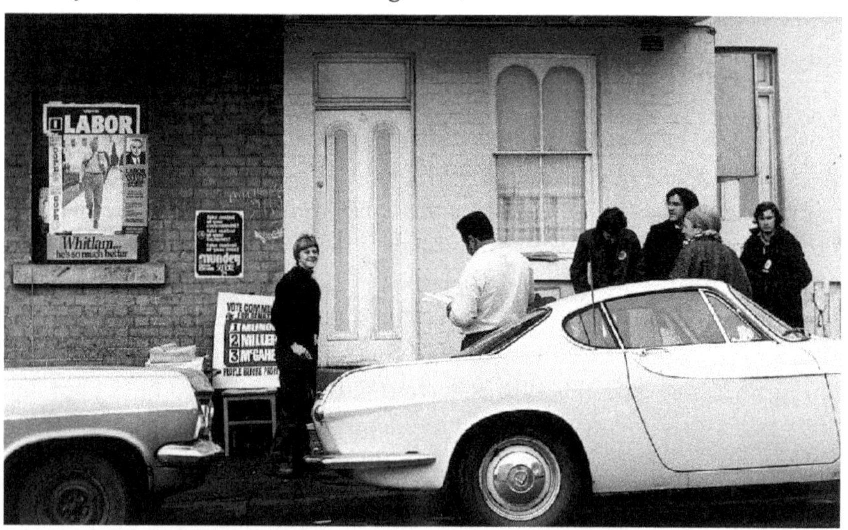

Gill Leahy at the Communist Party stand in Edward Street, 1974

New friends...

Gillian Leahy was a friend of Sue. She lived a couple of streets away from Edward Street. She had come into the Push some time while I was away, when some Push people had put aside their socially disinterested stance and become activists in alliance with at least some Communists. Hence the previously unlikely sight (opposite) of a Sydney Libertarian handing out Communist how-to-vote pamphlets. The times really were "a-changing".

Gill was about to enrol - maybe already had enrolled - in the Australian Film and Television School. She has since gone on to make some very good films. We became and have stayed good friends.

I had been writing to Abby with stories of the new life in Australia. I still held high hopes that she would come back to Sydney with Homer. In one of her letters to me she wrote: "*Trouble is still brewing here - like it could only happen in England - dispute after trivial dispute - volcanoes of bitterness/hate and repressed sexuality burst aflame every day.*" Surely, after a diatribe like that it would be only a matter of time before Abby, too, would give up on England.

Living next door to Sue were Peter, an actor and Virginia Bell. Virginia may have been an actor too at the time but she later became a barrister and after that a judge. I hardly knew Virginia and Peter. My reason for bringing them into the story is that they had a friend who frequently visited them: Katina Comino or Kay, as I came to know her. Kay was also an aspiring actress.

As autumn changed to winter Kay was planning to audition for a show. Since I had a portapak with me I offered to record her doing her audition piece so she could get an idea of how she presented. She did a song that had the refrain: "I want to make violent love to you."

I wasn't so egocentric as to think the words were directed at me, although a little later I must have complained to Sue that I was sexually lonely. Sue suggested to me (we were never mealy-mouthed in anything we said to each other) that Kay might welcome an advance from me (what made her think that?).

In the winter of 1974 the rain came pissing down. It was one of those rainy periods when all the rivers - up and down the coast and in the inland - swell up and flood over the countryside as far as the eye can see. Of course the rivers also spill over into any town unfortunate enough to be built on river banks, sometimes filling the streets with water almost to

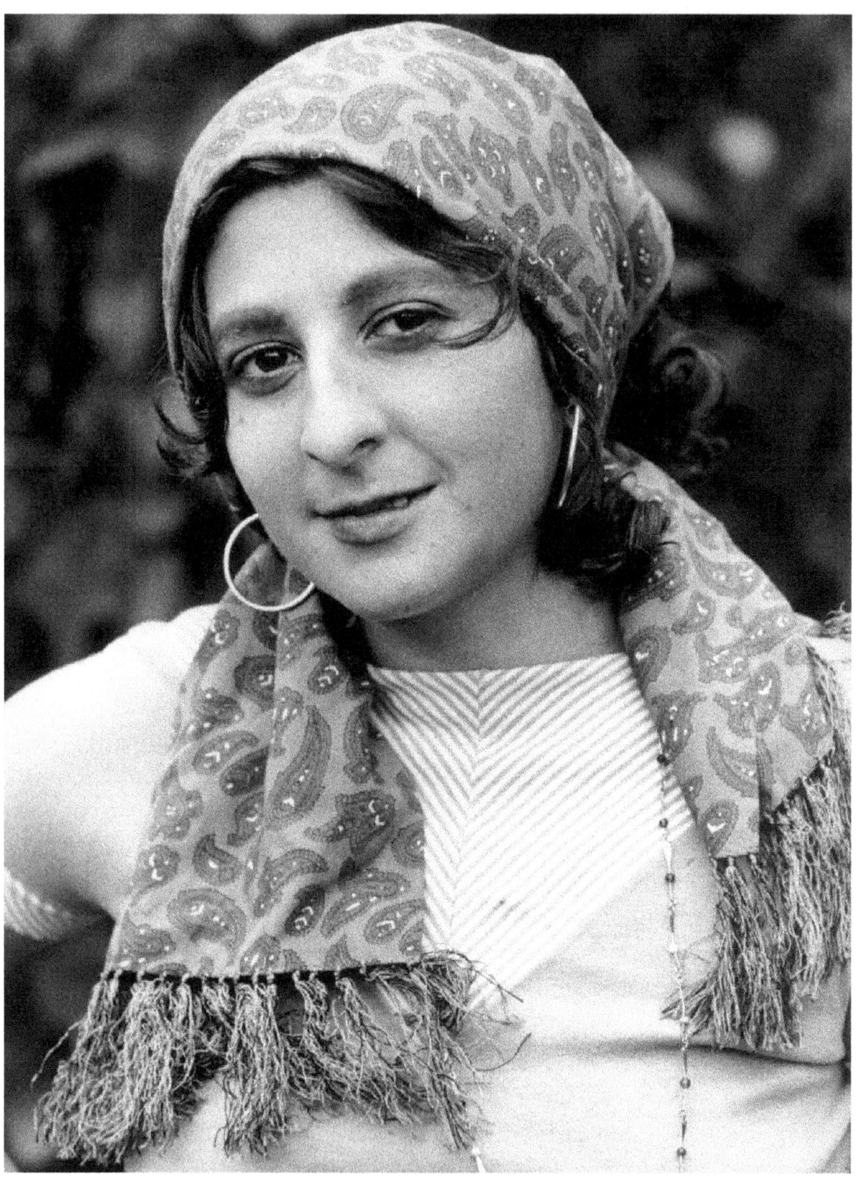

Kay Comino, 1974

the overhanging awnings. It was in such weather that I saw Kay dash out of a taxi towards Virginia's and Peter's front gate. Unchivalrously, or perhaps I just didn't have an umbrella, I stood in the door and called out to invite Kay in, almost certainly offering her a cup of tea. She was, of course, dripping wet. I got her a towel, started to dry her hair. With her so close to me and with my heart pounding, I asked her softly: "Would you like to fuck with me?" (If you think that plain English can't be spoken gently you're wrong.)

Kay smiled at me, saying: "I'll have to think about that." I don't think she took very long to think about it because by that evening we were in bed together.

Plenty of water and honest men ...

When I came back to Australia I was burning to make something of my experience of England, English people, my feelings about being a "colonial" and a sense of the injustices that the English had visited on what I was now convinced was my "homeland". Nor could I ignore any more the fact that having made a homeland of this place, I and everybody like me had contributed to the dispossession of the Aboriginal people. Nobody has the power to change the past but I wanted to tell something of what I had learned about the past and its pressure on the "present". I had been gathering images with portapaks and my still camera and an idea began to grow for a film that would bring all this, the past and the present, into some kind of feature film.

While I was away serious efforts had been made to develop funding mechanisms that had not existed when I left, so that by the mid-1970s it was possible for me to apply for a grant to research and write a script. All my friends encouraged me to apply, which I did, successfully.

I had been on the dole for a few months. One of the first things I did with my new-found income from the grant was to buy an old Morris 1100 car so that I could get around in the country near Sydney, which of course would be the location for much of the shooting. I also spent many weeks in the Mitchell Library reading old books and manuscripts. One of the most fascinating of these was a faintly-typed transcript (by Mitchell himself) of some letters written in the 1820s by a colonial bureaucrat with the grand name and title of Deputy Assistant Commissary General George Thomas William Blayney Boyes. Boyes' observations were fascinating to me. Written at the very time when the new colony could first be seen as having a real future, it felt to me that Boyes was describing experiences that could almost have been mine.

I wrote him into my script. The first few pages follow.

Fade in from black

A small cottage in the bush near Camden, NSW. A MAN in civilian dress is tending a garden or small field in the middle- ground. There are mountains in the far distance.
Occasional native bird-calls.

Moving closer to the cottage we lose sight of the man in the garden.

Very faintly at first, getting slightly louder as we approach the cottage, the scratching sound of a quill pen is heard.
Seen through a window of the cottage G.T.W.B. BOYES is writing a letter.

As Boyes writes the sound of his quill is heard louder now.

Sub-title: NEW SOUTH WALES, MARCH 16th., 1824

Boyes is now seen from the front, in close-up. He pauses in his writing, chews the end of his quill.

Sub-title: DEPUTY ASS'T. COMMISSARY GENERAL GEO. THOS. WM. BLAYNEY BOYES.

He begins to write again, and his hand and quill are seen briefly in C.U.

Boyes (voice-over): I am off to Sydney the day after tomorrow and have bidden adieu to my favorite river and its rocky banks, …

Tracking shot through wet bush. C.U's. of native plants after rain.

Boyes (voice-over continues): … and considering how many hours I have spent in rambling about the Nepean I cannot think of my departure with indifference. After raining heavily it cleared up this afternoon the lichens, the mosses, the Myrtles and Mimosas melted into balmy drops as I passed them each shrub shook fragrance on my head and perfumed my path.

Colour still photographs of bush scenes.

*The screen splits to show different images in two equal half frames, side by side*______________________

Left: L.S. Boyes climbs down a steep bank towards the Nepean.

Right: Home movie of a small [motor] boat on a creek, slowed to about ¼ speed.

*Full screen*____

A view across the Nepean river. The figures in this scene are distant though distinct. It is essentially a landscape with figures. The light is hard and clear. On the far bank Boyes removes his clothes and jumps in the water. While he is splashing about a ragged convict, wearing ankle chains, shuffles by. Boyes does not notice the convict, but the convict stares at Boyes.

Boyes *(voice-over continues): In these wild sequestered scenes there is nothing to remind you of England of animals, you meet with the Wallaby, the Kangaroo Rat, the Native Dog, the O'Possum, and the Native Cat, all differing from those of our country. The woods swarm with birds whose notes are entirely new to the European ear and are as various as they are discordant sometimes when I have been bathing in the Nepean River these feathered savages have set up all at once such yelling screams, shouting and laughter, that 50 natives, from whom perhaps they acquired their notes, could not have exceeded them.*

Distant sounds of native birds and the sounds of the convict's chains are heard beneath the voice.

Still photograph of boys fishing and swimming.

*Split screen*____

Left: Inside the cottage, Boyes continues his letter-writing. The room is lit only from the window and is barely furnished. There are several bookcases and one or two framed watercolour sketches on the walls.

Right: A small car in the bush. (From videotape.)

Boyes (voice-over continues): The mornings are fresh and sunny at every turn I discover something new in the prospect, or the same prospect seen under different feelings there will be everything in this colony in time except plenty of water and honest men.

Main Title (written as though with a quill pen, in dark blue ink on creamy paper):

PLENTY OF WATER AND HONEST MEN

The various interpolations and juxtapositions in the script represent my own point of view. I wrote the script for myself to direct and didn't feel the need to explain sub-texts. This may have made the script a bit more difficult to read, but I also knew that the difference between readings from the page and the screen is a product of skilled editing, which I also assumed I would be doing.

The main body of the script dealt with events in and around the tiny settlement of Port Jackson. It includes the relations between Aborigines and the English, showing a particularly galling debacle for the English, taken from the memoirs of Watkin Tench. From Tench, also, there is a cryptic account of a meeting between Tench and a young Aboriginal woman. There are scenes depicting the attempts by a few of the more intelligent officers to understand the environment they have occupied on the orders of the British government. There are two bloody battle scenes, one in Ireland, one in NSW which leads to reprisals that virtually bring to an end any thoughts of further organised rebellion by convicts.

All of that, based on many historical documents, was "book-ended" by the opening and closing scenes. The closing scene runs as follows:

Two men are riding in a horse-drawn sulky. One is G.T.W.B. Boyes, the other, MR. D'ARRIETTA, is thin, with dark hair,dark intense eyes and a deep suntan. Boyes is more relaxed.

The sulky bumps over large stones and deep wheel-ruts so that it is difficult to keep one's seat, let alone conduct a conversation. Nevertheless, Boyes and D'Arrietta do manage both things.

<u>Boyes</u>: It is a wonder (bump) -- it is a wonder to me, Mr.D'Arrietta (bump) that the revolutionary spirit of Europe (bump) has not taken hold (bump bump bump) -- has not taken hold here in a way it could not do in the Mother Country.

<u>D'Arrietta</u>: I do not understand (bump) -- I do not understand you.

<u>Boyes</u>: Well -- (bump) there must be, to begin with, a great proportion of people here with many grudges against Government(bump bump).

<u>D'Arrietta</u>: (bump) That is very true.

<u>Boyes</u>: Then, there are these vast forests that cover almost the entire land, it seems, (bump) which could never (bump) be fully patrolled (bump) even by all the armies of Europe. The lower people (bump bump bump) -- the lower people here are so deprived of advantages (bump) that one would think they have nothing (bump) to lose at all by taking to the forests in large bands (bump bump) -- in large bands that could descend on the military (bump) at a time of their own choosing.

<u>D'Arrietta</u>: Ah, Mr. Boyes -- they have tried it (bump).several times they have tried it. (bump) But always (bump)always it was a failure. (bump) They do not plan properly --and the plans they do make (bump) the plans -- there are always informers. (bump bump) The punishments! -- they are so awful (bump) you cannot imagine -- for most of them they think(bump) they think it is better to wait till they get emancipated and then get back to England (bump bump) as quick as possible. (bump bump bump) Those that do stay, they can make(bump) a lot of money (bump) one way or another -- or the rebellious ones (bump) they go into the bush (bump) and rob people (bump) whenever they can -- but they do it by themselves.That way (bump) that way nobody can tell their plans,at least. (bump) They are called bushrangers. (bump)

<u>Boyes</u>: Bushrangers? (bump) They are like (bump) like highwaymen then?

<u>D'Arrietta</u>: Yes. (bump) But they are called bushrangers here(bump) because there are no highways, only bush …

D'Arrietta has talked himself into a state of apprehension about bushrangers. The bumps lessen as they enter a softer, smoother part of the track.

<u>D'Arrietta</u>: … er, Mr. Boyes, are your pistols in good order --there is much danger of bushrangers in these very places we are going now. I could tell you horrible stories of what they do to peoples.

The gig travels on down the track, going smoothly now.

Home movie footage, blown up to full screen, of a comical[1970s] enactment of a bushranger scene.

Fade to black.

Boyes is again writing in his journal.

<u>Boyes</u> (V.O.): Mr. D'Arrietta has been so kind as to invite me to stay here on his farm for as long as I wish…

The scene shifts to a dinner party where Boyes, D'Arrietta and another man, DR. RUMKER, are eating a hearty meal of roast beef and a variety of vegetables around a table covered by a crisp white tablecloth. A single elegant lamp hangs over thetable.

A convict servant -- wearing a uniform of unbleached calico, starched and neatly pressed, buttoned right to the throat, and printed all over with stark government arrows -- comes forward to remove an empty wine bottle. Before he takes it he refills the mens' glasses from a new bottle. He behaves like a perfect waiter.

Boyes' narration continues over this scene.

<u>Boyes</u> (V.O.): … I expect I shall be staying here for a month or so. I am waiting for a house to become vacant before I take up my appointment. The Governor has played me such a dirty trick about an office that I had fully determined to return to England, when Lithgow arrived. Mr. Balcombe, who was sent out as

Colonial Treasurer, has not been acting at all like an English gentleman …

The narration now shifts seamlessly into naturalistic dinner table conversation.

<u>Boyes</u>: … He has taken the only eligible house for an office,after I had come to regular terms with the proprietor, and,what is more extraordinary, the Governor, who between ourselves is a great fool, has lent his name to the proceeding.

Rumker butts in, speaking with a heavy German accent. He is exceptionally untidy, his clothes are threadbare, his black hair very long and uncombed, his beard halfway down his chest.

<u>Rumker</u>: Ach! I could tell you some things about these Governors. I was once staying with Sir Thomas Brisbane when he insisted I should join him on a shooting party …

D'Arrietta laughs -- he knows the story.

<u>Rumker</u>: … Ach! Ja! You can laugh! Now, you know I have no love for the sport, and besides I did not know how to shoot,and besides I never fire off the gun in my life that I know of …

*As Rumker continues the screen splits*____

Left: The dinner party continues.

<u>Rumker</u>: … As we were going along we saw two magpie sitting on the tree. They were evidently man and wife. The Governor raised up the gun to give fire and kill one of the birds --Sir Thomas, he shoots very well. By god, I was so shocked at that, I threw down my shot belt, that he made me bring, and stamped about like mad. I never liked him since.

Boyes and D'Arrietta are greatly amused by Rumker's tale. By the end they are laughing uproariously.

Right: A montage of hangings, getting closer each shot.

Convicts with ropes around their necks. As they drop out of frame the ropes jerk tight. On the final drop the rope snaps.

This to synchronise with Rumker's words: "never liked him since" so that the laughter from the dinner party could be a reaction to the snapped rope.

*Full screen*____________________________________

The convict/servant is clearing away the plates. The laughter continues. Even the convict is amused. Rumker is bewildered.Boyes changes the subject.

<u>Boyes</u>: By God, D'Arrietta, this wine of yours certainly improves with drinking!

They all laugh then and D'Arrietta fills their glasses again.

Fade to black.

*Split screen*____________________________________

Left: Boyes is walking in the bush in the early morning, looking at plants, flowers, birds. He carries sheets of drawing paper and pencils.

Right: Shots from videotape of people in present-day Botanic Gardens, Sydney. Adults sit in the sun, some feeding the birds. Children play.Bush atmosphere, bird calls, insects etc. (for both halves of screen).

Left: Boyes sits on a rock, considers making a sketch. He looks up to a sound overhead. Bush sounds continue. Mix in the sound of a helicopter, quite loud as Boyes looks up.

Right: Reflections of plants in water and shots walking amongst tropical plants in the Botanic Gardens. These shots will be richly coloured by lab processes. The colours will be entirely un-naturalistic.

*Full frame*____________________________________

Boyes sitting on his rock. Behind him D'Arrietta comes out of the bush, startling him.

<u>D'Arrietta</u>: What are you thinking about?

Helicopter and bush sound begin to fade.
Full frame blow-up from videotape, C.U. Sally Haines.

Sub-title: SALLY HAINES, SYDNEY 1974.

From behind the camera [the Narrator] tells Sally about plans to make this movie and asks her if her parents talk about the arrival of Europeans in Australia. She dismisses the question and wants to talk about something else.

Full frame blow-up from videotape of Sally's sister, Brenda, standing in a bleak street eating an apple. Her clothes flap in the wind. All movements to be slowed to about one quarter natural speed by step-printing. The image is further processed photographically to produce a very harsh quality in tones of black, inky blue-black, blue, blue-green and white.
Bird calls, running water, children playing, distant traffic,and the fading sound of the helicopter.

Hold this shot for some time.

Very softly, the sound of wind.

Slow fade to black.

It's a sad fact - sad to me anyhow - that the film will never be made, at least not in the form outlined in the original script. Firstly its start was delayed by other things I was doing. By the time I should have been ready to start it, its time had well and truly passed. A number of movies about "white" Australia's history had already been made (although none in the way I was planning), the political situation had been turned on its head and thus the politics of film funding. And I found myself in a situation where I suffered something like depression, which I think was independent of politics.

When I finished the script I went back on the dole again. I knew of no possiblity then for a supporting parent's pension for men. Around this time Kay and I started living together when we moved to a small two storey house in Balmain. Although I think that Rachael sometimes felt

Kay was too strict with her - stricter than I was, that is - they formed a close relationship.

Before I moved away from Sue's, I had been thinking that I should brave Judy's anger and get in touch with our children. It seemed awful that I was now living in the same city and didn't have anything to do with them. My conflict was with Judy, not the children. I talked with Sue about it and I now think it's very strange that she advised me not to make contact. I don't know what her rationale was, I suppose she perceived that Judy could have had me put in gaol, although I can't see what that would have achieved, other than revenge; I was virtually penniless. The children were all teenagers by then and I can only speculate on how much better it would have been for all of us if I'd followed my first impulse and made contact. As it turned out it was seven or eight years more before Caitlin rang me up out of the blue and took the responsibility out of my hands.

In 1975 I applied for and was appointed to a position as "Film and Video Artist-in-Residence" at Griffith University in Brisbane. Professor Val Presley of the Humanities Department had ambitious plans to establish a place where students could do creative work outside of any academic structures, where they could just experiment with the media. Professor Presley had already organised the building of a large shed a little way from the main University building, under trees at the edge of the bushland that surrounded the campus. If I remember correctly the University flew me up to Brisbane to have a look around. Enthused, I came back to Sydney to draw up plans and to go on a shopping spree for equipment.

It was made clear to me, however, that I would have to put *Plenty of Water and Honest Men* on hold.

Queensland ...

Queensland had, when we went there, an atmosphere with some similarities to what I imagine Franco's Spain might have been like. Run by an ageing autocrat by the name of Joh Bjelke-Petersen, Queensland had, if you didn't scratch too deeply, a comfortably relaxed atmosphere. There were, however, murky undercurrents. I had an intimation of these before I left Sydney: I was in a bank, opening an account in which to receive my salary, when I heard that Malcolm Fraser had deposed the unfortunate Billy Sneddon as leader of the federal Liberal Party. The man who gave this news to customers and staff at large predicted that Fraser would be Prime Minister within six months. What he knew I don't know, but his prediction was accurate to within a week.

Griffith University was the first place I'd worked where I had to carry an ID card. I must have been very impressed by that. I've kept the card ever since. In 2004, looking at the image on it makes me wonder if any university now would employ such a "bolshie" looking person..

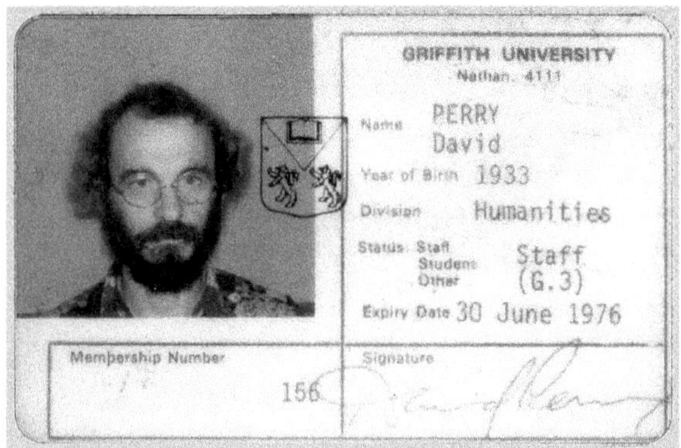

DP's ID card at Griffith University (photographer unknown), 1975

The Creative Arts Workshop, as the shed at Griffith was called, proved to be a very congenial place to work. When I arrived a carpenter and electrician were putting the finishing touches to the wiring and the

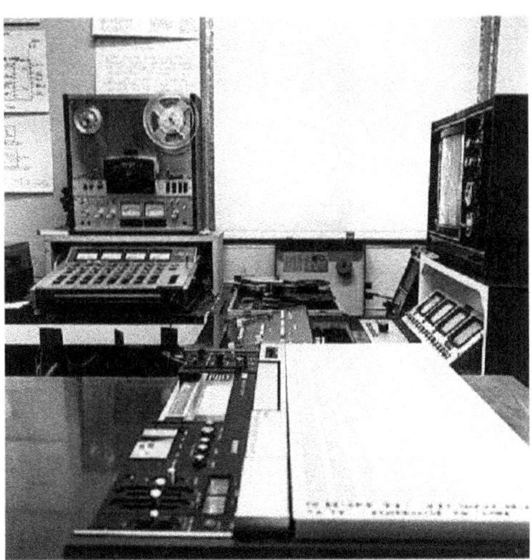

Side and front views of the equipment in place, Griffith Creative Arts Workshop, 1975

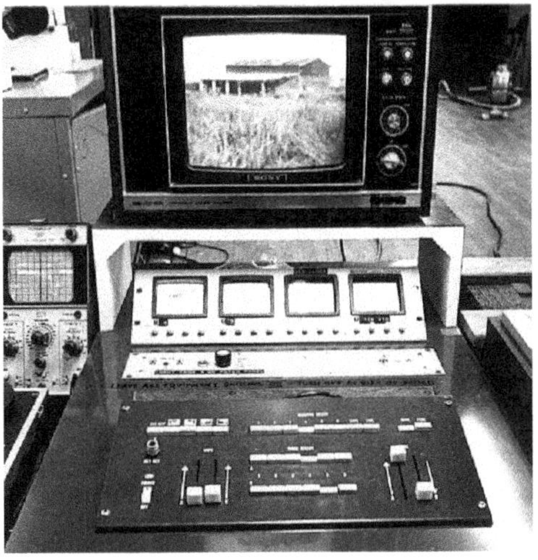

elaborate work bench that I'd designed. The electrician was amazed by the huge number, as he saw it, of power points needed.

By the time I'd installed most of the gear, with a lot of help from Kay, I gave her a crash course in soldering electronic connections and making up cables.

But after working for six months or so, although I had worked out a reasonably effective way of manually editing video images with the help of a stop-watch, I had to admit, to myself at least, that it couldn't approach film editing. I could never get closer to around a quarter to a half-second accuracy. Anyone who had tried it found the same, with the result that editing systems soon came on the market claiming plus or minus two frames accuracy. But even that is not really good enough. You really have to have frame-accurate edits, every time. Very expensive systems could manage that but more ordinary gear, which I often worked on subsequently, was extremely frustrating. It was only when computer based "non-linear editing" became available that videotape became a real competitor to film as a production medium.

I had to accept that I'd chosen video over film for the Griffith workshop way before its time. When I accepted its limitations, however, I came up with a short video piece that has stood the test of time and is still, I think, fairly highly regarded: *Interior with Views*.

The first thing I made at Griffith was a piece called *A TV Show,* in which I took advantage of the ability of portable videotape to gather large amounts of imagery and sound in various exteriors, including at night-time political demonstrations. I also recorded some off-air material, mostly news coverage of events leading up to the dismissal of the Labor Government and the subsequent election of Malcolm Fraser's Liberal Party with the Country Party (or was it by then the "National" Party) carried along in their wake. That of course was what the man in my bank in Sydney had predicted six months before. Whether or not *A TV Show* was an effective documentary (I don't think it was - too long and rambling), it is an interesting personal record of an extremely unsettled and unsettling time in Australia's politics. The events themselves left many people shattered. I was so stunned that I went home and cleaned and vacuumed every part of our house. Much later I met a man who said the only time in his life when he'd been happy was the three years when the Labor government was in power. I could have suggested that he "get a life" but that would have been too cruel. I have often thought that I was very lucky to have Rachael with me because the responsibility that my parenthood put on me, in spite of my lassez-faire attitude, obliged me at least to try to be a bit realistic and not to get entirely carried away by excesses of political or artistic adventurism, romanticism or whatever else a more bourgeois person might judge it. However, sexual adventurism was my greatest vulnerability. I have always loved making love and have always scorned any moralism, secular or religious, that constrained how or with whom love could be made.

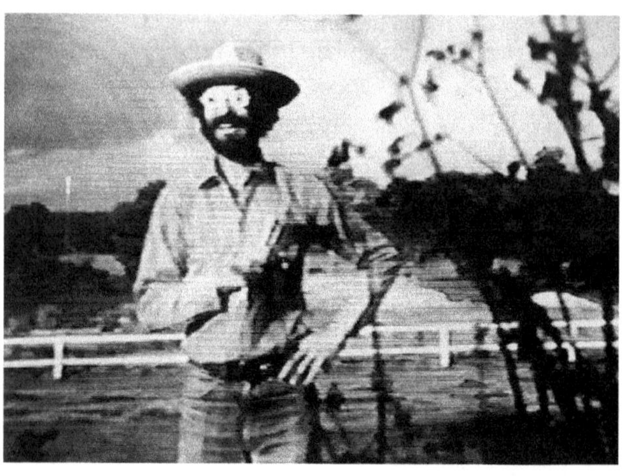

Screen shot from A TV Show, *1976*

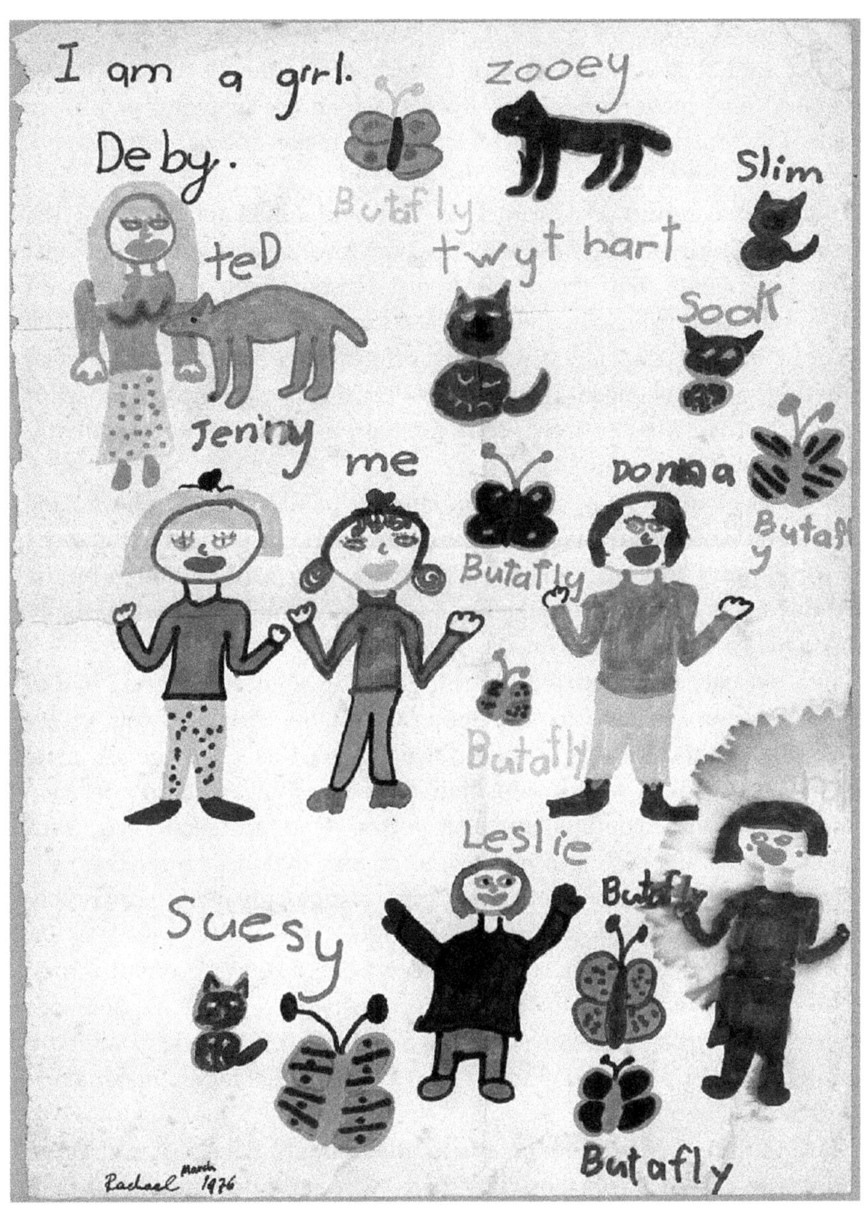

Me and my Friends, *drawn by Rachael, 1971 (dated in DP's handwriting)*

That said, I have known since I reached adulthood[8] that to "make love" can also make bonds (not always) which are (usually) painful to break. Obviously "making love" can also make babies (equally not always).

Before we moved to Queensland Kay and I had talked about the number of children I had fathered. I had obviously exceeded my personal "replacement rate" and thought I should do something about it. Since I was not about to consider giving up sex I had to find another way. The Family Planning Association was then offering free vasectomies to men in Sydney and Kay encouraged me to follow this up. We saw a counsellor who agreed we were entirely ready for the procedure and consequently arranged for it to be done.

My vasectomy was, as promised, entirely painless - at first. After the anaesthetic wore off it was a very different story. For the rest of the day I felt as though I had been kicked in the balls, very hard, although by the next day I was fine and from then on I was able to make love without any anxiety whatever about causing pregnancy.

Kay actually recorded the entire procedure with a portapak, in full frontal close-up (I have to say, though, that her shooting was pretty wobbly). At the Griffith workshop we edited Kay's footage. A male documentary maker, who was visiting at the time, did an audio interview with me to serve as commentary. This person, who incidentally has never acknowledged any virtue in my way(s) of film making, revealed a very widespread male anxiety about vasectomy being equivalent to castration. No amount of reassurance by me got through.

My year at Griffith proved to be a good one. I didn't produce a high volume of memorable work although in retrospect I am very pleased with *Interior with Views,* and with the large volume of material I shot on portapak and Super 8 that may yet prove to be valuable raw material for future work.

I don't think I gave as much attention as I might have to encouraging students to use the workshop, but there were no guidelines about that. Another factor that might have limited the number of students coming to the workshop is that there were no fine arts courses at Griffith that

[8] There are probably people who will say that I have never reached adulthood. I can hear them now, but have no intention of getting involved in arguments about it.

actually involved the making of art. There may well have been academic degrees offered but in the nature of such things practical creativity rarely seems to get much of a look-in. Of course, Griffith, like many other universities, had an extensive and valuable collection of modern

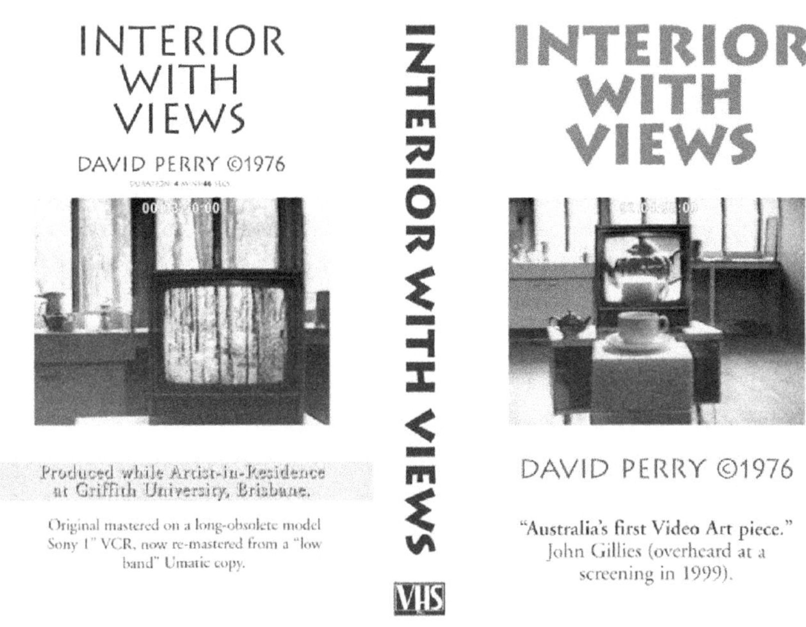

Videocassette cover design for Interior with Views, c.2000

Australian paintings. One evening soon after we arrived, the Vice-Chancellor and his wife showed Kay and me over the collection. The lights had been turned off (to save money?) and no one knew how to get them on, so our hosts were obliged to use cigarette lighters to illuminate the paintings.

As the end of my year's contract got closer I was approached by two academics from Darling Downs Institute of Advanced Education. These two men knew of my work and urged me to take a post that had become vacant: Lecturer in Film and Video within the School of Arts. (One should be very wary of any department with "Film and Video" in its name. What that usually signifies is that students will have access to limited and indifferent video equipment, but little or no access to professional quality film equipment. That's certainly what I found after I started at DDIAE.)

DDIAE ...

The Darling Downs Institute of Advanced Education, long since renamed the University of Southern Queensland (USQ), was on the outskirts of the large rural city of Toowoomba, capital of a very wealthy farming region, the Darling Downs. As you might imagine, the whole region, including Toowoomba, is very conservative.

I inherited a course structure designed by others. That's hardly surprising and as time went by I made submissions to the Board of Studies that put my stamp on things. Most importantly, I was able to order and install equipment away from the control of the ultra-conservative technicians who ruled the ill-equipped "resource centre", where the expression of any kind of creativity was scorned and derided.

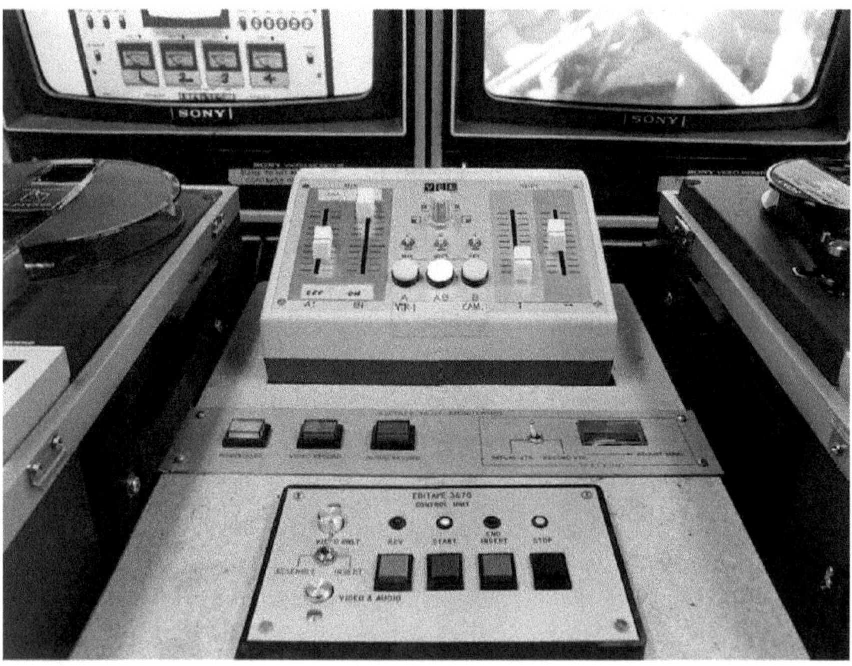

Half-inch video editing system at DDIAE, 1977

With newly available video editing equipment I set up a practical unit that went some way towards serving the needs of my students, of whom I had many, doing courses in school teaching, journalism, humanities and fine arts. (One of my fine arts students, John Gillies, went on to become head of the media department at the College of Fine Arts at UNSW. It's his quote on the videocassette label on p.183.)

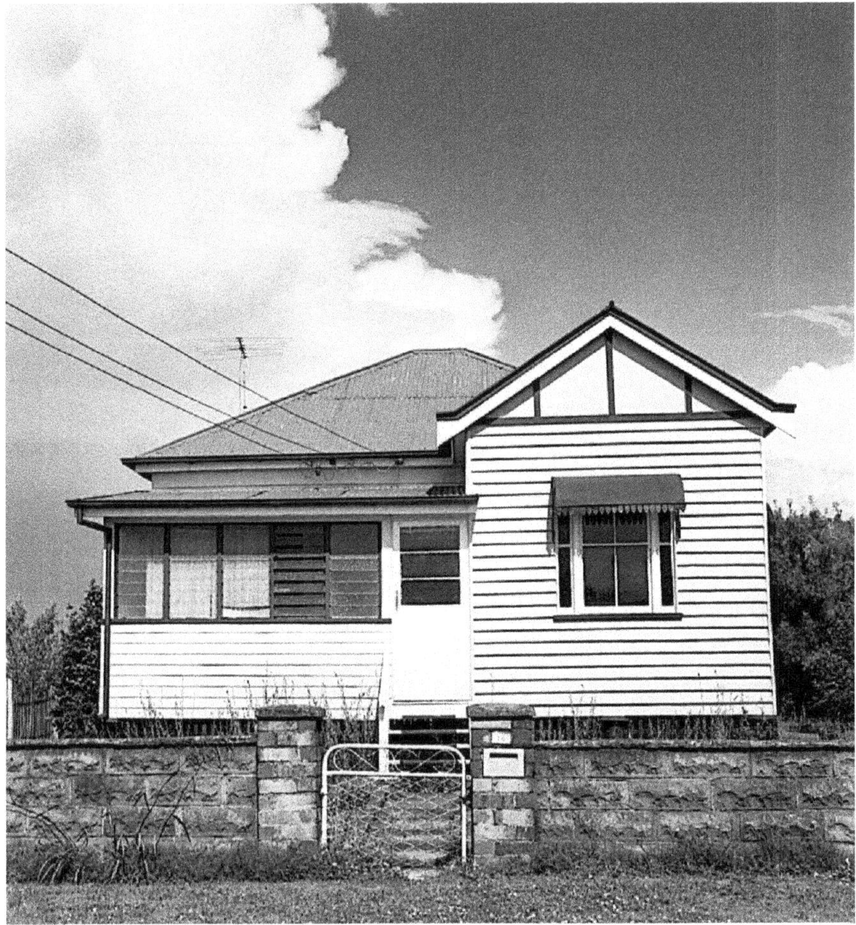

Our House in Bothwell Street, Tooowoomba, 1976

In advance of taking up the job in Toowoomba, we rented a house in Bothwell Street. It was a perfectly adequate place, if somewhat spartan. Being about 1,000 ft above sea level, Toowoomba can get very cold, even though it is on a similar latitude to Brisbane. Thus we needed as much heating as possible at night.. In the picture on the next page Kay is huddling close to a kerosene heater. These things were probably quite dangerous although safe enough if you treated them with respect.

The paintings on the wall are: on the left and mostly hidden, one from my exhibition at the Rocks Gallery before Abby and I went to England; and, behind Kay, a painting of a butchered tree, an image of my discomfort in London.

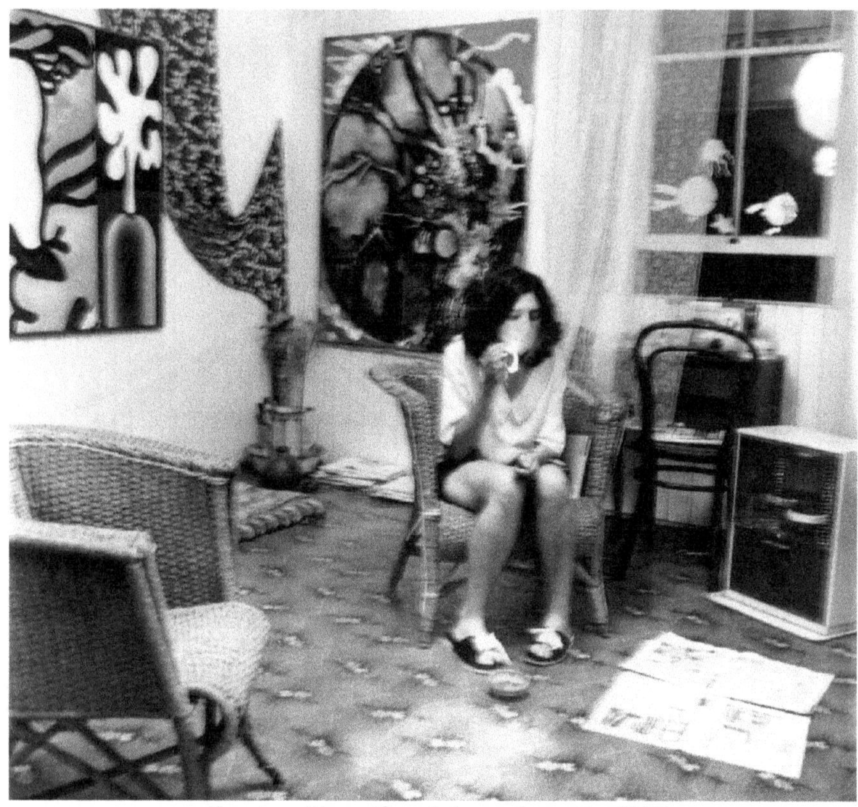

Kay, in cold weather, lights a cigarette, 1976

On the advice of my boss at the Institute, Robert Gist, we had enrolled Rachael in a very good state school named Gabbinbah, out on one of the corners of the grid of streets that was Toowoomba (it must be impossible to get lost there). Gabbinbah was good for Rachael, she made good friends with other girls there and did very well in her classes. (The weather must have warmed up by the time Kay took the picture on the next page.)

While still at the Griffith Workshop I had bought a secondhand Karmann Ghia (page 188). This car - built on a Volkswagen chassis and with a VW engine - had an enormous appeal to me. I saw it as a poor person's Porsche. In Toowoomba I compounded the romance of that by having the original, ugly orange paintwork redone to a shiny military green on the body and a white top to deflect the Queensland sun. I had some bizarre fantasy that I was the commander of a partisan detachment and this was my staff car. At one point I considered having a red star painted on the bonnet. It's a good thing I didn't, I might have been lynched. The region around Toowoomba, particularly, was home to radically conservative politics. There were a lot of guns there too. One weekend we heard a commotion on the street. Looking from our front door we saw a whole family - Mum and Dad plus the kids - all urgently bundling many rifles and shotguns into the back of their station wagon.

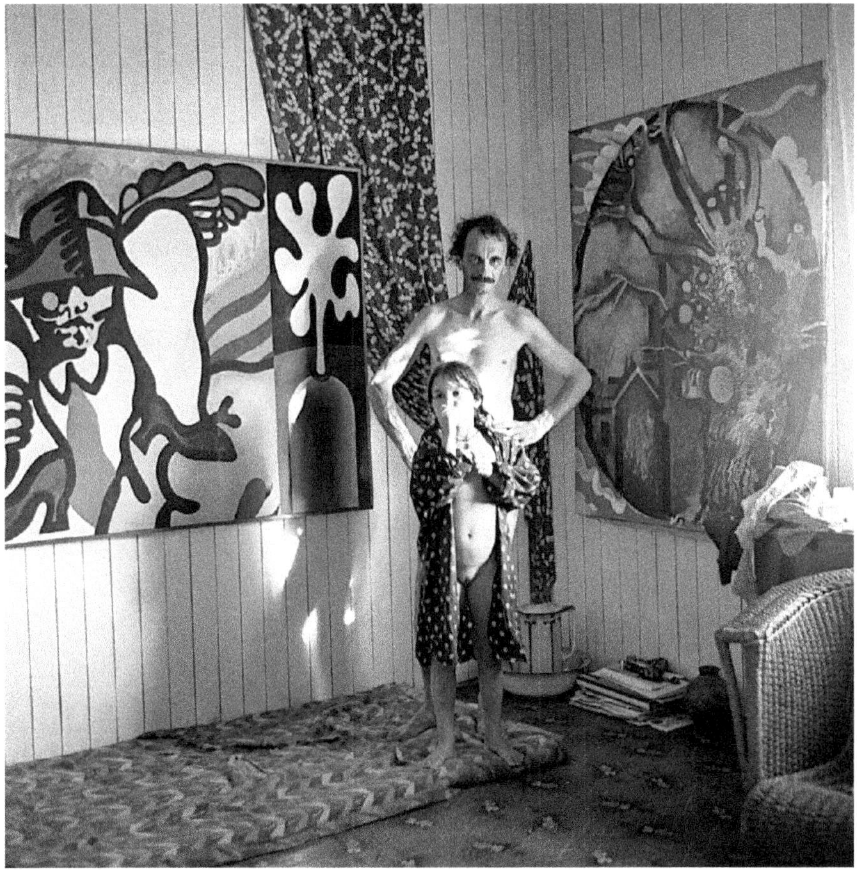

DP with Rachael, (photo by Kay Comino), c. 1976

They seemed a bit worried about something and we immediately fantasised that they had been warned of an imminent police raid looking for unregistered firearms. I think we could have been correct.

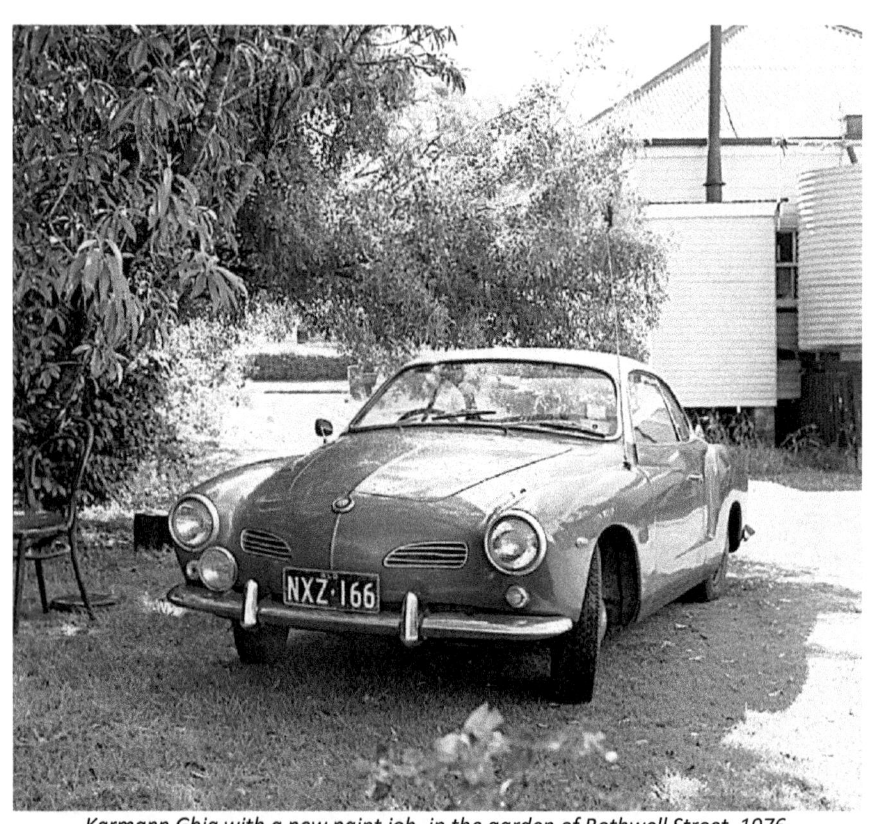

Karmann Ghia with a new paint job, in the garden of Bothwell Street, 1976

Home ownership made easy...

Having a tenured academic position, which I did, had the benefit of making it easy to borrow money. By 1977 I was earning enough to pay off a mortgage. For our deposit we borrowed some money from Kay's parents and my credit card. Then, to qualify as borrowers of most of the purchase price, we only had to answer two questions at the Toowoomba Building Society: "Where do you work?" and "How much do you earn?" No other questions, literally!

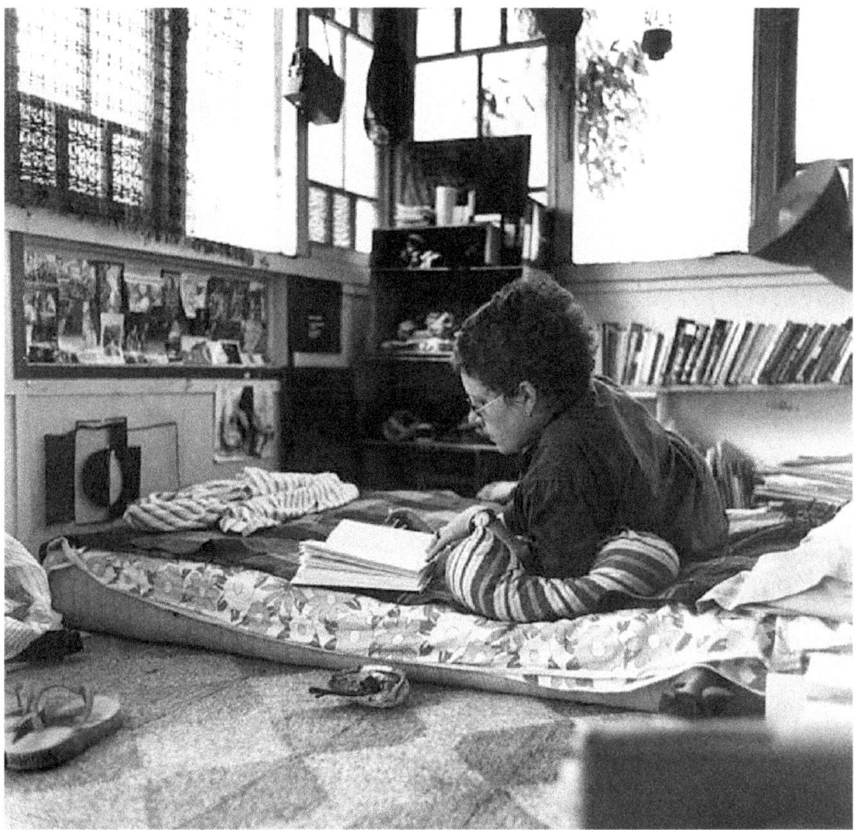

Lou on the verandah, c.1977

In a flash we were out on the street and around to the estate agent to get the keys to the small but nice "Queenslander".[9]

---

[9]A "Queenslander" is a single-storey weatherboard house raised up on brick stilts high enough to create a cool, usable space under the house. I couldn't find

We painted the house inside and out, put down "sea-grass" matting, and made the enclosed front verandah into a bedroom which we rented to Lou Hubbard, a fine arts (painting) student at the Institute.

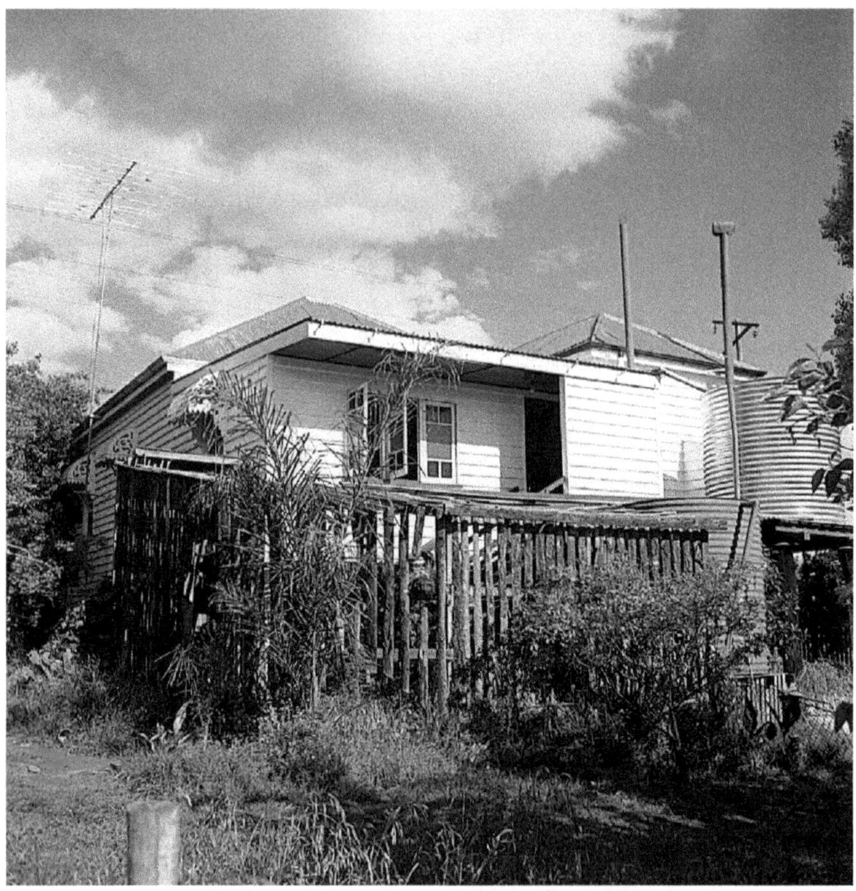

Our house in Mary Street, Toowoomba, c. 1 977

"Queenslander"- the house – in the Macquarie Dictionary although I think it should be there, along with "Under-the-House", which, as I understand it, is a specific location in the language of Queenslanders, the people, who *are* in the Dictionary.

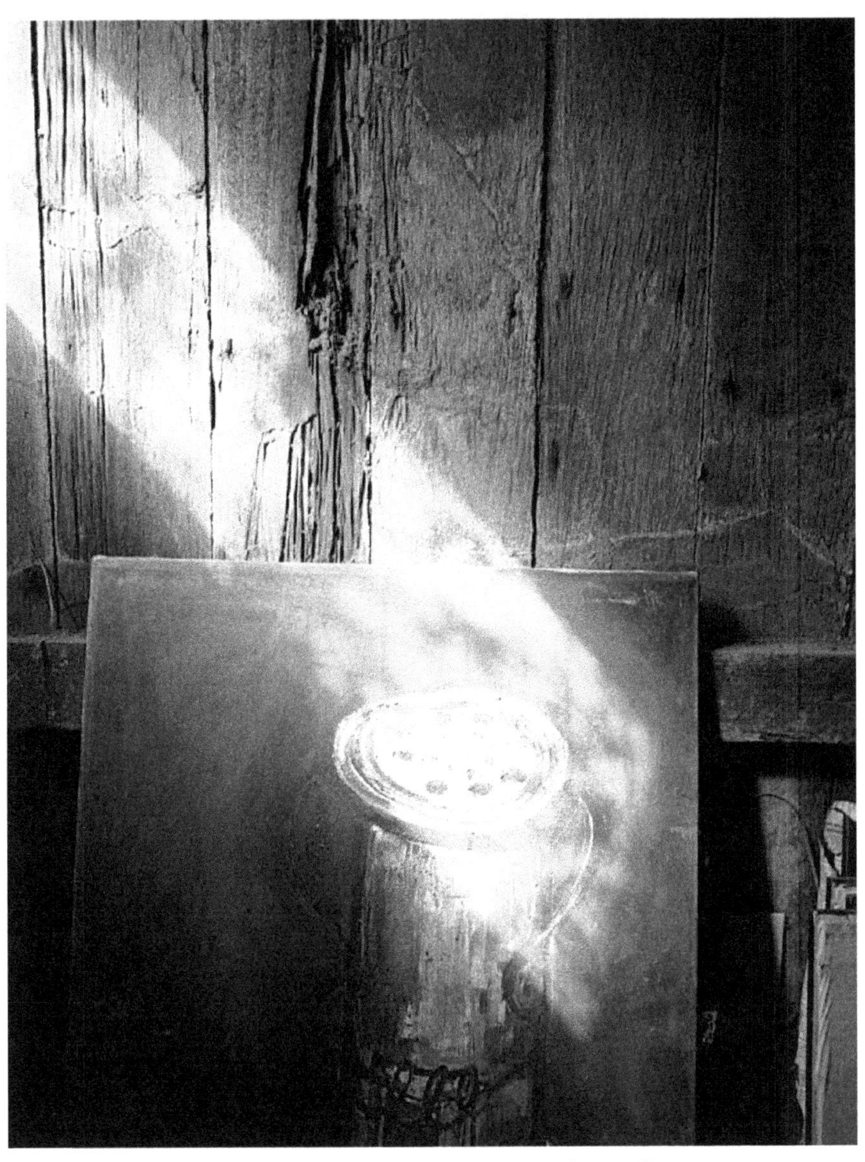

Under-the-house, Mary Street (old painting [c.1952]) , 1977

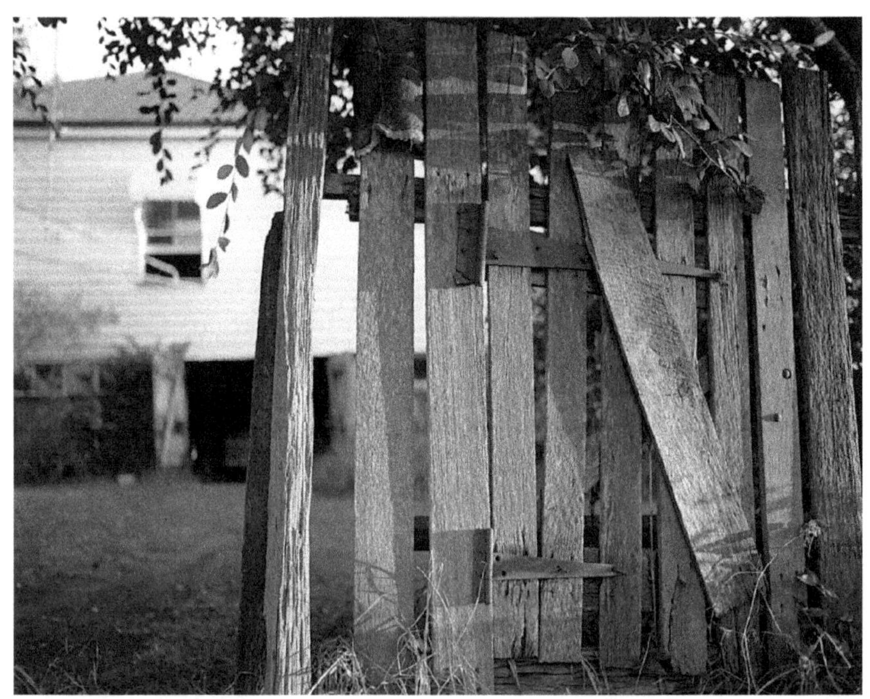

Side view, Mary Street ("under-the-house" half hidden by fence), c. 1977

Toowoomban politics ...

Politics in most parts of Queensland, particularly in Toowoomba, were conservative and paternalistic. Premier Joh Bjelke-Petersen knew what was best for the state and would tolerate no political protest at all. He scorned journalists and called the processes of press conferences "feeding the chooks". Pressed for answers to questions he often replied: "Don't you worry about that."

However, at universities, colleges

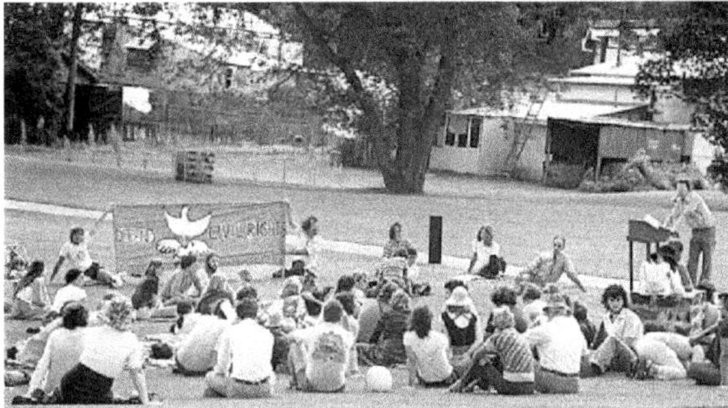

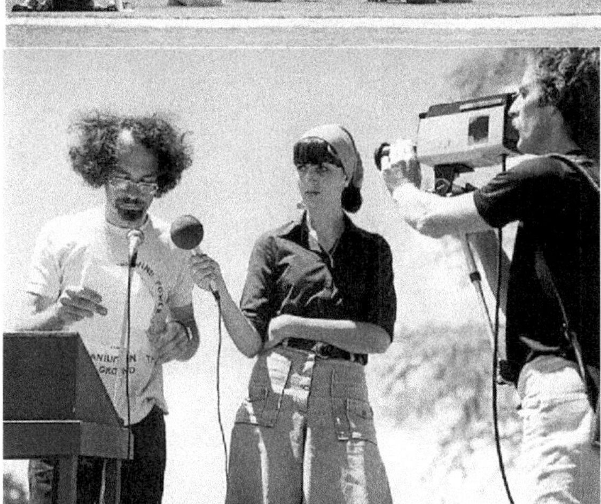

All photographs on this page – Protestors in Queens Park , Toowoomba, 1977

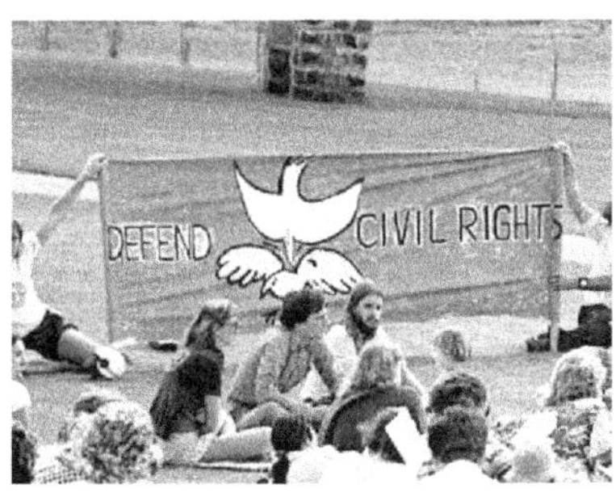

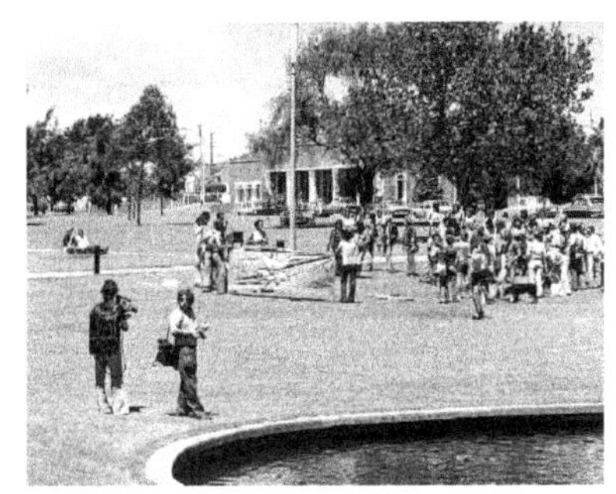

and DDIAE there were academics and students who, as you'd hope, protested about this. Of course, protesting, particularly in street marches, was severely restricted or, in effect, totally prohibited. At DDIAE a march was organised to protest about not being allowed to protest. Most of the people at the march were students and staff of the Institute. I painted a banner to be carried at the head of the march, having little doubt that it would be confiscated. The image on the banner was a crude reworking of the images from my 1964 film *Swansong in Birdland.*

As we expected, as soon as the banner was out on the street the cops moved in to confiscate it.

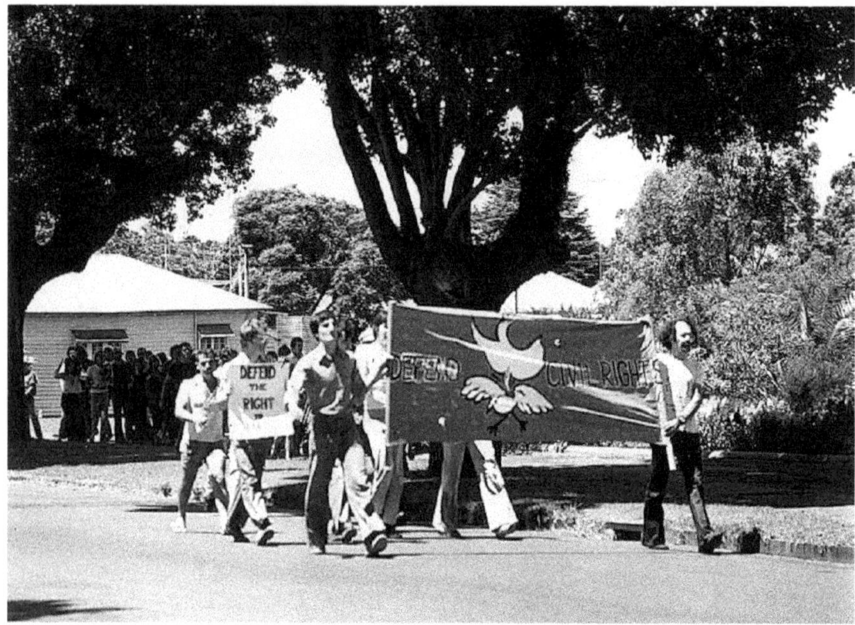

Carrying the banner out of Queens Park, 1977

I can't find the final shot from this sequence. It shows a senior cop grabbing the banner while the cameraman from the local TV station records the proceedings. This justified the whole exercise.

The pictures on these last two pages show a handful of people protesting against the political climate of the region, but that climate didn't really change - still hasn't. Much later, Pauline Hanson, a shopkeeper from Ipswich, a small town between Toowoomba and Brisbane, was elected to the Senate and began a campaign to glorify ignorance and every kind of prejudice. Joh Bjelke-Petersen might be long gone from the scene but his ghost lingers on into the present.

It seems to me that the prediction of G.T.W.B. Boyes is still true, that there'll always "be everything in this country except *plenty of water and honest men.*"

Around that time I involved many of my students in a production of Sophocles' Antigone. I had read E.V. Rieu's translation when I was very young, and have always loved the story. We did it in modern dress and in modern English in various locations around Toowoomba as well as in the "studio" of the dreaded Education Resource Centre. One of my students had a passing resemblance to Malcolm Fraser, the Prime Minister who deposed Gough Whitlam - an event ever so lightly touched on previously - so I asked this young man to play Creon, usurper of the Crown of Thebes, modelling his performance on Fraser. It was, I think, one of the best bits of casting in the production. There was a large and quite good drama department at the Institute and I drew on many of the students of that department who were also my students. Maybe I should have involved one or more of the lecturers as well to help with coaching the actors. I don't mind admitting that I was a bit out of my depth when it came to directing actors. I was, and am, more comfortable directing documentaries. There's no doubt that I wanted my *Antigone* to look like a documentary.

Having said that, perhaps the best bit of casting was in making the Chorus a single actor, playing the role as if a modern journalist addressing/warning King Creon from a video monitor. It's remarkable that for this to work I had to change very little of Sophocles' text. I suppose I cut quite a lot, but what I did use was remarkably effective.

Another part of this production that I remember fondly was the location for the "cave" where Antigone had been sealed up to die. For that we used a concrete tower projecting from the water of a large dam near Toowoomba. Creon, having relented, comes to release Antigone from the cave. He runs across a walkway over the dam to be met at the open door of the tower/cave by his son, Haemon, Antigone's lover, carrying Antigone's body. As in the original, she has pre-empted Creon by killing herself in the cave. Haemon then kills himself.

It's probably a good thing that this production was finished on the notoriously impermanent half-inch videotape. Apart from the bits I've described, the whole production was (how shall I put it?) not very good.

Abby comes to Toowoomba ...

Abby and I had kept up frequent correspondence and we arranged for her to visit us. I was still secretly, I suppose, in love with her when I met her and Homer off the plane at Brisbane. They must have been exhausted from the flight when I bundled them into the Karmann Ghia for the long drive back to Toowoomba. Rachael was with me and she and Homer rode in the back. I can't remember anything that was said during that trip and I can't remember what my feelings were like. Confused, no doubt.

Before they came I built double bunks for Rachael and Homer from hardwood planks fastened with bolts; it was incredibly solid. It would have lasted forever. It seems at this distance in memory that Rachael and Homer resumed the good friendship they had in London, as if they'd never been parted, although I can find no photographs from that time.

I think I've blanked most of it from my memory which makes me think I was having a hard time dealing with the situation. I don't think I knew what to say to anyone. No doubt that helps to explain why Abby, who always had plenty to say to everyone, eventually exploded in a tirade of abuse at me. It went on for a very long time, but what was it about? All my failings as a parent, of course, although I can't detail them now. I don't think I made any attempt to defend myself.

Perhaps too, although it's the one thing that Abby would not have admitted to herself and I have no material evidence for this I mean that she may have been jealous. Kay and I had a vigorous sex life and I'm sure that we weren't discreet about it. Abby must have heard us. I can only think how distressed I would have been if the situations were reversed.

Our argument can't have been pleasant for Kay, either. She took the children out into the garden and kept them occupied, but half of Toowoomba would have been entertained, horrified, or enlightened by what they must have heard. It may have been as soon as the day after Abby's blow-up that she took Homer back to England. That, of course, wasn't because of what had happened; the bookings had been made from the start.

I took Abby and Homer back to Brisbane and delivered them to the airport. On the way we stopped for a little while, had a cup of tea and talked amicably. I don't think much of import was said, I suppose from

Abby's point of view it had all been said. After she and Homer went into the departure lounge I drove my car around to the side of the airport, where in those days in Brisbane passengers entered planes by steps out in the open. Abby and Homer didn't know I was there but I watched as they climbed wearily into the jumbo-jet.

I've always felt, somewhere in the back of my mind, that Abby may have come to Toowoomba to see if there was a chance of us being re-united in some way; more likely, to take Rachael back to England with her. I know she was desperately unhappy about being separated from Rachael.

But both of us had made our beds and would have to lie in them. And Abby had a lover in London whom she subsequently married. It's amazing how everything changed after that visit.

I start to "lose it"in Toowoomba ...

My life was beginning to fall apart. Let's just say I was becoming unstable, again. Work at the Institute was unsatisfyng. I was isolated, the only person there teaching film. Perhaps the worst of it was that I wasn't doing any of the work that I was teaching. I was out of touch with what others in the field were doing. And although I kept up with what was happening in politics I was not a political activist. I could never get involved. As in London I remained detached. I was effectively an unemployed artist, even if I was getting a good income.

And I was drinking too much. Kay knew that I should get out of there, even if I had no idea what to do about it. Then Kay left Toowoomba to go to Sydney for a while. It became obvious later that she hoped this would force me also to leave.

Working in the office opposite mine there was a young woman, Beverly Hill, the same age as Kay, whom we had some time earlier invited to dinner at Mary Street. During that evening Beverly apparently told Kay that her astrologer(!) had told her that she would have an affair with an older man. I don't remember hearing that. Probably too drunk. I think that "prediction" unsettled Kay, as well it might.

In those days - if not to the present day - universities, colleges and art schools were hotbeds of affairs between staff, and very frequently between male staff and younger female students. Although I had been aware of the attractivness of some students I had never responded to that. I don't say this just to make out that I was virtuous, but I must have known even then that such attachments were usually unsustainable, at best; at worst, utterly destructive for both people.

No such constraints, however, seemed to apply to relationships between colleagues. After a party while Kay was away, Beverly and I made love, not just for one night but for a whole week. Rachael was furious with me.

During that week I took Rachael to school, went to work, collected Rachael from school, and in the evenings went to Bev's rented farmhouse or to Mary Street where Bev arrived as quickly as she could. It was mutual lust of high intensity. Somehow, in the midst of all this I managed to retain my sense of responsibility for Rachael, even though I know that moralists will dispute this.

At the end of that week I came home in the evening for the first time without Bev, fortunately to find that Kay had arrived unannounced. With a completely scrambled mind I had to confess all to her. There were tears all round. We tried to restart our relationship but, for me, it no longer worked. After a few weeks I had to tell Kay I didn't love her any more and wanted to be with Bev. Accepting the inevitable Kay returned to Sydney.

Soon after that a friend offered to look after Rachael for a weekend while Bev and I went to stay in a pub in Maleny, a little town in the mountains north west of Brisbane.

When we walked into the bar at Maleny all eyes turned on us. Someone called out loudly: "Sugar daddy!" This was a bit of a shock to me. I didn't think I was showing my age and I didn't (didn't want to?) acknowledge the age difference between us, a difference close to 20 years. Anyhow, we ignored the comment and retired to our room where we had urgent business to attend to.

In the morning after breakfast we explored what there was to see in and around Maleny. The most spectacular sight was the Glasshouse Mountains, east of Maleny. The weather was stunningly beautiful, as it often is in Queensland.

Photographs from that time illustrate something that was a feature of our relationship: we often photographed each other in places we went. At first Bev borrowed my camera, although she soon after bought one for herself. She became an avid student of techniques of photography: developing and printing, handling the camera, taking pictures, and so on. If we hadn't had that as a cement between us I don't think our relationship would have lasted as long as it did.

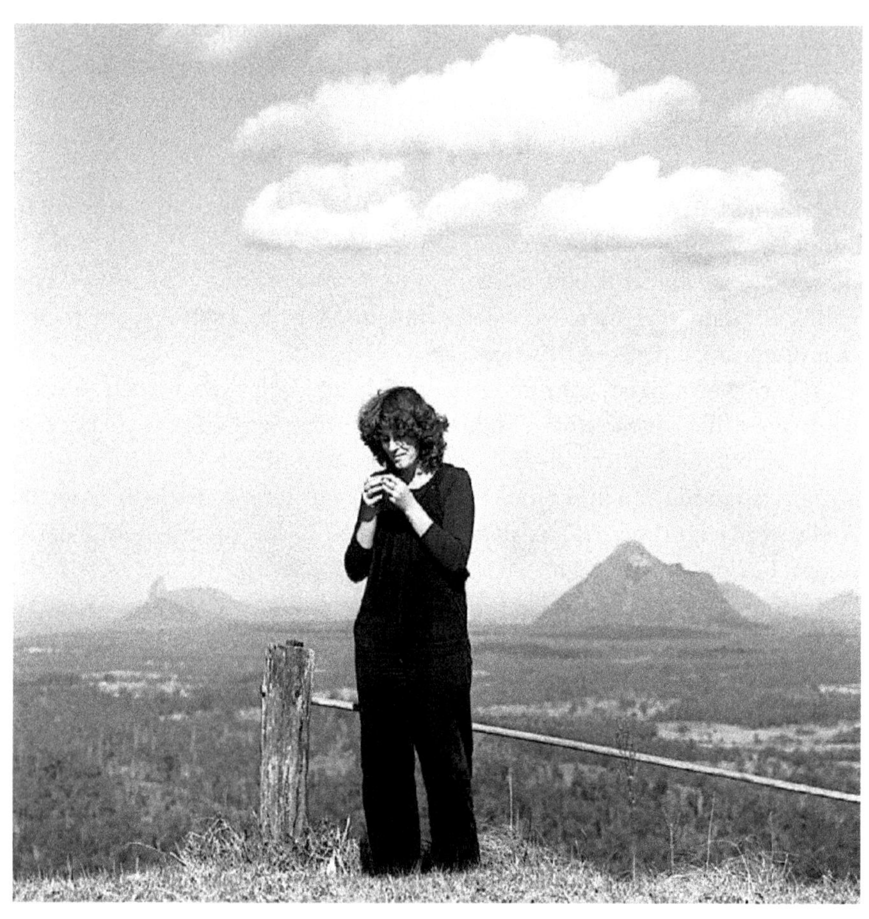

Bev rolling a cigarette near Maleny, c. 1978

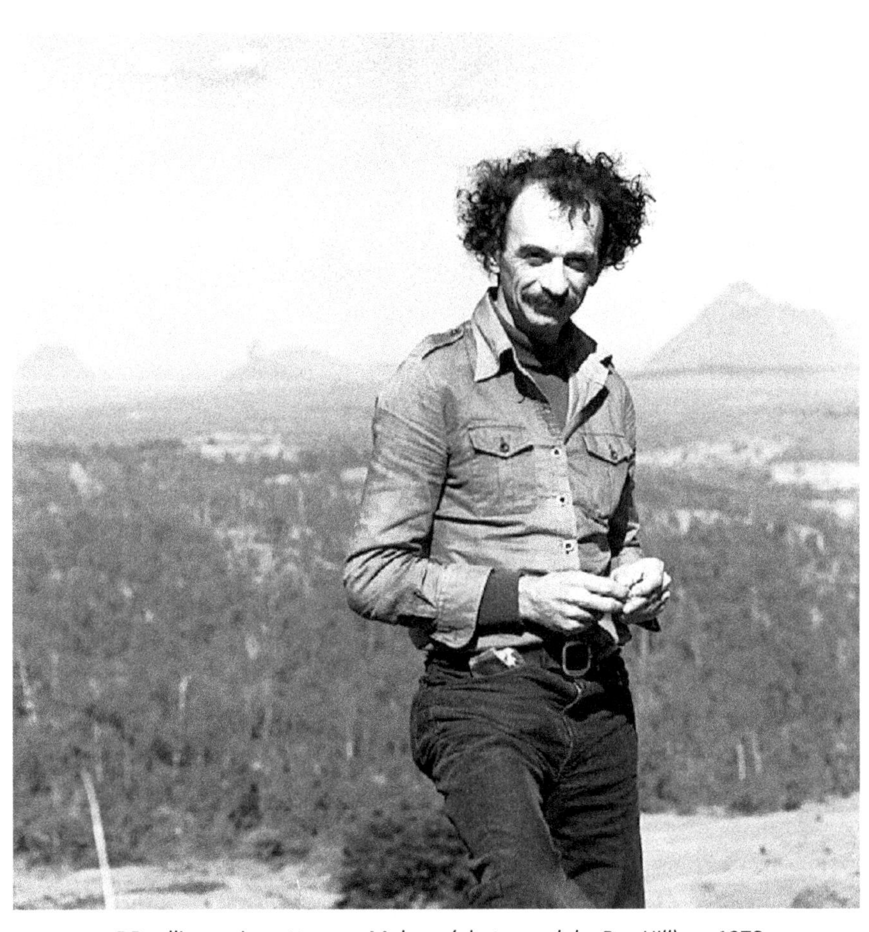

DP rolling a cigarette near Maleny, (photograph by Bev Hill), c. 1978

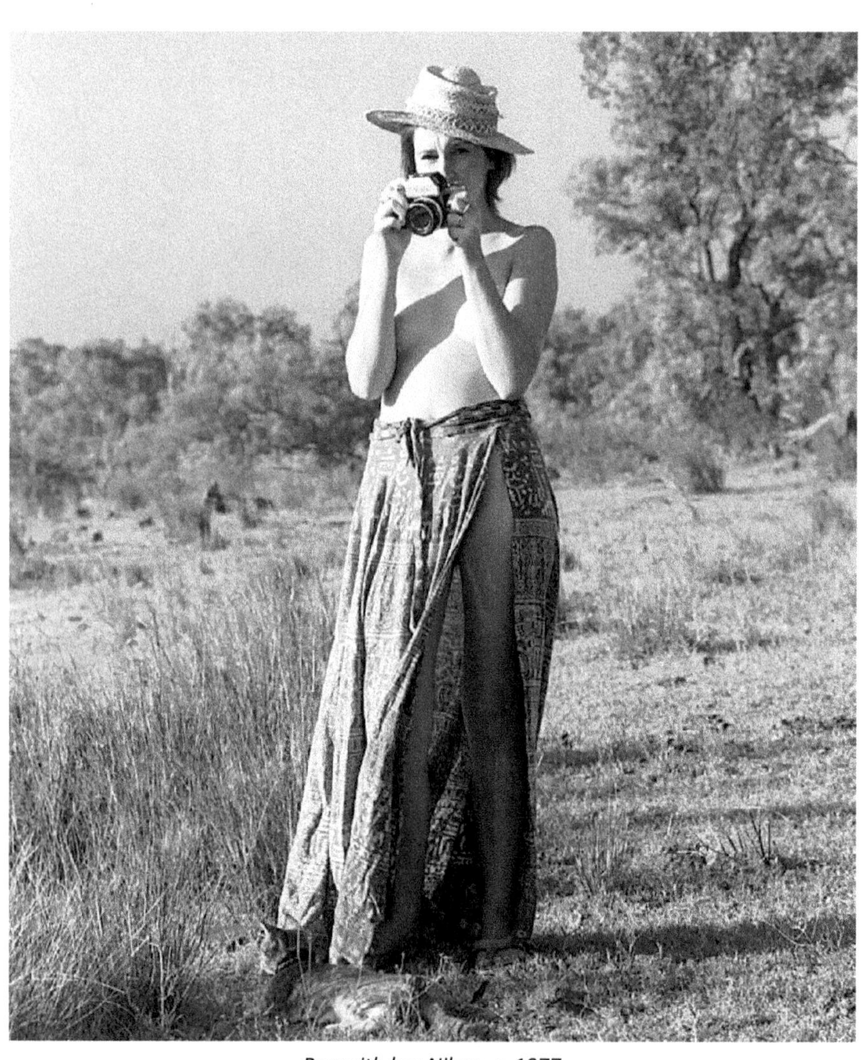

Bev with her Nikon, c. 1977

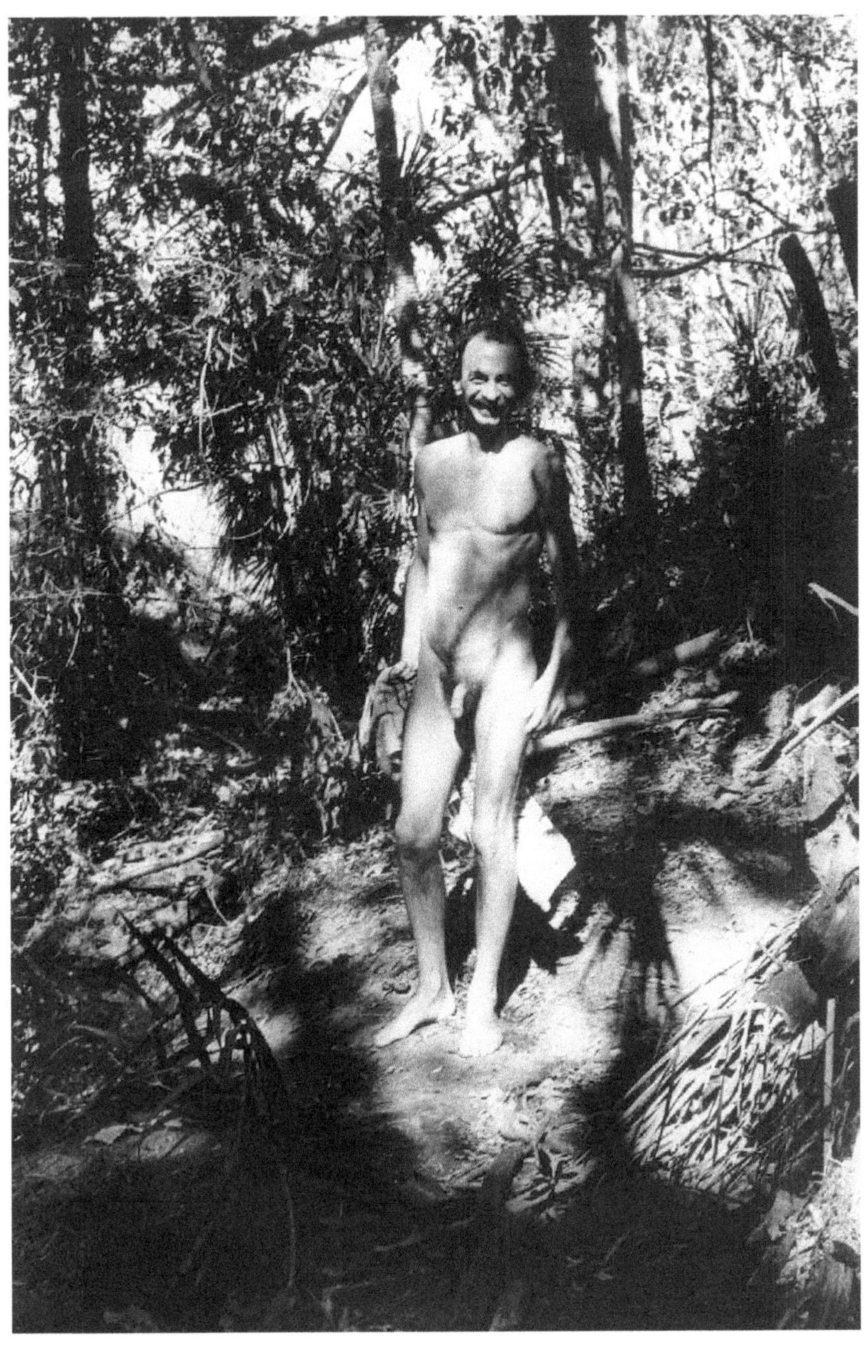

In the bush, North Queensland (photograph by Bev Hill), c. 1977

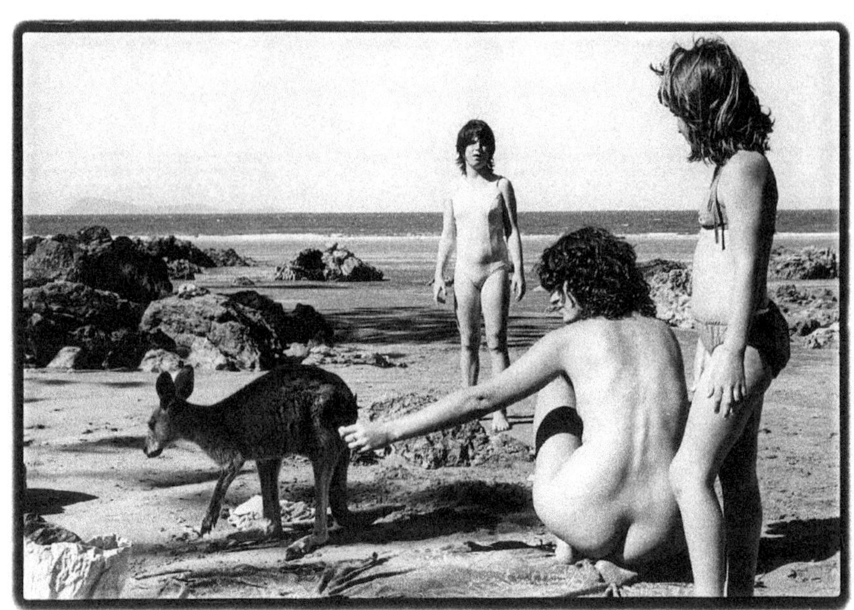

On a beach near Mackay (1), c. 1977

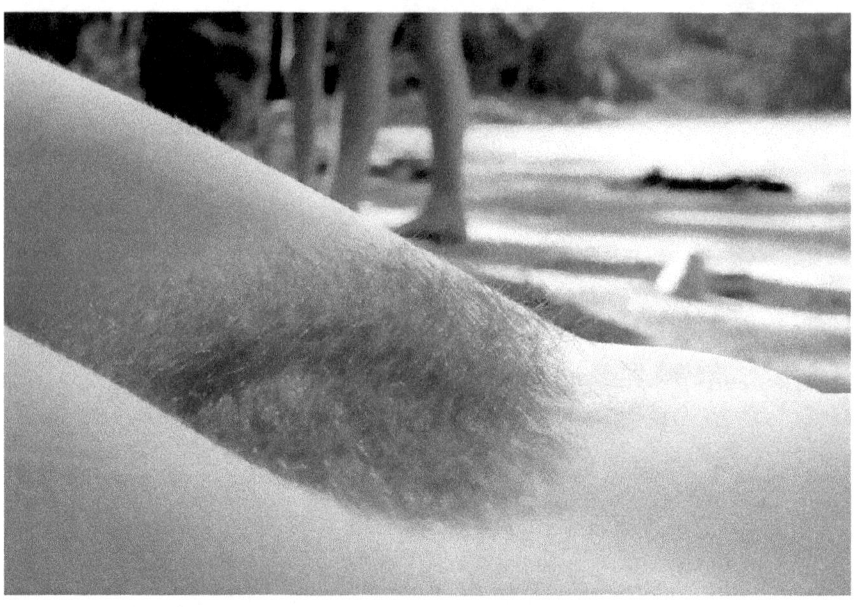

On a beach near Mackay (2), c. 1977

At Mary Street I set up a darkroom in the kitchen. I became, perhaps for the first time, conscious of still photography having a prestige equal to painting and drawing, neither of which I'd done very much of since returning to Australia.

Then I bought a Pentax 6x7 SLR camera with a marvellous, massive wide-angle lens. That lens on that camera could, with care, produce images so sharp that they could be enlarged to a very high degree. I started using the Pentax in a more self-conscious way. I took a number of photographs of Bev in her farmhouse by torchlight. I used a technique based on architectural photography, where buildings in total darkness are "painted" with light by walking around them with a flash set off at points that will pick out details. This time, with the Pentax on a tripod and using a hand-held electric torch, I asked Bev to hold her pose in the dark while I walked around her, painting her, and her setting, with the beam of the torch.

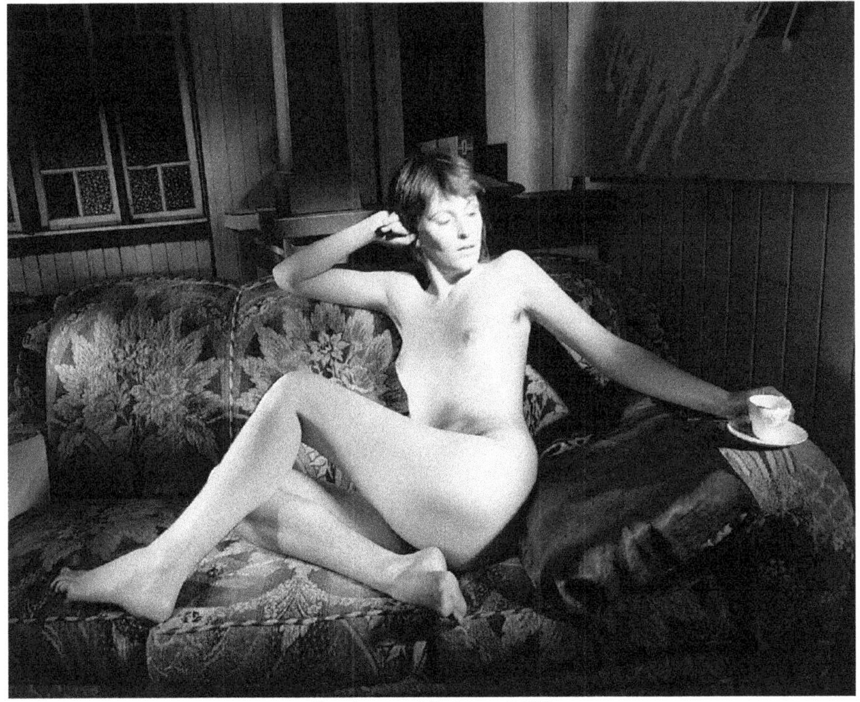

Bev by torchlight, c. 1978

For this still-life set up on the ironing board at Mary Street I used the same technique I'd used to light Bev's portrait. The "Universal Grinder" was an old meat grinder (mincer) that I never actually used, I just liked the look of the thing.

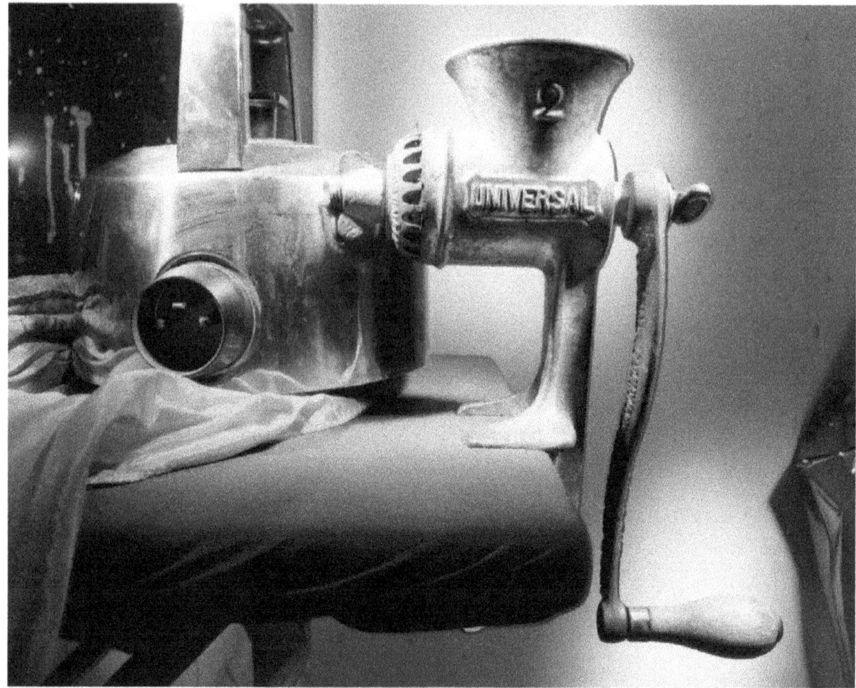

The Universal Grinder, c. 1978

Leaving Toowoomba...

Beverly's contract at DDIAE was a finite one, which of course meant that she would move away from Toowoomba. I could have stayed there forever but the prospect was not appealing, to say the least. And I should have accepted that the relationship with Beverly had a limited life. I could see - but refused to accept -that she wanted to move on. When she did move on I determined to follow her. That, of course was the worst of reasons to move, but motivations can often be plural, some good, some not. If I could only ignore the obsession with Beverly there were other, and very practical reasons for moving: Rachael's schooling and my career as a film maker, for example. So I arranged to put Mary Street up for auction, resigned from my position at DDIAE and in a very short time set off for Sydney.

The house at Mary Street sold for the same price we'd paid for it. Allowing for inflation and other factors, we had made a loss on it. I had made contact in Sydney with Sue Howe and we had agreed to share a flat in Macleay Street, Potts Point, in a marvellous solid old twelve-storey apartment block. Beverley left Toowoomba several weeks before I did and found herself a flat in Paddington. Of course it would have been better if we'd made a clean break in Toowoomba. After a few unhappy months our relationship ended, "not with a bang, but a whimper". For a long time after this , although it wasn't a conscious decision, I effectively withdrew from sexual relationships. A psychologist might say that was a necessary step.

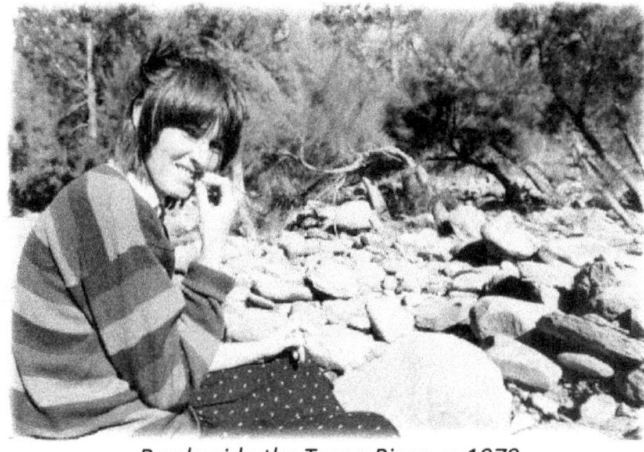
Bev beside the Turon River, c. 1979

When my relationship with Beverly was in the process of ending, we went for a long drive to Hill End, where we stayed overnight at the pub. On the way back we stopped beside the Turon River, where I took this photograph. As if to prove my theory about photographs recording the relationship between photographer and subject, it's obvious that there was a palpable distance between us. We had little more to say to each other.

Back in Sydney...

I enrolled Rachael at Darlinghurst Primary School which was within walking distance of the flat. Most mornings, when I walked Rachael to school through Kings Cross, the street cleaners were out hosing down the footpaths outside strip joints, night clubs and so on. The "Cross" was a bit seedy but really quite safe.

From our sunny, enclosed verandah on the third floor of the Potts Point flat, we had a view over an excavated vacant block next to the Chevron Hotel, waiting for who knows what addition.

The Chevron's glamour had long-since faded, but I love faded glamour and my beloved Pentax came into its own for shots of my new surroundings - exteriors as well as still-lifes.

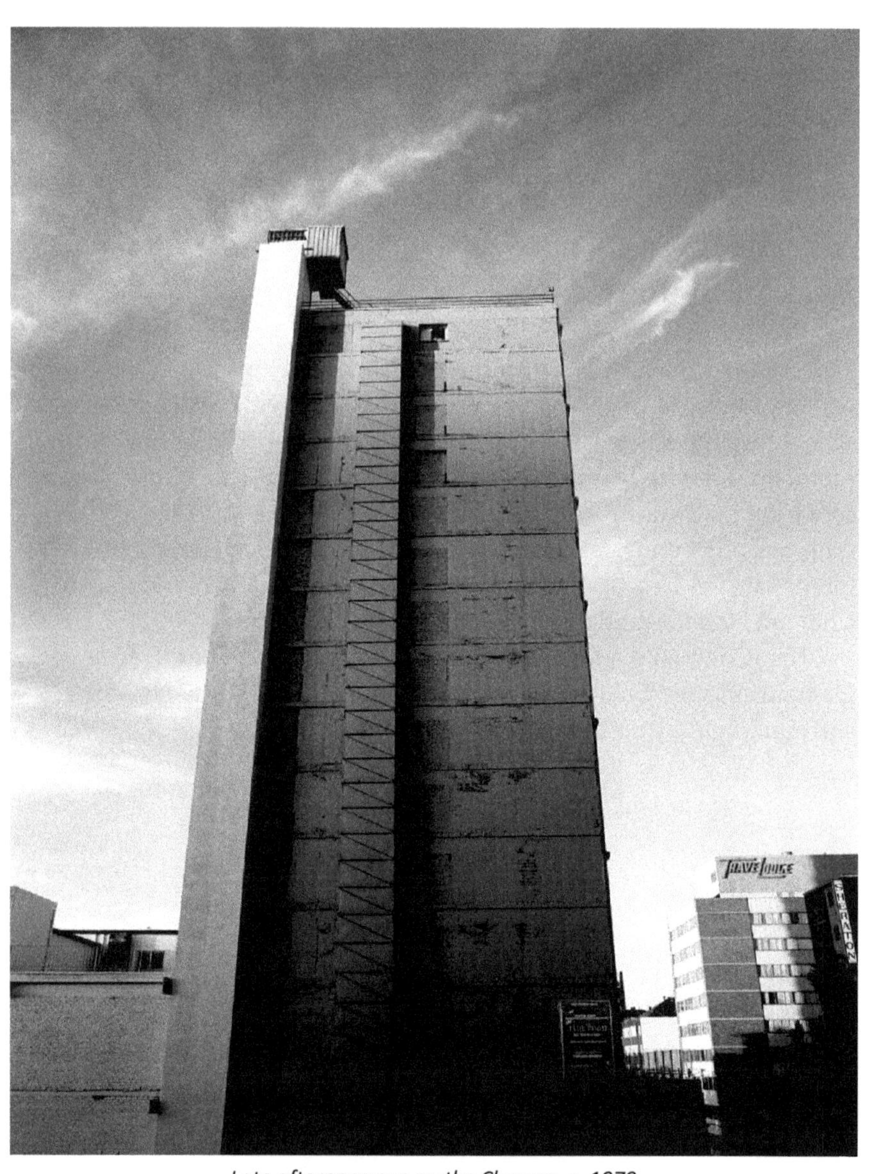

Late afternoon sun on the Chevron, c. 1979

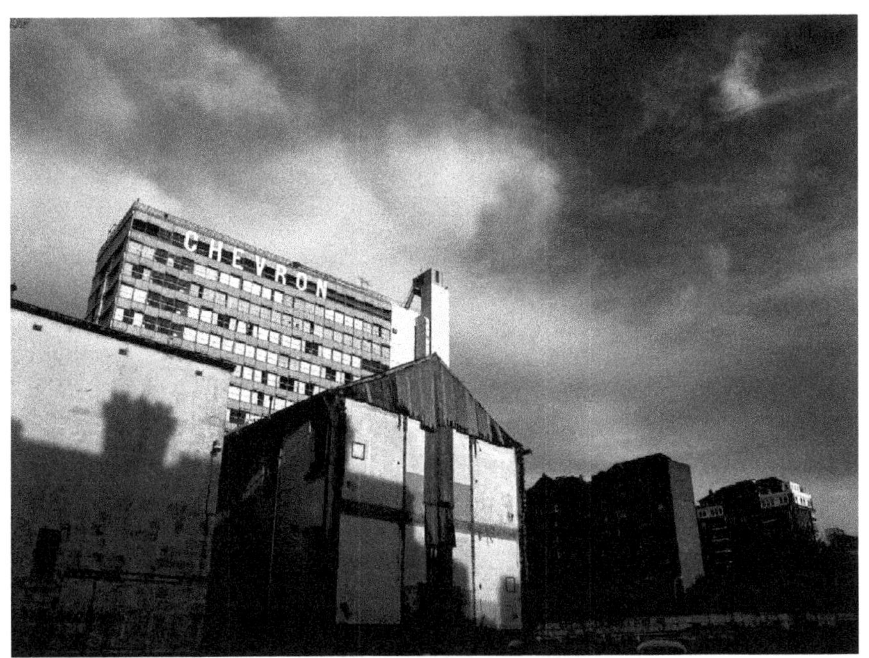

Rear view of the Chevron, c. 1979

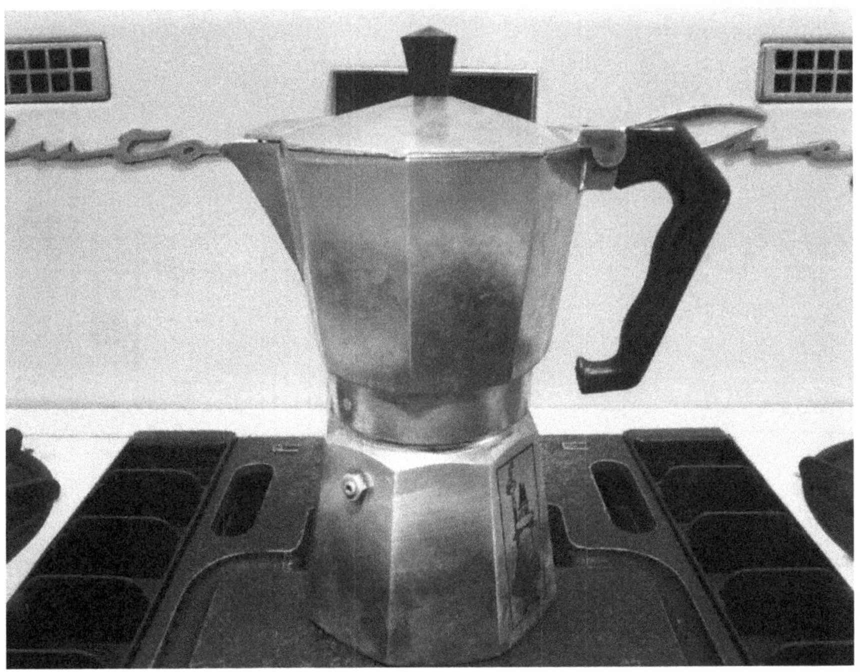

Sue's coffee pot, c. 1979

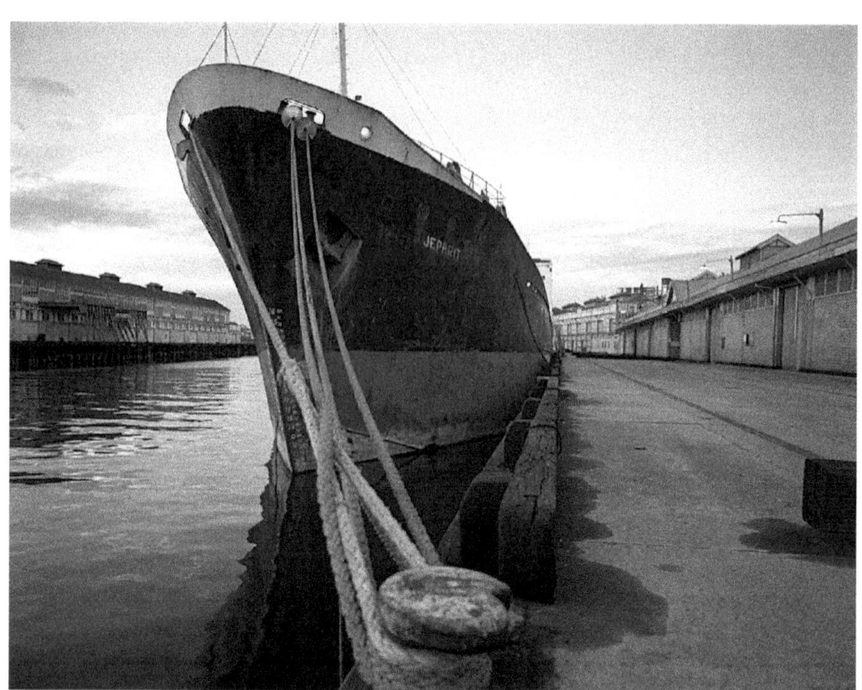

The Jeparit *anchored at Woolloomooloo Bay, c.1979*

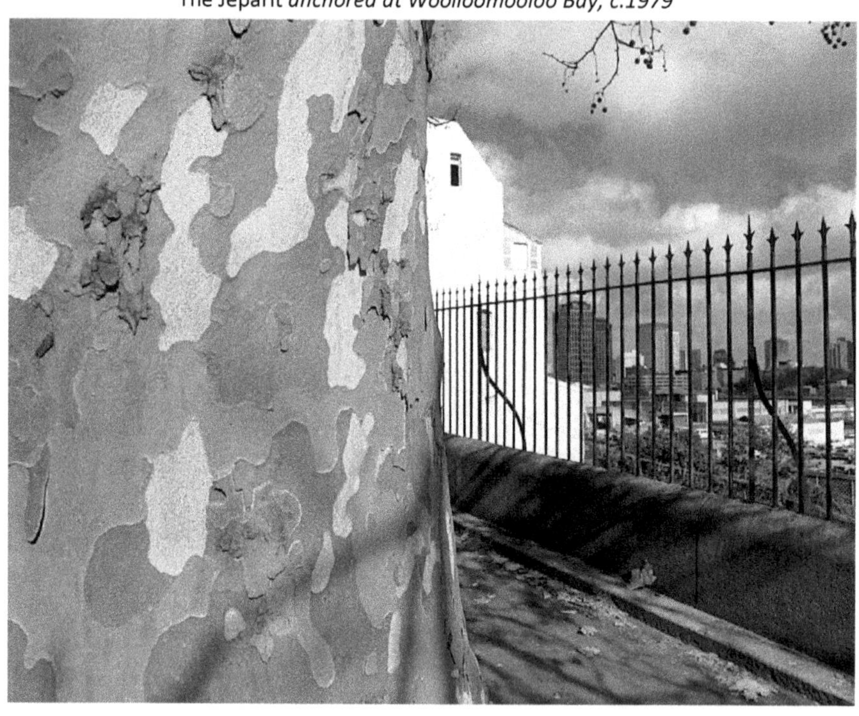

North end of Victoria Street, Potts Point, c. 1979

A short walk downhill from Potts Point was Woolloomooloo Bay, the place where as a young apprentice I had made drawings and photographs that were the beginnings of my career as a "dedicated amateur". There was an atmosphere of romantic melancholy about the place, which

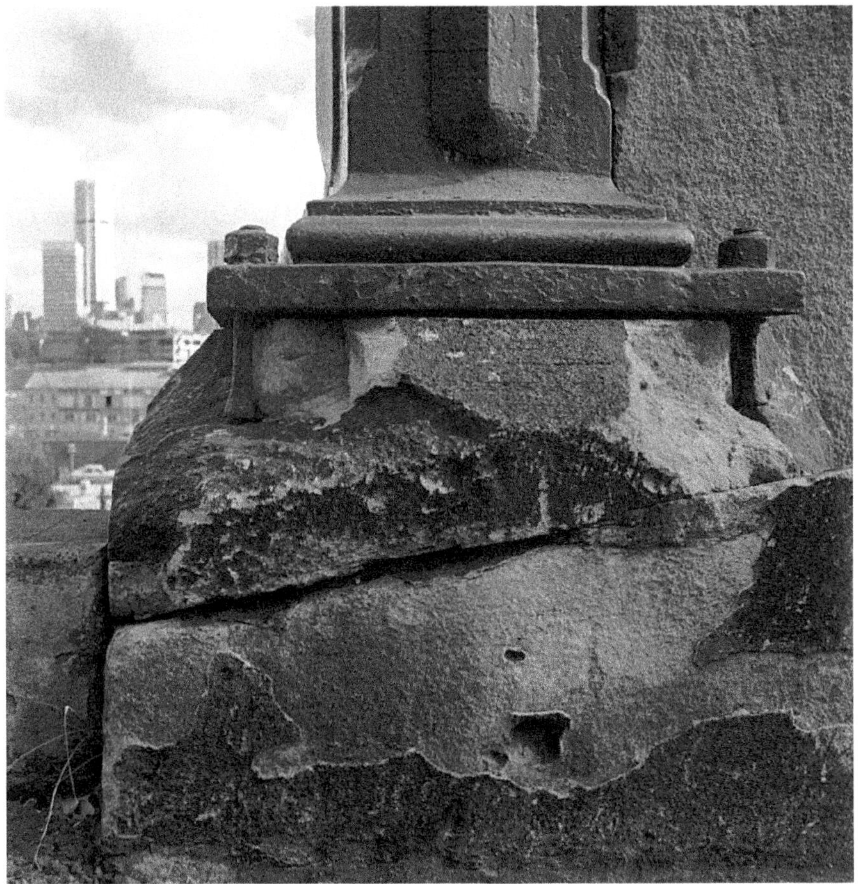

The city from the top of McElhone Stairs, Victoria Street, Kings Cross, c. 1979

seemed in keeping with my self-defined status as returning prodigal. The ship at anchor here was famous, perhaps notorious for being the site of a long-running struggle between unionists and ship-owners. One evening around that time I had a visit from an Australian film maker I had met in London. With him was a woman friend who , I think, might have been "interested" in me, although I didn't reciprocate. While we were all talking on the lounge Sue came home. We were all stunned when she exploded: "Who's this floozy?"

Sue had been a good friend to me for many years, and more recently she had become very attached to Rachael. Now Sue must have thought I was about to start yet another love affair. Perhaps she thought she had to protect Rachael from my irresponsibility.

Whatever the truth or otherwise of that I had to find somewhere else to live. We moved into a house in Glenmore Road, Paddington, sharing with a woman who was a friend of Kay's friend, Debbie.

Debbie, who lived almost under the Sydney Harbour Bridge, had in her flat a small but very workable darkroom. She offered me the use of the darkroom, even giving me a key so I could get in at any time.

In my travels to and from the darkroom I had to walk under the Harbour Bridge which brought me into intimate contact with its structure, which in turn brought me to take photographs of the bridge and its approaches. I was getting to know the Pentax well and with my Harbour Bridge photographs I started to think in series (pages 216 to 217).

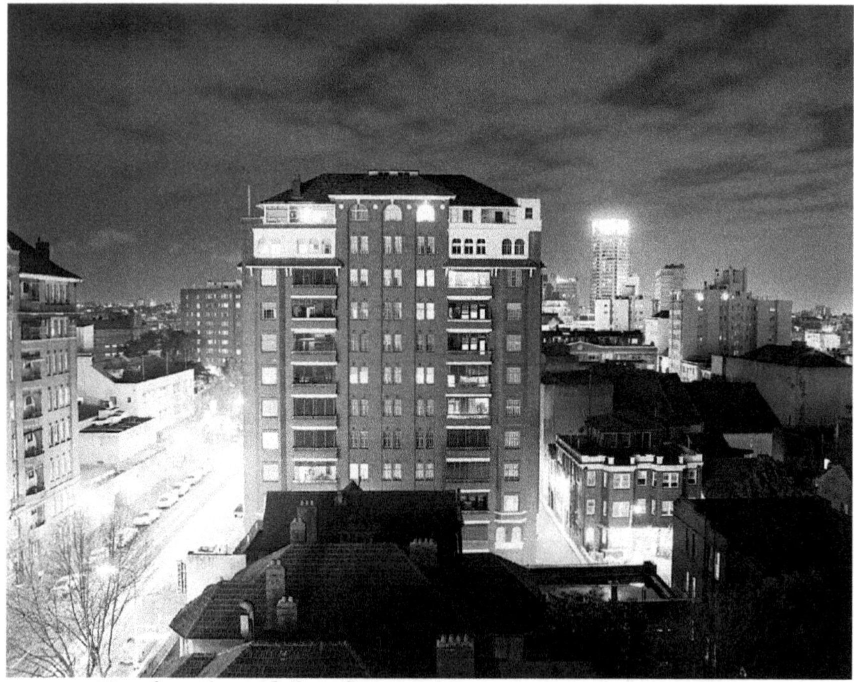

View from the roof of our flats, Macleay Street, Potts Point, c. 1979

The Harbour Bridge Series ...

This section shows four of the eight photographs in this series - the full series can be seen on the website gallery.

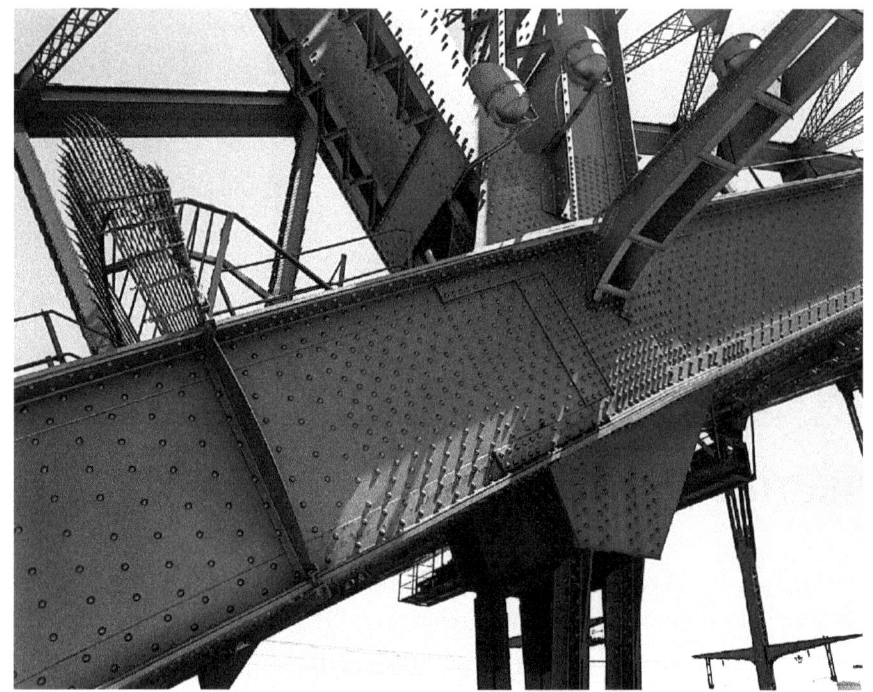

Harbour Bridge detail, c. 1980

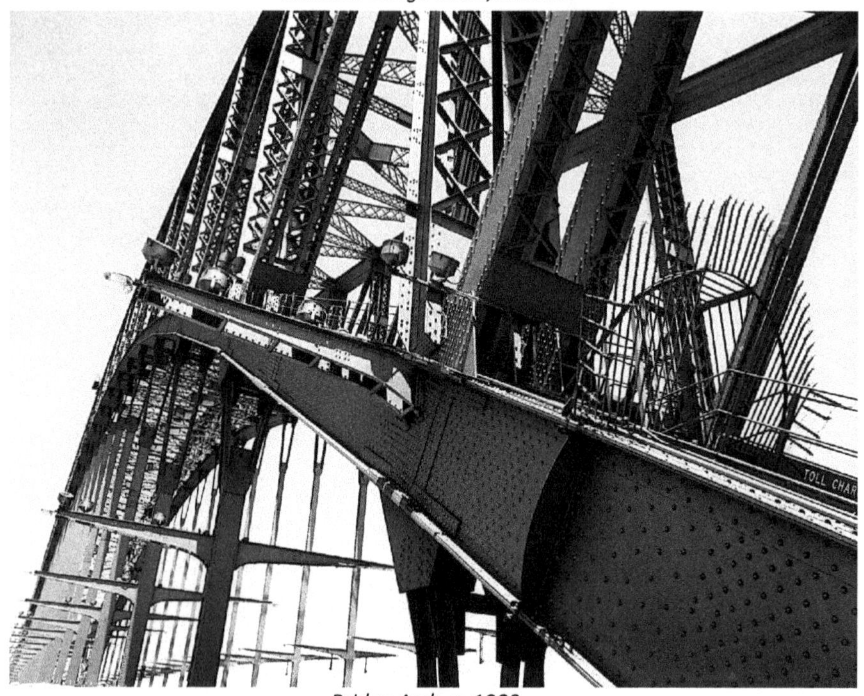

Bridge Arch, c. 1980

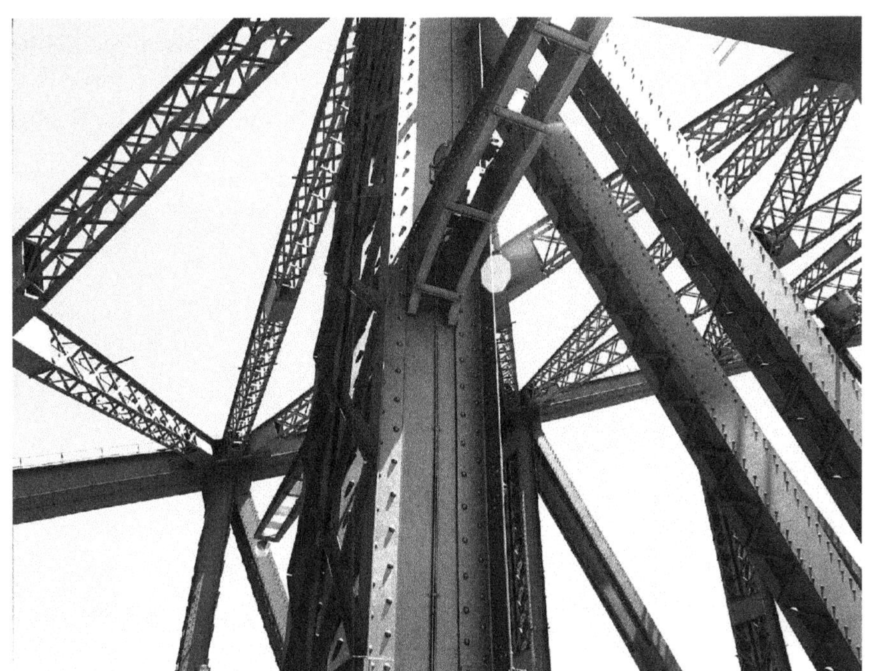
Harbour Bridge detail (1), c. 1980

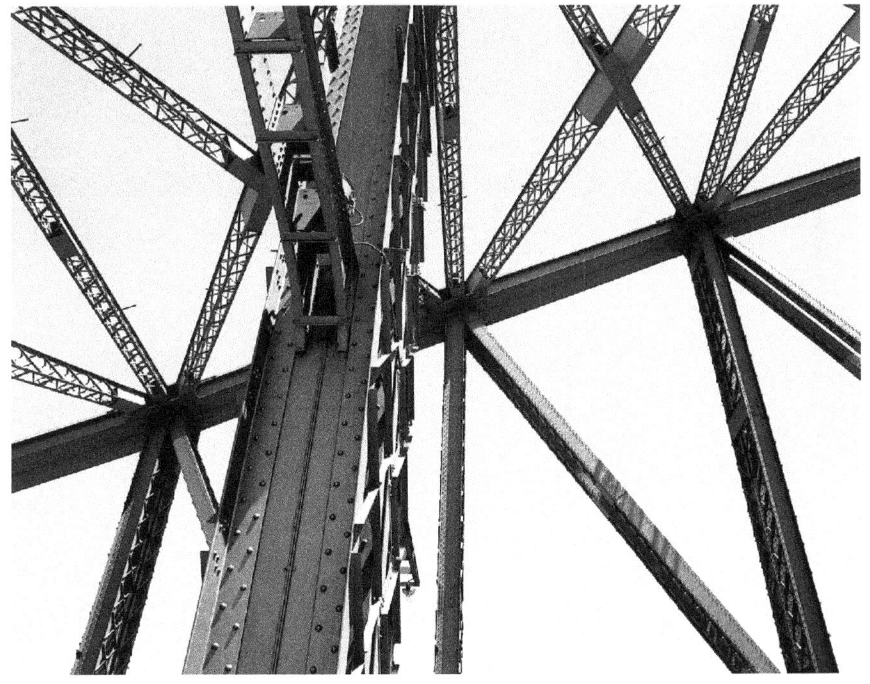
Harbour Bridge detail (2), c. 1980

Then I started wandering around Paddington at night with the Pentax on a borrowed tripod. Some of the exposures were very long, more than 30 minutes in some cases, which must have meant I could have been mistaken for a weirdo loitering in shady places.

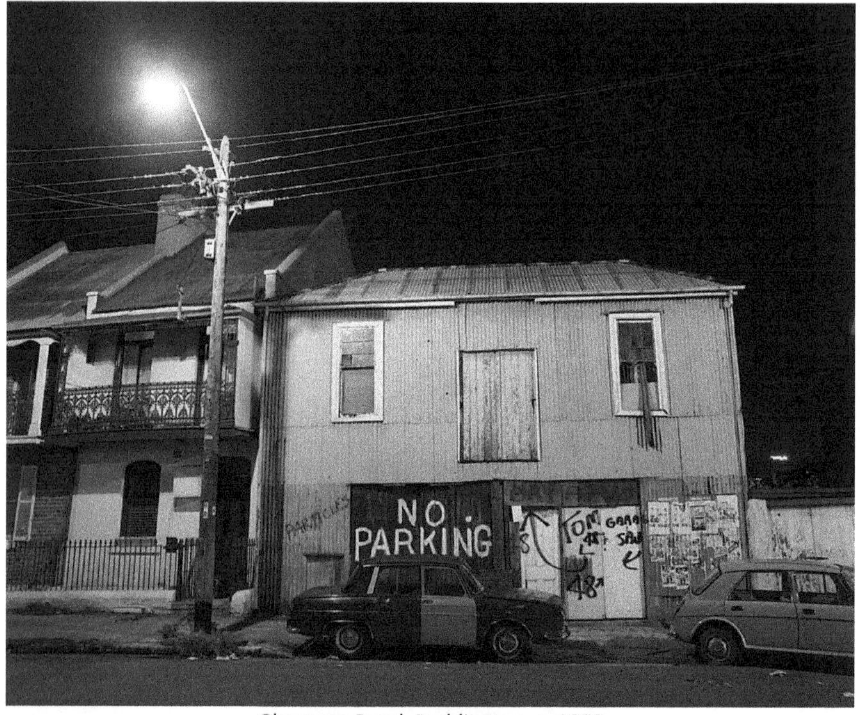

Glenmore Road, Paddington, c. 1980

The Pentax gets stolen…

I had just bought a diopter for the Pentax. This was a large chunk of glass that screwed over the front of the 50mm lens and allowed me to focus on objects very close, so close that an image could be life-size or larger on the negative and thus much larger than life-size on pretty well any print. The miniature cacti in the image below were photographed with that.

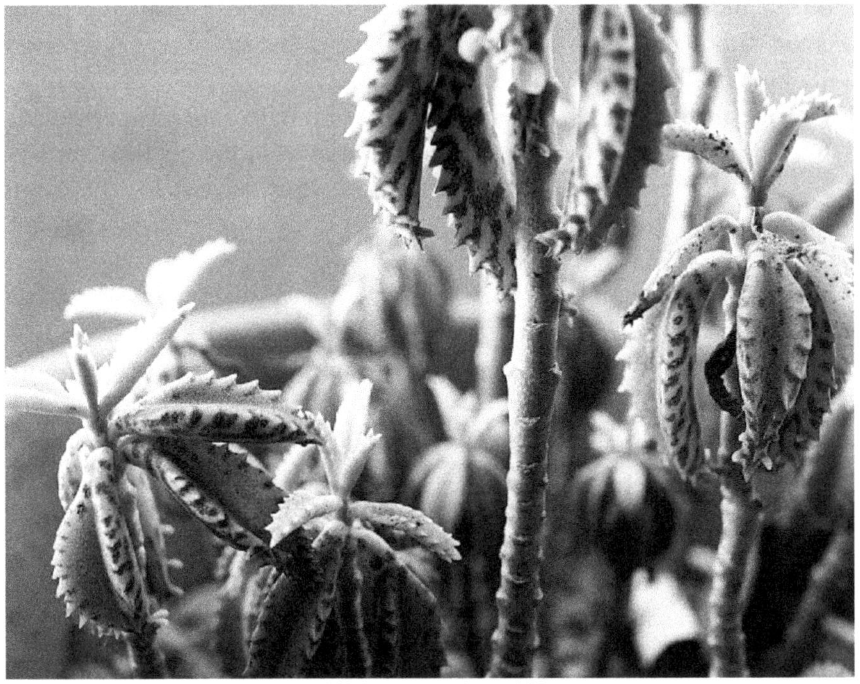

Miniature cacti, c. 1980

The roll of film this shot was on was the last I used in the Pentax. After taking the close-ups and taking the film out of the camera, I left the camera on my bed and went out. This wasn't as silly as it sounds, since the only access to the house was through the front door which was usually closed and anyone entering would have to pass the woman I shared with who lived on the ground floor.

However, when I came home later in the afternoon the Pentax was missing. When I asked my house-mate if she had any idea of what could have happened to it she said she didn't. A day or so later another friend, who also knew the woman downstairs, made a cryptic remark about "leaning on" somebody to get the camera back. It's a measure of how naively trusting I was of these people that I didn't come to the immediate conclusion that whoever took the Pentax must have known the woman downstairs and been alerted by her to its presence in my room. As far as I knew, these people didn't have expensive drug habits. To cut this dismal story short, I never recovered the camera. Of course, it wasn't insured.

There was no way I could afford another Pentax, but I immediately went to a second-hand camera shop in Kings Cross and bought a Mamiya RB67, a SLR camera that could in some respects just about match the Pentax, although a wide-angle lens like the one just stolen was completely out of my reach, even if it had been available.

Around this time I had found a job working as part of a Drug and Alcohol Education team, as one of two film makers there. The other film maker was John Baird who was an escapee from advertising. John was responsible to a public hospital in Sydney and I was responsible, through the Education Team, to the Health Department. At first we were lumbered with the most abysmal equipment and surrounded by various counsellors and social workers whose experience and knowledge, if in fact many of them had any of that, was utterly incompatible with ours, especially mine. In spite of that, over a year or so John and I managed to get the Education Team to buy enough equipment to set up a reasonably workable "non-broadcast" production outfit. Generally speaking, I designed the layout, and John and I together built it up, including all the carpentry, electrical and electronic wiring. (Looking back on my history of building similar set-ups it seems clear that one part of me is a technophile "nerd".) I must say that most of the work we did with that equipment was utterly forgettable. Occasionally we got a brief that led to something interesting and/or useful, but for a while it looked as though my career as a creative film maker was even less viable than it had been in Toowoomba. I channelled virtually all of my creative energy into still photography.

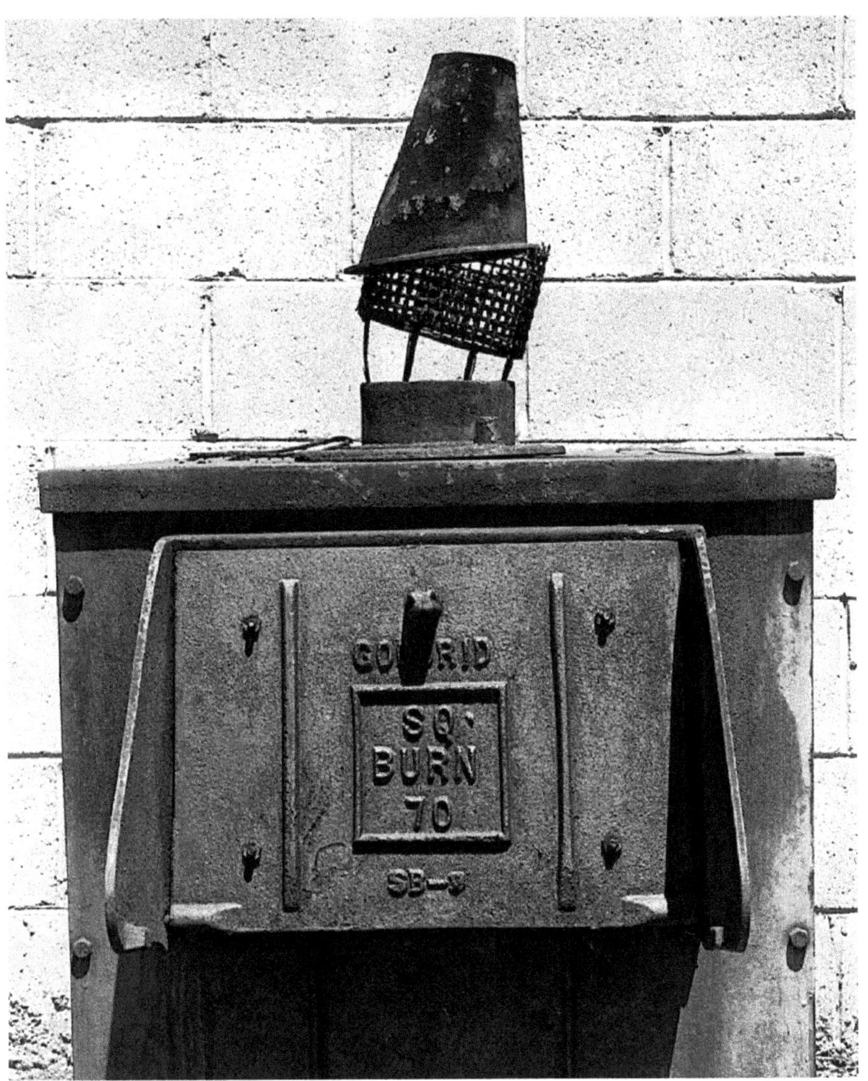

Incinerator, c. 1981

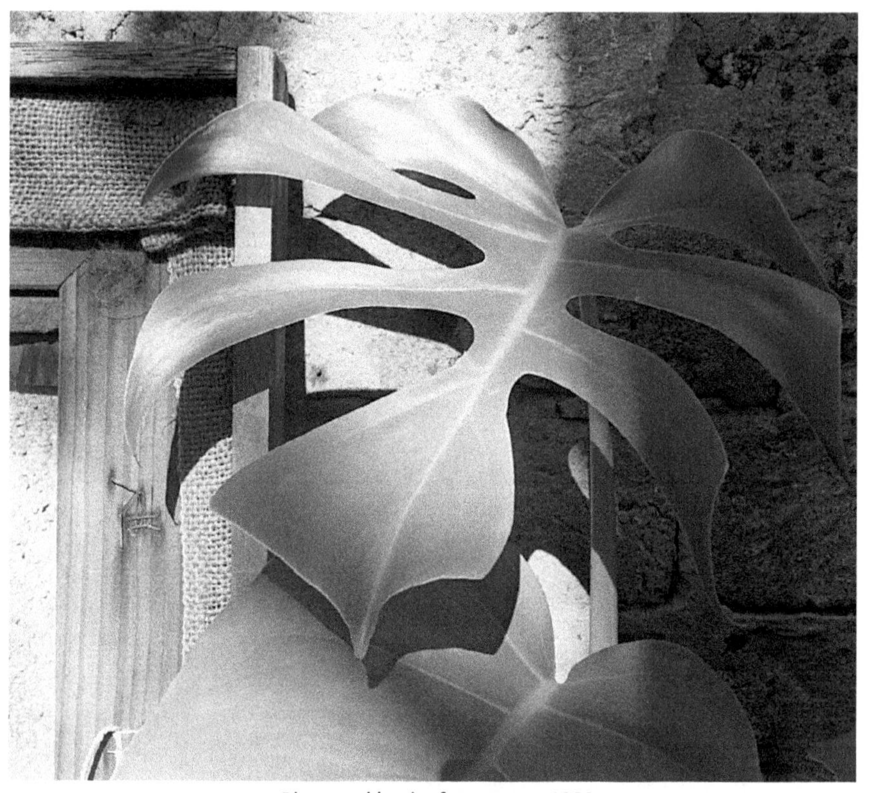

Plant and back of canvas, c. 1982

Rachael had been doing very well at Darlinghurst Primary and as it was her last year before going to high school I thought it would be a nice idea to photograph all the boys and girls in her class. I got permission from their teacher to take the kids into the school grounds in various sized groups to make the shots. The school had a good darkroom and I got permission to use that after hours for making the prints, which I bound into a book showing all the kids and various views of the school's grounds and buildings and presented the book to the school .

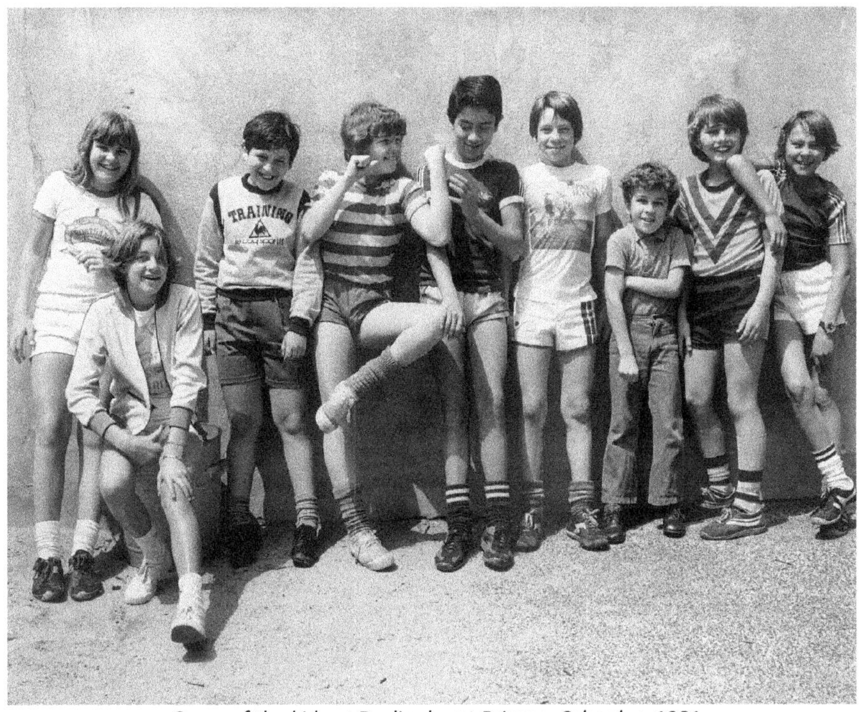

Some of the kids at Darlinghurst Primary School, c. 1981

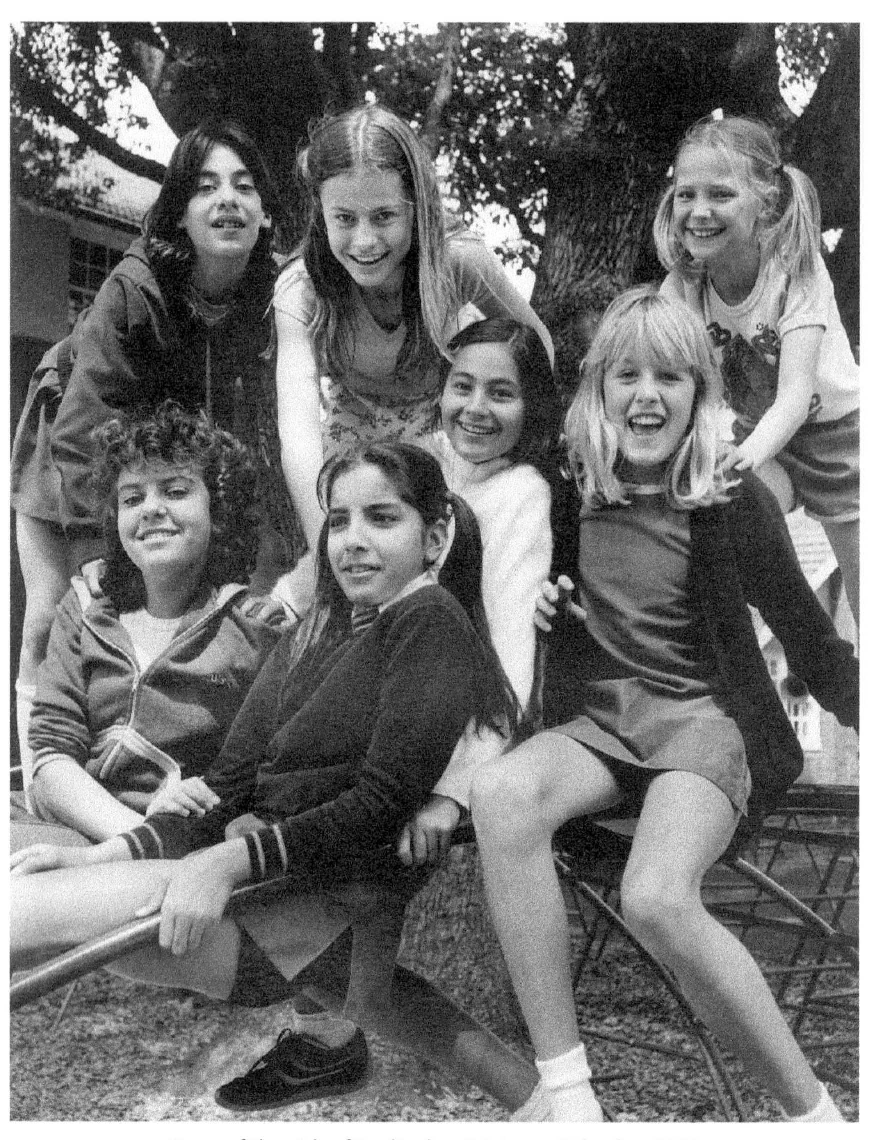

Some of the girls of Darlinghurst Primary School, c. 1981

Fairlight...

Rachael did very well in her HSC which made her eligible to go to a selective High School. While we lived in Paddington the nearest selective school to us was Sydney High, so that's where I enrolled her.

Some time in 1981, I think it was, Looby told me he was looking for someone to rent his house at Fairlight, near Manly, while he and his partner, Kerry Gregan, went overseas. I took up his offer and Rachael and I moved in. In the laundry I set up a darkroom where I could only work at night, which wasn't a problem since I was usually at work during the days.

Rachael had a long way to go to school across the Harbour by Manly ferry, then a bus across the city but she wasn't the only one. She had several friends who all made the same journey each day, so they formed a tight-knit group.

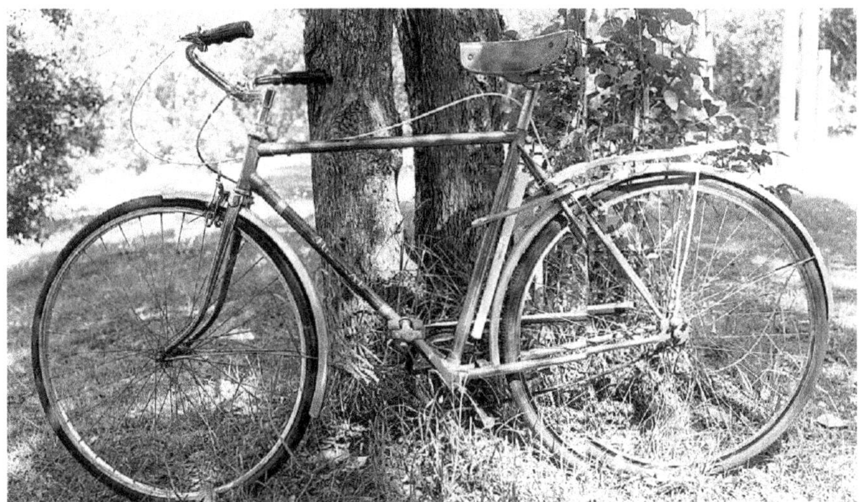

My bicycle, c. 1981

I bought myself a bicycle which I rode often, sometimes going long distances out past the northern beaches, once at least out as far as Bayview on the shore of Pittwater - not such a long distance to a serious cyclist, but I found it incredibly invigorating and satisfying.

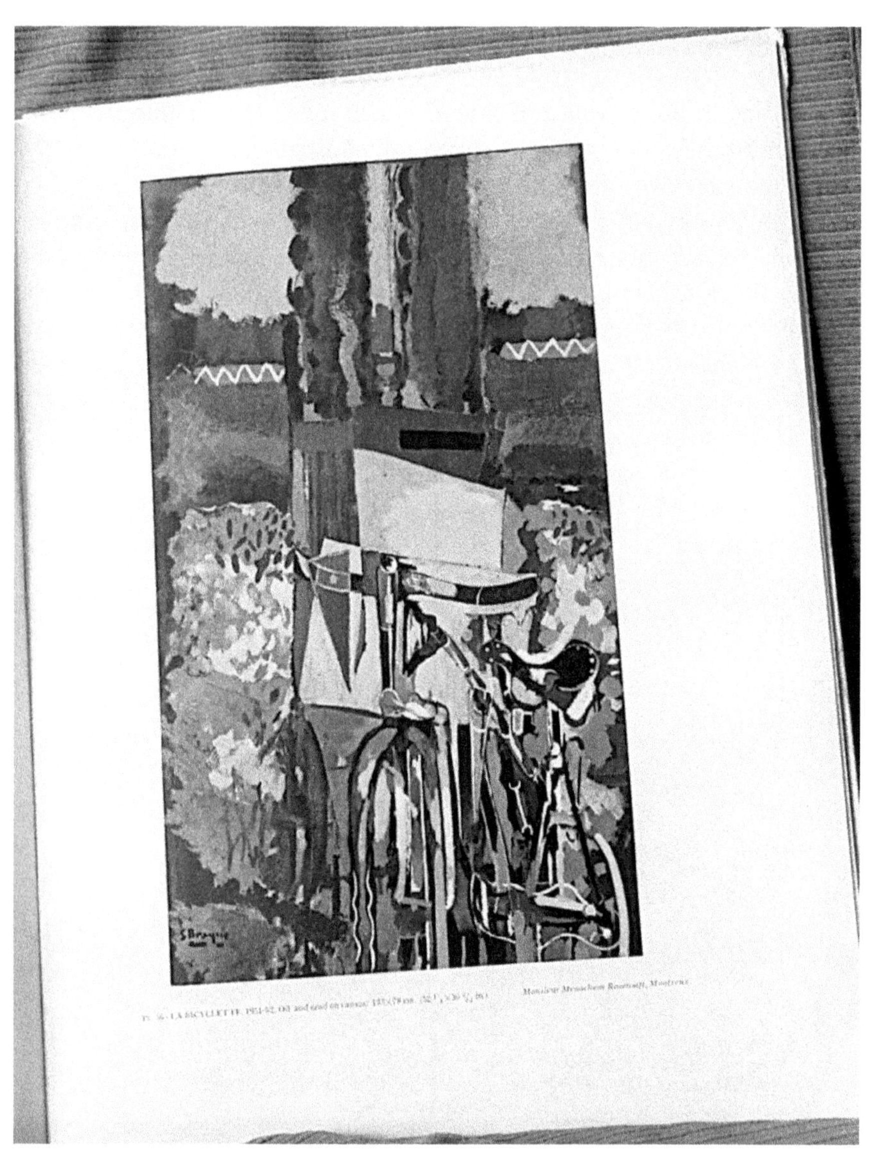

Page of an art book (Braque's bike), c. 1981

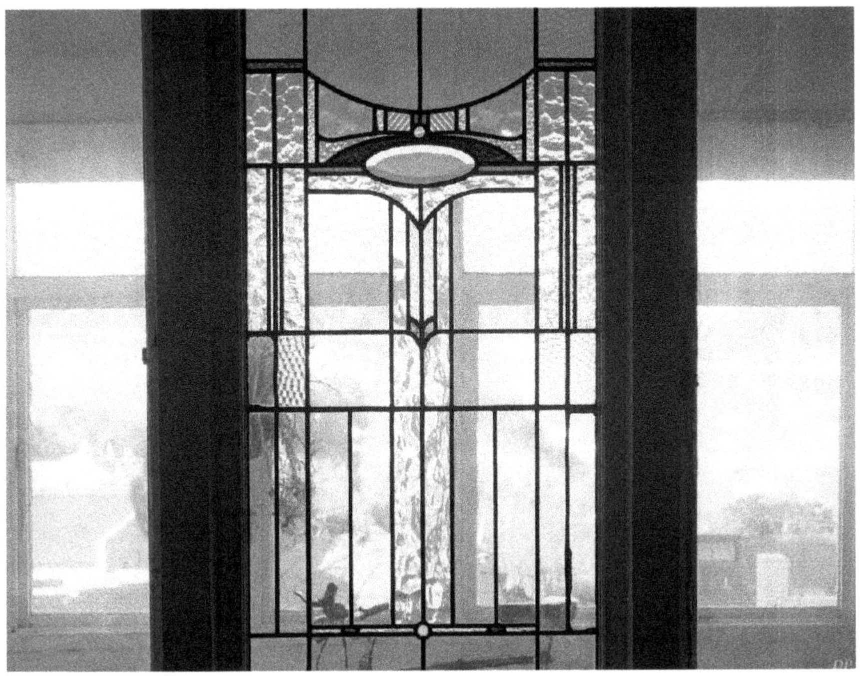

North Harbour through the windows at Fairlight, c. 1981

My bike is just visible at the bottom of this photograph. The one on the previous page is a composite made of three close-ups spliced together which accounts for the disjunctures, especially through the back wheel. (The technique of making composite panoramas is something that I did more of a little later, and with computer editing programmes can be done almost seamlessly.)

Throughout the late 1970s and early 1980s I did very little painting or drawing. The pastel drawing of *Manager Death* (next page) was something of an anomaly amongst all the photographs I was doing, often with ambitious seriousness.

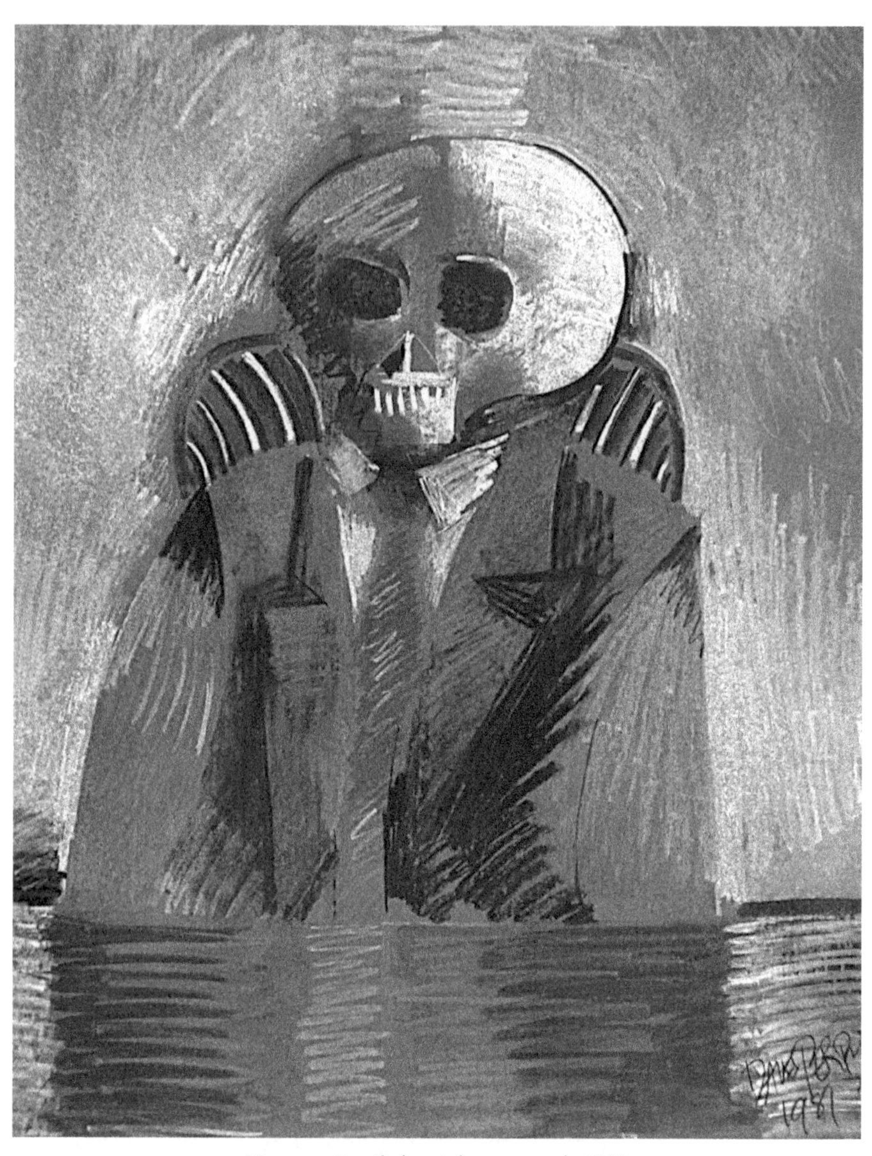

Manager Death *(pastels on paper), 1981*

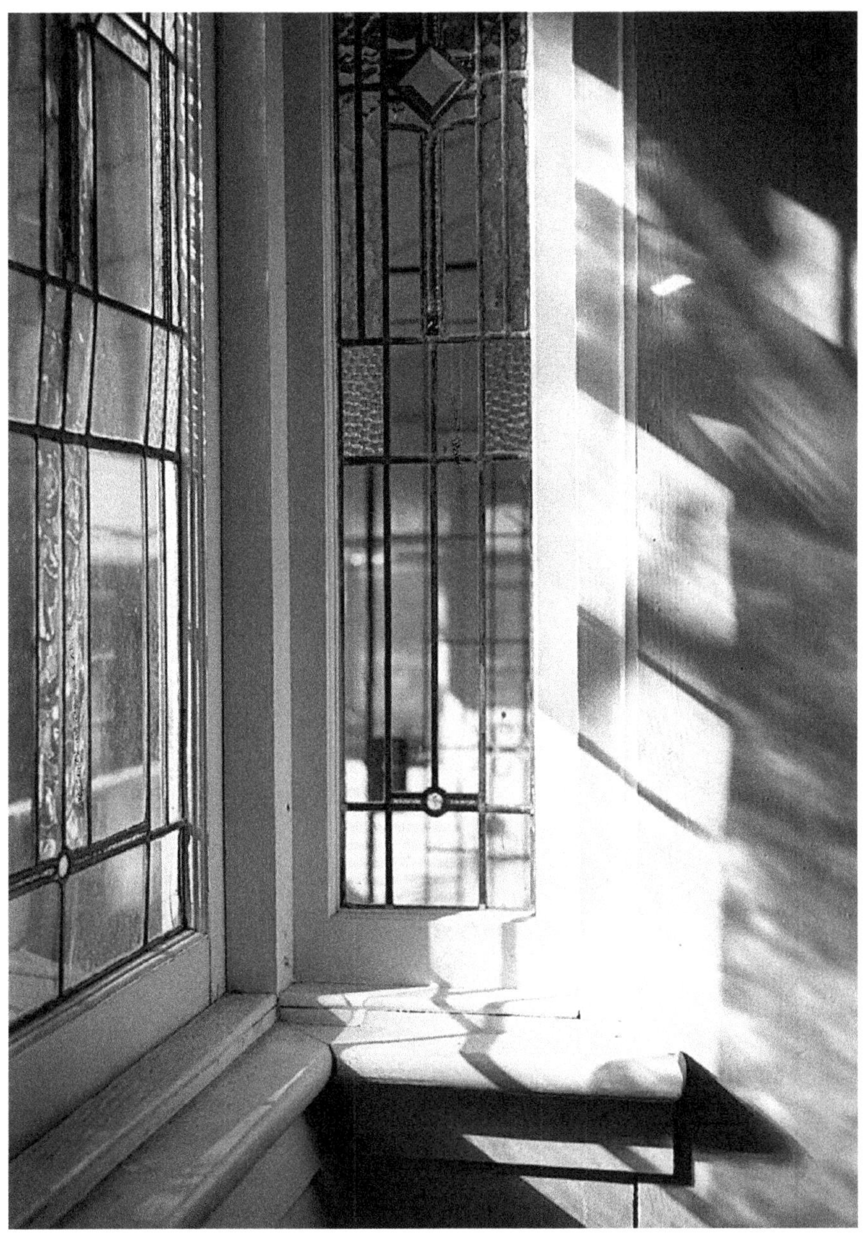

Sun through the leadlights at Fairlight, c. 1981

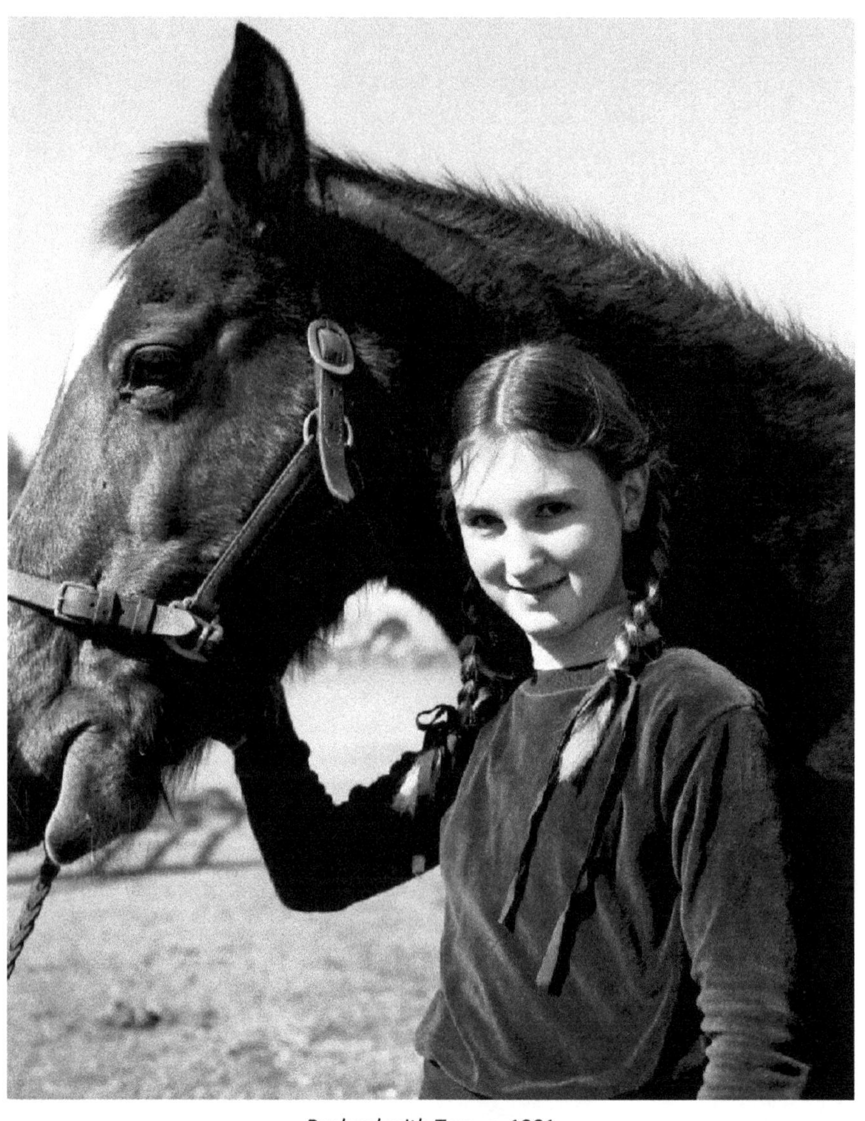

Rachael with Tom, c. 1981

On one occasion I applied to the Australia Council for funding that I hoped would make it possible for me to compile a series of very high quality prints and to seek an exhibition of some of this work. I was interviewed by a project officer who said, when he saw examples of the work which was not unlike what's here, including portraits of Rachael: "We don't fund family photographs."

Kerry Gregan's young son Karl left his toy gun at Fairlight while Kerry, Looby and Karl were overseas. When I found the gun lying around the house I liked its almost antique character and was driven to photograph it.

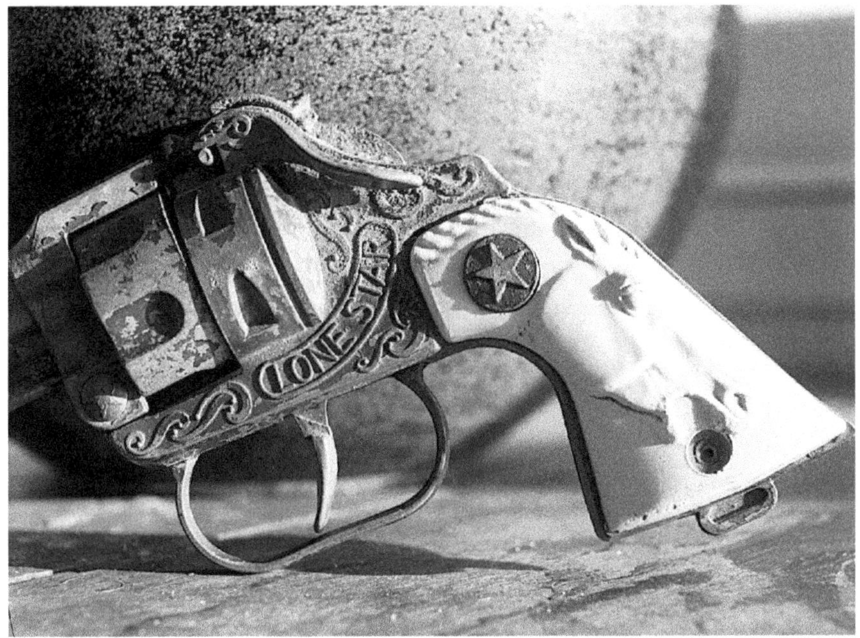

Karl's gun, 1982

When Looby and Kerry returned from overseas Rachael and I had to move to a self-contained flat at the top of the house, which was perched high on a hill overlooking Sydney Heads and the Harbour. It's hard to imagine a more spectacular location. From the window of the flat we had a one hundred and eighty degree view. I do think that views are for looking at rather than photographing, although when the light was right I was able to make a few adequate scenic shots.

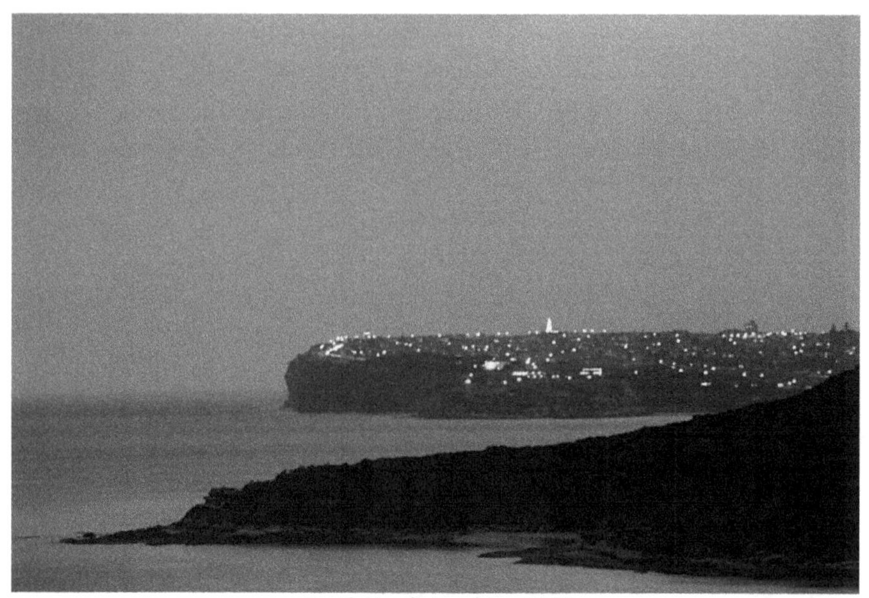

South Head at night, c. 1982

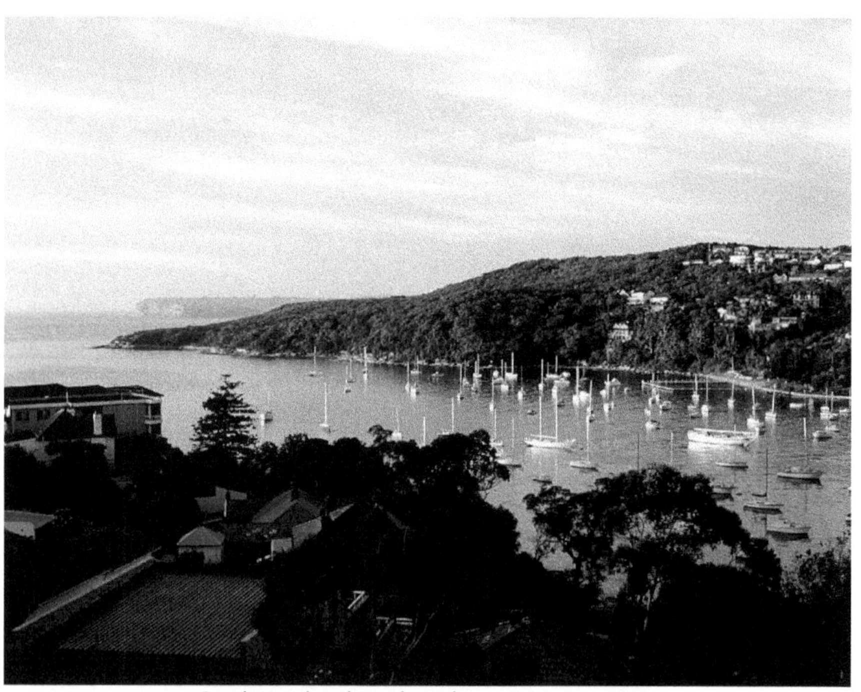

South Head and North Harbour at sunrise, 1982

I was starting to use colour occasionally, and in the case of the top one here, a borrowed 35mm camera. I don't think this photograph - nor the one below it for that matter - has much going for it except that it illustrates something about where we were living. Of course if I really wanted to illustrate things I would have been a photo-journalist. That's something I am/would be hopeless at. It seemed that like a lot of artists,

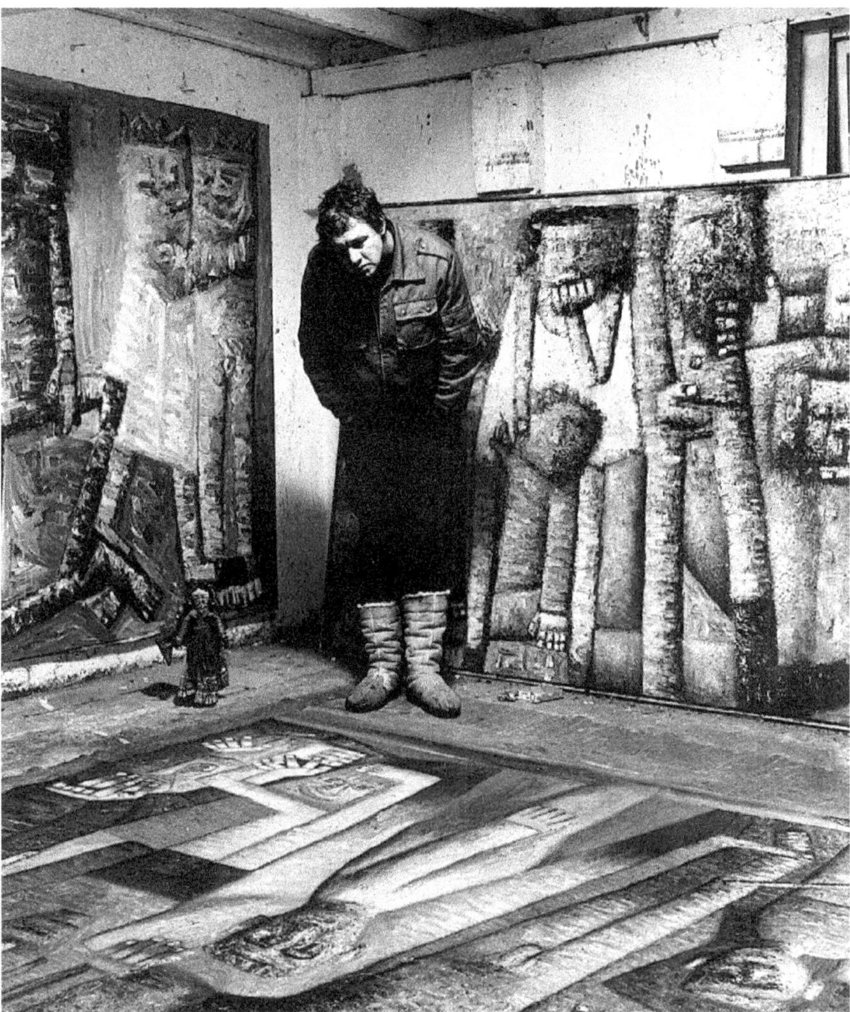

Looby in his Fairlight studio, 1982

Looby's idea of photographers was that they are only illustrators (I don't hold that against him) so one day he asked me to take a photograph of him at work to illustrate the catalogue for a forthcoming exhibition of his paintings in Melbourne.

Looby's exhibition was reviewed for Melbourne's *The Age* by a critic who didn't like Looby's work at all. In a calculated insult to Looby, the critic claimed that my photograph of him (previous page) was the best thing in the show. Back-handed compliment to me as it might have been, I was moved to write indignantly to *The Age* in the following terms (the letter wasn't printed):

18th. August, 1982

Dear Sir,

I have only just seen the review (The Age, 4/8/82) of Keith Looby's exhibition at Realities. The review is remarkable in the intensity of its scorn for the painter.

My reason for writing at this late stage is that the reviewer has used my photograph of the painter as ammunition for her attack on him. In doing this she has misinterpreted the photograph, asserting that its purpose "is to locate Looby in a context of high modernist seriousness."

In fact, my purpose in taking the photograph was to record the light and character of Looby's studio, and to locate Looby in only one context, that of his own work.

All technical preparations were made when he wasn't there, then I simply asked him to "stand there now look at that painting." I took three shots, the one in question is the third, the whole operation took maybe twenty seconds of Looby's time. There was no question of his striking a pose as the reviewer insultingly claims.

The reading which your reviewer imposed on it is inexplicable and could not be derived from the photograph.

Yours sincerely,
[Signed David Perry.]

Contact remade ...

One day, out of the blue, I had a phone call from a young woman asking: "Is this David Perry?" Naturally, since I was he, I said: "Yes." It was none other than Caitlin, the youngest of the three children I had so callously abandoned 12 years earlier. We agreed to meet at a café in the city.

I think I was very nervous about this meeting. Of course I was guilty about the intervening years. But there were no accusations, just a clear need to make contact. I can't remember all that we talked about, although I do remember Cait telling me that she was a member of the Communist Party. As a member of the Sydney Push, which was essentially a group of dedicated non-joiners, I thought, nevertheless, that having a Commie daughter was a really nice thing.

I think I would have recognised Caitlin even if the meeting hadn't been planned. Although she was well into her twenties then, she was very much the same person I remembered, especially her eyes. Caitlin gave me her sister Jane's phone number so I nervously rang her. Jane was by then married and had a young daughter (next page). She invited me to visit her and when I did she was at first very tearful. Nothing could have told me more clearly of how my absence had been felt.

A little later Simon came to visit. At that time he was editing a motor-cycle magazine, a job that required him to write all the copy each month as well as to take all the photographs. Simon's interest in photography was already there in 1970 (see image on p.89). He arrived on his first visit on a huge motor bike. Simon looked fairly big too, but when he took off his helmet and padded jacket his physique was not unlike mine at the time.

I have never been able to overcome the guilt I feel about my treatment of these children. I think they were innocent victims of my anger at their mother. Unreasonable, no doubt, but it leaves a shadow.

No doubt, also, Judy was aware of a similar kind of shadow cast by me.

Some people might think I am very hard-hearted, but I think the best thing to do when people are angry is to just walk away, either for a day or forever, if necessary. If you don't you will continue to be hurt.

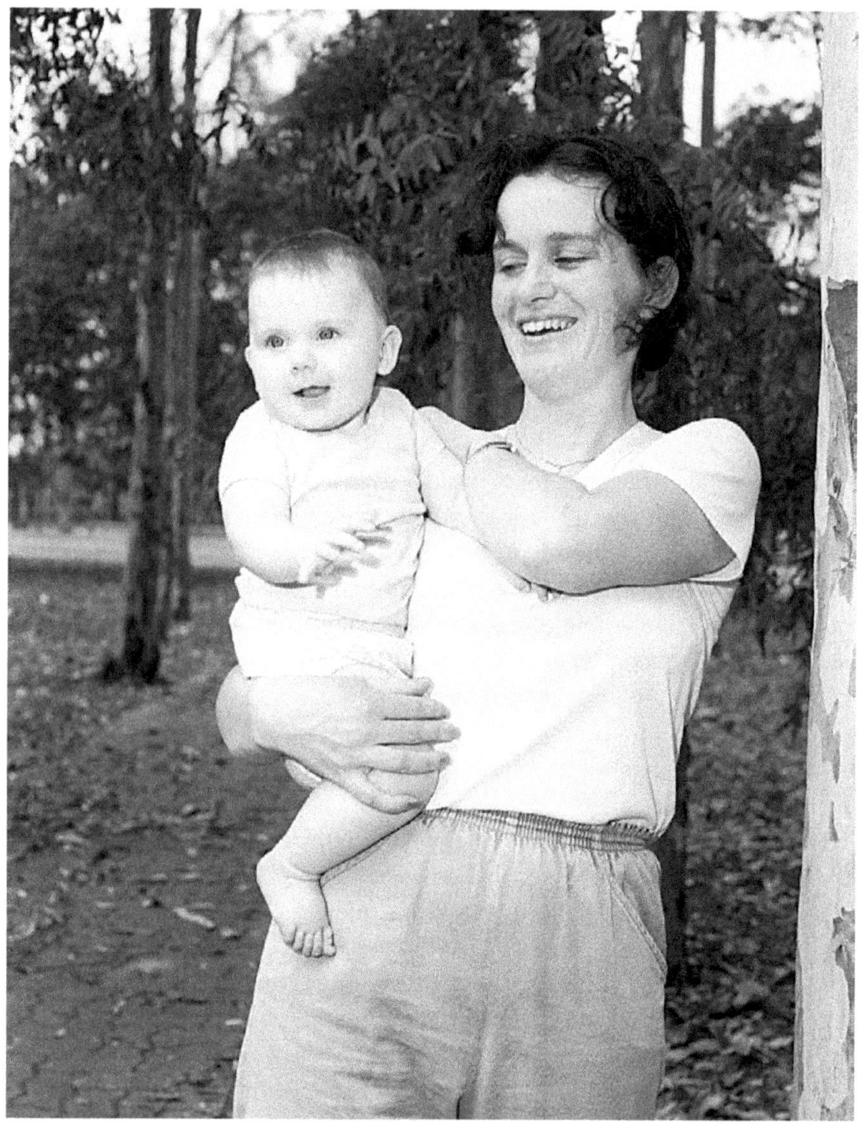

Jane with Rebecca, 1982

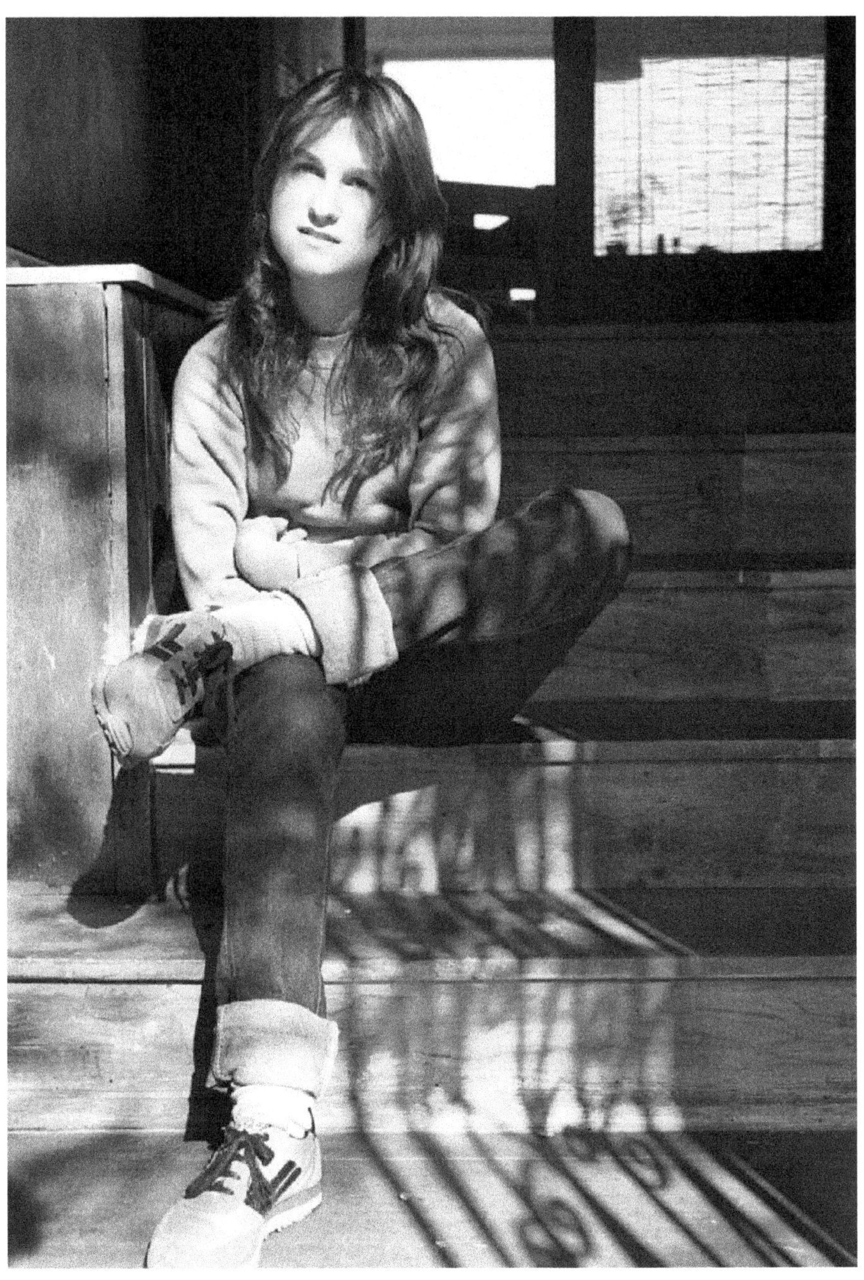

Rachael in the sun on the steps at Fairlight, 1982

In the 1980s Rachael was rapidly growing up and I took many photographs of her. There is one of her sitting on the steps to the Fairlight flat that is my favourite from this period (previous page); it seems to have caught her thoughtfulness and something of her attitude to me: "What is he up to now?" We had frequent rows, usually about what I could afford to buy at the supermarket or at clothes shops, but all-in-all I think I managed single parenthood well enough.

However, work for the Health Department at Chatswood was only irregularly rewarding. I don't think any of the other people in the building had any idea of why I was there. In fact I was only there to serve the woman in charge's empire-building. She loved power above anything, but her little empire wasn't as strong as she thought.

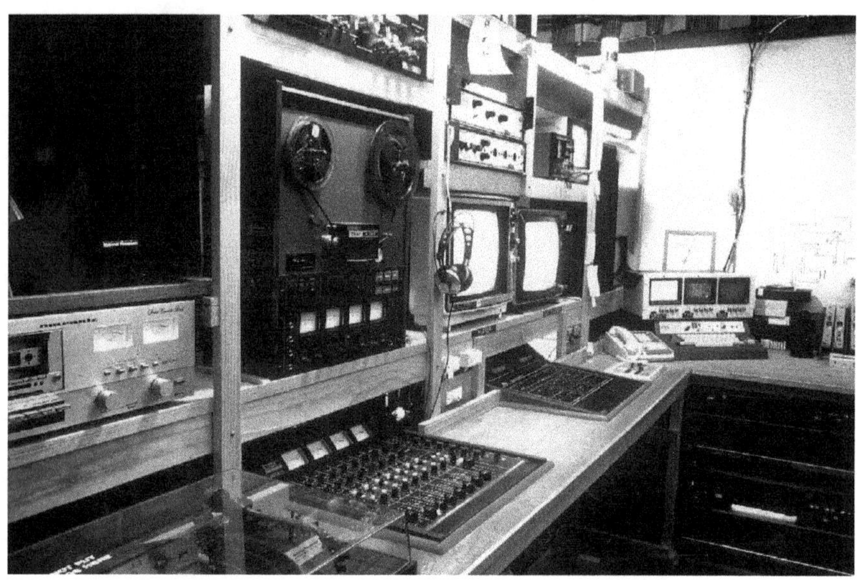

Video and sound editing system before dismantling, c. 1982.

The Health Department was, of course, undergoing funding cuts and rationalisations. To complicate matters the equipment that John Baird and I had assembled was funded from disparate sources and one day the people who had paid for a significant part of the equipment said that they intended to take it to their own building on the other side of the city. What had been a functional system became virtually useless.

One day as I walked down the corridor at Chatswood I heard my name called. Lydia Gautier, as I'd known her in the 1960s, had recognised me from behind. Lydia, a psychologist, was visiting the psychologists at Chatswood. We got to talking and Lydia, knowing that I was a photographer, asked me if I'd take some photographs of her and her two girls. A time and place was arranged and I duly took the photographs. When I was leaving her house I was remembering the afternoon in 1965 when she had come to my bedroom in Darlington. We had made love just once, but the sensations came back to me strongly. As Lydia was about to open her front door to say goodbye I felt an almost irresistable urge to put my arms around her and kiss her. I restrained myself, as much as anything because I knew there was another man in the picture but also because I was living an almost-celibate life and almost enjoying it. A few days later I delivered Lydia's prints and put her out of my mind.

Manly ...

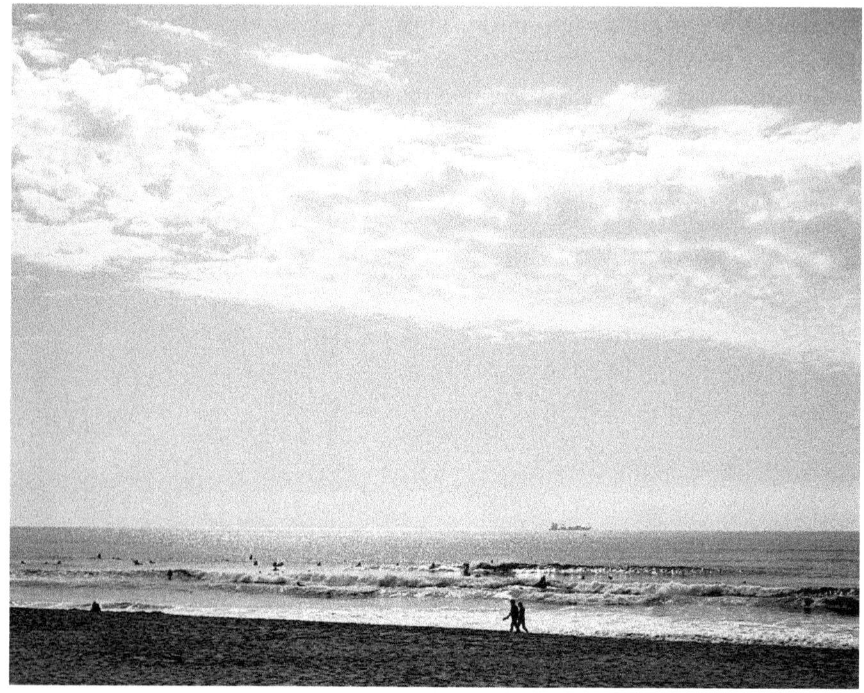

Early morning, Manly Beach, c. 1983

Around that time, Rachael and I moved to a pleasant little sandstock terrace house in Steinton Street in Manly. The old Manly ferry, the *Baragoola,* had become my favourite way of getting to the city. It was soon to be phased out of service and a much more modern ship was to take its place. Before we moved out of the Fairlight flat I sometimes saw the two ferries, the old and the new, passing each other as they crossed the open water between Sydney Heads. Several times I set up the RB67 on the window ledge, waiting for the two ferries to cross paths with no land in sight. I eventually got such a shot, but although it showed what I wanted it to show, it was a very boring photograph. I'm not even sure if I've kept it.

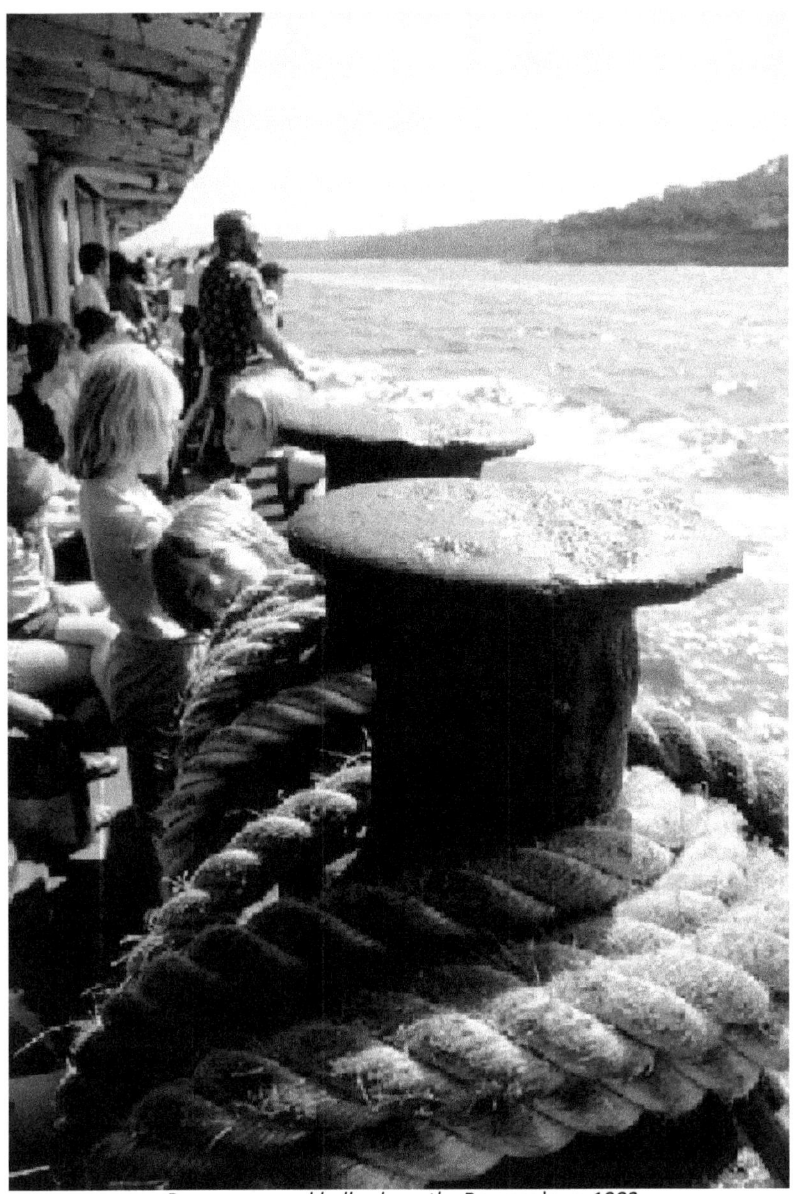
Passengers and bollards on the Baragoola, *c. 1982*

I remembered the huge waves that in rough weather rolled in from the open sea and made a ferry ride to Manly so exciting when I was a young teenager. Now Rachael and her friends on the way to and from school enjoyed the same thrills.

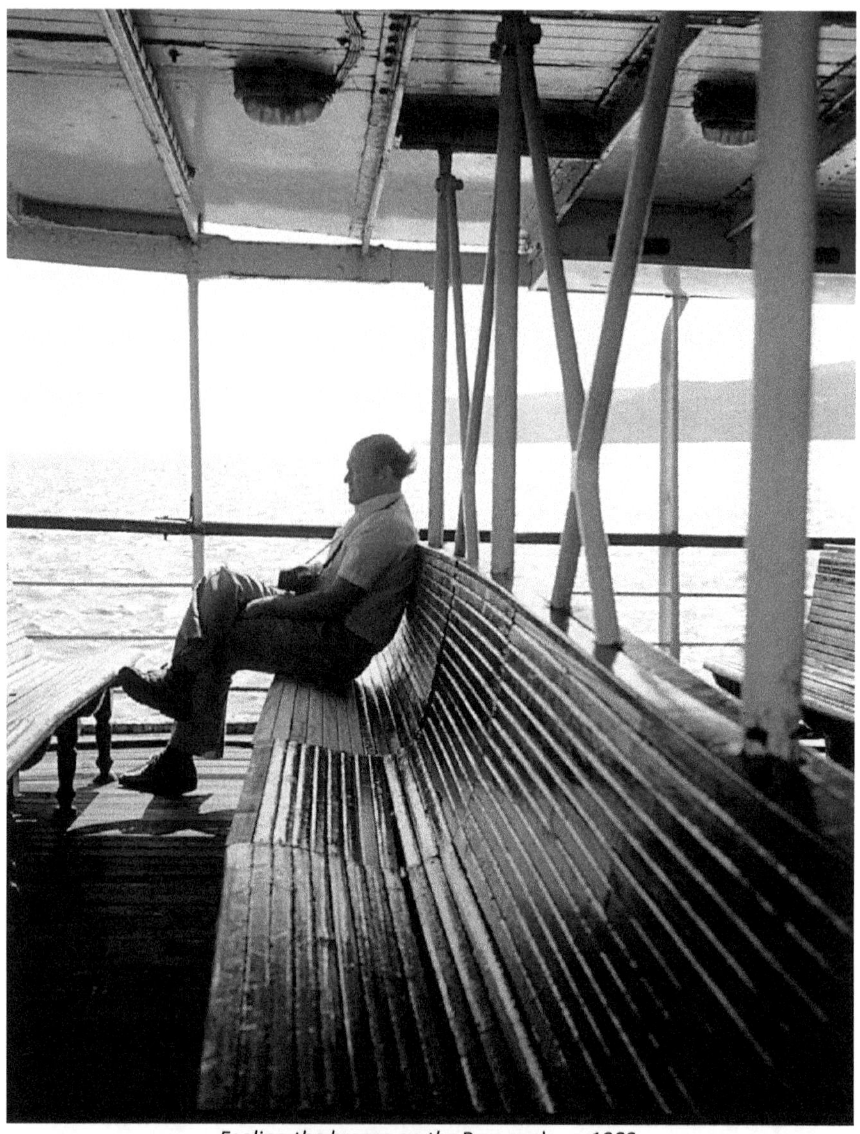

Feeling the breeze on the Baragoola, *c. 1982*

Now that Rachael was becoming independent I was becoming freer to "do my own thing", which of course, at the time, was photography. I had set up a darkroom at Fairlight but at Steinton Street I had a better one. In a small room I covered the window and got perfect black-out at any time of day.

My Karmann-Ghia had long since faded away, been sold for not much to a collector who probably made a lot of money on the deal. For transport I now used my bike with a luggage rack for my camera case.

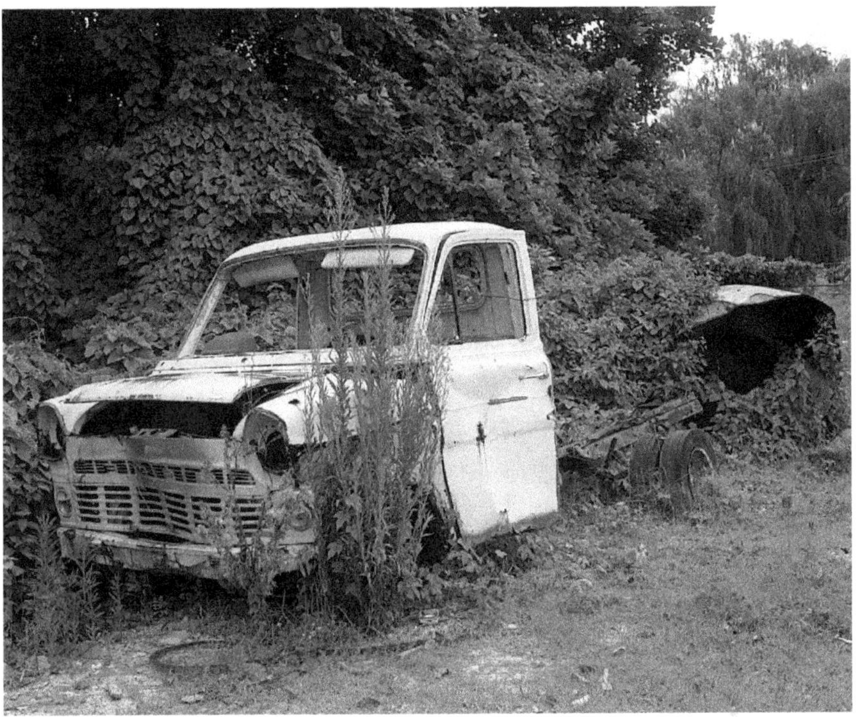

Decaying truck, Warriewood, c. 1983

Out at Warriewood, where Rachel's Tom was stabled, I found this old truck. I am clearly a romantic, attracted to old and decaying things and places.

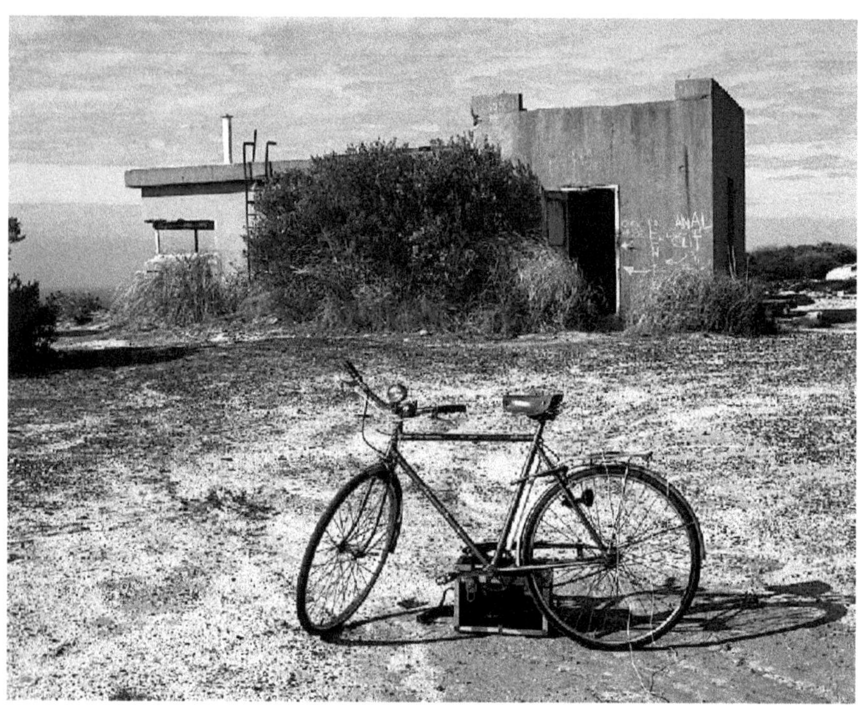

Bunker on North Head, c. 1983

The Bunker Series...

At a remote place close to the cliffs of North Head, I found this old structure, a part of the fortifications to defend against a feared Japanese invasion by sea in one of the worst times of World War II for Australia. On the roof there was a large steel turntable which had once supported a cannon to be fired at the approaching warships.

Living as a child in East Lindfield I was somewhat insulated from the worst fears of that time. Even so this place evoked for me the atmosphere of imminent attack that we had all lived with. It also invoked memories of my national service and my training as a "layer" on 25-pounder cannons. For all these reasons, as well as the obvious more recent use of this place for clandestine rendezvous of a clearly sexual nature, I was drawn by its photographic possibilities but repulsed by its reality.

This composite view, below, shows two adjoining walls. The right angled corner has been flattened to show two perspectives in one image, a device borrowed from the cubist painters in an earlier era. There's another connection for me there - with Australian art history - the image makes me think of the view from inside Ned Kelly's armour. I must say that when I was inside this bunker I couldn't help thinking that it would have offered little enough protection against a direct hit by a large bomb or naval shell . Probably the protection offered by this bunker and the others nearby would have been as effective as the protection offered by Ned's armour: pretty well worthless.

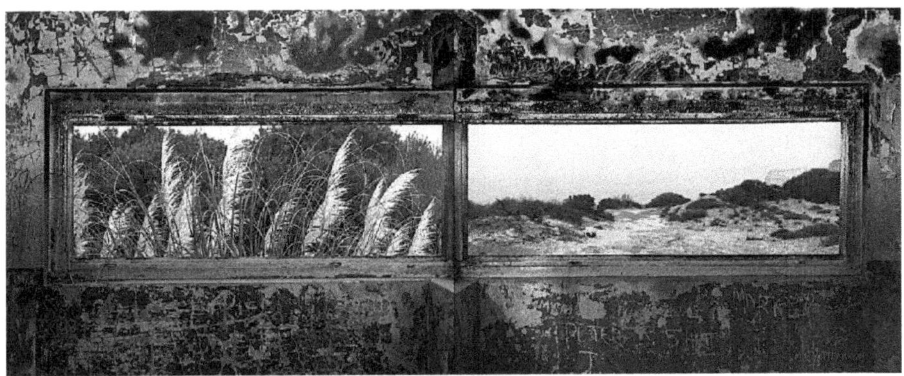

View from inside the bunker, North Head, c. 1983

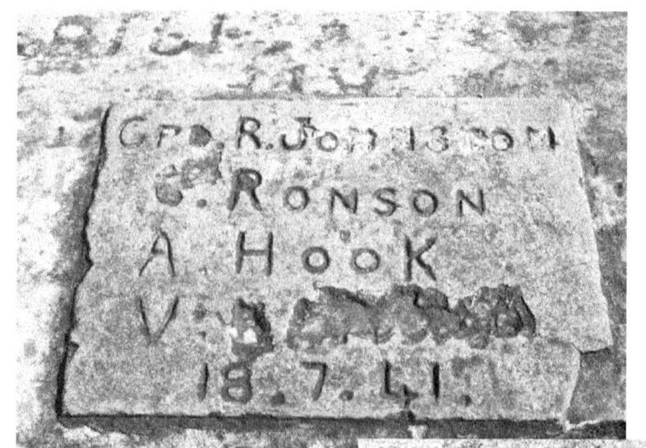

I found these names on cement plaques on the rock outside the bunker. I wondered if the damage to this plaque at left was the work of time (not likely) or if the person had "blotted his copy-book" (how?) and been cut out of memory, or if later vandals had done it. (If photography is evidence of "something" it's a very non-specific something without knowledge from outside the photograph.).

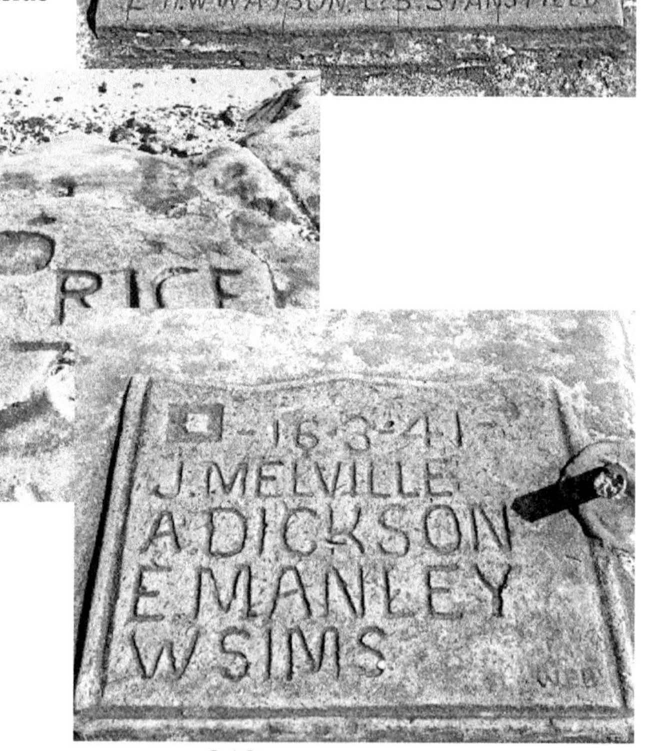

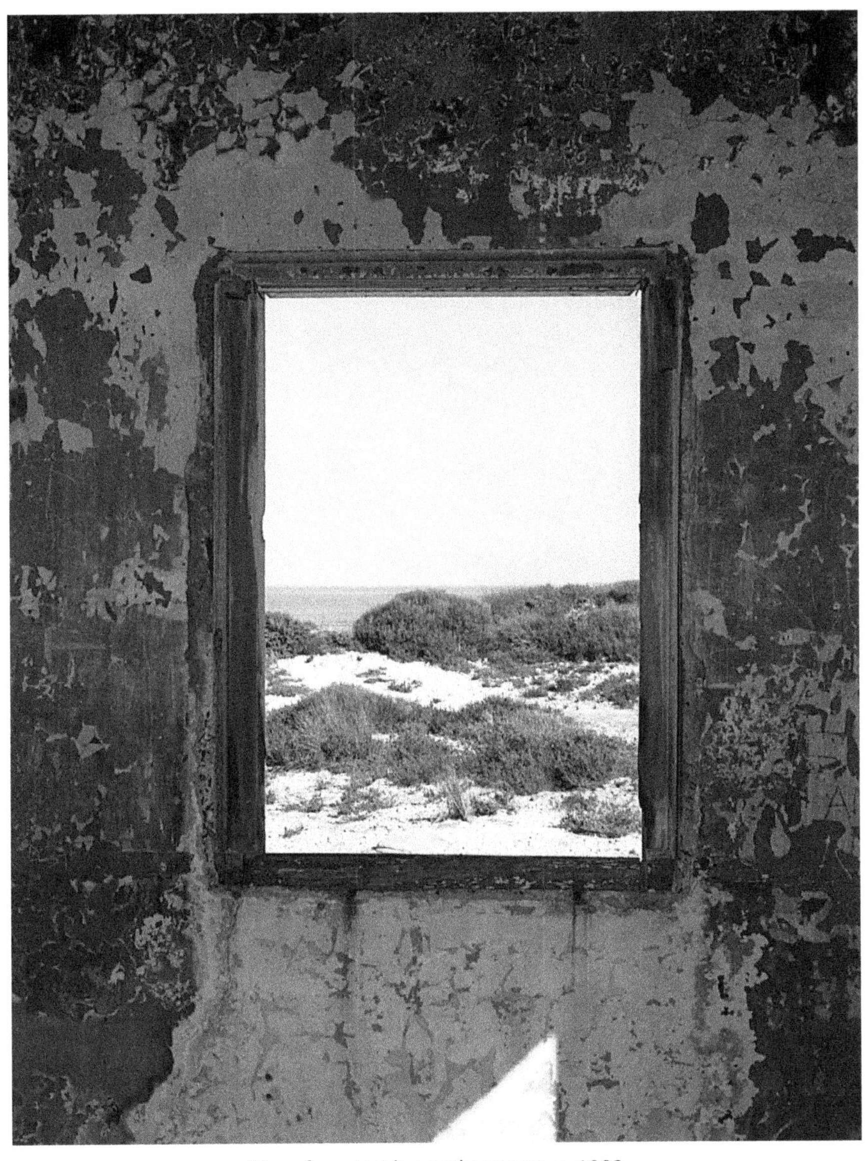

View from inside another room, c. 1983

The full Bunker series can be found on the website gallery.

Panoramas...

Around this time I took up the idea of making panoramas to capitalise on the large amount of detail that can be captured on the relatively large film frames of a camera like the Mamiya RB67.

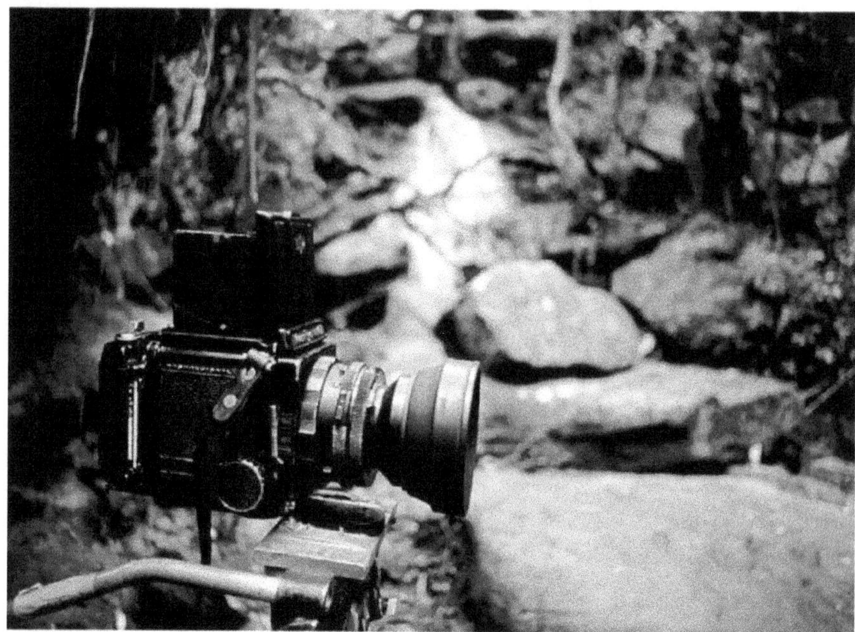

The Mamiya set up for shooting a panorama, c. 1983

I had read somewhere that for this to be successful, the pivot point for the camera must be directly under the optical centre of the lens. Since the optical centre, not the same as the physical centre, wasn't marked on my lens, I had to guess it. If the optical centre is correctly located, I had also read, the sides of each frame in the panorama will meet seamlessly. I must have guessed reasonably accurately because when I joined the prints, the objects at the edges of the frames matched not perfectly but well enough..

Most of the photographs in this book are not reproduced from prints but from scans of original negatives or transparencies, so when I scanned the trannies for the frames in the panoramas it was possible to fudge the joins by making the sides of the frames slightly soft. There is however, another proviso, to avoid "key-stoning" in individual frames the camera's line of sight must be truly horizontal.

I made a number of trips to the Blue Mountains to get panoramic shots of the effect of the seriouos bushfires on the landscape (see website). To get that panorama I drove a rented car up Bells Line of Road till I found the turn-off to the "Walls Lookout." Soon after arriving I took a set of frames late in the grey overcast afternoon (not my favourite images), slept in the car and got up before dawn to be ready to shoot the panorama of cliffs and fog. The continually shifting fog and light made the joins between the frames impossible to hide, but I quite like the effect, as well as the harshness of the foreground which was emphasised by the huge difference in exposure readings for the sky and land.

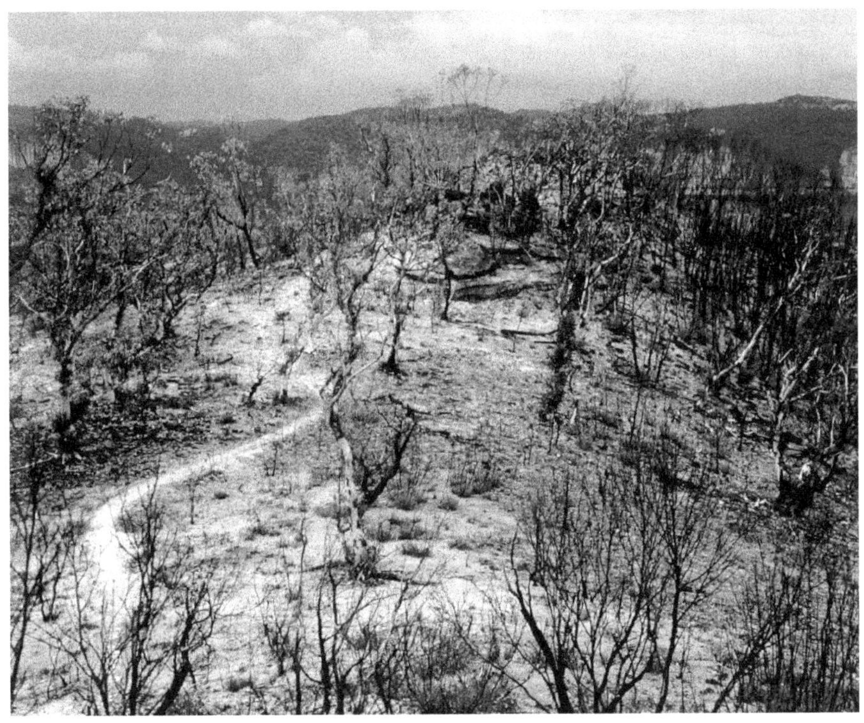

Blue Mountains after bushfire, c. 1983

Now the Mamiya is stolen ...

You might offer various old sayings to explain why I couldn't have two cameras stolen but, of course, they would all be nonsense. The truth is that I almost invited some junkie to steal the Mamiya. I took it into The Domain one day to take some close-up details of bark on trees, intending to extend the panoramic technique to a vertical format. After drawing attention to the equipment by looking into the viewfinder up close to several trees for maybe half an hour, I locked the camera in its shiny case inside the borrowed van I was driving and walked into the city to do whatever I had to do. It was only hours later, after I'd driven away from The Domain, that I noticed the camera's loss. No doubt the creep who took it sold it for a song.

Of course it wasn't insured. The cost wasn't really the point, anyhow. I was so dispirited by the loss of not just one, but two marvellous instruments that I felt unable to continue with the kind of work I'd been doing. A little while later I bought a second-hand Nikon, but I only ever used that for snapshots. When the Pentax went I had at least taken the film out of it. When the Mamiya went my last roll of film went with it. I just didn't have the heart for taking new shots after that. The image on the next page is probably the last medium-format photograph that I have a record of.

However I continued to work in the darkroom, making Cibachrome prints from colour trannies and black-and-white prints from negatives, some of them quite old. It's probably around that time that I began the process of looking back over old work that is culminating in these memoirs.

And at last my libido was coming out of hibernation. Through work at the Health Department I had met several women I was attracted to but nothing came of this. Then I met a single mother of a sensible age for me to form a relationship with. We went out once and got on extremely well. I was inspired to write a love letter to her which she was touched by, but my intensity seemed to frighten her. Once again I had to accept my single status, at least for a while longer.

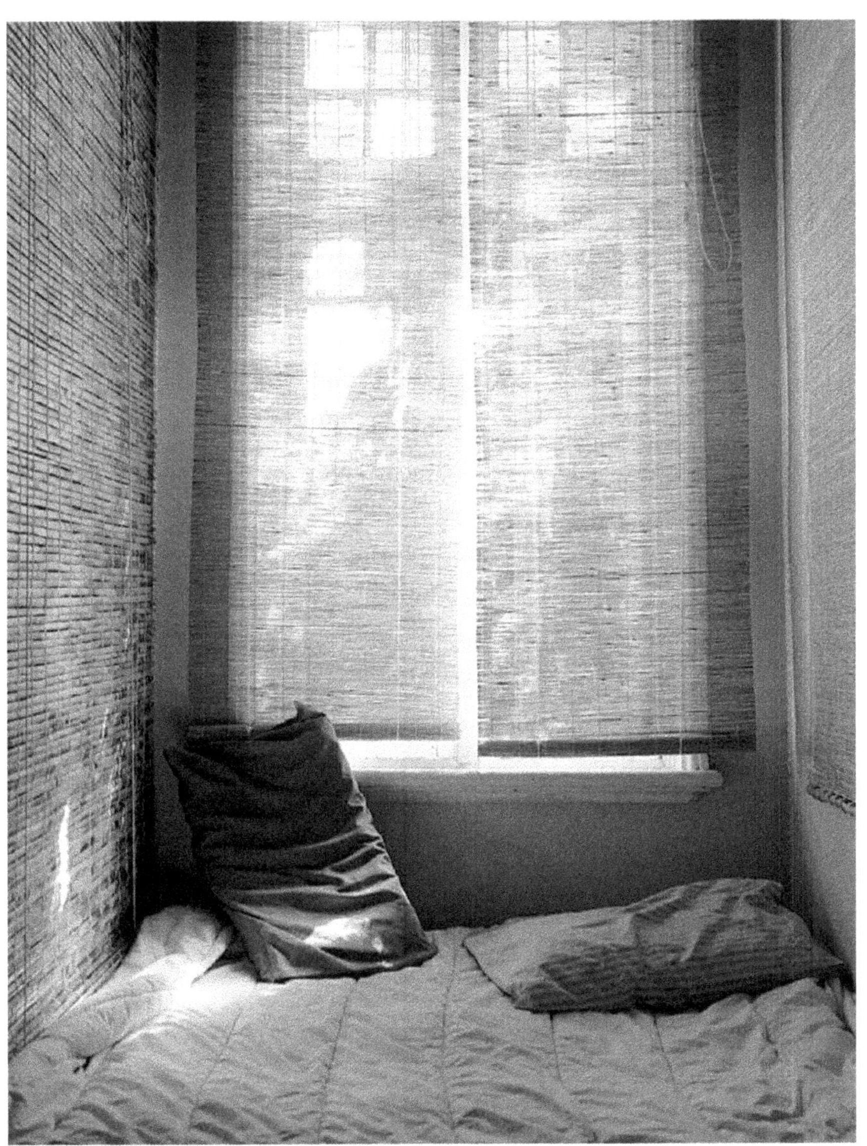

My bed at Steinton Street, c. 1983

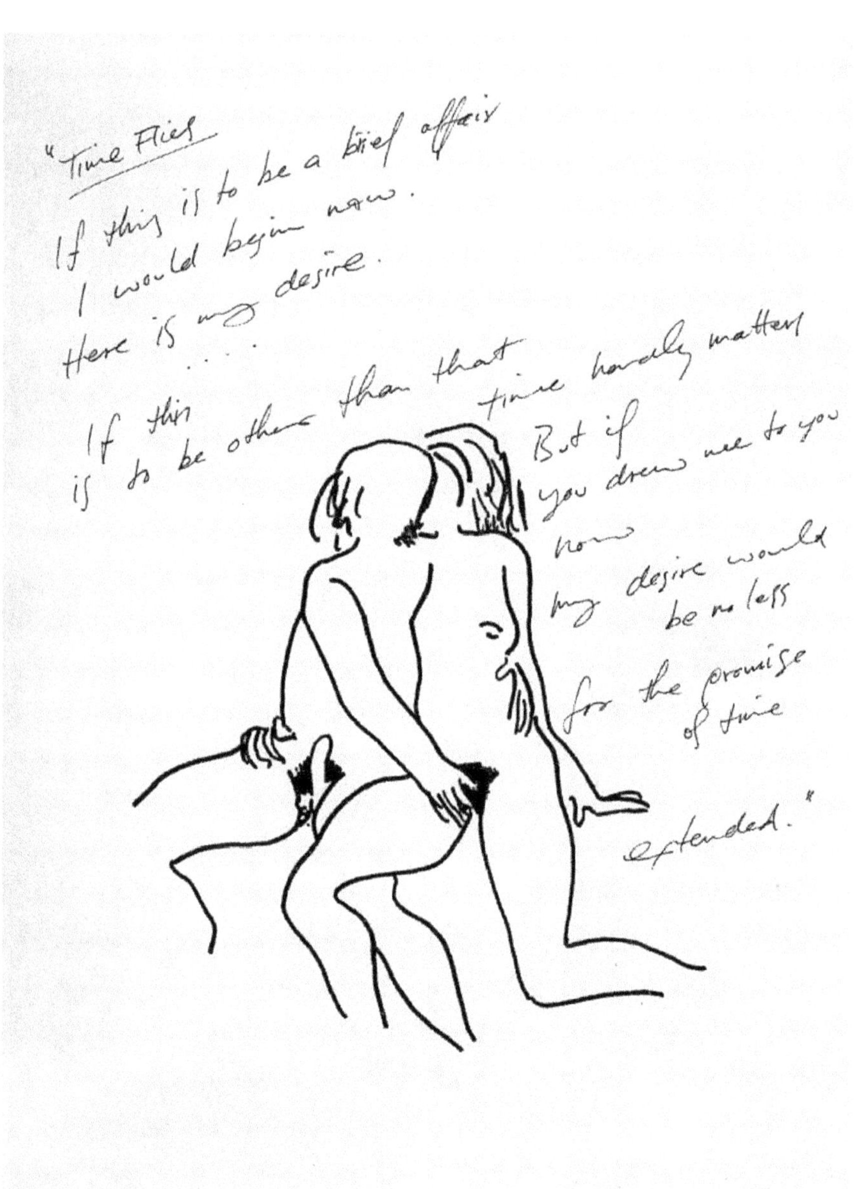

Love Notes, page 2, (photocopy on paper), c. 1983

Lydia ...

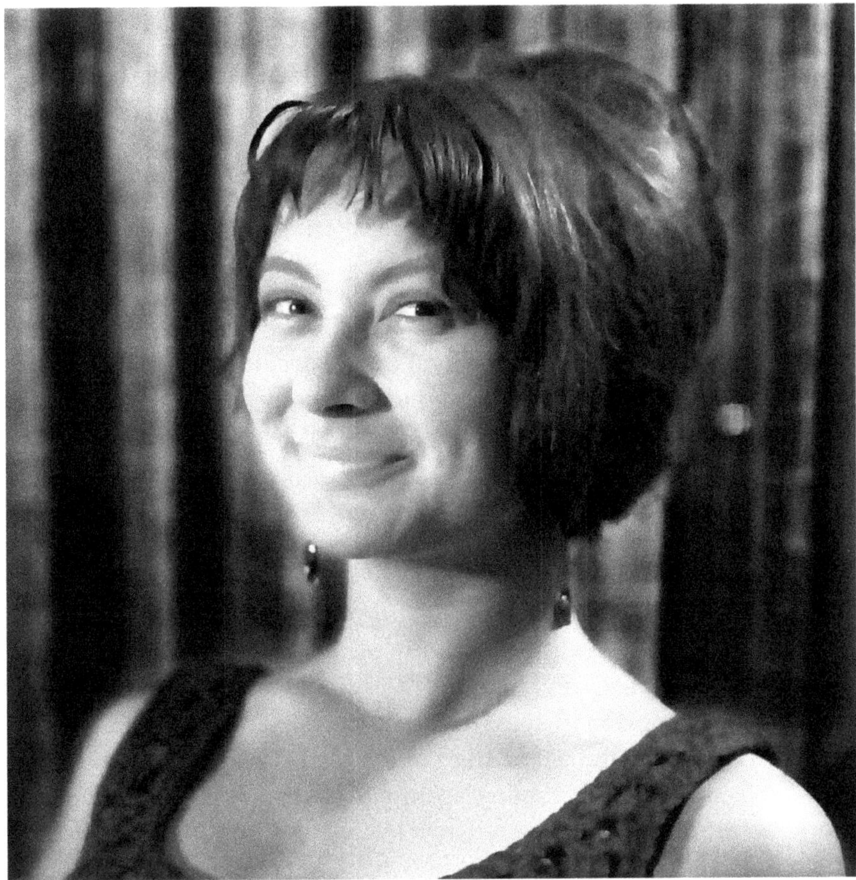

Lydia dressed and made-up for a commissioned portrait (toning and effects added later), 1966

The love note on the previous page wasn't written to Lydia. I think she would have found it horribly precious and I only put it there as an example of how singleness had affected me.. Nor is Lydia the single mother I spoke of a couple of pages back.

I could not have put Lydia out of my mind as much as I thought I had, when I took her new prints to her a year or so earlier. One day I rang the number she'd given me when we met at the Health Department and invited her to dinner at Manly. I can't remember what I cooked for her but I think we sat on the carpet in the living room, talking about work, hers and mine, and no doubt about our children. Lydia had two daughters, both younger than Rachael. We got on very well but eventually it was time for Lydia to go.

Once again I had a strong desire to kiss her but instead I asked her if she'd have dinner with me again the next week and told her, now, that I wanted to make love with her. Possibly, probably, my language was earthier.

Lydia *did* come to dinner the next week, and we did make love. From that night on we have been lovers. The portrait here is one that I made in 1966, although I don't think I printed it then. In 2003 I dug out the old negatives and scanned and modified the image.

Because work at Chatswood was no longer practical, John Baird, whose position was based at the local public hospital, invited me to join him there, where we built a new production facility and worked generally on projects commissioned by doctors, surgeons, psychologists and social workers, amongst others.

Having put the worst experiences of my earlier life behind me, and inspired by my friend Gilly Leahy's film, *My Life Without Steve,* I wrote a proposal for a film to be called *Love and Work.* I submitted the project to the AFC for production funding, intending it to be shot on 16mm film and to incorporate many optical effects. I hoped at last to be able to emulate the "look" of *Album,* my film of 1970, but this time with sufficient funding, using moving images.

The AFC offered me only a third of the funds I had asked for, which I very foolishly accepted, hoping against hope that it could be made to work using video. I suppressed my knowledge that in the mid-1980s video was not a practical medium for what I wanted to do. Looking back now I think that the years since the collapse of *Plenty of Water and Honest Men* - and all those years in low-grade academia and the Health Department - had utterly sapped my confidence. In spite of a marvellous performance by John Flaus as Phil Bute, my "double", *Love and Work* was only effective in parts, and not many parts at that. Dramatically it was a complete failure.

Life with Lydia ...

Lydia had bought a house in Cremorne which she invited me and Rachael to share with her and her girls. There wasn't really enough room for all of us so we agreed that we would extend the house. I raised the necessary mortgage for this which gave me some equity in the property. A wonderful aspect of the extensions was that we would build a self-contained studio for me at the back of the land, separated from the main house by a small paved courtyard.

At first all went well. Rachael was in her final year at high school and she and Lydia's girls got on well. But Sasha, Lydia's eldest, was clearly unsettled by what was going on. The atmosphere between Sasha and me became openly hostile. It was unpleasant for me and no doubt for Sasha, and extremely difficult for Lydia, and it rubbed off on Rachael. It got to the point where I seriously thought of moving out. I told Rachael, but she said I shouldn't do it, that she'd be alright.

Eventually, together with a couple of friends, Rachael took off to North Queensland where she got work and established her independence.

Many years later, long after this story ends, my relationship with Sasha became a good one. I sometimes wonder how Lydia and I survived the intervening years, but we did. Lydia's younger daughter had a much more manageable attitude to me, far less fraught. I once heard her refer to me as: "My mother's current lover."

Threaded through this long story there have been numerous accounts of relationships. If I had been a "professional" artist instead of a "dedicated amateur" I would, I'm sure, have had a similar history of relationships, but would those relationships have been so much in the foreground? No professional artist that I know of would let such things have much, or any, bearing on his or her "career path".

I'm not about to ask readers to analyse my work psychologically. With my old friend Albie Thoms, I am deeply suspicious of attempts to explain any work of art by recourse to any psychological theory. In the first place, understandings of psychology by most writers are profoundly shallow (!). In the second place, to attempt to analyse the physicality, the actual nature of a work even a body of work by references to non-physical

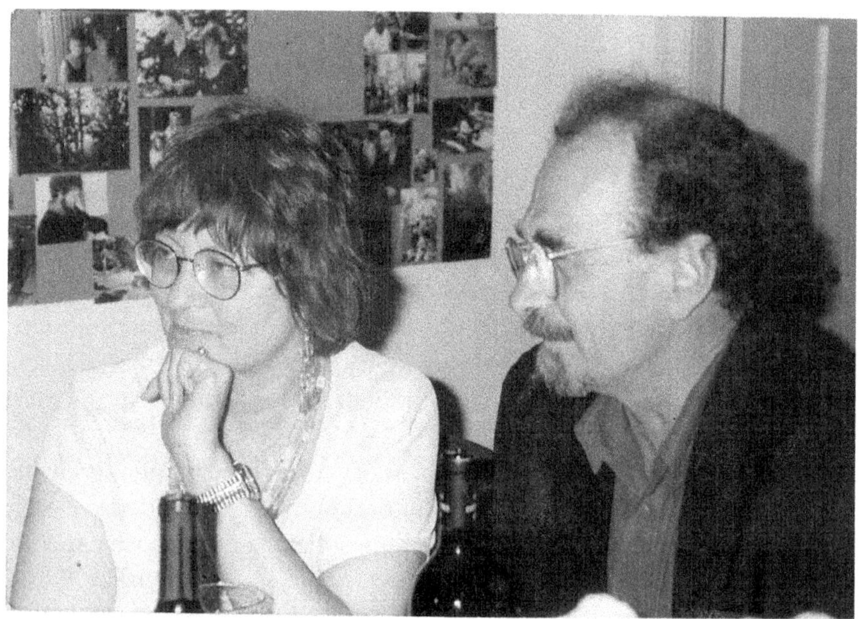

Lydia and David, 1994 (Photographer Elizabeth Perey)

physical, therefore imagined or "intuited", characteristics, is just so much verbiage. It flies in the face of everything that I understand as realist philosophy.

It is however true that my relationships have had a major bearing on my work, in the sense that they have necessitated many practical adjustments I've had to make during my life: financial adjustments, adjustments to physical and/or cultural circumstances, adjustments to other people's needs. These are practical things that I imagine many (most?) other artists have also dealt with, without having such disparate careers. The reasons that I haven't done this to the same extent are no doubt psychological, but they are nobody's business but my own, and cannot explain the "meaning" of a single product of my output.

Lydia's parents had come from Russia to China, where Lydia was born during the Japanese occupation. Her father's family seem to have left Russia to escape the Revolution; her mother's family, who were Jewish, left before then to escape the czarist pogroms. Her mother had died before I joined up with Lydia but her father I did meet. He seemed to have something of a scoundrelly past, though I'm not suggesting criminality. I got the distinct impression that his attitudes had been formed by the politics of the early days of the Russian Revolution. I got on well with him and I don't think I'm misrepresenting him by saying that he seemed to have a lot of sympathy for the aims of that Revolution.

Amongst the many books on Lydia's shelves there was a battered old one called *Picture History of Russia*. In retrospect I can see that, although it's in English for western readers, its perspective is a Bolshevik one. Published in the USA of all places (and originally in Russian) in 1945 and revised in 1956, at least half of the book's pages are devoted to the period from the Revolution to the book's present, a very short period measured against all of Russian history. Particularly fascinating to me was a graphic made in 1918, reproduced overleaf, showing the top Bolshevik leadership at the time.

I subsequently found that almost all of the people on that banner as I choose to call it, were murdered during the Stalinist purges of the late 1930s. Two were sidelined to relative obscurity, one died in what to me are suspicious circumstances.

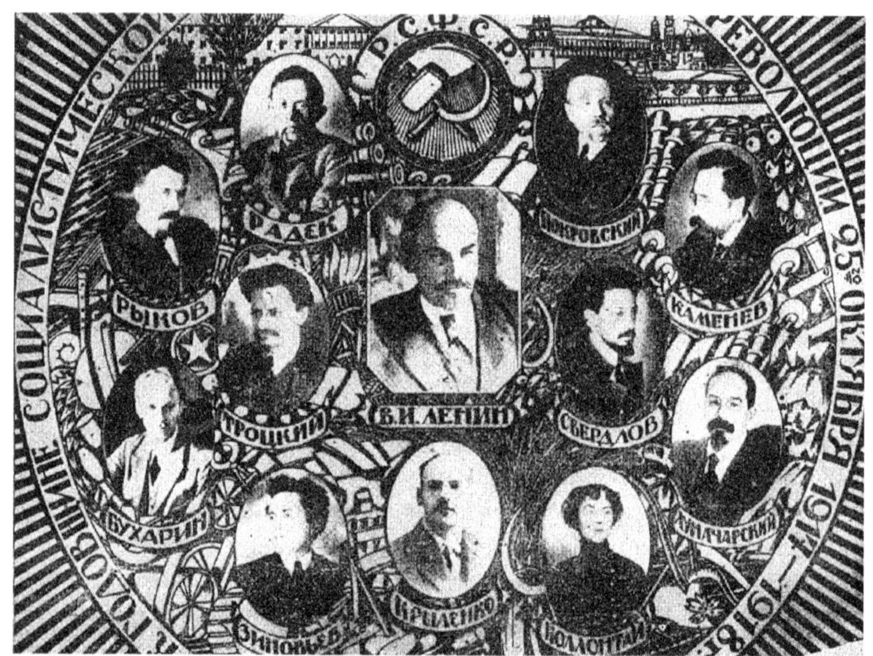

Leadership of the Bolsheviks in 1918, reproduced from Picture History of Russia, (© 1945 and 1956, Crown Publishers Inc., USA)

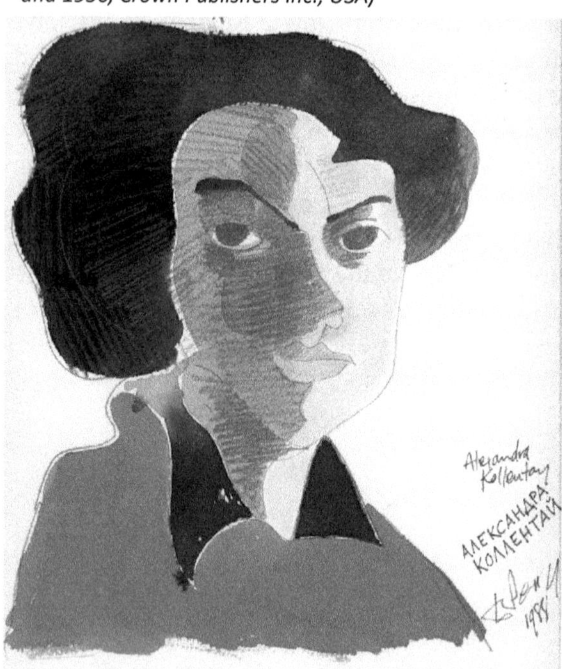

Study for portrait of Alexandra Kollontai, (watercolours on paper, [name mispelled in both languages]),1988

I became fascinated by Lydia's history, and read a number of histories of the subject. I learned (superficially) the Russian language, and am thus able to read the names on the banner. They are, around the outer circle from top right Pokrovsky; Kamenev; Lunacharsky; Kollontai; Krylenko; Zinoviev; Bukharin; Rykov; Radek. In the centre is Lenin, to his right (our left) Trotsky; to our right, Sverdlov. As I read on I gathered stories about all of these people, even the obscure historian, Mikhail Pokrovsky.

Eventually, in my newly-finished studio, I began work on what became a series of 15 watercolour portraits, which I called collectively (and unsurprisingly) *The Bolsheviks*. Some of the portraits were based on the smudgy images on the banner, others on photographs reproduced in one history book or another. The first character I attempted was the intriguing Alexandra Kollontai.

The terrified look on Bukharin's face can't be seen on the banner, it wouldn't have been there in 1918, but it certainly would have been visible by 1936.

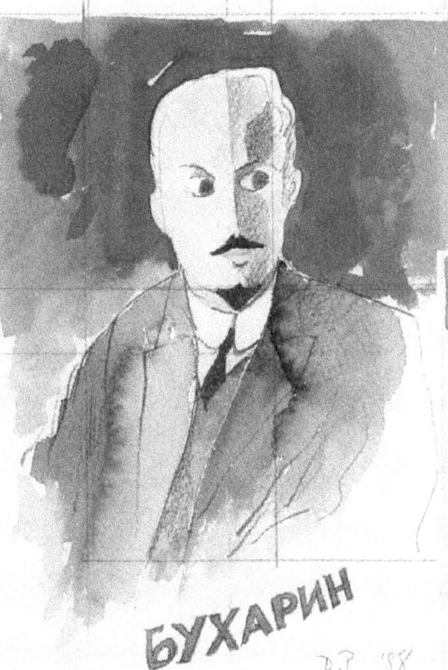

Study for portrait of Nikolai Bukharin (water-colours on paper), 1988

All of *The Bolsheviks* were painted during 1988 which was the bi-centenary of the settlement/ invasion/occupation of Australia by the British. My view of Australian history is jaundiced enough for me to joke to myself that these paintings were my Bicentennial Gift to Australia.

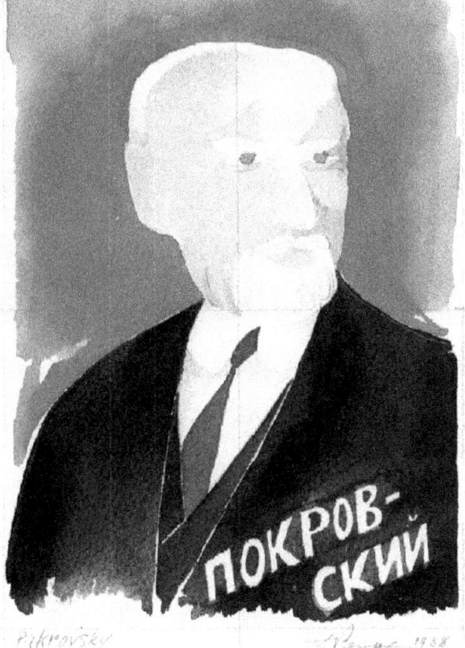

Study for portrait of Mikhail Pokrovsky (water-colours on paper), 1988

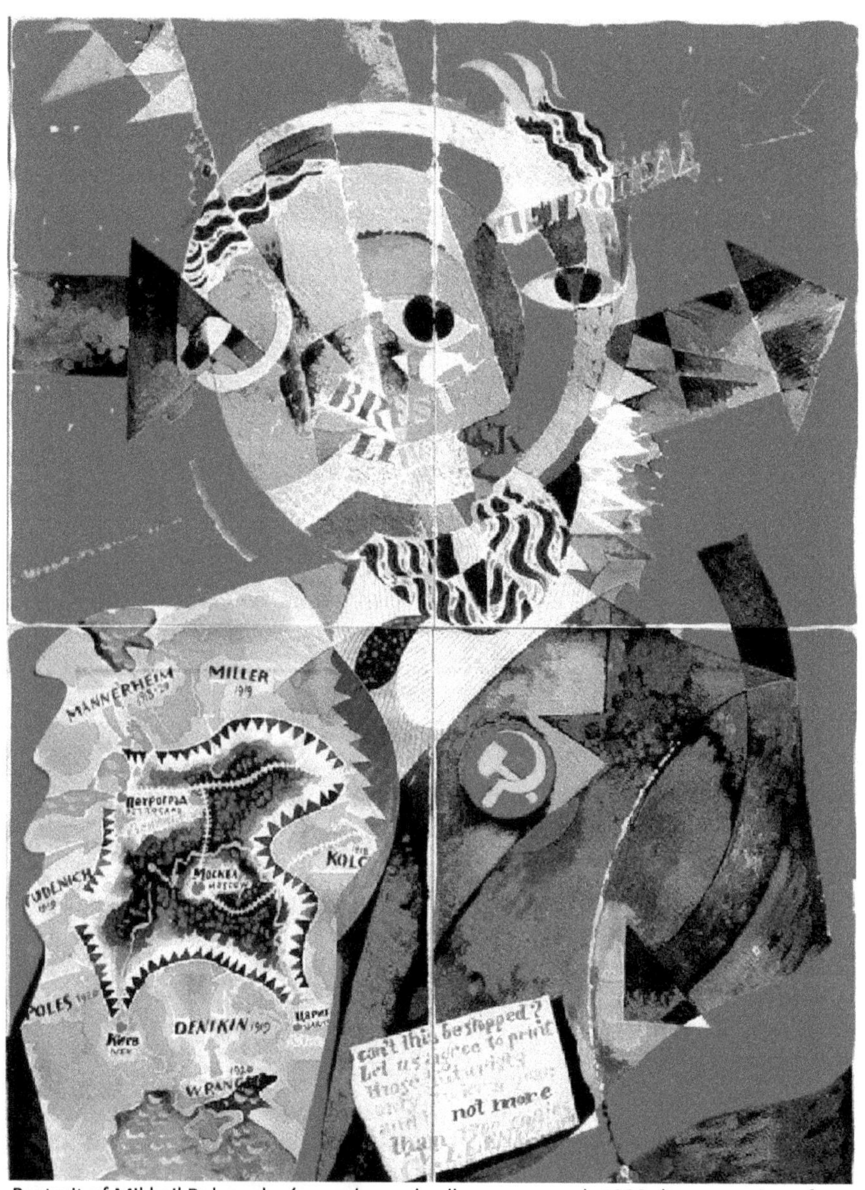

Portrait of Mikhail Pokrovsky *(gouache and collage on paper), 1988. (In possession of Albie Thoms' estate.)*

Pokrovsky was a particularly "over-the-top" character. One of the histories I read told of how, when he was a delegate to the Brest-Litovsk "peace" conference, he lectured the Prussian officers on the other side of the table about Liberty, Equality and Fraternity. Lunacharsky, shown opposite, was Commissar for the Arts in the early days of the Revolution.

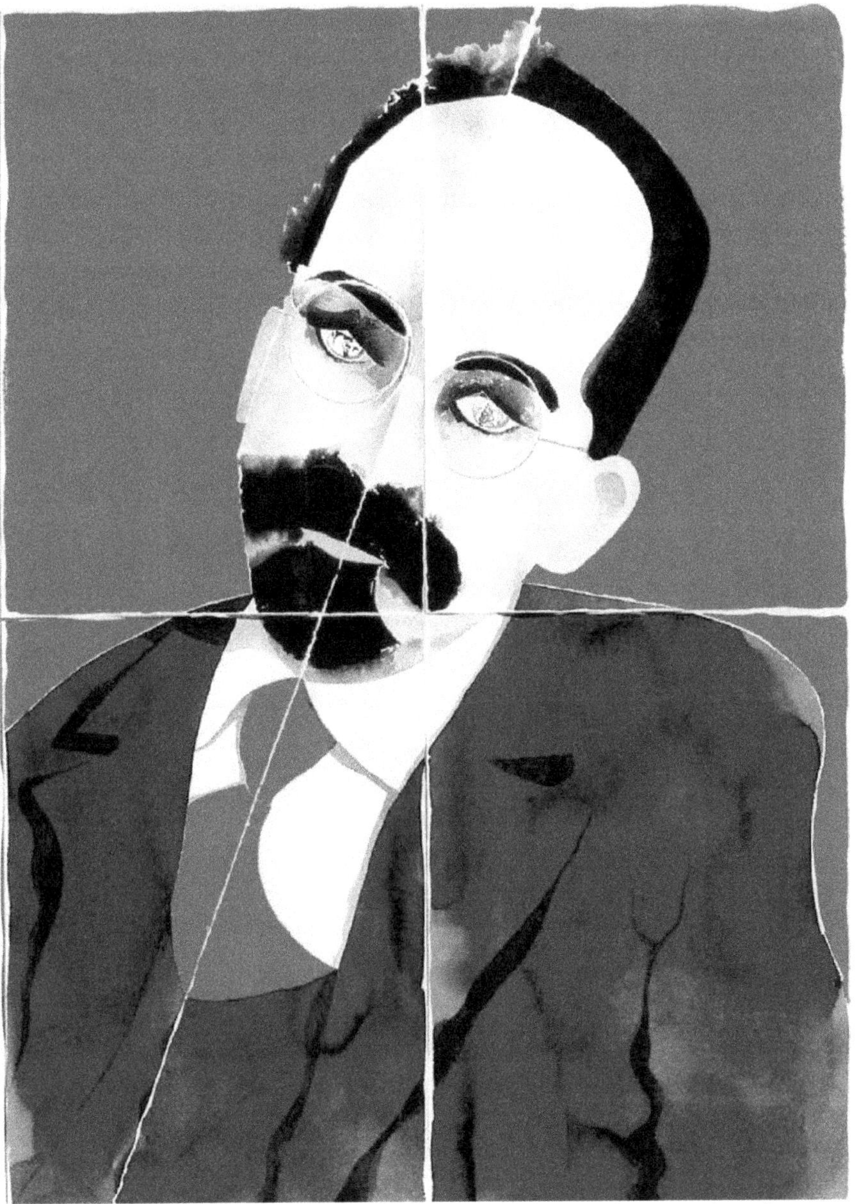

Portrait of Anatoly Lunacharsky *(coloured inks on paper), 1988. (Present whereabouts unknown.)*

He too was a supporter of the avant-garde. Drawn in his eyes are tiny versions of a Malevich painting and Tatlin's plans for the Monument to the Third International.

The ragged lines cutting across all the paintings in this series are due to the fact that in making the first one I had used small sheets of paper butted together to make a larger image. I so liked the effect that I used it for all the others. Lunacharsky was one of the few "old Bolsheviks" to escape the purges of 1936-37. He was appointed ambassador to the Spanish Republic and died of food poisoning on the way to take up the appointment - a very suspicious circumstance, in my view.

In around 1995 *The Bolsheviks* and other related paintings were shown at the Ray Hughes Gallery, where they sold like hot cakes, not to put too fine a point on it.

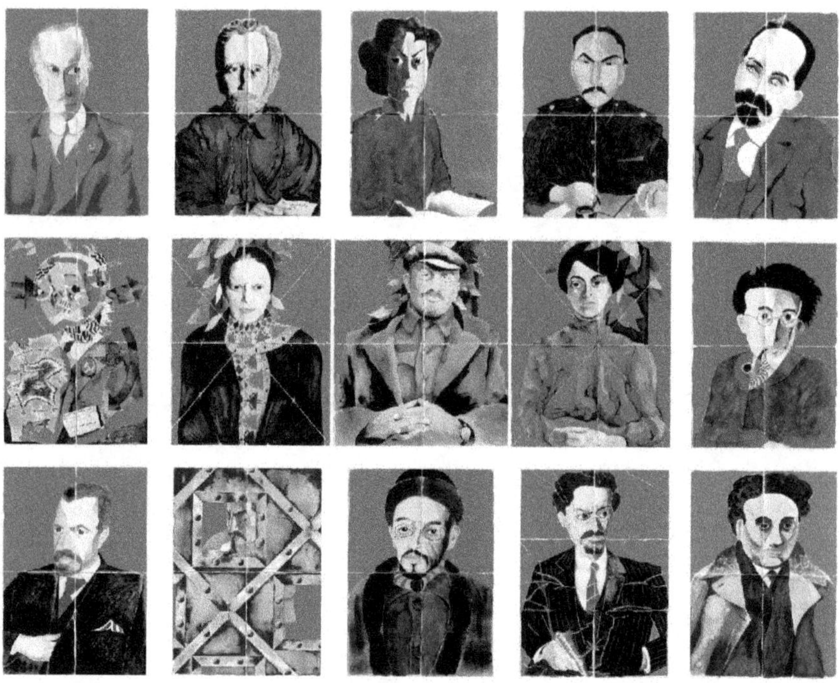

The Bolsheviks, *1988. All individual portraits in full colour on website*

In the exhibition the paintings were arranged pretty much as they appear above. The figures in these paintings are (top row, left to right): Bukharin; Kamenev; Kollontai; Krylenko; Lunacharsky; (middle row) Pokrovsky; Nadezhda Krupskaya; Lenin; Inessa Armand; Radek; (bottom row) Rykov; Stalin; Sverdlov; Trotsky; Zinoviev.

After completing *The Bolsheviks,* I did several paintings on the theme of "exile" and also attempted a very large oil painting. This painting gave me hell. No matter how I changed it I couldn't make it work. I worked on it for at least six months and still I couldn't make it work.

As the image on the next page shows, the subject was an artist at work, using a "socialist realist" woodcut of heroic reconstruction for his model and reinterpreting it as a brightly coloured abstraction. But no matter what I did, I couldn't integrate the three parts, and eventually, in desperation, I sawed the plywood panel into pieces. All that remains of the painting now are the photograph and some studies I made before I started it and some while I was struggling with it. Up in the far right corner you can see a little bit of *trompe-l'oeil,* an image of a piece of paper pinned to the surface containing the Russian phrase: *shto delat?* ("What is to be done?"), the title of Lenin's famous pamphlet of 1917.

The photograph of that painting (see next page) shows *What is to be Done?* just before I destroyed it. It tells me, if no one else, why I could never have made it work. Apart from its attempt at "grand narrative" its formal structure was against it; or more accurately, its colours. (Interestingly, in black-and-white, it almost works.) The right hand third, the still life by a window, was in bright greens, pinks and yellows. The middle the "soviet realist" woodcut was in greys. The "new painting", in the left third, went through more permutations than I like to think of. That's where I had most of my trouble: on a bright blue ground, the abstract construction, where I attempted to emulate the dynamic diagonals of political "art". That also brought me deep embarrassment. At one stage I had two large bright yellow zig-zags on the blue background. Just then we had several Russian visitors and I proudly showed them what I was up to. They were transfixed by the double zig-zags. In horrified tones they asked me (or possibly they asked Lydia in Russian): "SS!?"

It wasn't what I'd intended, but it sure as hell was what was understood. I was reminded once again of just how variable "meaning" can be and, as well, of just how awful was the memory for Russions of the Nazi invasion.

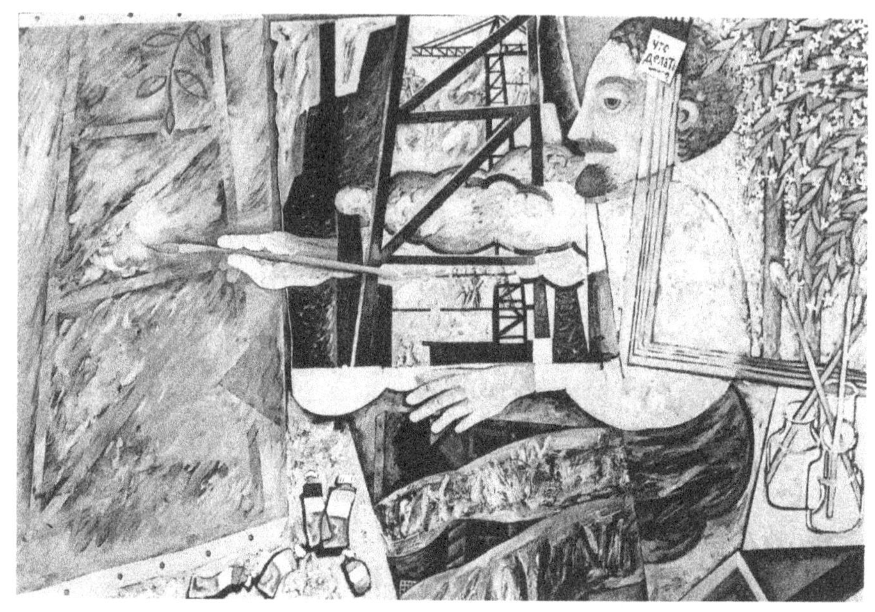

What is to be Done (oils on plywood), 1989

Following are three other paintings from that exhibition.

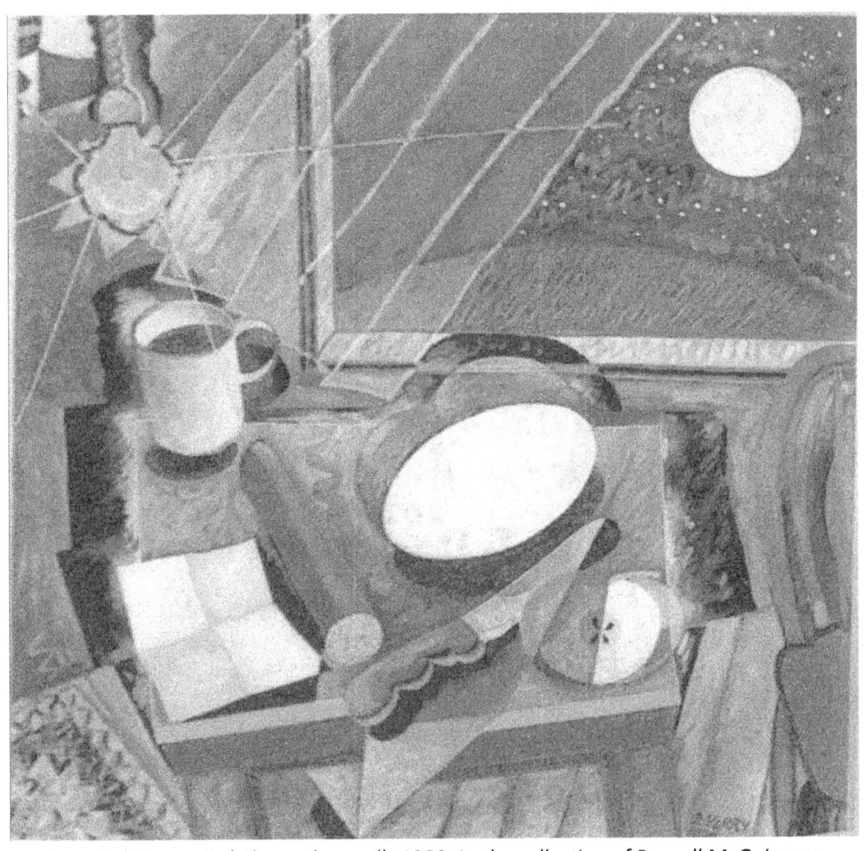

The Exile's Room II *(oils on plywood), 1989. In the collection of Parnell McGuinness.*

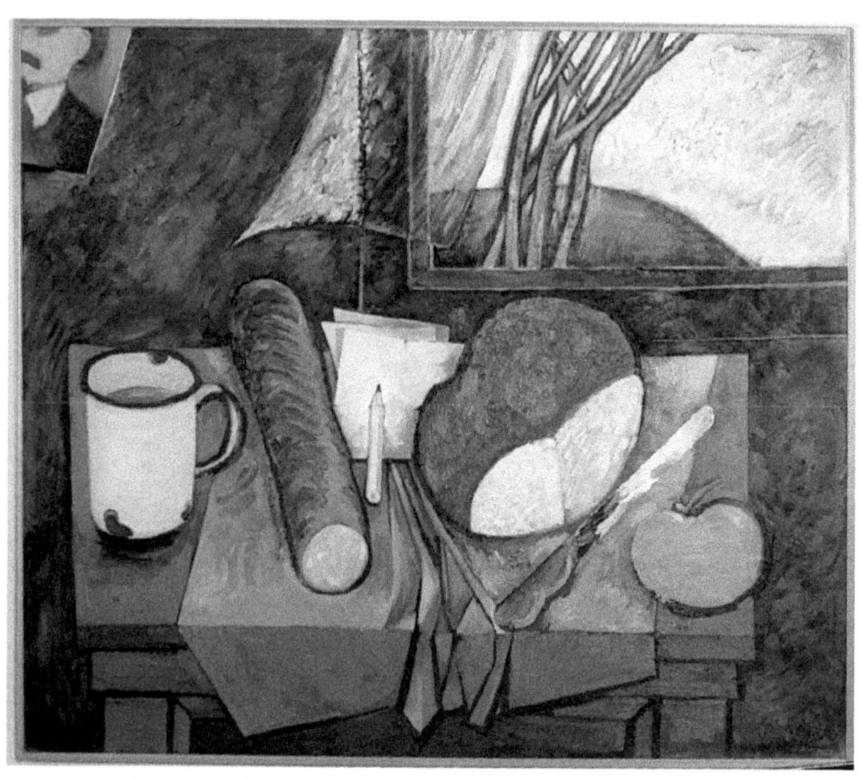

The Exile's Room I *(oils on plywood), 1989. In the collection of Carolyn Barkell.*

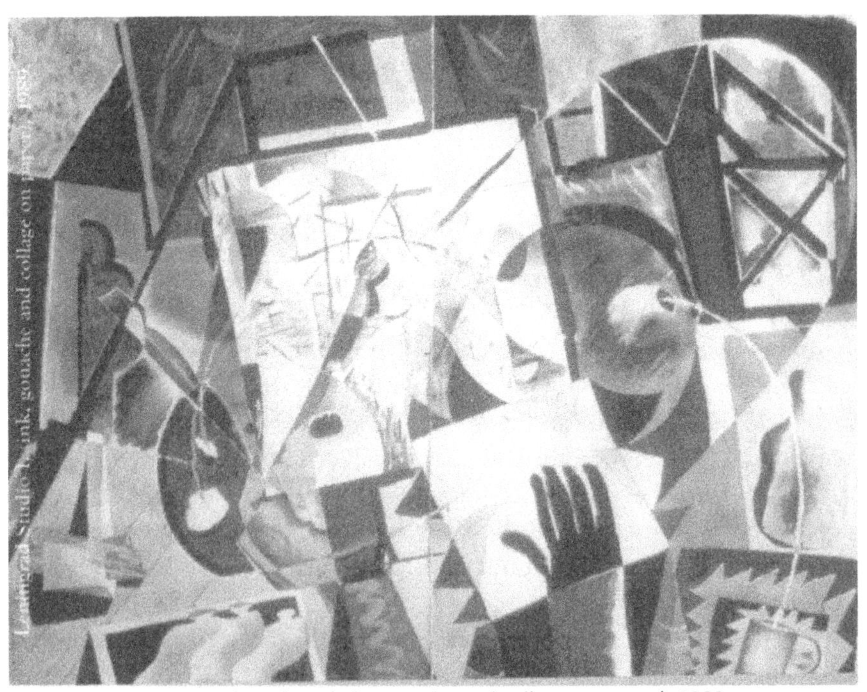

Leningrad Studio 1 *(Ink, gouache and collage on paper), 1989*

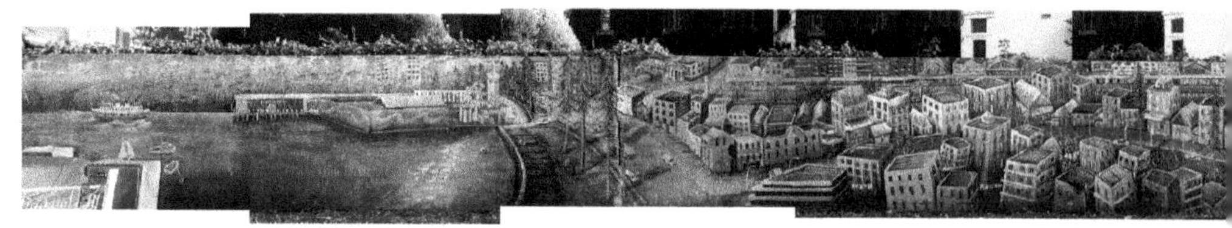

Car park mural at Manly, photographed 1989

The Manly Mural Project ...

While still living at Manly I had become intrigued by a mural painted along the entire back wall of the council parking area at the corner of Wentworth Street and Darley Road. Completed in May, 1980, by Ian Walker, it seemed to me a tragedy that the mural, a detailed (if somewhat kitschly distorted) record of the centre of Manly from the ocean to the harbour, was doomed by the council's intentions to redevelop the site, still as a car park but larger. I only know about the mural's history from an article that appeared in the *Manly Daily* when the artist was finishing his work. I also learned there that Ian Walker felt very aggrieved by the fact that he'd been unable to sell any of his paintings and had consequently burned them all in his backyard. I sympathised with his disappointment but I couldn't agree with his destruction of his own history.

In August 1989, possibly in an attempt to distract myself from the problems of *What is to be Done?*, I decided to photograph Walker's mural. Lydia drove me to Manly early in the morning, which was the only time that the entire wall would be lit by the sun, while I hoped against hope that there would no cars in the car park.

Since the Mamiya had been stolen I only had my 35mm Nikon, which would have to do the job. Loaded with fine-grain Kodachrome film it did the job very well. Unlike the landscape panoramas of the early 1980s I couldn't cover this subject from a fixed position by panning. What works well with a three-dimensional subject wouldn't work at all with a two-dimensional one. (That would push even photography's ability to create optical illusions beyond breaking point.)

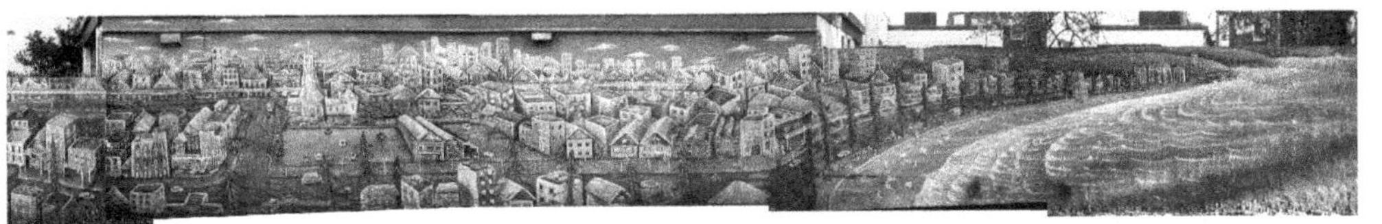

To get the result I wanted I first had to decide on a distance from the wall that would allow me to fit the highest part of it within the height of the horizontally-mounted camera's frame. That became the distance that each part of the mural had to be photographed from, to maintain correct scale from one part to the next. Then I moved systematically along the mural, photographing it in slightly overlapping sections, each section taken from the same pre-determined distance and with the camera's back parallel to the wall as nearly as I could estimate.

Before I acquired the very good computer and software system that I now have, I had A4 colour photocopies made from the Kodachromes. With a bit of cutting and pasting I assembled a draft version of the image, similar to but much larger than the image below. I took the photocopies to show to a person at Manly Library, hoping to apply for funding to make large, high quality photographic prints which could be assembled to create a large and reasonably accurate record of the mural. The library person was hardly interested in the proposal which I thought was pretty strange, considering it was a record of an already lost part of Manly's heritage. She did, however, give me a photocopy of the *Manly Daily* article.

Luckily I'm not as angry as Ian Walker - I didn't destroy my work - and eventually assembled it in my computer in a version that can one day be printed to approximately three metres across, a shadow of the original work but impressive nevertheless.

The Refracting Glasses ...

For a time I retired to my studio where I concentrated on making paintings and drawings. Some of these were quite large in all kinds of media. Many of them were interpretations (certainly not copies) of paintings and woodcuts in a Soviet-era book called *Artists of the Blockaded City* (my translation). The city was Leningrad. I'd found the book in the now defunct Soviet Bookshop in Sydney.

Long before then a friend, Maree Delofski, had seen The Bolsheviks at our house. She thought there might be a film in the paintings, and as she worked for the AFC at the time she urged me to put in an application for funding. I'm not sure what Maree expected but what she got was a detailed script for the first two-thirds of an experimental feature film about a very odd character with the odder name of Constant Malernik.[10] I wrote the character for myself to play. Just before the final third of the story, I introduced Lydia as a subject for a "documentary". Lydia had heard all sorts of stories about Russia, but had never actually been to her family's homeland. I proposed to take her there to record some of her reactions as well as Constant's reactions to the realities of his dreamland.

The last page of my script said something to the effect: "We'll go to Russia and see what happens." I doubt if anyone could get away with such a vague proposal these days, even if the assessor(s) took into account as they did then, my track-record since the 1960s. The end result was that I was offered the most substantial, the most realistic funding I have ever had to the present day.

If only people had known I was going to get material about the first weeks after the collapse of the Soviet Union. If only **I'd** known what I was going to get (!): not journalistic material but extremely personal reactions by Lydia, her aunt whom she had never met before, people on the street (Red Square, actually) and, I mustn't forget, Constant Malernik.

This time I was going to shoot almost all of the *The Refracting Glasses* on 16mm film with one interview to be shot on video for transfer to film

---

[10] "Constant" from Constant Lambert, musician son of the Russo-Australian artist George Lambert, as well as Constant's inconstancy as an artist. Malernik is an unlikely compound of the German word for painter, "maler", with the Russian suffix "nik" often applied to an adjectival noun to create a name that describes a person's profession. The composer Mahler is also in there somewhere.

and one section to include special effects to be shot on 35mm for reduction to 16mm before final printing.

The part of the story that used those special effects was the Ern Malley sequence, based on my youthful experience when I first came upon the poetry of Ern Malley. Young Constant is on a train going to somewhere unspecified in the country. When the train pulls into a station at night Ern and Ethel Malley come into Constant's compartment. Almost immediately Ern begins haranguing Constant with his, Ern's, life history. Virtually all of Ern's lines were taken from his poems.

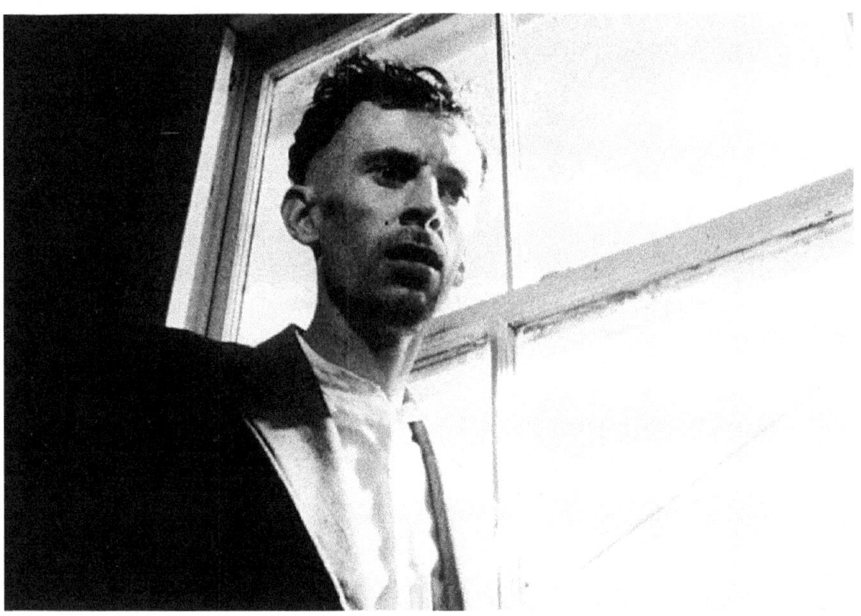

Iain Gardiner as Ern Malley in The Refracting Glasses *(Frame blow-up Cantrills Filmnotes.)*

Ern Malley in fact never existed. He was the creation of James McAuley and Harold Stewart - good, if conservative poets - who were appalled by what they considered meaningless rubbish produced under the influence of surrealism. They created a lot of parodies of their hated surrealism by, they claimed, randomly selecting lines, phrases from all sorts of "non-poetic" sources (for example, a handbook on the control of malarial mosquitoes). The problem for our hoaxers was that, being good poets, they couldn't help but create some good work, even though they devoutly believed they were composing "rubbish".

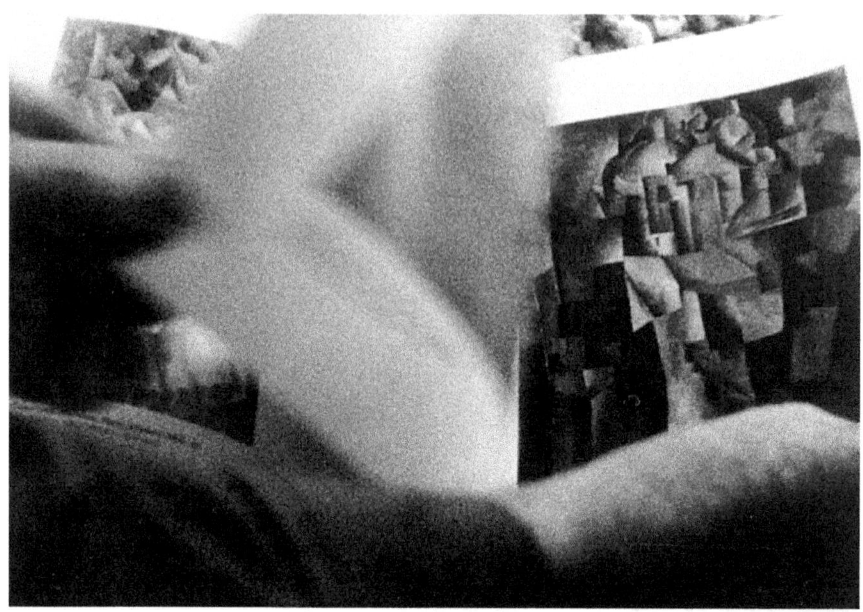

Constant looks at the catalogue to the Cubist Exhibition in The Refracting Glasses. *(Frame blow-up by Cantrills Filmnotes.)*

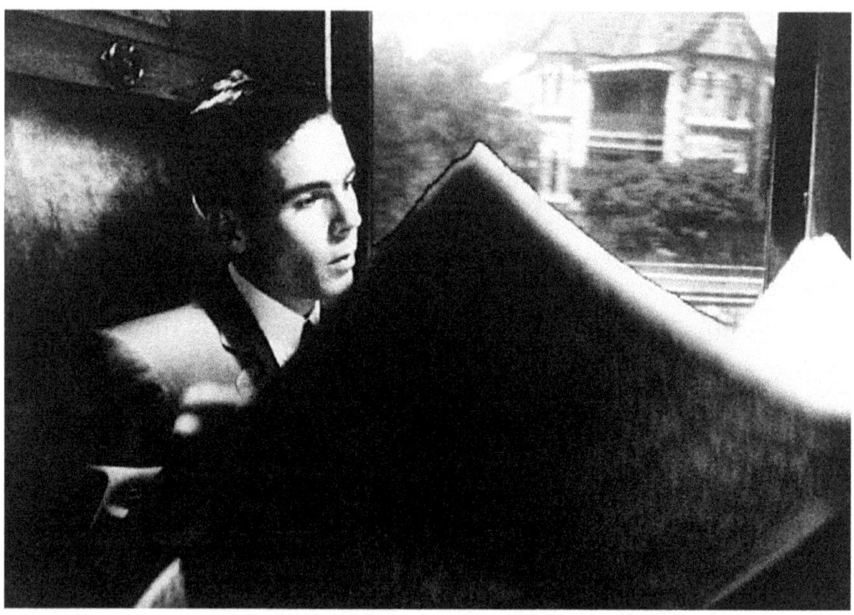

Constant reads a newspaper report of the death of Stalin in The Refracting Glasses. *(Frame blow-up by Cantrills Filmnotes.)*

Not only did they create Ern's poetry, they also created his character and sketched a life history for him. They had him die of Grave's disease, which is rarely, if ever, fatal, although it did create a marvellous parody of a tortured and ignored genius.

Finally they created Ern's sister, a dull bourgeoise Ethel and, with a covering letter from her, sent a manuscript of the poems to Max Harris, editor of *Angry Penguins*, a little modernist magazine in Adelaide. As the saying goes: "The rest is history." A version of that history can be found in *The Ern Malley Affair* by Michael Heyward, published by UQP in 1993, a book that retrospectively confirmed my instinct to include Ern in *The Refracting Glasses*, although obviously it couldn't have had any influence on my plans.

The connections between modernism and revolution are well documented but lesser known may be the anti-leftist feelings lurking behind McAuley's and Stewart's parodic pastiche. The following lines are not in the film, but they are, I think, a plausible invention by the poets that invokes and sends up the left-wing beliefs of many real artists of the 1940s.

I have been bitter with you, my brother
Remembering that saying of Lenin when the shadow
Was already on his face: "The emotions are not skilled workers"

Much later in the story, just before Constant and Lydia are due to leave for the Soviet Union, Ern materialises at the door of Constant's studio and speaks the following warning:.

I have heard them shout in the streets
The chiliasms of the Socialist Reich
And in the magazines I have read
The Popular Front-to-Back.
But where I have lived
Spain weeps in the gutters of Footscray
Guernica is the ticking of the clock
The nightmare has become real ...

Constant listens to these lines impassively while tapping them into his primitive computer, a tribute by me to Cocteau's film Orphée, where

Orpheus takes down lines of poetry coming from his car radio which he then publishes as his own work.

When I wrote the script I had Constant, while posing as an artist/worker, working on the paintings of *The Bolsheviks* in some ill-defined location, an imagined socialist industrial estate that included a drum factory. My production manager, John Prescott, who was in fact my co-producer, found a run-down estate in Sydney where there was a real drum factory. After looking at the place we decided it was ideal and John negotiated for us to shoot there for a couple of days.

It was only after we got to the Soviet Union that I realised how well chosen this location had been. On the banks of the Neva River in Leningrad we saw grotty little sheds that had the same atmosphere as the drum factory. At the back of the factory, there was a dingy little room where I set another scene in which a young woman was working on a painting while a supervisor (a commissar?) peered approvingly over her shoulder at her work-in-progress.

In another part of the estate Constant Malernik, worker/artist, was putting the finishing touches to his Bolsheviks portraits. This entire sequence was driven by the closing passages of Shostakovich's *Symphony No. 5*, a piece of music that I'd long admired.

At the finale of the drum factory sequence, the young woman, with the help of other workers, has placed two big drums on a raised platform outside the factory. As Shostakovich's music comes to its crashing finale the young woman bangs on the drums. A sweeping crane shot takes us behind and above her, when we finally see what she has been painting: a portrait of Stalin which has become a drum skin. In time with the closing drum beats, the young woman pounds angrily on Stalin's image. Shostakovich wrote his symphony in 1937, possibly the worst year in Soviet history, when people that Shostakovich knew were disappearing into the camps, when Shostakovich feared that he too would disappear.

Earlier in the story, Constant had shown, on the steps of his studio, a painting that honoured Shostakovich, his symphony, and one of his friends, Marshal Tukhachevsky, shot in the early stages of the purge of 1936-37.

Throughout the film I scattered references and/or homages to early Soviet cinema, cubist painting, and particularly to two projects of the constructivist artist, Vladimir Tatlin. The construction, from the ground up, of Tatlin's gigantic (but in fact never built) *Monument to the Third International* was animated for the film by computer artist Pavel Kyral.

Towards the end of *The Refracting Glasses,* Constant is taken to an air force museum where he is able to see a relic and written records of Tatlin's other major project, his plans to mass produce an "air bicycle", the *Letatlin,* a play on his name and the Russian word *letat,* to fly.

I wrote the part of Constant Malernik and played him as best I could, as though he were a naïve innocent which is how conservatives saw many members of the Australian Communist Party and their "fellow travellers", who, in the words of the slogan I photographed in England in the early 1970s, "carried a new world in [their] hearts". I wish, with just a corner of my own heart, that I wasn't the skeptic that I am, that I could have believed more. Perhaps then my own work might have had more consistency, a greater unity. Who knows?

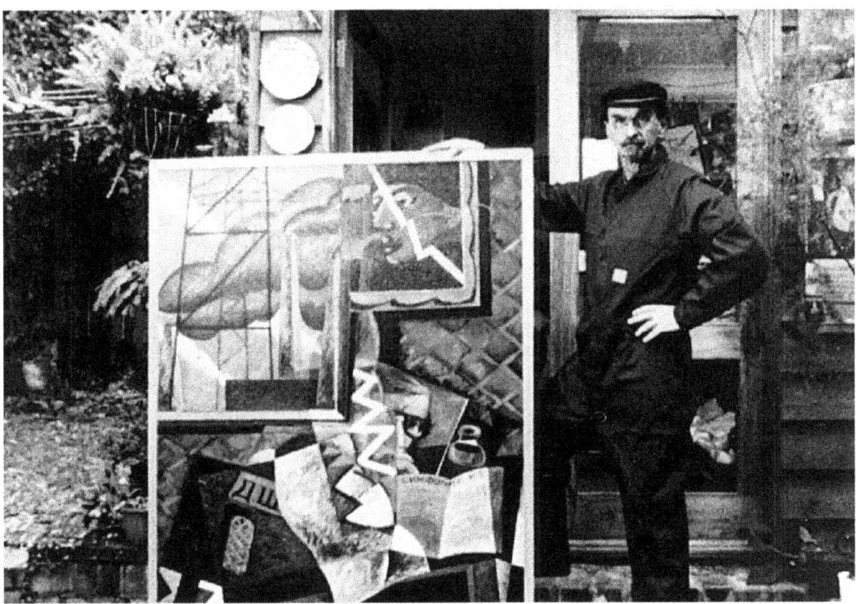

Constant, artist/worker shows his painting of Shostakovich and Tukhachevsky. (Frame blow-up by Cantrills Filmnotes.)

Lydia had to return to Sydney two weeks before I did, so I had to cope alone. I think I did that adequately. At least my Russian lessons in Sydney had prepared me to read Cyrillic street signs, bus and train destination signs (thank you, Alla Constantinovna). Anyhow, on my last morning in Moscow, when I was no longer Constant Malernik but just myself waiting outside my apartment building for the car to Sheremetyevo Airport, I was approached by a young boy carrying in his hands two small squares of

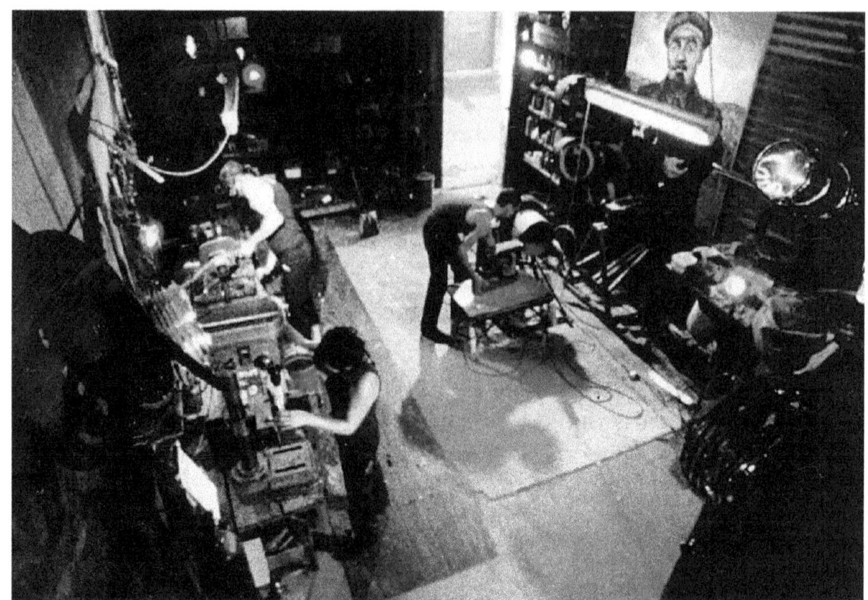

Inside the drum factory in The Refracting Glasses. (Frame blow-up by Cantrills Filmnotes.)

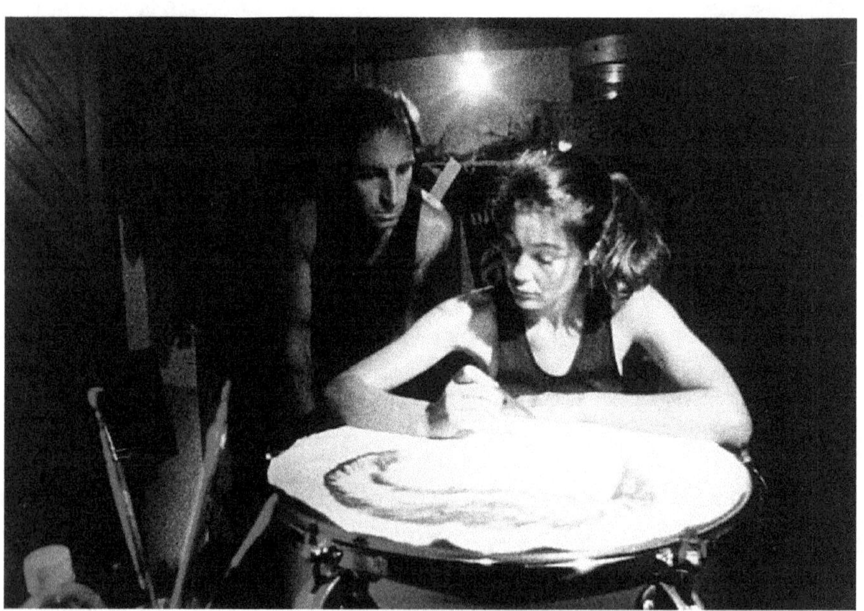

Young woman painting in the drum factory in The Refracting Glasses. (Frame blow-up by Cantrills Filmnotes.)

cake on pieces of wrapping paper. He held one of these out to me. He clearly realised that I wouldn't understand his words because he said nothing. I signed to him: "For me?" He nodded and I took a piece of cake. I may have said to him in an accent he probably wouldn't have understood: "Spasibo" or "Spasibo bolshoi". Anyhow, while I ate the cake, which was delicious, the boy just faded out of sight. It's a scene that I might have had in a dream, but I know it really happened.

Aeroflot got me safely to Singapore (on the flight I was surrounded by Russian Mafia dripping with gold bracelets and clutching fistfuls of dollars), and Qantas got me to Sydney, where a few weeks later I briefly got back into character as Constant and re-enacted the scene of the boy and the cake with projected images of Moscow apartments behind me. The numerous small and large kindnesses shown me in Russia had to be acknowledged. And finally, in the last shot of the film you might be able to see that Constant is able to acknowledge the bleakness of the late Soviet Union.

Speaking only for myself now, I think that the failure of the Soviet Union had little to do with economics. I think it was psychology that put the nails in the coffin. I don't think the Russian people ever recovered from the purges or from the smaller but even more pervasive insults of the judgementalism that was characteristic of so many members of the Communist Party.

The Refracting Glasses had its first public showing at the Sydney Film Festival in 1992 and following that, a one-week season at the Chauvel Cinema in Paddington where, frankly, it didn't pull much of an audience. It sank like a modernist stone in a post-modernist ocean.

A short while after showing it in Sydney, I took it to Melbourne for a screening at a festival which pulled the right kind of audience - for one night only, of course. I like visiting Melbourne. I'm not sure if I could live there, it has a totally different atmosphere to Sydney. I decided then that I'll always call Melbourne "the Leningrad of Australia". It has something of Leningrad's "left-wingness", it has the same faded grandeur, although nowhere near the scale, and a distinctly European feel, something that's capitalised on in advertisements for Melbourne as a tourist destination. Melbourne also had *Cantrills Filmnotes,* a very long-lived journal of alternative views of the cinema, which on a number of occasions had been very supportive of my work.

On a later visit to Melbourne (now *really* outside the scope of this story), I stayed with Helen Beresford and Jan Senbergs. One afternoon, walking back to their house I was moved to make this little sketch (below) of the Victoria Markets on a scrap of paper that I found in my pocket. You can see the print on the other side showing through.

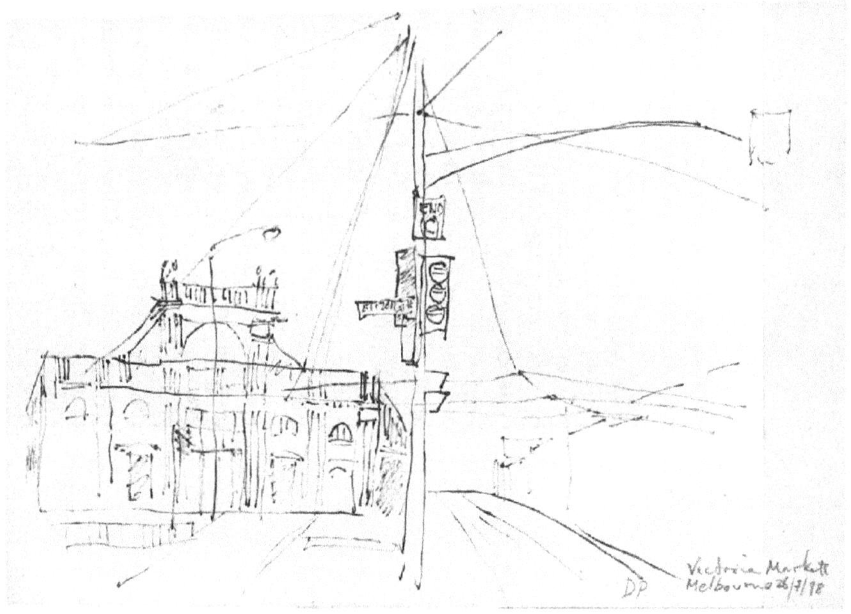

Victoria Markets, Melbourne (ink on paper), 1998

Doctor Jazz, an exhibition, another script ...

I did many things after being in Russia, and I felt that our "free" capitalist culture wasn't immune to the mistakes the Bolsheviks had made. Many ex-Trotskyites are now influential in right wing politics here and an authoritarian mood frowns over much in our lives.

I dug out my old script for *Plenty of Water and Honest Men* and, imagining it had actually been made, incorporated it as a "lost film" into a dystopian science-fiction called *Water Under the Bridge,* about the future of Sydney. That occupied at least two years of my life (I was by then living on a small amount of superannuation). To make that film would require many millions of dollars, and since I know no one in Australia would risk funding me to that extent, I have put that aside too. If that seems to be an ending "not with a bang but a whimper" I can only say: it's not the end.

It was during that period that I held my exhibition at the Ray Hughes Gallery, *The Bolsheviks and All That Jazz,* from which a number of images were reproduced in the "Life with Lydia" section of this book.

My love of jazz re-flowered, leading to a lot of colour photographs (see next two pages) and a film, *Dr Jazz,* which was bought and shown by the ABC. I also shot several films for Albie Thoms.

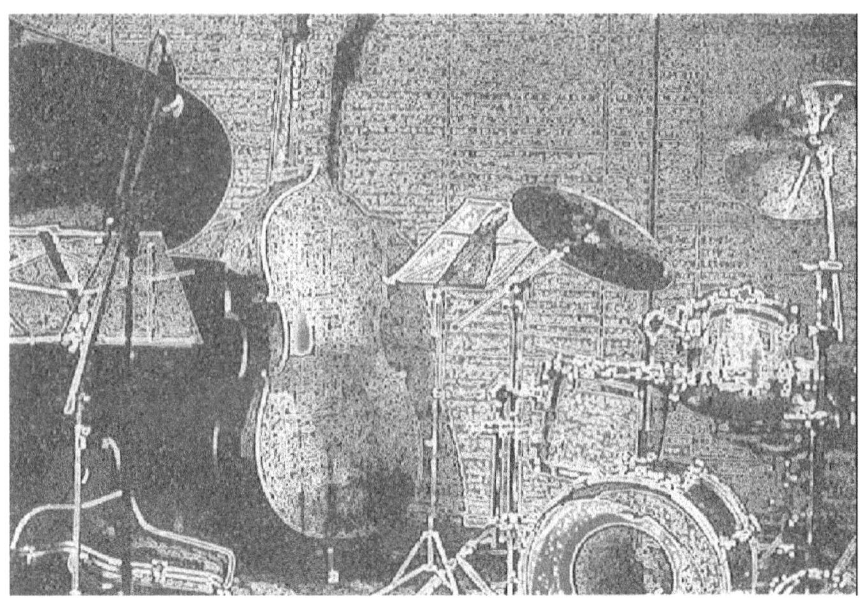

Instruments during the break at the Strawberry Hills Hotel, 1995

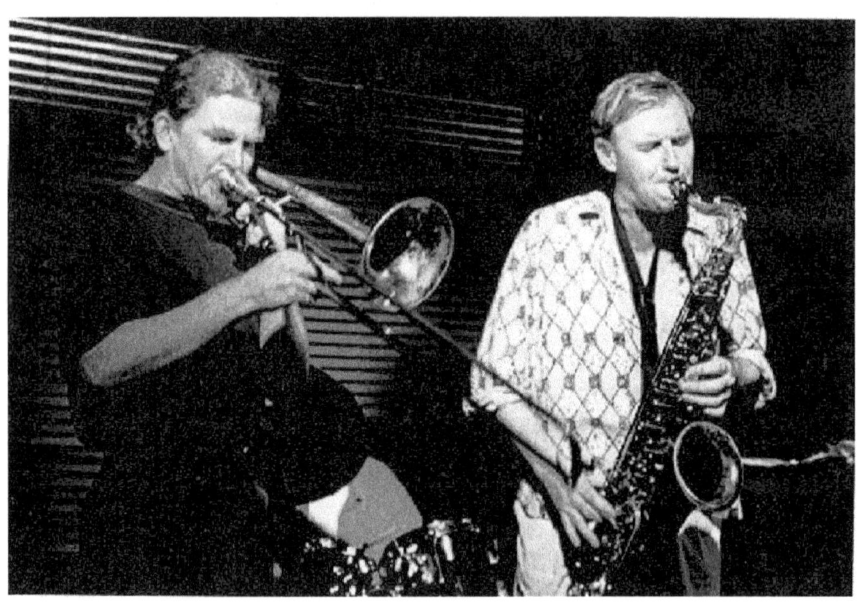

James Greening and Mark Simmonds at the Strawberry Hills Hotel, 1994

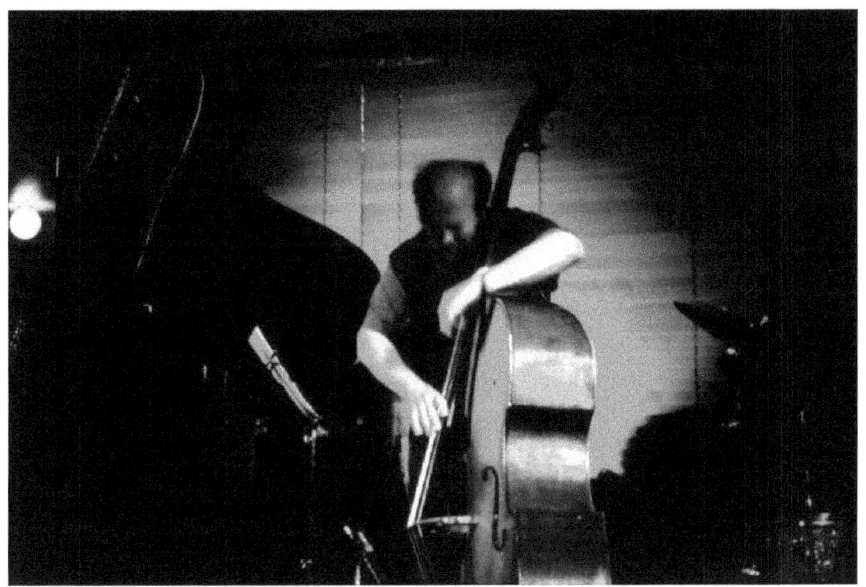

Craig Scott at the Strawberry Hills Hotel, 1994

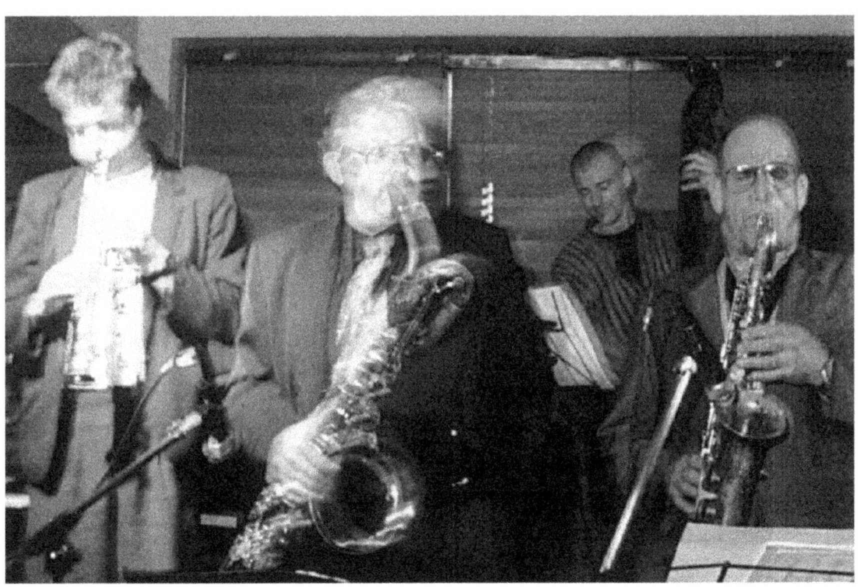

Roger Frampton, Bob Bertles, Steve Elphick and Bernie McGann playing with Ten Part Invention *at the Strawberry Hills Hotel, 1994*

Hill End ...

In 2001 I wrote an application for the short-term position of Artist-in-Residence at Hill End, an historic gold mining town about an hour's drive out of Bathurst in the mid-west of NSW.

I heard nothing more for many months and had almost forgotten about it when I had a letter saying that I had a choice of dates in 2002, from which I selected March/April, which I thought offered the most pleasant weather. I proposed I would do some drawing but that my major aim would be to make a documentary film about Hill End.

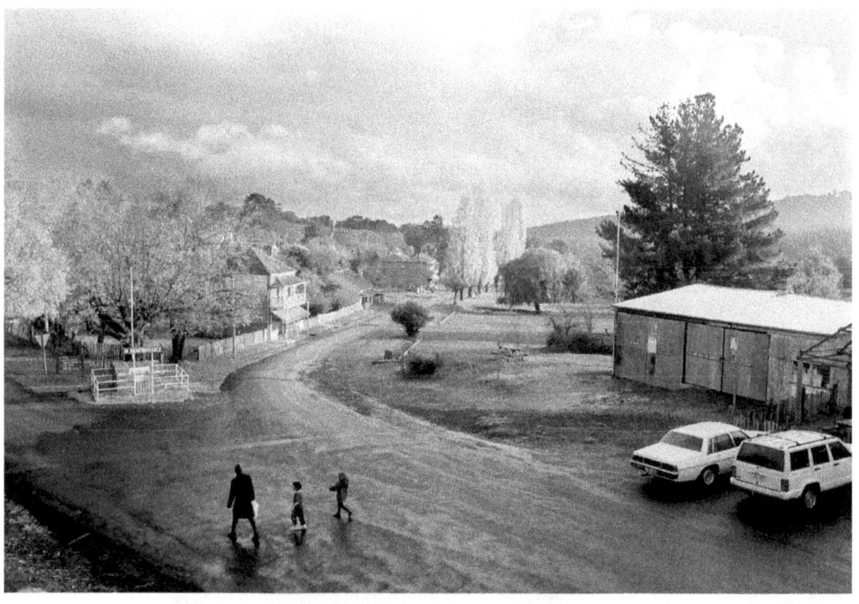

Early morning, Hill End, c. 2005

One of the things that attracted me to the town was what my mother had told me, when I was a child, about her trips by sulky to Hill End, when *she* was a child. In the doco that I eventually made, I included a sequence that represented my mother's point-of-view as her sulky bounced over the very rough road that connected Windeyer, her home town, to Hill End. To achieve the POV, I mounted my video camera on the bonnet of my Ford Laser and later on a plank looking out of a rear side window. These mountings used a lot of gaffer tape and padding. In spite of the padding the jolting journey caused the camera's microphone to disconnect so that before I could finish the doco I had to ask Lydia who was coming up later to spend some time with me to bring two attachable mics.

One outcome of our time in Hill End was the creation of several lasting friendships with people from the town, including artist Luke Sciberras and Sheena Goodwin, daughter and grand-daughter of notable early residents going as far back as the gold rush of the 1870s.

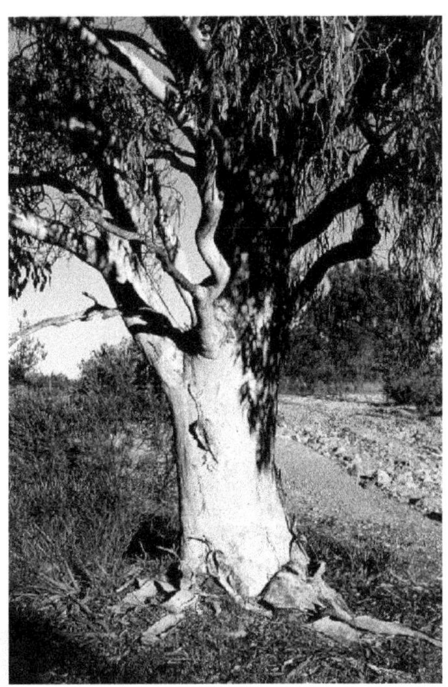

Late sun on a tree trunk, Hill End, c. 2000

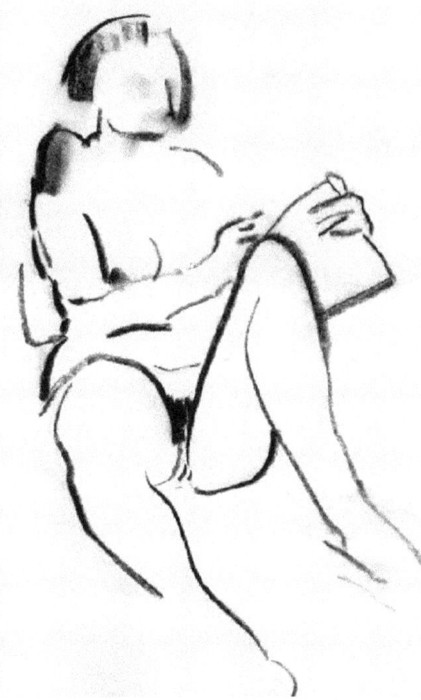

Study No.4 (charcoal on paper), 2005

Of course the other outcome was my short doco, *Notes from Hill End*. I held the "World Premiere" of that work in the Royal Hall, next to the pub, to which many people came from Sydney and further afield.

In subsequent years I went back many times to take photographs and make paintings and drawings.

At other times, as well as during my residency, I made drawings and a few paintings of Hill End and the country round about. At such times it was impossible to forget the earlier presence in Hill End of Donald Friend and Russell Drysdale, as if I would want to forget them, those artists were very important to my own awareness of myself as an artist.

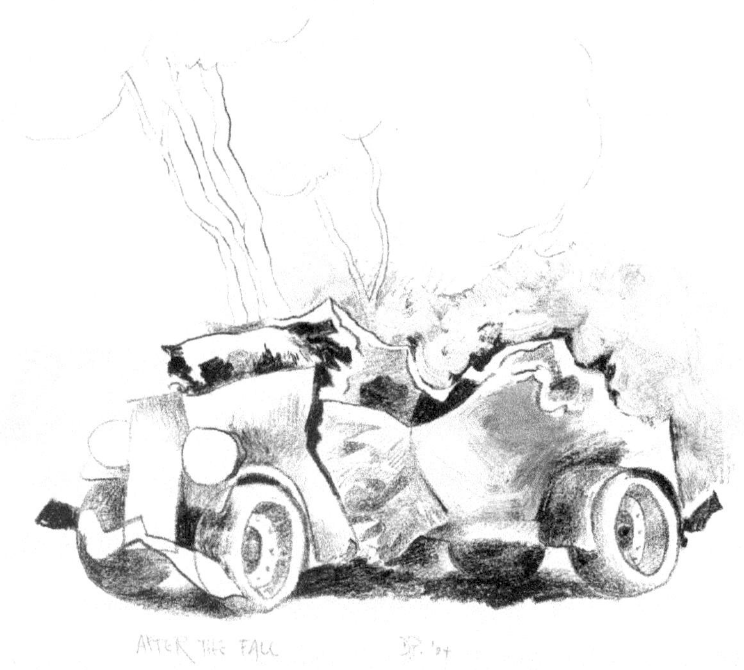

After the Fall (Car over the Cliff), crayon and acrylic on paper, 2004

On the last day of one of my later visits there was a lot of activity: a helicopter circling overhead; then a fire truck and a farm vehicle came past the pub, towing a seriously smashed-up car. The car (see drawing above), it turned out, had rolled off the very rough and steep road up from the Turon River. The driver, it was said, was lucky to be alive and there were suggestions of marital problems (I know that here I'm just re-telling gossip).

Lydia in China ...

Some time in 2004, I think it was, Lydia told me she wanted to go to China, the country where she was born, to explore her family history and her own childhood. I told her I'd only agree to go if I could make a film of her adventure, since that was what it promised to be.

Lydia paid both our fares (first class, no less, on Air China) and accommodation in Harbin, Xian and Shanghai, while I rented a marvellous compact digital video camcorder for the time we expected to be away.

I cannot claim to be a dedicated traveller and although I have had some very mind-expanding experiences outside Australia, I think I have to say that China was the most mind-expanding of them all.

Harbin was not part of Lydia's childhood but it was closely connected to her parents. Harbin was a refuge for many Russians after 1917 but I think it had earlier been a refuge for Russian Jews after czarist pogroms in the 19th century. That seems to be how Lydia's mother's family came to be there.

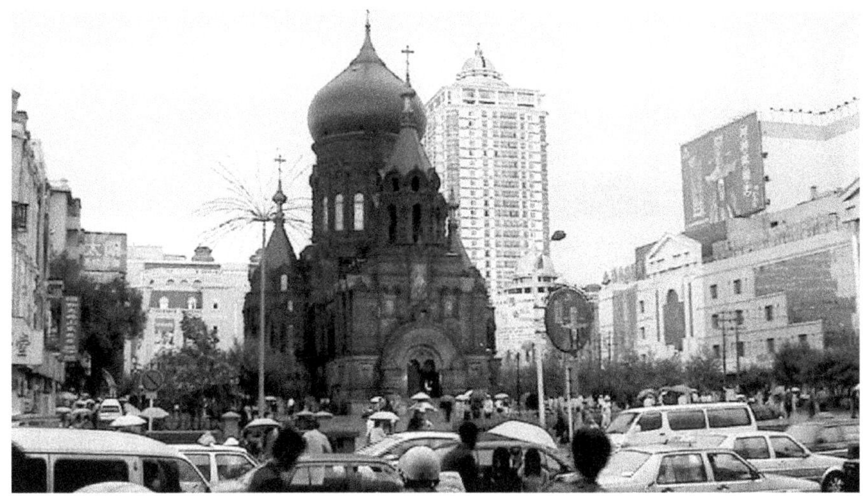

Russian Orthodox cathedral in Harbin, 2005

The Russian Orthodox cathedral in Harbin, by the time we saw it, had been somewhat restored after being vandalised during the Cultural Revolution.

But as well as its connections with the past, Harbin showed all the signs of a thriving, booming economy that we saw wherever we went in China.

In Harbin we went to a conference about Jews in China which, not to put too fine a point on it, consisted mostly of many rambling papers by very amateurish speakers. I recorded parts of many of those presentations, fragments of which might have ended up in a movie called *Lydia in China*. The material is relevant to Lydia's search for her Jewish roots passed down from her mother.

Lydia's mother died before I came on the scene. Her father, who we called "Papa", graduated as an engineer from the Harbin Polytechnic. We spent several days searching amongst the tertiary institutes of Harbin

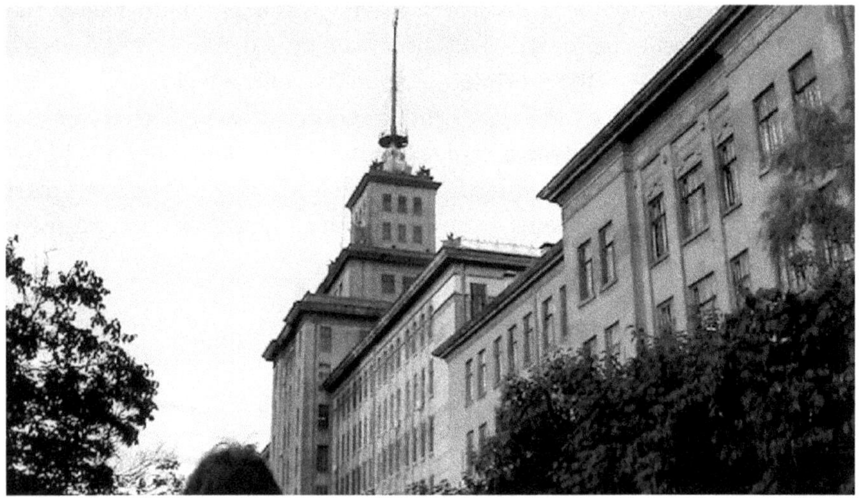

Where Papa studied, Harbin, 2004

until we eventually found this one which we immediately recognised from photographs in old copies of Papa's professional journals. The photographs here are, in fact, "frame blow-ups" from the video footage I shot on our trip.

Most of my successful shooting happened in Shanghai, a place that excited me greatly. An "odd-one-out" from the blow-ups might be the shot of the Peoples' Liberation Army entering Shanghai in 1949 on the next page, but in fact I collected it, without permission , with my video camera from a display in a Communist Party museum just across from our hotel in Shanghai.

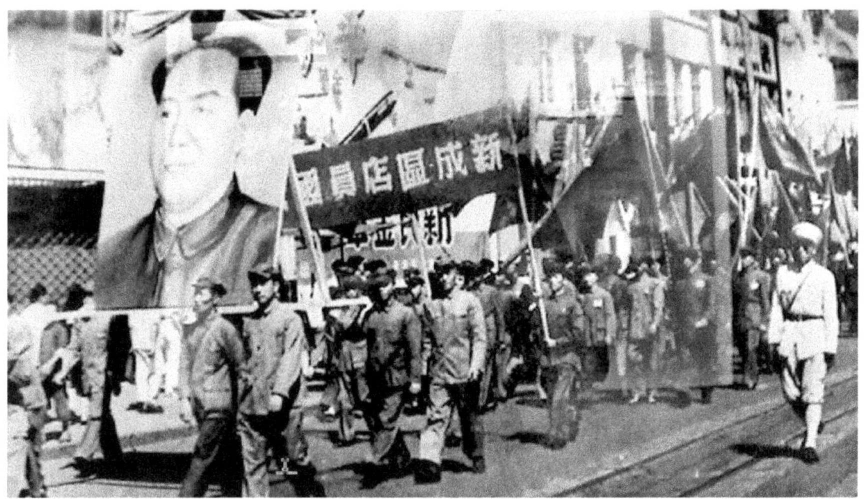

Red army entering Shanghai, 1949

Shanghai is the only place in China that Lydia remembers from her childhood and it was in Shanghai that I'm sure I got the best material for *Lydia in China,* especially her search for her primary school, the so-called "British School". I thought that her reactions, which I caught on tape, were so striking as to be very strong evidence indeed that she was right, even though she met people in Shanghai who contradicted her belief.

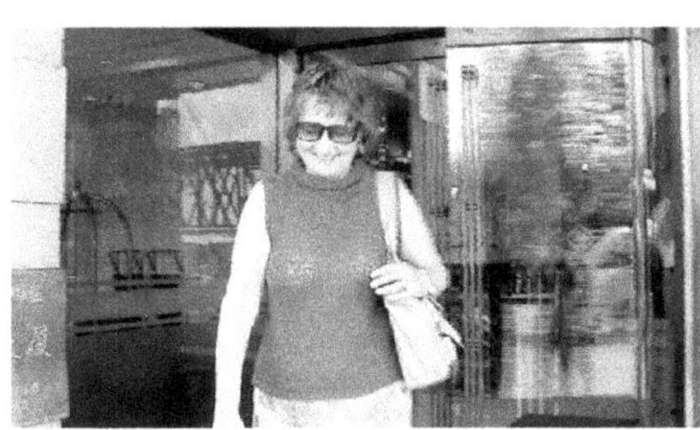

Lydia stepping out, Shanghai, 2004

Overall we both enjoyed ourselves enormously in China. This shot of Lydia setting out on one of our many forays into Shanghai, seems to me to exemplify that. For Lydia the journey allowed her to make many connections back to her childhood and into her family history. And it allowed me see China, I hope with unclouded eyes, as well as allowing me to get raw material for what turned out to be a fairly ordinary documentary.

An exhibition proposed ...

In mid-2006 I had a very satisfactory meeting with Tony Geddes, the director of the Mosman Art Gallery. I originally met him to propose an exhibition of photographs covering my work from the early 1950s to the 1980s, that time-span being brought to an end by the thefts of my cameras.

However Tony thought it would be far better to include items from all the fields I had worked in up until the time of the exhibition (proposed to be mid-2009). We brought Albie on board to help in curating at least the film and photographic sections.

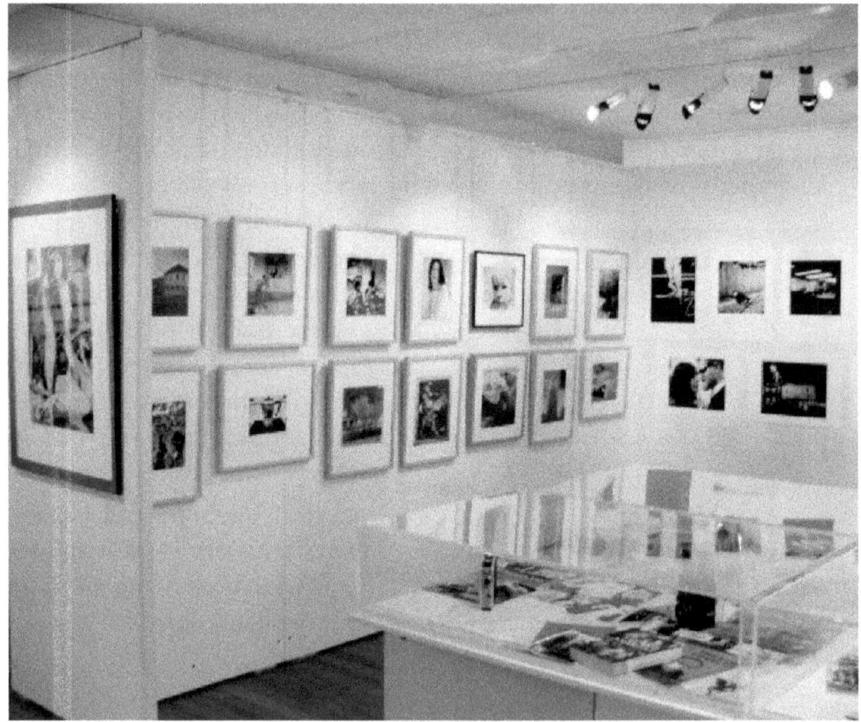

A small section of the exhibition at Mosman, 2009

I wanted to give the exhibition a name similar to these memoirs, calling myself "a dedicated amateur," but Tony, not recognising the irony, wanted to call me "a dilettante."

Although limited in size by the space of the gallery this promised to be a truly retrospective show. It gave me a lot of work to do, locating and borrowing paintings, drawings and graphics, especially those done in the 1960s and 1970s.

Postscript (by Lydia Fegan)

Much has happened since David wrote this memoir, so David has asked me to write a sequel to complete the narrative and explain what has been happening in his life since.

The retrospective art exhibition did go ahead and was very successful. It looked really good in the Mosman Art Gallery space. Not only was there a large number of examples of his paintings, drawings and photographs from the early years right up to the present, but some of his artworks and prints associated with Ubu films were also displayed in glass cases, and his short films and videoworks were shown in a small side gallery on a continuous loop.

Unfortunately it was a very disturbing and distressing time for David and both Albie and I were quite worried about him. He found it very difficult to organise himself or to remember where things were, so I had to take over and find where all his works were scattered around the house or who had various paintings and drawings that had to be collected so that Albie could then put everything in order and basically curate the whole exhibition. It has to be said that without Albie that exhibition would never have happened, and throughout his artistic life David is forever indebted to the encouragement and support of Albie Thoms, and his wife Linda Slutzkin.

You can see from the photograph on the previous page that the Mosman exhibition contained not only a number of works already included in these memoirs, but also very many more, one of which is shown on the next page.

The exhibition ended up being called 'Then and now and everything in between', and the catalogue included four articles which shed light on different aspects of David's work. The one by Albie Thoms "David Perry: a lover of art and life" was particularly illuminating. With his characteristic indifference to self-promotion, David has not even

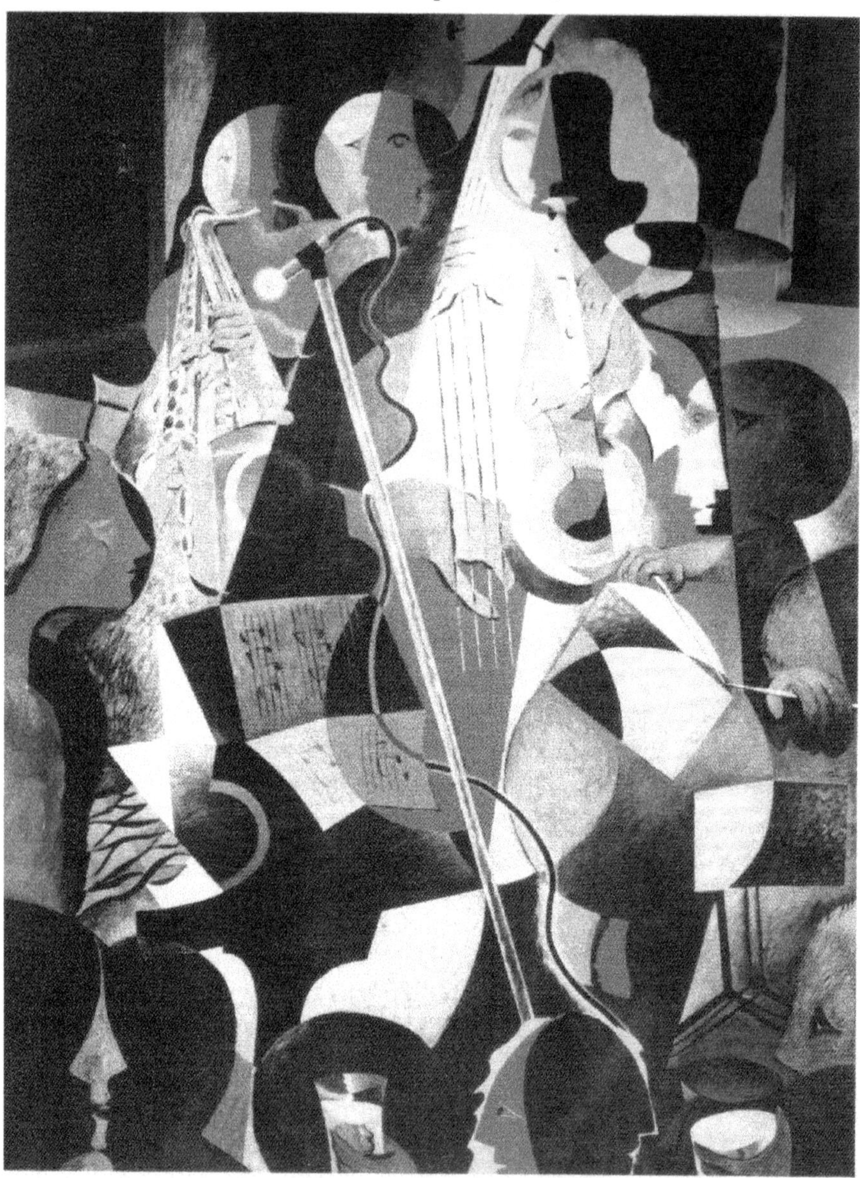

Piece for pub, jazz band and the city outside *("Big jazz"), 2001*

mentioned in these memoirs that *Album* premiered in the International Underground Film Festival at London's National Film Theatre; nor is there any mention of his comedy *The Tribulations of Mr. DuPOnt Nomore* which had the Australian censors in a flap.

And in the end, in the catalogue, Tony Geddes did refer to David as "a dedicated amateur", not a dilettante!

It was soon after this that David was diagnosed with hydrocephalus and after h e got a shunt, his memory and organisational skills improved. Unfortunately, a couple of years later he had a mild stroke which set him back a little more.

Early in 2012, David's short film *Walking* (1951-54) was shown on continuous loop in an exhibition at Damien Minton Gallery called "Five Bells", a group exhibition celebrating Sydney Harbour and the poem of that name by Kenneth Slessor.

The interesting thing is that these days David has been recognised by a younger generation for his video artworks. Over the past few years David's video works have been shown in various international video art festivals and conferences, at the Museum of Contemporary Art, and at the NSW Art Gallery. In 2012 he was asked to give the opening address at an international conference in Brisbane called "Parallel Universes" where one of his works, *Mad Mesh* (1968), was also displayed. This short videowork demonstrated how the manipulation of the mechanics of the black and white television camera, together with the use of the hand-held camera could produce abstract images unknown until then. It was the beginning of the convergence of art and technology (these days encompassing computer technology) which can be seen in every art gallery and exhibition in the world today.

It could be said that David Perry was one of the "founding fathers" of the interweaving of various emerging technologies in his case in his time, the technology of video, and later, the computer, with art and film. In David's case, in his video works he used *"many of the methods commonly associated with what we used to call underground films, methods such as rapid repetition, juxtaposition of disparate styles and images, and a rejection of narrative continuity."*[11] But all his film, video and even photographic works reveal his basic artistic sensibility, and his interest in abstraction.

David still puts down his intellectual development and political ideas to his encounters with the Push, although he recognised that the Push, apart from a few notable exceptions, was uninterested, and even scornful, of anything to do with "art". The Push led him to read widely in areas

---

[11] Opening address by David Perry, "Parallel Universes", 2012.

not covered by his art, and also helped to form his political ideas. Some of these can be seen in many of his works, particularly his interest (if not obsession) with communism and bolshevism, as well as his horrible fascination with Nazism. His remarkable watercolour portraits of the Bolsheviks were a huge hit at the exhibition at Ray Hughes' Gallery (1997).

He was also interested in jazz, but especially modern rather than trad jazz, because it was the closest to abstractionism in art, as shown in a number of his paintings, drawings, photographs and culminating in his videowork, *Dr. Jazz* (1997-98), which led to a number of friendships which David still values today.

Another area of interest has always been history. In fact a great number of his works have had an autobiographical content, and his interest in his own history broadened into an interest in history as it impacted on his life from his earliest memories, that is, particularly that of World War II.

In 1997 he was invited to give a talk at a conference in Melbourne, "Screening the Past: Film and the Representation of History". David's paper was entitled "Letatlin and Ern Malley: History Refracted through 'Impossibility' and Hoax", in which he describes his film *The Refracting Glasses* which, among other things, explores the absolute and fiercely-held belief that David has always had that in no way any artistic medium, either art, film or photography, can be said to portray "reality". As he quotes Picasso, *"Art has always been art and not nature"*. In fact, although David's works have almost always had, more or less, a narrative content, narrative has never been his primary interest (except in his truly abstract paintings).

It is primarily form, structure, technical considerations, and the juxtaposition of imagery, light and shade which have been David's lifelong fascination, and not narrative. I would like to quote from David's paper as it gives us a glimpse into how he views art, whether it is painting, photography or film/video work:

"What an artist intends is usually to do first of all with structural or stylistic matters. One way or another these are practical things, vessels into which meaning flows as if by intention. Unless an artist scrupulously avoids any suggestion of imagery, meanings will almost certainly arise.... And the meaning is given to the work by the reader or viewer, and not necessarily the one that the author or artist intended."

He also quotes from B. Kazansky: *"The cinema possesses its own laws of geometry, mechanics, physics, under which the most impossible situations become possible".*[12]

David is still a "dedicated amateur" and his interest in art, particularly abstraction, his interest in history, and his close friendships with a number of people from his Push days, will go on till the end.

The way David continues to see himself is graphically illustrated in the following image, which was intended as the cover for an earlier version of this manuscript. The tube of paint and the photograph of David with his movie camera is very symbolic for David, as he feels that they epitomise the main passions in his life (apart from women) - painting and making films.

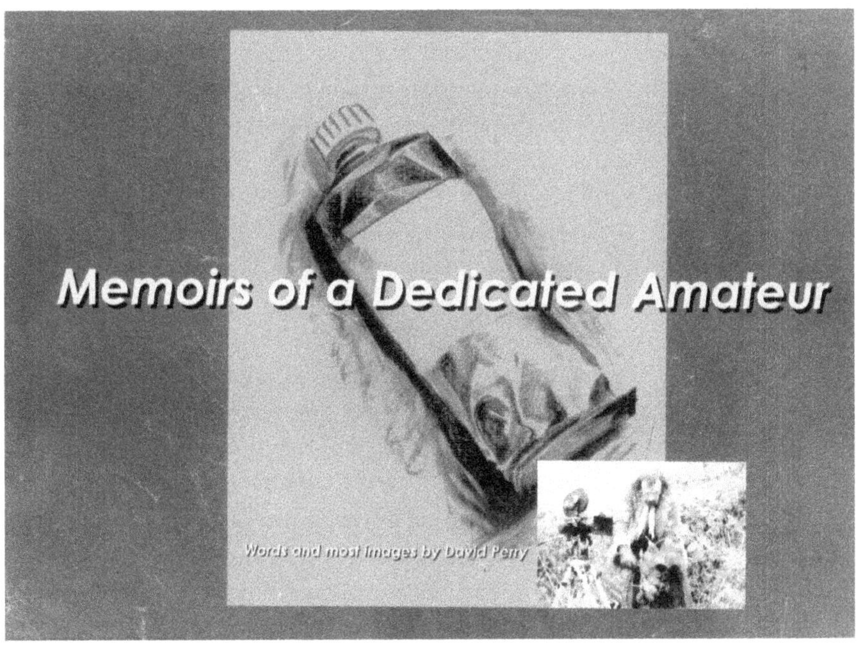

Early manuscript cover, 1971

[12] From 'The Nature of Cinema' (1927); quoted in Herbert Eagle (ed.), *Russian formalist Film Theory* (Dept Of Slavic Languages, University of Michigan, 1981)

A few words to end with ...

When I think of formative moments in my life there's an anecdote that always rises to the top: it was at primary school; we were sitting in the warm winter sunshine, one of Sydney's most seductive aspects. There were several of us there, mostly boys but maybe one or two girls. We had our backs to the weatherboards at the rear of the lunch shed. I would guess we were about ten years old.

One of the boys was Werner Czerezansky (I hope I've spelled it right). We had just been to a "scripture" lesson. These lessons each week were taken by variously weird protestant ministers from local churches. The Catholics were insulated from such contradictions, they always had the same priest. Werner was the only Jew at our school, where scripture lessons were compulsory. It must have been considered the least inapppropriate option for a Jewish boy to be put with the Protestants.

Somehow Werner's family had escaped from Czechoslovakia and found their way to Australia (this was in the early 1940s). Werner — who seemed to have taken a liking to me — once told me of how he'd been bashed over the head by a German soldier's rifle butt.

We all found Werner rather strange. He was taller and skinnier than the rest of us, had a mop of curly hair and wore short trousers down to his knees, made of brown velvet! Ours were of grey serge, and much shorter. Werner also played the flute. Mr Brown, the headmaster and one of our only two teachers, had co-opted Werner into playing his flute as all the rest of us marched up the steps into school. I don't think this was a regular event, it may have been unique, but anyhow it's stuck firmly in my memory. Another thing I remember about Werner is that his father made fireworks. On at least one occasion Mr Czerezansky put on a wonderful "cracker night", otherwise known as "Empire Day". I've sometimes wondered just what Werner's father did with his skills with explosives in Europe before the War.

But all that's a digression. The "formative moment" was when, after the scripture lesson, Werner told us: "We don't believe in Jesus." All at once Werner had introduced me to Doubt. Following that came

Skepticism. I can't tell you how liberating that felt. It must have been a major part of my preparation for the Sydney Push, although Werner can't take all the credit for that. Some of the credit's due to my family.

My parents never invoked the authority of religion, and I've only recently learned, from my sister Diana (who knows everything about our family), that my paternal grandfather was an early supporter, if not an actual member of the Australian Communist Party. But it was skepticism, not communism, that I carried into my adult life.

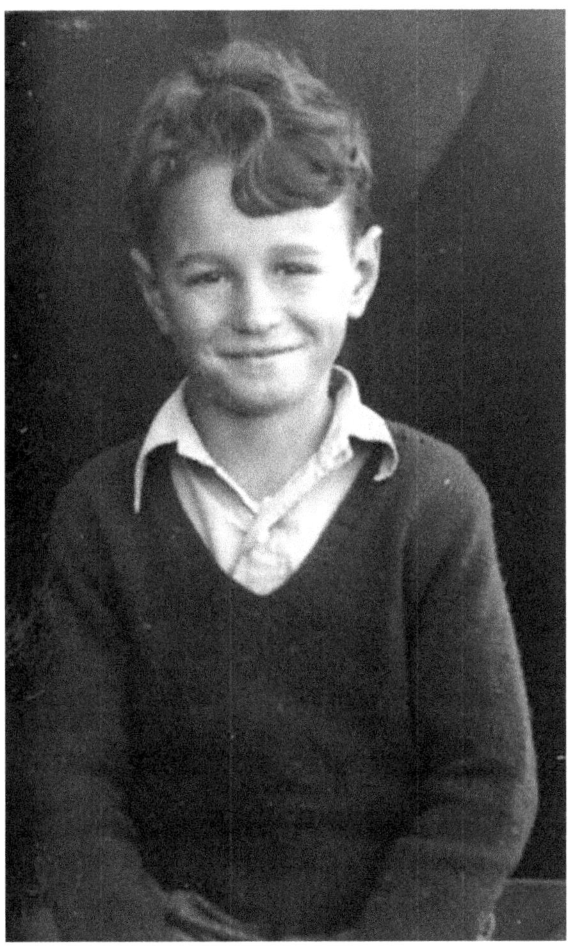

DP at the onset of skepticism (photographer unknown)

David Perry
Mosman, 2014

Some of the images in *Memoirs of a Dedicated Amateur* were originally in colour. These can be viewed online in colour at the Valentine Press photo gallery: **http://valentinepress.com.au/?page_id=553**

A large collection of images of other works by David Perry which are not contained in this book can also be viewed in the online gallery.

A Reader Comments page has been included on Valentine Press website where your feedback on *Memoirs of a Dedicated Amateur* would be welcomed: **http://valentinepress.com.au/?page_id=562**

INDEX OF IMAGES

Paintings and Drawings

After the Fall (Car over the Cliff) (crayon and acrylic on paper), 2004 284
A Rural Tragedy (acrylics on hessian), 1970 104
A story by David Perry, *Ubu News* double page spread, 1969 98-99
Bacchus at Balls Head (felt pen on paper), 1974 158
Bacchus falling for Ariadne (felt pen on paper), 1974 159
Backs of houses in Opotiki (Indian ink on paper), c. 1957 45
Birds of a Feather No. 5 ("Unpleasant Bird"), monotype using oil paint on newsprint, 1964 54
Blue Mountains Landscape (oils on canvas), 1956 29
City (gouache, wash and Indian ink on paper), 1957 43
Cow (Indian ink on paper), 1956 36
Drawing for the cover of Sydney Film Makers' Co-operative Catalogue (Indian ink on paper), 1970 101
Farm workers (Indian ink on paper), c.1957 44
Flying out of Tehran, 1974 163
Girl in the bush (pencil on paper), 1966 77
Girl in a wind (pencil on paper), 1966 77
Girl waving (pencil on paper), 1966 77
Icarus making his wings (quill pen and Indian ink on paper), c.1957 40
Instruments during the break at the StrawberryHills Hotel, 1955 280
Jazz (quill pen and Indian ink on paper), 1957 42
Jazz band (quill pen and Indian ink on paper), c. 1957 41
Judy (Indian ink on paper) 1957 38
Leningrad Studio 1 (ink, gouache and collage on paper), 1989 267
Love Notes, page 2, (photocopy on paper), c. 1983 252
Manager Death (pastels on paper), 1981 228
Nightmare in Queensland (photocopy and coloured pencils on paper), 1977 161
Obverse of Our Truck 'The Cynic'(quill pen and Indian ink on paper), c. 1957 40
Old English penny (pencil on paper), 1970 111
Opotiki (Indian ink on paper), 1956 36
Our Truck (Indian ink on paper), 1957 39
Piece for pub, jazz band and the city outside ("Big jazz"), 2001 290
Portrait of Anatoly Lunacharsky (coloured inks on paper), 1988 261

Portrait of Bill Psychs (pastels on card-board, c.1962 53
Portrait of Johnny Earls (oils on hardboard), 1963-64 48
Portrait of Mikhail Pokrovsky (gouache and collage on paper), 1988 260
Portrait of Richard Appleton (oils on hardboard), 1962 49
Rome (felt pens on paper), 1971 114
Rome 2 (felt pens on paper), 1971 115
Self Portrait (Indian ink on paper), c. 1955 1
Sergeant Phuqnukle (felt pen on paper), 1973 143
Sergeant Phuqnukle in a house (ballpoint on paper), 1973 143
Simon (Indian ink on paper), 1957 37
Study for portrait of Alexandra Kollontai (watercolours on paper), 1988 258
Study for portrait of Mikhail Pokrovsky, (watercolours on paper), 1988 259
Study for portrait of Nikolai Bukharin (watercolours on paper), 1988 259
Study No.4 (charcoal on paper), 2005 283
The Bay of Plenty (Indian ink on paper), 1957 35
The Bolsheviks,1988 262
The coast of Brittany (acrylics on canvas), c.1973 129
The Comet, 1970 102
The Exile's Room I (oils on plywood), 1989 266
The Exile's Room II (oils on plywood), 1989 265
The Intruder (oil-stick on paper), 1972 142
Victoria Markets, Melbourne (ink on paper), 1998 278
View of Texel (pencil on paper), 1971 133
Vote Informal Poster, 1966 50
What is to be Done (oils on plywood), 1989 264
Woman I, (proof), 1963 69
Woman III, (gouache proof), 1963 69
Woolloomooloo near Sungravure (oils on canvas), 1953 9

Photographs by David Perry

Abigayl at Goodhope Street, 1967 75
Abigayl in kitchen at Goodhope Street, 1967 75
Abby bathing new Rachael, 1968 88
Abby feeding Homer, 1971 131
Abby napping while reading Women's Estate, 1972 139
A drunk sleeping it off in Lindfield, 1954 12
A ruined chateau, 1971 125
A small section of the exhibition at Mosman, 2009 288
Autoportrait at the ABC 78
Barbara Segal, Billy Tuck and Tony Skillen shopping in France, 1971 124
Bev beside the Turon River, c. 1979 207
Bev by torchlight, c. 1978 205
Bev rolling a cigarette near Maleny, c. 1978 200
Bev with her Nikon, c. 1977 202
Bill Pope at Darlington Road 62
Blue Mountains after bushfire, c. 1983 249
Bridge Arch, c. 1980 216
Bunker on North Head, c. 1983 244
Caitlin, Jane and Simon, somewhere in the Blue Mountains, c.1970 89
Caitlin and Simon, c. 1970 90
Car park mural at Manly, photographed 1989 268-269
Carrying the banner out of Queens Park, 1977 194
Cat (Henrietta) on a Sofa, Hartley Vale, 1970 105
Cement plaques, four photos, bunker series, 1983 246
Chinon, 1971 127
Craig Scott at the Strawberry Hills Hotel, 1994 281
Decaying truck, Warriewood, c. 1983 243
Demolition in Darlington, 1966 61
DP setting up for the installation, 1972 119
Early morning, Hill End, c. 2005 282
Early morning, Manly Beach, c. 1983 240
Edward Street, Redfern, 1974 162
Ellen White 62
Etchers at Sungravure, c.1953 10
Family home in East Lindfield 4
Feeling the breeze on the Baragoola, c. 1982 242

Fireworks on Sydney Harbour celebrating the Queen of England's first visit to Australia, February, 1954 13
Fishing boats in Woolloomooloo Bay, c.1953 11
Geoffrey Whiteman's place at 125 Darlington Road, c. 1965 57
Gill Leahy at the Communist Party stand in Edward Street, 1974 164
Glenmore Road, Paddington, c. 1980 218
Gopala on the roof outside his top floor flat, c.1972 136
Half-inch video editing system at DDIAE, 1977 184
Harbour Bridge detail, c. 1980 216
Harbour Bridge detail (1), c. 1980 217
Harbour Bridge detail (2), c. 1980 217
Homer and Rachael in the communal garden 145
Homer asleep, 1971 130
Homer in London, 1973 146
Homer pissing, Gloucestershire, 1973 154
Homer with Abby in London, 1974 160
Hornsey corridor 1, 1971 120
Hornsey corridor 2, 1971 120
Hornsey corridor 3, 1971 120
Incinerator, c. 1981 221
James Greening and Mark Simmonds at the StrawberryHills, 1955 280
Jane, c. 1970 90
Jane with Rebecca, 1982 236
John (Dufaycolor transparency), c.1954 16
Judy with Simon early 1957 44
Jumping In (to our favourite swimming hole at "The End" of Middle Harbour), c.1954 14
Karl's gun, 1982 231
Karmann Ghia with a new paint job 1976 188
Kay, in cold weather, lights a cigarette, 1976 186
Kay Comino, 1974 166
Keith Looby & painting, *God Made All This*, photo 1968 84
Kings Lindfield in the early 1950s. 5
Late afternoon sun on the Chevron, c. 1979 210
Late sun on a tree trunk, Hill End, c. 2005 283
Leaving Sydney sites 1 108
Leaving Sydney sites 2 108
Looby in his Fairlight studio, 1982 233
Looby's painting *Last supper*, photo 1968 85

Lou on the verandah, c.1977 189
Lydia dressed and made-up for a commissioned portrait, 1966 253
Lydia stepping out, Shanghai, 2004 287
Miniature cacti, c. 1980 219
Muswell Hill under snow, 1970 116
My bed at Steinton Street, c. 1983 251
My bicycle, c. 1981 225
Near Brunel University, c.1971 121
Nisa, c.1972 137
North end of Victoria Street, Potts Point, c. 1979 212
North Harbour through the windows at Fairlight, c. 1981 227
On a beach near Mackay (1), circa 1977 204
On a beach near Mackay (2). C 1977 204
Our house in Bothwell Street, Toowoomba 185
Our house in Mary Street, Toowoomba, c. 1 977 190
Page of an art book (Braque's bike), c. 1981 226
Passengers and bollards on the Baragoola, c. 1982 241
Patricia (Trish), early 1950s 17
Plant and back of canvas, c.1983 222
Paul, c.1954 19
Previous manuscript cover 299
Protestors in Queens Park , Toowoomba, five photos, 1977 193
Rachael asleep in a French forest, 1971 128
Rachael in France, 1971 126
Rachael in Gloucestershire, 1973 153
Rachael on the steps in the sun at Fairlight, 1982 237
Rachael with Tom, c. 1981 230
Rear view of the Chevron, c. 1979 211
Red army entering Shanghai in 1948 287
Roger Frampton et al playing at Strawberry Hills Hotel, 1994 281
Rowing on Middle Harbour, c.1954 15
Ruined car in a ruined street, c.1973 143
Russian Orthodox cathedral in Harbin, 2005 285
Self-portrait in new clothes, 1952 or '53 8
Self-portrait with painting, *Table in a Bar of Sunlight*, c.1960 48
Side and front views of most of the equipment in place,
Griffith Creative Arts Workshop, 1975 179
Side view, Mary Street, c. 1977 192
Simon tries out the Bolex 66

Some of the kids at Darlinghurst Primary School, c. 1981 223
Some of the girls of Darlinghurst Primary School, c. 1981 224
South Head and North Harbour at sunrise, 1982 232
South Head at night, c. 1982 232
Sue Howe & Aggy Read at Boxing Day dinner at Goodhope St, 1966 68
Sue Howe and Albie Thoms at Goodhope Street, Paddington 63
Sue's coffee pot, c. 1979 211
Sun through the leadlights at Fairlight, c. 1981 229
Sunset in Darlington, 1966 60
Tanya and Rachael on tour, Barbara Segal in background, 1971 128
The cheapest wine in France (and the roughest?), 1971 127
The city from the top of McElhone Stairs, Victoria Street,
Kings Cross, c. 1979 213
The entrance to our building, c.1972 138
The Mamiya set up for shooting a panorama, c. 1983 248
The Universal Grinder, c. 1978 206
The Jeparit anchored at Woolloomooloo Bay, c. 1979 212
Tim and his son in Gloucestershire, 1973 150
Under-the-house, Mary Street (old painting [c.1952]) , 1977 191
View from inside another room (bunker series), c. 1983 247
View from inside the bunker, North Head, c. 1983 245
View from the roof of our flats, Macleay Street, Potts Point, c. 1979 214
View of Sydney from Darling Harbour, 1966 74
Where Papa studied, Harbin, 2004 286

Photographs (and other images) not by David Perry

DP (far right) at a Sydney restaurant with two other "chocos", c.1955 21
DP and Homer in London, 1973 (photograph by Linda Slutzkin) 155
DP arranging "dingle" for a student film in London, c.1971 117
DP as an apprentice retouching paper negatives in the early 1950s 6
DP at the onset of skepticism (photographer unknown) 295
DP rolling a cigarette near Maleny (photograph by Bev Hill), c.1978 201
DP with microdensitometer, c.1969 (photo by Scott Meynert/ABC) 94
DP with Rachael, (photo by Kay Comino), c. 1976 187
DP's ID card at Griffith University, 1975 178

Homer, DP and Rachael in Gloucestershire (photograph by Tim) 151
In the bush, North Queensland (photograph by Bev Hill), c. 1977 203
Leadership of the Bolsheviks in 1918, reproduced from Picture History of Russia, c. 1945 and 1956, Crown Publishers Inc., USA 258
Lydia and David, 1994 (photographer Elizabeth Perey) 296
Me and my Friends, drawn by Rachael, 1976 181
My mother and me, 1933 132
Myself with Simon early 1957 (photographer probably Judy) 44
Outside Lindfield catholic church, 1956 30
Portrait of DP (photograph by Gopala), c.1972 135

Films and Plays

A break in rehearsals for *Theatre of Cruelty* 59
Aggy unpacking lights for Looby shoot, 1968 83
Building a set for *Theatre of Cruelty* 58
Clem Weight (part of a publicity series for *Marinetti*), 1969 91
Constant, artist/worker shows his painting of Shostakovich and Tukhachevsky in *The Refracting Glasses* (Frame blow-up) 275
Constant looks at the catalogue to the Cubist Exhibition in *The Refracting Glasses* (Frame blow-up) 272
Constant reads a newspaper report of the death of Stalin in *The Refracting Glasses* (Frame blow-up) 272
Early manuscript cover, 1971 293
Ellen White (publicity still for *Harbour*), 1966 72
Filmstrip from *Halftone*, 1966. Photographed by Peter Mudie 70
Flyer for screenings of *American Underground Movies*, 1968 86
Frame blowup from *A Sketch on Abigayl's Belly*, 1968 87
Frame blow-up from *Album*, 1970 106
Frame blow-up from *Album*, 1970 107
Frame blow-up from *Swansong in Birdland*, 1964 55
Frame from *Poem 25*, 1965 71
Front page of Ubu News No.15, June 1969 96
Iain Gardiner as Ern Malley in *The Refracting Glasses* (Frame blow-up) 271
Inside the drum factory in *The Refracting Glasses* (Frame blow-up) 276
In the Science Museum (screen shot from *Fragments*), c.1973 141
Johnny Earls in London (screen shot from *Goodbye Richard Nixon*), original recording 1973 148

Marinetti World Premier Poster 1969 92
Mary Patterson on the cover of *Squire*.......... 65
Rita clothed, publicity still for *Rita and Dundi*.......... 67
Side and front views of the equipment in place,
Griffith Creative Arts Workshop, 1975 179
Screen shot from *Fragments*, c.1973 140
Screen shot from *A TV Show*, 1976 180
Setting up to shoot *Bolero*, 1967 (Photo, Matt Carroll) 79
Shooting *Blunderball* 64
Sue Robertson, *Blunderball* publicity still.......... 65
Theatre of Cruelty, Simon in mask 59
Ubu logo.......... 64
Video and sound editing system before dismantling, c. 1982 238
Videocassette cover design for *Interior with Views*, c. 2000.......... 183
White Bird high over the land (Frame blow-up from
Swansong in Birdland), c.1964 55
Young woman painting in the drum factory in *The Refracting Glasses*
(Frame blow-up).......... 276

www.ingramcontent.com/pod-product-compliance
Ingram Content Group UK Ltd.
Pitfield, Milton Keynes, MK11 3LW, UK
UKHW020145250726
13967UKWH00002B/872

9 780987 506344